SECOND HISTORICAL SURVEY OF WOMEN'S EDUCATION IN INDIA 1988-1994

CONCEPTS IN COMMUNICATION INFORMATICS & LIBRARIANSHIP (CICIL)

For a list of titles in this series, please see. pp 414 at the end of the book

About the Authors

S.P. AGRAWAL (b. 1929), was Director, National Social Science Documentation Centre, ICSSR, and Member Secretary, Indian Association of Social Science Institutions. He was also the Vice-Chairman of the Asia and Pacific Information Network in Social Sciences (APINESS). In 1988 he was awarded the degree of Doctor of Philosophy in Education *(Honoris Causa)* by International University Foundation. Presently, he is Member, Round Table on Research in Reading, IFLA, and Member, International Committee for Social Science Information and Documentation. He is also Member of Board of Studies of National Archives of India and Hindi Advisory Committee, Ministry of Coal, Government of India. Born and brought up in the cradle of freedom movement which he joined at the tender age of twelve, he gained an insight into political problems and developed a sense of responsibility which bore fruit as an information scientist committed to Gandhiji's philosophy and action-plan in the field and its social concept. He has written extensively on various aspects of education, Indian Polity and library and information science.

J.C. AGGARWAL (1928), a retired Deputy Director of Education/Executive Director, Delhi Bureau of Textbooks, Delhi Administration, is a known writer and has been writing extensively on education, contemporary economic and political affairs. Some of his recent publications on education include: *Landmarks in the History of Modern Indian Education; Development and Planning of Modern Education; Second Historical Survey of Educational Documents in India; Educational Planning in India; Educational Administration, Management and Supervision; Learning without Burden; Education Policy in India, 1992, etc.* Shri Aggarwal has authored singly/ jointly about 150 books.

Concepts in Communication
Informatics & Librarianship-73

General Editor: **S.P. Agrawal**

SECOND HISTORICAL SURVEY OF WOMEN'S EDUCATION IN INDIA 1988-1994

Present Status, Perspective Plan, Statistical Indicators with a Global View

S.P. AGRAWAL
J.C. AGGARWAL

CONCEPT PUBLISHING COMPANY, NEW DELHI - 110059

ISBN-81-7022-544-2

First Published 1996

S.P. Agrawal (*b.* 1929)
J.C. Aggarwal (*b.* 1928)

Published and Printed by
Ashok Kumar Mittal
Concept Publishing Company
A/15-16, Commercial Block, Mohan Garden
NEW DELHI - 110059 (India)
Phones : 5554042, 5504042

GENERAL EDITOR'S INTRODUCTION

The women in India, who were revered in ancient India but were the most neglected lot decades ago, have now been receiving increased attention. It is being increasingly realised that all out effort should be directed towards building up society where men and women live on equal terms, where women have the same facilities and the same opportunities to develop themselves and the same economic and social status as that of men. It is gratifying to note that through governmental involvement and the efforts of some of the dedicated voluntary organisations we are moving towards the realisation of this goal. In the post-Independent period we have made appreciable progress in this direction—still much remains to be done. Society is far behind in educating them and in raising their social and economic status and thus integrating them in the so-called men-dominated world of today. In this connection it may also the pointed out that whatever the achievements that we find in the sphere of women pertain to the urban women. The progress made in regard to rural women is painfully slow. They are still in economic and social bondage; they are still denied the right to educate themselves.

In the past not long ago it was considered that women are cut out only for the profession of home-making and that their education and training should be geared to this aspect only. Now things have changed considerably. The urban women are entering into the men's preservations and their performance in this sphere is no longer inferior to that of men. As a result of their entry into special fields we have known women engineers, women scientists, women technocrats and women lawyers. We have women politicians as well. However, the rise of some women into high political position should not be understood that the women have joined politics in a big way. The ground realities are quite different. Despite modernisation the powerful male still dominates the scene. It would take quite some time for women to catch up the men in social, economic and educational spheres, even in an urban sector. The rural scenario is quite depressing and disheartening. In many areas and regions things are very much difficult for the women. There is much resistance for girls' education. Moreover, since the girls are burdened with heavy domestic chores and also help their family in struggle for survival, they have no time to spend—even a few hours, for learning. Early marriage also makes heavy toll of their education. Alarming drop-out rate in the case of women also tells its own story.

The present publication in CICIL series is the continuance of the previous one entitled "Women's Education in India: Historical Review, Present Status, Perspective Plan with Statistical Indicators (1992) which has shown the position of women in ancient India, the Constitutional provisions for them in new India and the governmental effort to raise their status and improve their position through the deliberations of the various Committees and Commissions set up from time to time. The preceding volume has also indicated the National Perspective Plan for Women's Education (1988 to 2000 AD) and has provided statistical indicators in regard to enrolment of girls in all levels of education during the British regime and the independent India upto 1986-87. This volume is a step forward in the direction of women's education. It provides an overview of the state of women's education in India since 1988 in all its aspects in the light of National Policy on Education (NPE) (1986), and its Programme of Action (POA). It also provides detailed information about the recommendations relating to women's education of the Ramamurti Committee (1990) which was set up to review the implementation of NPE, 'Education for All 2000' (1990) prepared by the National Institute of Educational Planning and Administration (NIEPA) New Delhi, and the Comments of the Central Advisory Board of Education Committee known as Janardhan Committee on the recommendations of modified NPE and POA on the basis of which the Central Government may take its decisions on the matters pertaining to women's education. It also provides statistical indicators relating to women's education.

The other special feature of this publication is the global view of women's education highlighting the programmes being followed in other developing countries and the efforts of the U.N.O. bodies in accelerating the pace of development in this regard. Appendices include, among others, sources of financial support for Research.

S.P. Agrawal

CONTENTS

General Editor's Introduction 5

PART I

Recent Developments in Women's Education in India since 1988

1. Overview of Women's Education in India 17
2. Ramamurti Committee for Review of National Policy on Education, 1986 25
3. Education for All by 2000 (1990) 56
4. Central Advisory Board of Education Working Group on Education for Women and other Disadvantaged Groups (1991) 60
5. Programme of Action of National Policy on Education (1992) 63
6. Janardhan Committee to Review Implementation of NPE (1992) 72
7. Workshop on the Need of Women's Education in the Teacher Education Curriculum (1992) 75

PART II

Statistical Indicators: India (as a whole) States Scheduled Castes and Scheduled Tribes Districtwise Women's Literacy (1991)

8. India (as a whole) 81
9. States 101
10. Scheduled Castes and Scheduled Tribes 147
11. Districtwise Women's Literacy (1991) 181

PART III
Global Overview Select Documents Women's Education: Comparative Indicators

12.	Women : Challenges to the Year 2000 (1991)	201
13.	SAARC Decade of the Girl Child (1991)	210
14.	Literacy, Education and Women (1992)	223
15.	Women in Development (1992)	230
16.	Women in Literate World (1992)	248
17.	UNICEF and Girl's Education (1994)	252
18.	International Responses to Women's Education and Allied Issues	256
19.	United Nations and Women's Education Including Allied Issues: Retrospect and Prospect	263
20.	Women's Education : Comparative Indicators	268

Appendices

I	Women's Education in Ancient India	279
II	Girls: NCERT Study (1986)	281
III	Women's Education and Fertility Behaviour: A Case Study of Rural Maharashtra, India	293
IV	Education and Sex-Gap	297
V	Sexwise Distribution of Nobel Laureates, 1901-1989	298
VI	Women's Development Task, Strategies and Initiatives of Government of India	301
VII	Seminar on Declining Sex Ratio: Implications for Education and Media (1991)	304
VIII	Sources of Financial Support for Research in India	307
IX	Education of Women and Girls in India: A Case Study	355
X	Women's Literacy Works	358
XI	Council of Europe: Education of Women in Austria	361
XII-1	1995 World Conference on Women	364
XII-2	Women's Studies Project	365
XIII	Working Women in India	366
XIV	Focal Points/Bodies Dealing with Question Relating to Women's Development Issues	368
Select Bibliography on Women's Education and Allied Topics		395
Index		406

LIST OF TABLES

2.1	Girls' Access to Education: An Overview	33
2.2	Distribution of Districts Having Combined (For All Levels) Gross Enrolment Ratios for Girls Less Than 50 per cent and Rural Female Literacy Rates Less Than 10 per cent,	40
2.3	Status of Women through Curriculam: Middle School: Class VI - VII Elementry Teachers Handbook, NCERT, 1982	42
8.1	Women Literacy Rates in India, 1951 to 1991	81
8.2	Percentage of Sex-wise and State-wise Literates to Estimated Population Age Seven Years and Above	81
8.3	Sex-wise Enrolment by Stages/Classes Since 1951: School Level	83
8.4	Girls Enrolment 1950-51 to 1991-92	83
8.5	Percentage of Girls Enrolment to Total Enrolment at the Primery Stage : Classes I to V, 1950-51 to 1991-92	84
8.6	Percentage of Girls Enrolment to Total Enrolment at the Middle/ Upper Stage : Classes VI to VIII 1950-51 to 1991-92	84
8.7	Percentage of Girls Enrolment to Total Enrolment at the High/Higher Secondary Stage: Classes IX to XII, 1950-51 to 1992	84
8.8	Percentage of Girls Enrolement to Total Population in the Age Group 6 to 14, 1951 to 1992	85
8.9	Percentagwe of Sex-wise Enrolment in Respective Age Group Population in classes I to VII since 1987-88	85
8.10	Students Flow in School Classes I-VII and Retention Rates, 1964-65 to 1986-89	86
8.11	Girls Retention Rate upto Class V and Class VIII, 1964-65 to 1988-89	88
8.12	Enrolment of Women and Their Number Per Hundred Men in Higher Education	89
8.13	Enrolment of Women and Its Percentage to Total Enrolment in Different Classes, 1986-87	90
8.14	Enrolment of Women and Its Percentage to Total Enrolment in Different Classes, 1987-88	91

8.15	Enrolment of Women and Its Percentage to Total Enrolment in Different Classes, 1988-89	92
8.16	Enrolment of Women and Its Percentage to Total Enrolment in Different Classes, 1989-90	93
8.17	Enrolment of Women Its Percentage to Total Enrolment in Different Classes, 1990-91	94
8.18	Percentage of Women Enrolment to Total Enrolment in Different Classes, 1987 to 1990-91	95
8.19	Distribution of Teachers by Sex and Types of Schools since 1951	96
8.20	Number of Women Teachers Employed in Various Types of Schools, 1950-51 to 1980-81	97
8.21	Number of Women Teachers Employees in Various Types of Schools, 1986-87 to 1990-91	98
8.22	Percentage of Female Teachers to Male Teachers of Different Levels of Education, 1950-51 to 1985-86	99
8.23	Students Going Abroad by Sex-wise, 1970-71 to 1985-86	100
8.24	Female Students Gone Abroad by Field of Study, 1981-82 to 1985-86	100
9.1	Distribution of Population, Sex Ratio, Density and Growth Rate of Population	101
9.2	Sex Ratio : Females per 1,000 Males, 1901-1991	104
9.3	Female Literacy : Six Top States / Union Territories	106
9.4	Female Literacy: Six Most Backward States/ Union Territories	106
9.5	States and Union Territories Arranged in Descending Order of Literacy Rate among Persons: Females and Males, 1991	107
9.6	Sex-wise and State-wise Enrolment Ratio in Primary and Middle Classes, 1991-92	109
9.7	Sex-wise and State-wise Enrolment in Pre-Basic / Pre-Primary in 1990-91	111
9.8	Sex-wise and State-wise Enrolment Ratio in Classes I-V and Classes VI-VIII of Schools to General Education, 1990-91	112
9.9	Sex-wise and State-Wise Enrolment in Classes I - V and Classes VI-VIII, 1990-91	114
9.10	Sex-wise and State-wise Girls Enrolment in High/ Post-Basic Classes IX-X	116
9.11	Sex-wise and State-wise Enrolment in Pre-University	

	and Higher Secondary Classes (10+2), 1990-91	117
9.12	Sex-wise and State-wise Girls Enrolment in Intermediate/ Junior Colleges, and Pre-Degree/Pre-University Classes 1990-91	119
9.13	Sex-wise and State-wise enrolment in Polytechnic Institutes and Technical, Industrial Arts and Crafts Schools, 1990-91	121
9.14	Sex-wise and State-wise Girls Enrolment in Teacher Training Schools.1990-91	123
9.15	Sex-wise and State-wise Enrolment in B.Ed/B.T. and M.B.B.S. 1990-91	124
9.16	Sex-wise and State-wise Enrolment in B.Com (Hons) and B.Sc (Engg.) / B.Arch, 1990-91	126
9.17	Sex-wise and State-wise Enrolment in BA/BA (Hons)/ BSc (Hons), 1990-91	128
9.18	Sex-wise and State-wise Enrolment in M.Sc/ M Com 1990-91	130
9.19	Sex-wise and State-wise Enrolment in /Ph.D/D.Sc/ D.Phil, and 1990-91	132
9.20	Sex-wise and State-wise Dropout Rates upto Class X, 1988-89	134
9.21	Sex-wise and State-wise Number of Teachers, 1991-92	137
9.22	Sex-wise and State-wise Number of Teachers in Primary/Junior Basic Schools and Percentage of Trained Teachers 1990-91	139
9.23	Sex-wise and State-wise Number of Teachers in Middle/Senior Basic Schools and Percentage of Trained Teachers, 1990-91	140
9.24	Sex-wise and State-wise Number of Teachers in High/ Post Basic Schools and Percentage of Trained Teachers, 1990-91	141
9.25	Sex-wise and State-wise Number of Teachers in Higher Secondary / Junior Colleges (10+2 New Pattern) and Percentage of Trained Teachers, 1990-91	143
9.26	Indian Female Student Gone Abroad by State/ Union Territory, 1970-71 to 1985-86	145
10.1	Sex-wise Rural-Urban and SC and ST Literates and Illitrates in India, 1981-91	147
10.2	Percentage of Sex-wise SC Enrolment in Classes I-V and Classes. VI - VIII	147

10.3 Percentage of Sex-wise Enrolment in Classes 1-V and Class VI - VIII 148
10.4 Percentage of Sex-wise Enrolment: General, SC and ST Classes I to V and Classes VI to VIII, 1991-92 148
10.5 Enrolment of SC Women and Its Percentage to Total SC Enrolment in Different Classes, 1986-87 149
10.6 Enrolment of SC Women and Its Percentage to Total Enrolment of SC in Different Classes, 1987-88 150
10.7 Enrolment of SC Women and Its Percentage to Total Enrolment of SC in Different Classes, 1988-89 151
10.8 Enrolment of SC Women and Its Percentage to Total Enrolment of SC in Different Classes, 1989-90 152
10.9 Enrolment of SC Women and Its Percantage to Total Enrolment in Different Classes, 1990-91 153
10.10 Sex-wise and State-wise Enrolment Ratio of SC Students in Primary and Middle Classes, 1991-92 154
10.11 Sex-wise and State-wise Enrolment Ratio of ST Students in Primary and Middle Classes, 1991-92 155
10.12 Sex-wise and State-wise Enrolment Ratio of SC and ST Students at the Pre-Primary/ Pre-Basic Stage, 1990-91 156
10.13 Sex-wise and Statewise Enrolment Ratio of SC Students in Primary and Middle Classes, 1990-91 157
10.14 Sex-wise and Statewise Enrolment Ratio of SC Students in Classes I to VIII, 1990-91 158
10.15 Sex-wise and Statewise Enrolment Ratio of SC Students at the Primary Stage Classes I-V, 1990-91 159
10.16 Sex-wise and Statewise Enrolment Ratio of SC Students at Middle Stage Classes VI-VII, 1990-91 160
10.17 Sex-wise and State-wise Drop-out Rates of SC upto Class X, 1988-89 161
10.18 Sex-wise and State-wise Drop-out Rates of ST upto Class X, 1988-89 162
10.19 Sex-wise Statewise Enrolment of SC and ST Students in Classes IX and X, 1990-91 163
10.20 Sex-wise Statewise Enrolment of SC and ST Students in Classes XI and XII, 1990-91 164
10.21 Sex-wise Statewise Enrolment of SC and ST Students at Pre-University (One-Year Course), 1990-91 165
10.22 Sex-wise Statewise Enrolment of SC and ST Students at Pre-Degree Pre-University (Two Year Course), 1990-91 166

10.23 Sex-wise Statewise Enrolment of SC and ST Students in Intermediate/Junior Colleges, 1990-91 167
10.24 Sex-wise Statewise Enrolment of SC and ST Students in MBBS, 1990-91 168
10.25 Sex-wise Statewise Enrolment of SC and ST Students in Teacher Tranining Schools 169
10.26 Sex-wise Statewise Enrolment of SC and ST Students in Technical Industrial Arts and Crafts Schools, 1990-91 170
10.27 Sex-wise Statewise Enrolment of SC and ST Students in Polytechnic Institutes, 1990-91 171
10.28 Sex-wise Statewise Enrolment of SC and ST Students in BE/BSc (Engg) / B.Arch, 1990-91 172
10.29 Sex-wise Statewise Enrolment of SC and ST Students in B.Ed/BT, 1990-91 173
10.30 Sex-wise Statewise Enrolment of SC and ST Students in B.Com / B.Com (Hons), 1990-91 174
10.31 Sex-wise Statewise Enrolment of SC and ST Students in BSc/BSc (Hons), 1990-91 175
10.32 Sex-wise Statewise Enrolment of SC and ST Students in BA/BA(Hons), 1990-91 176
10.33 Sex-wise Statewise Enrolment of SC and ST Students in M.Com, 1990-91 177
10.34 Sex-wise Statewise Enrolment of SC and ST Students in M.A., 1990-91 178
10.35 Sex-wise Statewise Enrolment of SC and ST Students in M.Sc, 1990-91 179
10.36 Sex-wise Statewise Enrolment of SC and ST Students in Ph.D/ D.Sc/ D.Phil, 1990-91 180
11.1 Women Literacy Rates Districtwise 1991: Andhra Pradesh 181
11.2 Women Literacy Rates Districtwise 1991: Arunchal Pradesh 182
11.3 Women Literacy Rates Districtwise 1991: Assam 182
11.4 Women Literacy Rates Districtwise 1991: Bihar 183
11.5 Women Literacy Rates Districtwise 1991: Delhi 184
11.6 Women Literacy Rates Districtwise 1991: Goa 184
11.7 Women Literacy Rates Districtwise 1991: Gujarat 184
11.8 Women Literacy Rates Districtwise 1991: Haryana 185
11.9 Women Literacy Rates Districtwise 1991: Himachal Pradesh 185

11.10	Women Literacy Rates Districtwise 1991: Kerala	186
11.11	Women Literacy Rates Districtwise 1991: Madhya Pradesh	186
11.12	Women Literacy Rates Districtwise 1991: Maharashtra	187
11.13	Women Literacy Rates Districtwise 1991: Manipur	188
11.14	Women Literacy Rates Districtwise 1991: Meghalaya	188
11.15	Women Literacy Rates Districtwise 1991: Mizoram	189
11.16	Women Literacy Rates Districtwise 1991: Mizoram	189
11.17	Women Literacy Rates Districtwise 1991: Nagaland	189
11.18	Women Literacy Rates Districtwise 1991: Orissa	190
11.19	Women Literacy Rates Districtwise 1991: Punjab	190
11.20	Women Literacy Rates Districtwise 1991: Rajasthan	191
11.21	Women Literacy Rates Districtwise 1991: Sikkam	191
11.22	Women Literacy Rates Districtwise 1991: Tamil Nadu	192
11.23	Women Literacy Rates Districtwise 1991: Tripura	192
11.24	Women Literacy Rates Districtwise 1991: Uttar Pradesh	193
11.25	Women Literacy Rates Districtwise 1991: West Bangal	194
11.26	Women Literacy Rates Districtwise 1991: A and N Islands	195
11.27	Women Literacy Rates Districtwise 1991: Chandigarh	195
11.28	Women Literacy Rates Districtwise 1991: Dadra and Nagar Haveli	195
11.29	Women Literacy Rates Districtwise 1991: Daman and Diu	195
11.30	Women Literacy Rates Districtwise 1991: Lakshadweep	196
11.31	Women Literacy Rates Districtwise 1991: Pondicherry	196
11.32	Women Literacy Rates Districtwise 1991: Women Literacy Rates : 10 Top Districts in India	196
11.33	Women literacy Rates: 10 Bottom Districts in India	196
11.34	Female Literacy Rates: Top District in Each State	197
16.1	Adult Literacy Rates by Sex 1990	249
20.1	Women's Education World Comparision	268
20.2	Regional Summaries: Women's Education	273
A-4.1	Percentage of Females to Total Enrolment	297
A-5.1	Sexwise Distribution of Nobel Laureats 1901-89	298

PART I

RECENT DEVELOPMENTS IN WOMEN'S EDUCATION IN INDIA SINCE 1988

Overview of Women's Education in India

Documents on Women's Education

1

Overview of Women's Education in India

Since the formulation of the National Policy on Education (NPE), 1986 Government of India, Ministry of Human Resource Development, Department of Education, has taken several measures for the promotion of women's education in the country. An overview of the state of women education in India, is provided in the following pages:

1.A Education for Women's Equality

4.1.1 The National Policy on Education (NPE) and Programme of Action (POA) commit the entire educational system to work for women's equality and empowerment. The modified, 1986 and its POA give high priority to the education of women, being a factor of the equity package. Besides, this issue is also of economic importance. Education is a major factor in developing and thereby optimising the contribution of this large segment of society towards socio-economic development. The POA, 1992 has identified a number of specific programmes in this area keeping in view the experience in implementing the previous POA.

4.1.2 Significance has been greatly attached to actually operationalising the NPE's Programme of Action and in a series of regional meetings with the State governments, a special review of gender issues in education was undertaken. At the same time it was emphasized to the States, that gender concerns must be built into all educational processes. A monitoring committee for women's/girls' education at the Ministry of Human Resource Development level monitors the indicators of gender concerns in all policy and projects. The State governments have been advised to set-up similar monitoring committees at the State

---

Annual Report 1992-93, Ministry of Human Resource Development, Department of Education, Government of India, 1993

Note : Paras refer to para numbers of Chapter 4.

Secretaries' level to ensure that this perspective is incorporated and implemented in the education system. Emphasis has been laid on eurolment and retention of the girl-child in formal and non-formal schooling; recruitment of rural women teachers and removal of gender bias in the curriculum.

4.1.3 A heartening feature of the decadal census figures of 1991 is the improvement in the literacy rate of women compared to that of men. As per these figures 39.4 per cent of women are literate compared to 29.8 per cent in 1981. The literacy rate in case of females during 1981-91 increased by 9.6 per cent points as compared to 7.5 per cent in case of males. While these figures are still way behind the figures of men, the decadal growth rate of women literacy is higher than that of men.

4.1.4 The enrolment of girls as a ratio of total enrolment during 1991-92 is 39 per cent at primary stage, 33 per cent at middle stage, 28 per cent at secondary and higher secondary stage and 23 per cent at higher education stage.

4.1.5 Special provisions have been incorporated for the benefit of women under the existing schemes of the Department. Under the Operation Blackboard scheme, the revised policy formulations stipulate that at least 50 per cent of teachers recruited in future should be women. Under this scheme, Government of India have provided assistance since 1987-88 for creation of 1,22,890 posts of primary school teachers, mainly to be filled by women. According to the latest reports, 69,926 posts of teachers have been filled of which 57.39 per cent are women teachers. A scheme of hostels for enabling girls to benefit from secondary education is being operationalised.

4.1.6 Under the Ministry's scheme of NFE 90 per cent assistance was given for NFE centres exclusively for girls. The cumulative number of NFE centres for girls is 82,000.

4.1.7 By conscious action, admission of girls to the extent of 28.44 per cent in Navodaya Vidalayas has been ensured. The total number of girls in these Vidyalayas is 22,222 as against total of 78,149 as on March 1992.

4.1.8 In the total literacy campaigns the theme of empowerment of women is receiving special focus. Since the female literacy rate in the country is strikingly lower than for men it happens that the women learners under TLCs out number male learners. The social awakening in terms of empowerment of hitherto deprived sections has been significant as evidenced by the movements in some of the districts for payment of fair wages for construction workers, sale of kharis directly to the workers, closure of liquor shops, and uniform increase in the demand for enrolment of children in all the campaign districts. This is mainly due to the literacy of women. In the adult education and post-literacy education centres, special attention was given to enrolment of women.

4.1.9 There has been phenomenal expansion of educational opportunities for women in the field of higher education — both general and technical. Women's education at the university and college levels has been diversified and reoriented in tune with the changing requirements of the society, industry and trade. The number of women enrolled in institutions of higher education increased from 40,000 in 1950-51 to about 14,37,000 in 1990-91, recording an increase of more than 36 times over the forty-year period. The number of women enrolled per hundred men enrolled during this period has gone up more than three times from 14 in 1950-51 to 48 in 1990-91. The enrolment of women as a percentage of total enrolment increased from 27.7 per cent in 1981-82 to 32.5 per cent in 1990-91.

4.1.10 The University Grants Commission has been providing financial assistance to universities for undertaking well-defined projects for research in women's studies and also for the development of curriculum at the undergraduate and post-graduate levels and relevant extension activities. The Commission has also created 40 positions of part-time research associateships for women candidates in Science and Humanities including Social Sciences and Engineering and Technology. Twenty-one research projects relating to the theme of women's studies were approved for assistance upto September, 1992. Also, the Standing Committee on Women's Studies, after examining various proposals, recommended assistance to 21 universities and 11 colleges/university departments for setting up women's studies centres and cells respectively.

4.1.11 Under the polyvalent adult education programme of Shramik Vidyapeeths (SVP) during the calendar year 1992 UNICEF has provided special assistance to 10 selected Shramik Vidyapeeths for conducting skill-based literacy programme. One thousand women/girls are to be made literate by each SVP. By the middle of 1993, 10,000 women will not only be made literate but will also be empowered with skill in a popular trade.

4.1.12 A number of specific programmes were launched by the Department for women's education and empowerment. The Mahila Samakhya (Education for women's Equality) was launched in April, 1989 with Dutch Assistance. This project was formulated in pursuance of the National Policy on Education, 1986. The constraints that have prevented women and girls from assessing educational inputs, is the main focus of the project. This project seeks to begin by addressing issues of self-image and self-confidence of women and societal perception about them. Mahila Samakhya Project presupposes that education can be a decisive intervention towards women's equality. Its overall goal is to create circumstances to enable women to better understand their predicament, to move from a state of object disempowerment towards a situation in which they can determine their own lives and influence their environment, and simultaneously create for themselves and their family an educational opportunity which serves the process of development. The Mahila Samakhya component is being made part of the strategy for women's education in UP. Basic Education Project and Bihar Education Project.

4.1.13 The programme covers 10 districts in Uttar Pradesh, Karnataka and Gujarat. During the Eighth Plan period it is being expanded to another 10 districts as well as three districts in Andhra Pradesh. Encouraged by the success of the Mahila Samakhya strategy, it is being incorporated in several other basic education projects in the country.

4.1.14 The POA, 1992 provides for the establishment of a women cell for monitoring the programmes for education in the Department of Education. A Cell has already been set-up in the Planning Bureau of the Department for this purpose.

4.1.15 POA, 1992 also provides for a high level Inter-Ministerial Committee for Women's Education in the Department of Education, Ministry of Human Resource Development to review the implementation of POA; advise the government on policies and programmes related to girls' education and to acclerate planning mechanism to ensure provision of essential support services that will enhance girls' and women's participation in education. Such a Committee has been duly constituted and the States have been requested to set up similar committees.

4.1.16 The NCERT has conducted special programmes on women's education. A study on 'Factors for Continuance and Discontinuance of Girls in Elementary Schooling' has been completed in the NCERT. The Council has initiated a major integrated multi-level research-cum-training project in Haryana where 300 education personnel will be oriented on universalisation of primary education among girls and disadvantaged groups in rural and remote areas. Guidelines for removal of sex bias from textbooks, handbooks for teachers for promoting equality between sexes and a training manual on women's education, are being developed. A programme was also organised by the Council in collaboration with Howrah Teachers Forum to prepare a set of guidelines for universalisation of primary education for rural girls. Three gender sensitization workshops for teacher educators and educational administrators were conducted, two for Delhi and one for West Bengal on request.

4.1.17 Concretely, an attempt would be made to operationalize the POA, 1992 on the following lines:-

(i) A nation-wide gender sensitization programme will be undertaken to cover a large number of educational personnel to include educational administrators, teachers and teacher educators. Complementary to this strategy, would be media campaigns and parental awareness programmes for generating a positive climate for girls' education. Mobilization of women's groups would be intensified around basic issues of women's empowerment and girls' education.

(ii) All teachers and instructors will be trained as agents of women's empowerment. Training programmes will be developed by NCERT, DAE, SRCs, DIETs, SCERTs and the university system. Innovative training programmes will be designed with the assistance for concerned organisations and women's groups.

(iii) The NCERT would undertake a study of problems of recruitment and posting of women teachers in rural areas to identify the bottlenecks and workable solutions.

(iv) Steps would be taken to enhance access of girls to vocational, technical and professional education at all levels, breaking gender stereotypes.

(v) Stress would be laid on convergence of schemes and programmes of various departments for creating supportive services that will release girls for education. Active cooperation of the Department of Women and Child Development and of State Governments be sought.

(vi) Legal literacy materials developed by Department of Women and Child Development will be disseminated far and wide so that these become part of the school curriculum, literacy campaigns and women's mobilization. Media support would be sought especially from the Ministry of Information and Broadcasting.

(vii) Distance education will be enhanced to increase girls' access to middle and secondary education. The National Open School has been able to draw girls into distance education and the linkage will be increased to support more middle school girls into education.

(viii) Accent will be on promoting and documenting innovative programme on women's education.

1.B State of Literacy (1991)

Illiteracy or the absence of literacy in our country is regarded as the greatest single impediment to social and economic progress of the masses. Literacy acts in a number of ways. Where literacy rates are higher, population growth rates are low, making the rate of economic growth faster even with limited resources. In India, better sex ratios exist in high literacy pockets (except where there are reasons for selective migration). Literacy makes the task of social transformation relatively easier. Diversification of economic activities opens up new opportunities of gainful employment but it is possible only if the prospective employees are literate.

The 1991 Census registered a literate only one who could both read and write. Children below 7 years of age were left out of the calculations. Since age tables were not available, estimated number of population between 0-6 has been deducted for purposes of calculating literacy rates. The available information shows that between 1951 and 1991 the literacy rate improved from 18.33 per cent to 52.11 per cent of the population (excluding 0-6). Male literacy improved from 27.16 per cent to 63.86 per cent while in case of females the percentage of literate population increased from 8.86 in 1951 to 39.42 in 1991. (Population for purposes of literacy rates excluded 0-4 age group in 1951).

Broadly speaking, it could be said that increase in literacy rate between 1981-91 has been higher than that observed in the preceding decade.

While percentage figure may offer some consolation, this is not the correct picture. The absolute number of illiterates has increased considerably. In 1981, only 301,933,000 persons were illiterate. The number swelled to 324,030,000 in 1991. While this increase was only 5,792,000 in case of males, it was 16,305,000 in case of females.

Literacy rates have ranged from 38.54 in Bihar to 90.59 in Kerala. While over half the male population is registered as literate (the lowest being 51.10 for Arunachal Pradesh), the picture is rather dismal in the field of female literacy. Rajasthan has just 20.84 literacy percentage. Among women Kerala is again at the top with 86.93 per cent of its women as literate.

There are 8 States and U.Ts that have a literacy rate lower than the All India rate of 52.11. Among males, 11 States and U.Ts are below the national average. Since even the national average is very low (39.42) in case of females, 8 States and U.Ts have an average literacy rate which is lower than the national average.

Statewise Literacy rates with sex classification are given in Table 8.2.

Haryana is one of the bigger (population over 10 million) States that has shown the maximum increase in literacy rate. Among other States and U.Ts, Daman and Diu has the highest increase in the literacy rate. Female literacy has increased faster except in Rajasthan. Bihar showed only marginal increase in its literacy rates both in the male and female sectors. Comparisons from 1981 figures reveal that the country has a very long distance to travel to be able to reach the goal of 100 per cent literacy. Rajasthan had 13.99 females as percentage of literates to estimated population between 7 years and above in 1981. Today it is 20.84. Four-fifth of the female population in such a big state is illiterate. Utter Pradesh has an almost similar story. The figure of 26.2 broadly indicates that three-fourth of the female population in the State is illiterate. The position in Bihar is even worst with the figure being just 23.1 for 1991. Madhya Pradesh is only slightly better with 28.39 per cent women literate among 100 estimated population between 7 onwards. Even the male literacy figures are no better. The national average for male literacy in 1991 stands at 63.86 on the basis of estimated population (age 7 and above) but Bihar, Madhya Pradesh, Rajasthan and Uttar Pradesh are well below that mark. These States are big in size, both in area and population. Unless they cross the hump there is very little hope for the All-India average to rise substantially.

There is a great disparity in female education in districts. While female literacy is as high as 94 per cent in Kottayam District in Kerala, it is as low as 12.82 per cent in Badaun district in Uttar Pradesh. Nine top districts in female literacy are in Kerala alone. Of the ten most backward districts in female literacy, 5 are in Uttar Pradesh, 3 in Rajasthan and one each in Bihar and Madhya Pradesh.

The regional concentration of female illiteracy is highlighted by the fact that 155 of the 247 districts whose female literacy rates are lower than the national average are in Uttar Pradesh (51 districts), Madhya Pradesh (38 districts), Rajasthan (27 districts) and Bihar (39 districts). The gender disparity is even more conspicuous among the SCs and STs.

1C. Expansion of Education Facilities for Girls and Women

Enrolment of girls increased from 54 lakh to 424 lakh from 1950-51 to 1991-92, at the primary stage, showing an increase of about 7. 8 times against 4.3 times in the case of boys. Percentage of girls to total enrolment increased from 28.12 per cent to 41.73 per cent. During the same period enrolment of girls in Classes VI to VIII increased nearly 24 times as against 8.3 times in the case of boys. In Classes IX to XII, the percentage of enrolment of girls went up to 33.01 per cent from 13.33 per cent.

Despite this level of expansion, vast ground is yet to be covered. Drop-out rates are significant, retention of girls in schools is low. Wastage is considerable.

There has also been a phenomenal increase in the enrolment of women in higher education. Their number increased from 40,000 in 1950-51 to 15.10 lakh in 1991-92, showing an increase of 38 times.

In 1950-51, the enrolment ratio of women to men, was 14 per hundred men. In 1991-92 it was 49 per hundred men.

The enrolment of women students to total enrolment was the highest in Kerala (53.0 per cent), followed by Punjab (48.2 per cent), Delhi (46.3 per cent), Haryana (42.2 per cent), Meghalaya/Nagaland/Mizoram (39 per cent), Tamil Nadu (38.5 per cent) and West Bengal/Tripura/Sikkim(38.4 per cent). The enrolement of Women was the lowest in Bihar (16.4 per cent).

2

Ramamurti Committee for Review of National Policy on Education, 1986

Introduction

In May 1990, the Government of India (National Front Government), appointed a Committee to review the complementation of the National Policy on Education (NPE), 1986 formulated by the Congress party which was then in power at the Centre.The Review Committee consisted of 17 members with Acharya Ramamurti as its Chairman. The Committee submitted its report under the title: Towards an Enlightened and Humane Society."

The terms of reference of the Committee were as under:

(a) To review the National Policy on Education, 1986 and its implementation;
(b) To make recommendations regarding revision of the policy; and
(c) To recommend action necessary for implementation of the revised policy within a timeframe.

In Chapter 2 entitled "Approach", the Committee highlighted its general concerns and in Chapter 4, it made detailed observations and recommendations on various aspects of girls' and women's education. Relevant text of the NPE,1986 is also given for recapitulation.

National Policy on Education, 1986 (Extract from Part 4)*
Education for Women's Equality

4.2 Education will be used as an agent of basic change in the status of

* Committee for Review of National Policy on Education, 1986, *Towards Enlightened and Humane Society*, Ministry of Human Resource Development, Department of Education, Government of India, New Delhi, 1991.
* *National Policy on Education*, 1986, Ministry of Human Resource Development, Department of Education, Government of India, New Delhi, 1986.

women. In order to neutralise the accumulated distortions of the past, there will be a well-conceived edge in favour of women. The National Education System will-play a positive, interventionist role in the empowerment of women. It will foster the development of new values through redesigned curricula, textbooks, the training and orientation of teachers, decision-makers and administrators, and the active involvement of education institutions. This will be an act of faith and social engineering. Women's studies will be promoted as a part of various courses and educational institutions encouraged to take up active programmes to further women's development.

4.3 The removal of women's illiteracy and obstacles inhibiting their access to, and retention in, elementary education will receive overriding priority, through provision of special support services, setting of time targets, and effective monitoring. Major emphasis will be laid on women's participation in vocational, technical and professional education at different levels. The policy of non-discrimination will be pursued vigorously to eliminate sex stereo-typing in vocational and professional courses and to promote women's participation in non-traditional occupations, as well as in existing and emergent technologies.

EXTRACTS FROM CHAPTER 2 ENTITLED 'APPROACH' OF THE RAMAMURTI REPORT

2.2.4 The rural areas in general, and the tribal areas in particular, have suffered in terms of resources, personnel and infrastructure facilities. This phenomenon of regional disparities in educational development has acquired a major political dimension in the current Indian scene. It is reflected in the regional and sub-regional movements. Therefore, the need of the hour is planning for, and implementation of, educational development programmes in terms of disaggregated targets and, area, community and gender specific activities. This would mean concrete programmes being established on ground for the disadvantaged groups - SCs and STs, women, the educationally backward minorities and the handicapped with appropriate budgeting for the same. No doubt, there have been special component plans for the SCs and sub-plans for the Tribes. But these plans have largely remained exercises on paper, not concretely provided for in the budget documents. The consequence has been that these plans have not had any impact on the educational standards of the SCs and STs in terms of enrolment, retention and reduction in drop-out rates. Excepting for the implementation of a small scheme, "The Integrated Education for the Disabled", the handicapped do not significantly feature in the educational programmes of the Centre or the States. The Programmes for the educationally backward minorities have not been significant, having been construed as the almost exclusive domain of the States.

2.2.5 In order to promote participation of the girls and women in education at all levels, there is need for an integrated approach in designing and implementing the schemes that would address all the factors that inhibit their education. Mere implementation of disaggregated schemes such as Opening of Non-Formal Education Centres for Girls, Adult Education Centres for Women etc. by themselves are not adequate. In this context special mention may be made of inter-action of Early Childhood Care and Education (ECCE) with primary education. Education of women is not to be construed of a question of mere access but of empowering them through education of all on equality of sexes.

EQUITY, SOCIAL JUSTICE AND EDUCATION*

Section A: Education and Women's Equality

4.1.1 The evaluation of policy in relation to women's education needs necessarily to be made in the larger context of the socio-cultural reality in which women live; and the educational situation that is sought to be addressed and subsequently redressed.

4.1.2 At the time of the formulation of NPE, 1986, the existing data on the state of education (Government Reports and the Census of India 1981) clearly indicated the following trends in the educational situation of women. The NPE/POA also make reference to some of these.

— The rate of illiteracy among women is 75 per cent as compared to 53 per cent for men. Illiterate women predominate in villages and particularly among the under-privileged sections of society. The illiteracy rate is as high as 90.1 per cent among SC women and 92 per cent among ST women (Census, 1981);

— Regional disparities in the state of women's literacy are also pronounced. While illiteracy among women in Kerala is 34 per cent, it is as high as 89 per cent in Rajasthan and 86 per cent in Bihar;

— While about 42 per cent of boys in the age-group of 6-14 years at an all-India level are not attending schools, almost 62 per cent

Note: 1 Full text of chapter 4.
2 Recommendations are serially numbered.

of the girls in the same age-group do not go to schools. This gender disparity is further accentuated if one views the rural population separately. About 47 per cent of the rural boys in this age-group do not attend school. In contrast, the proportion of rural girls outside the ambit of formal education is as high as 70 per cent. Even in the urban areas, more than one-third of the girls are outside the school system;

— While 70 per cent of non-enrolled children are girls, the majority come from rural areas. Enrolment rates are poorest among girl children who belong to communities which suffer from social and economic discrimination i.e., the Scheduled Castes, Scheduled Tribes and other educationally backward communities;

— Although precise data are not available, it is widely acknowledged that the percentage of girls belonging to certain minority communities going to schools may be as low, as in the case of SC/ST girls, if not lower.

— While the drop-out rate of both male and female school children increases with the stage of education, it is more acute among girls at each stage. Here again, dimensions such as the urban-rural, socio-economic status and ethnic background are important;

— The representation of women in higher education is as low as 31 per cent. Data show that, of all the women enrolled in higher education, 55 per cent are in arts courses and only 20 per cent in science courses. Women also tend to join lower professional courses as compared to higher professional courses. For example, only 6 per cent of students enrolled for engineering courses are women;

— The proportion of women amongst teachers engaged at Primary, Middle and High/Higher Secondary levels in 1987-88 was as low as 26.3 per cent, 32.2 per cent and 31.2 per cent respectively.

— It is recognised that women are poorly represented at higher levels of the decision-making process in the education system, though information on this issue is yet to be compiled.

The Status of Women in Indian Society—Implications for Education

4.1.3 Research available on the education of women in India points to a number of socio-cultural and economic factors that influence the participation of women in the system of education and have a bearing on the above-mentioned trends.

4.1.4 The prevailing cultural norms of gender behaviour and the perceived 'domestic' and reproductive roles of women tend to adversely affect the education of girls. Negative attitudes towards sending girls to school, prejudices against retaining them in school, restrictions on mobility especially after puberty, early marriage, pressures to enter 'womanly' courses etc. are known to affect the nature of participation of women in education. These are reflections of the patriarchal values and attitudes which are dominant in society. The effect of gender bias varies in different social and economic groups and is particularly harsh on communities which suffer discrimination and those in certain minority groups. Among poor families, the economic role of the girl child and her responsibilities in the household are obstacles to schooling. The gender bias existing in society has a direct bearing on many aspects of the education system. These include inadequate facilities for girls' education at different stages, unequal access to non-traditional' courses, gender stereo-types in both the 'official' and 'hidden' curriculum, negative attitudes of teachers and administrators, and poor representation of women in positions of authority and decison-making. Education policy must, therefore, address itself to the larger socio-economic and cultural context that affects education of girls.

4.1.5 At the same time, it must be recognised that poor enrolments and large drop-out rates among girl children are not a result of social, economic and cultural factors alone, but are also the product of the policy and its priorities. For example, it is policy which determines the nature of the available educational facilities, their coverage and quality. This in the above context can either accentuate existing problems of girls' education or facilitate their participation.

NPE/POA Stipuilations

4.1.6 Referring to women's education, the NPE clearly states that education will play a positive, interventionist role in the empowerment of women.... foster the development of new values through redesigned curricula, textbooks, the training and orientation of teachers, decision-makers and administrators....'. The thrust of the policy lies in intervening within the education system, as is also evident from the policy parameters listed in the POA. The socio-economic and cultural constraints that lie outside the school system and have a direct bearing on girls' education are not adequately addressed. The larger context of the nature of development and the scant economic opportunities available to poorer and socially discriminated sections of society among whom girls enrolment is the lowest, do not seem to have informed strategy enunciation. The NPE seemingly construes education alone as an agent of basic change in the status of women'. The concern for support services', such as water, fuel, fodder, child-care and hostel facilities, has not been adequately operationalised in the POA. This is also reflected in the POA's acceptance (without question) of the official norms regarding the distance at which schooling should be available in rural areas. For instance, the official norms of 1 km. and 3 km. as 'walking distance', at which primary and middle schools respectively are to be made available, may still not be suitable for girls.

4.1.7 Further, even if education is to play an interventionist role, it is crucial that a gender perspective is reflected throughout the policy.* This implies that all dimensions of the education policy should reflect a well-conceived edge in favour of 'women' in order to neutralise the accumulated distortions of the past'. There is, however, a gap between the policy statement and the POA. Other than the part where the focus is on Education for Women's Equality', the education of the 'female half', of the population receives only scattered references in the POA. The POA as a whole, does not reflect a holistic treatment of women's education in all its aspects.

4.1.8 In the discussion that follows, the Committee reviews the NPE and POA in the context of women's education and makes recommendations with regard to the following dimensions**:

- Access to education and quality of learning,
- Content of education and gender bias,
- Vocational education,
- Training of teachers and other educational personnel,
- Research and development of Women's Studies,
- Representation of women in the educational hierarchy,
- Empowerment of women,
- Adult education,
- Resources, and

* By this we mean that education "... must address the structures and attitudes that have prevented women's equality till now, and have perpetuated and strengthened patriarchal values and institutions that subordinate women". Education must also play "... an active role in promoting the new values of equality in the division of roles, rights and responsibilities between men and women in *every sphere*",

** Many of these concerns are relevant for school children in general. However, this chapter focuses specifically on the education of girls.

Management.

Access to Education and Quality of Learning

4.1.9 The education of children in general and the girl-child in particular, has to be viewed within the larger context of development. In addition to the socio-economic and cultural factors referred to earlier, the education of girls is in a very real sense linked to the availability of water, fuel, fodder and child-care facilities to individual families. As much as 29 per cent of the entire time of a girl-child in rural areas is spent in the collection of fuel and 20 per cent in fetching water. Care of siblings also accounts for a significant proportion of a girl's time. This is particularly so in poor rural families. For instance, it was observed that in eastern UP, 30 per cent of the household burden and 20 per cent of the agricultural work is shared by girl-children.

(a) Water, Fuel, and Fodder

4.1.10 The release of the girl-child for schooling thus requires an improvement in the access of house-holds to water, fuel and fodder, and this should invariably inform the Policy. Further, it should also stress that efforts in the direction of social forestry, drinking water supply and greening of village common lands should be viewed not merely as eliminating drudgery from women's lives' (POA, Para 12) but as necessary inputs to improve girls' access to and retention in schools. In the POA, the mention of support services appears to have no operational link with the Primary School.

(b) Early Childhood-Care and Education (ECCE)

4.1.11 As already emphasised in the chapter on ECCE, easy access to organised and holistic early child-care is crucial if families, especially among the under-privileged, are expected to relieve girl children of this responsibility and spare them for schooling. Without providing full-fledged day-care services, particularly for the 0-3 age group, no school programme can hope to become accessible to older girls in the 6-14 age group. Although both the NPE and POA do mention the need for early child-care facilities, the criticality of the link between this support service and the access and retention of girls in schools is not adequately stressed. The POA Chapter on 'Education for Women's Equality' makes no specific reference to its link with the need for child-care for the 0-3 age group. While a passing reference is made to early childhood education as a support service, no attempt is made at strategy enunciation in this regard. In the POA on ECCE, this matter receives a hesitant reference, "Girls in these groups (under-privileged) may require support services like child-care, sometimes in very small units" (Para 7).

4.1.12 Apart from older siblings, women teachers may also require child-care facilities to enable them to attend schools regularly. The POA doesn't refer to this aspect.

4.1.13 Detailed recommendations for providing ECCE services, especially to the under-privileged sections of society, have already been discussed (see the chapter on ECCE). In the context of women's education, the Committee re-emphasises the following aspects:

(c) The Availability of Schooling

4.1.14 The POA states that there will be a shift in emphasis from enrolment to retention in elementary education (Chapter II, Para 13). While retention in schools needs to be emphasied, concerted drives aimed at increasing enrolment of girls, especially those from under-privileged social groups, must continue.

4.1.15 The availability of facilities for schooling within easy reach is crucial for access to and retention of girls in schools. At present, 48.6 per cent of the habitations representing about one-fifth of the country's rural population do not have Primary Schools. These include habitations which have population of more than 300 persons and hence according to the official norms should have already been provided with primary schooling. Although almost 95 per cent of the rural population, according to official figures, are served by a primary school either within or up to a 'walking distance' of one km., this should not give rise to grounds for complacency as far as girls' education is concerned. It is necessary to recognise that the involvement of girls in sibling care and domestic chores and other socio-cultural constraints may make even one km. beyond 'walking distance' for them. These factors become more important when it comes to middle schooling where access to education is poorer than at the primary stage. Only 13.3 per cent of habitations have middle schools. The poor availability of middle schooling may be a major constraint in the retention of girls in schools. Parental fears at sending girls outside the village particularly with the approach of puberty cannot be dismissed. Girls belonging to SC, ST and other discriminated social groups are particularly vulnerable. In other words 'the socio-cultural threshold' beyond which girls have to venture to receive education makes easy availability of schooling of critical importance. The official target of providing a middle school within 3 kms of the habitation, hence, will not ensure accessibility of upper primary education to all girl children. (see Table 2.1).

TABLE 2.1: Girls' Access to Education : An Overview

Factors which will facilitate girls' education	Reasons	Recommendations
I. Linking Early Childhood Care and Education (ECCE)	Prepares girls in in the 0-6 age group for Primary Schools Relieves older girls from the responsibility of sibling care. Positive impact of ECCE's child-centred approaches on the learning environment in school. Enables women teachers also to avail of day-care facilities for their children and attend school regularly.	(i) Locate ECCE centres in proximity to the Primary School and adjust their timings to include school hours. (ii) Teacher Training programmes and redesigning of curricula for Classes I-III should incorporate ECCE approaches. (iii) Co-ordination between Anganwadi worker and school teacher. (see Chapter on ECCE for further details)
II. Providing Easier Access to Water, Fuel and Fodder	Relieves girls-children from the responsibility of gathering fodder and fuel and fetching water from distant sources.	Make water, fuel and fodder easily accessible on a priority basis, to those habitations or communities whose enrolment and retention rates for girls in schools are below the State average
III. Primary School within Habitations	The 1 km. official norms for 'walking distance' is inappropriate from the standpoint of girls due to their involvement in	(i) Provide each habitation with a population of 300 or more with at least one Primary School by the year 2000 (this implies an additional

Factors which will facilitate girls' education	Reasons	Recommendations
	activities of the household within and outside the home. Primary School within easy access may enable parents to spare children for schooling. Security for very Small girls	1.22 lakh schools as per 1986 data). In the meantime, each of these unserved habitation may be linked to the nearest Primary School through a para-school' (see the chapter on Universalisation for details). (ii) A network of para-Schools', linked to the nearest Primary School should be started such that all unserved habitations with population of less than 300 would be served by at least one para-school' by the end of the Eighth Plan. (iii) Habitations having enrolment and retention rates for girls below the State average must be given priority.
IV. Middle Schools (especially for girls) within easy Access, i.e., within 1 km.	The present norm of of 3 kms. for 'walking distance' places the Middle School beyond the reach of rural girls who carry heavy household responsibilities at this age. Hence, proximity of the school is important for girls. Very real problem of security and apprehension of parents in this regard*	(i) Provide each habitation with a population of 500 or more with at least one Middle School by the year 2000 (about 2.5 i.e., lakh additional schools as per 1986 data). In the meantime, each such habitation may be served by a para-school', linked to the nearest Middle School. (ii) For unserved habitations with a population of less than 500 each, a network of 'para-school'

* The CWDS document states that even 3 kms is a distance that makes parentas apprehensive of sending girls in this age-group to schools.

Factors which will facilitate girls' education	Reasons	Recommendations
	Restrictions relating to puberty regarding mobility, interaction with men.	linked to the nearest Middle School should be started, such that every child has access to a 'para-Middle School' within one km. of residence by the end of the Eighth Plan.
		(iii) Priority should be given to habitations where enrolment and retention rates for girls are below the State average.
V. Non-Formalising the school, making the formal school less rigid Involvement of Village Education Committees formalising school.	The rigidity of the formal school in terms of the school hours and the school calender is a deterrent to the enrolment and retention of girls involved in activities within and outside the home. The rigidity of the curricula and the formal learning environment discourages children from the school.	(i) Shortening and staggering of school hours, particularly for girls and working children. (ii) Flexible timings of the school and matching the school calender with the local agricultural seasons and cultural festivals would be necessary. (iii) Recruit Para teachers' (e.g., Shiksha Karmis) from within the habitation to organise 'para-schools' (linked to the Primary/Middle School), thereby enabling the school to reach out'*
	Children who shift place of residence during seasonal migration cannot avail of formal schooling	(iv) In the context of the above, local educational needs will have to be identified. The Educational Complex and the Village Education Committees will be in the best position to decide how how to effectively open up the school', to recruit para-

* See the chapter on Universalisation of Elementary Education for details regarding 'para teachers'.

Factors which will facilitate girls' education	Reasons	Recommendations
		teachers' and to identify teachers who can be persuaded to help in this process* (v) To meet the needs of working children, drop-outs, children of seasonal migrants, street children etc., creative and non-formal methods, e.g. the ECCE approach, should be designed. (vi) Legal measures be adopted to make employers send their child workers to schools to be especially set up for the purpose.*
VI. Other measures to Attract Girls to Schools	Girls [illegible] labour may require 'opportunity cost' in order to be able to attend school regularly. Older girls and their parents are often uncomfortable with male teachers.	(i) Provide scholarships to deserving girls from under- privileged groups. (ii) Provide uniforms, textbooks etc. to all girls (iii) Increase the number of women teachers. (iv) Complaints regarding sexual abuse of girls in school should be taken seriously.
VII. Secondary and Higher Secondary Schools Better transport facilities. Increase in the number of schools for girls.	Poor transport facilities, particularly in rural areas, contribute to inaccessibility of schools. This is especially true for girls who are discouraged, to use the bicycle or return late in the evening	(i) Educational Complexes should mobilise, on rental, public bus transport facility or private transport (tempo, mini buses, rickshaws, etc.). Rental should be paid by the parents. Bus timings in rural area should be coordinated, as far as possible, with school hours. This will

In the view of the Committee the practice of child labour is a product of the inequitous economic system and should be discontinued. However, as long as the practice continues these children cannot be denied the basic right to education.

Factors which will facilitate girls' education	Reasons	Recommendations
Residential facilities for girls near Secondary and Higher Secondary	Parents are often hesitant to educate older girl children if schools are co-educational or teachers are male. Some parents may be prepared to send girls for schooling if hostel facilities are available. The element of security is important.	benefit students as well as teachers. Innovative methods need to be evolved to enable girl-children to attend schools at greater distances. (A suggestion of having school mothers' as escorts has been made CWDS document) (ii) Increase the number of single sex schools. The possiblity of having two shifts in a school, one for girls and the other for boys can be explored.
	Women teachers will find it convenient, if hostel facilities are available.	(iii) Increase the number of women teachers in co-educational schools and in general. (iv) Hostel facilities must be made available for girls at all levels and women teachers (with one women teacher as warden). Existing accommodation in a village/ town can be hired for this purpose to increase the facility at minimum cost. Free residential facility should be made available for SC/ ST and other under-privileged groups.
VIII. Higher Education Increasing opportunities for women in higher and professional education.	There is need to expand facilities for higher education, especially in subject streams and geographical regions where the representation of women is poor.	(i) Increase in facilities for higher education for women, particularly in the technical professions, in streams and regions reflecting gender disparity with respect to the representation of women.
Incentives for women to pursue further studies,	Special incentives such as scholar-	(ii) Scholarships should be given to encourage

Factors which will facilitate girls' education	Reasons	Recommendations
especially in areas that are non-traditional'	ships, will encourage women to enter streams such as medicine, veterinary sciences, engineering, law etc. Women from poorer families will require freeships, free textbooks, and other such incentives to pursue their studies. Creches, hostels and such other support services will enable women to continue their education.	women to enter non-traditional', high technology courses. (iii) Special financial incentives in the form of freeships, free textbooks etc. should be provided for women from under-privileged sections. (iv) Creches and hostel facilities should be provided to facilitate women to continue education. (v) Relaxation of age-limit and the possibility of continuing education and re-entry into the mainstream, after a break, especially for women who have left studies due to various reasons (see provision for multiple-entry and exit points, as envisaged for Secondary and Higher Education).

(d) Regional Disparities

4.1.16 In addition to state-level disparities in education, district and block-level disparities are also critical dimensions of planning and resource allocation in education. It is observed that districts with the lowest rural female literacy rates, also report poor participation of girls in primary schools. There are 123 districts where the enrolment ratio for girls in primary schools is less than 50 per cent and literacy rate is bleow 10 per cent (See Table 2.2) ; 87 per cent of these districts are concentrated in the five States of Andhra Pradesh, Bihar, Madhya Pradesh, Rajasthan and Uttar Pradesh. This dimension has not been taken into account in the strategies enunciated by the POA.

Content of Education and the Gender Bias

(a) The Curriculum

4.1.17 Serious thought needs to be given to the restructuring of the curriculum so that the objective of women's equality in education is facilitated. While there can be a *women's component* in the curriculum to begin with, the larger goal should be to bring a *gender perspective into the entire curriculum,* whatever be the latter's components. The POA, however, does not reflect such an approach. There is no reference to women or gender in the entire chapter on 'Content and Process of School Education', except for a mention that 'Equality of Sexes' is to be one among the ten core curriculum areas (Pars 6). While the chapter on 'Education for Women's Equality', mentions the incorporation of values commensurate with the new status of women; in the core curriculum it does not present any framework reflecting a gender perspective.

4.1.18 The POA, however, recommends that the NCERT Women's Cell will be given the responsibility for preparing the component of the core curriculum relating to women's equality' (Para 5g). The POA also mentions that this Cell should accelerate its work of eliminating sexist bias and sex stereo-types from school text-books. In the view of the Committee, a gender perspective in the content of education means more than the elimination of sexist bias and sex stereo-types from text-books. A study of NCERT text-books commissioned by the Review Committee showed a distinct gender bias, a greater visibility of male as compared to female characters, portrayal of women as passive and mainly in domestic roles and men in positions of power and authority. The study also observes that such textbook examples cannot be viewed in isolation of the larger context of social reality which gives rise to such stereotypes. Indeed, the mere creation of a Women's Cell in NCERT does not necessarily imply that gender bias will be removed.

4.1.19 The task of bringing a gender perspective into the curriculum is a complex one and requires research input, discussion and debate. Some suggestions made by CWDS in 1985, need to be deliberated upon. These recommendations are modified and given at the end of this chapter.

(b) Stereotypes in Textbooks and the Hidden Curriculum

4.1.20 Given the everyday social reality in which children continuously imbibe gender-biased messages, the school further reinforces these in

TABLE 2.2: Distribution of Districts Having Combined (for all levels) Gross Enrolment Ratios for Girls Less Than 50 Per Cent and Rural Female Literacy Rates Less than 10 Per Cent

States	Number of Districts
Andhra Pradesh	8
Arunachal Pradesh	4
Bihar	14
Haryana	1
Jammu and Kashmir	8
Karnataka	1
Madhya Pradesh	29
Orissa	2
Rajasthan	25
Uttar Pradesh	31
TOTAL	123

Note : Computed from figures provided in GOI/MHRD, 1989, Report of the Working Group on Early Childhood Education and Elementary Education Set-up for Formulation of Eighth Five Year Plan and Census of India, 1981.

Source : Kurrien, J., October, 1990.

terms of both the hidden curriculum (teachers' attitudes, daily activities, peer influence, etc.) and 'the official curriculum'. Examples of the 'hidden curriculum' in a primary school:

(a) "Boys, you must study, the girls will get married anyway."
(b) "Chattan (a boy), if you continue to trouble, you will be made to sit with the girls".

The above examples reflect a gender-bias rooted within the attitudes and behaviour of teachers (this will be dealt with-in the Section on the training of teachers).

4.1.21 Several examples of sex stereotypes even in recent NCERT textbooks have been reported. Reflecting on the image of women that the education system is projecting through textbooks, the Shramshakti Report observes that girls and women are rarely portrayed in roles associated with economic activity. By and large, even mere references to women are minimal, and poor women projected even less. Although the POA affirmatively states that the NCERT Women's Cell should take active help of all persons the role of women's studies centres and women activist groups in eliminating sexist bias in school textbooks is left vague and undefined. Many educational institutes are not even aware of their possible role.

4.1.22 It is important to introduce a note of caution regarding recommendations that give institutions a blanket responsibility for preparing the component of the core curriculum relating to women's equality (POA, Para 5 g). It would be useful to review the work done by such institutions in the area of elimination of gender bias in text-books. In 1982, for instance, NCERT designed Teachers'Handbook entitled 'Status of Women Through Curriculum'. An example from one handbook given in Table 2.3 suggests that mere mechanical changes infact reinforce existing gender roles in 'sophisticated' ways.

(C) The Role of the Media

4.1.23 The powerful role that the media plays in reflecting and perpetuating dominant societal values, such as gender inequality, is well known. Hence efforts by the education system to incorporate a gender perspective and promote women's equality need to be accompanied by intervention in the domain of media as well. To the extent that the media continues to project women in subordinate and exploited roles, and ignores their very presence as well as contribution towards economic activity, it will be difficult to achieve values of gender equality through the educational system alone. While the POA states that "... clear policy guidelines should be developed by Radio and TV in 1986-87 and measures taken to persuade films and other media on these lines" (Para 5 e), it fails to establish media's crucial link with the larger objective of creating gender equality. Although it is not known that such guidelines were ever prepared, in accordance with the suggestions of the POA, no impact is visible in the projected images of women through the media.

Vocational Education

4.1.24 Even though the policy-makes a positive statement on the elimination of sex stereotyping in vocational and professional courses and to promote women's participation in non-traditional occupations ..' the POA in fact makes a negative statement in this regard. It states that .... while girls will continue to receive preferential treatment in trades/ occupations, for which they are particularly well-suited (e.g. teaching and nursing), this will not become a barrier for their participation in technical

TABLE 2.3: Status of Women Through Curriculum of Middle School
Class VI-VII Elementary Teachers' Handbook, NCERT, 1982

Value	Topic	Ideas to be projected	How to project it
Basic knowledge and skill is equally required and applied by men and women	Motion, Force and Pressure	The laws of motion, force and pressure are equally applicable to all. The basic knowledge and skills pertaining to these principles are required by both men and women in their daily life...	Some examples* of motion, force pressure in the household are listed below : (i) *Motion* : *Churning of milk* by churner is an example in which the hands move in linear motion whereas the wheel moves in rotational motion. In sewing machine the rotational motion. of wheel is converted to transiatory motion of sewing-needle. Grinding-wheel and the swing (jhoola) are examples of vibrational motion. (ii) *Force* : For frictional force, the examples of scrubbing, striking match, sharpening knife and cleaning vessels should be cited. (iii) *Pressure* : Cooking by pressure, use of knife and cutters, syringe, handpump, cycle pump and grinding stone, etc., should be used as illustrations.

These examples are from household work traditionally associated with women. The guide book could as well given alternative examples concerning work common to men and women.

and professional courses of higher level .... ' (POA, para 18(i).

4.1.25 In practice it has been observed that options for scientific and technical professions are rarely available to women. Existing polytechnics for women offer only traditional 'women-oriented' courses, such as fashion designing, cookery, nursery teachers' training, beautician, interior decoration, steno-typing etc., thus reinforcing the sex-stereotypes.

4.1.26 Given the present low educational status of women, and high drop-out rates, it is desirable to develop a wide-range of vocational courses at the 'Plus Class VIII' (i.e secondary stage) level so that such opportunities would be available to a larger segment of girls than would be the case if such courses were available only at +2 level. Such courses should be linked with placement opportunities and entrepreneurship.

4.1.27 In this context, POA's emphasis on exposing girls to a variety of vocational training activities, at each stage in school education itself, is particularly welcome. POA also suggested that skill development amongst girls and women would be a continuous process starting from the NFE and AE centres and carried further by the Continuing Education Centres. There is no evidence that these positive aspects of NPE for promoting gender equality have been implemented during the post-policy period.

Training of Teachers and other Educational Personnel

4.1.28 Teachers, themselves being products of society, bring with them gender-biased stereotypes and images which they communicate (often unconsciously) to students within and outside the classroom. An awareness of gender discrimination, stereotypes and biases, both in the 'official' and 'hidden' curriculum, can help the teacher to consciously attempt to practise gender equality within the constraints of the class-room situation. In this context the committee has in mind the concrete teaching context where teachers (especially in elementary rural schools), working under trying conditions, are extremely vulnerable, have little autonomy and are bound by a rigid curriculum. However, since the pedagogical relationship does give the teacher a position of authority vis-s-vis the student in the class-room and the fact that teachers can and do wield influence over children and their parents, gives rise to possibilities for intervention in education. Although this interventionist potential of teacher, as also of decision-makers and educational administrators, is implied in NPE/POA, it needs to be explicitly stated and incorporated in strategies. It is here that the training of teachers becomes crucial. In the context of gender, training implies a re-orientation of the content and practice of teaching towards a perspective of women's equality. This pertains not only to the 'official' curriculum but also includes an understanding of how gender bias is communicated and reinforced within the school through the 'hidden' curriculum, an aspect not mentioned by the POA.

4.1.29 The implementation of measures suggested by POA (Paras 5 b, c and h) regarding training and sensitisation of educational personnel at all levels has hardly received attention so far. While there is no evidence that NIEPA has taken any step in organising programmes for administrators and planners on women's issues, the work reportedly being undertaken by NCERT/SCERTs/DIETs has yet to become visible. This lack of priority may itself reflect a gender bias.

4.1.30 Training and sensitisation has been viewed by the POA as a highly centralised activity, with too much expectation from NCERT's Women's Cell, NIEPA and UGC. No concrete participatory role has been envisaged for the Women's Study Centres or women's organisations in decentralising training, sensitisation and curriculum evaluation programmes.

Research and Development of Women's Studies

4.1.31 Recent developments in research and the teaching of Women's Studies offer a method and an instrument in transforming the role of the educational system in active promotion of new value.

4.1.32 Although the POA refers to four dimensions of the Women's Studies programme in terms of teaching, research, training and extension (Para 6) , it essentially views it in the limited context of higher education and specific non-formal approaches to women's development. Research on Women's Studies makes available rich sources of data that can be incorporated into the very structure and process of education. Such research can be a major input in incorporating women's issues, concerns and perspectives at all stages of education. Concrete inputs should be in the areas of curriculum development and training and sensitisation of teachers and other educational personnel. Data collection and monitoring, particularly on the progress of girls' education, as part of Women's Studies, can provide a continuous link between research and educational practice. Women's Study Centres should involve women's organizations in their programmes so that concrete issues affecting the lives of women can be discussed, researched and analysed within the centres. This can pave the way for action research as well.

Women's Studies Courses

4.1.33 Although the POA refers to the incorporation of issues relating to women's status and role in the foundation course proposed to be introduced by University Grants Commission for all under-graduate students and incorporation of the women's dimension into courses in different disciplines (Para 6), it is not known what steps have been taken to concretise these recommendations.

Extension Services

4.1.34. Developing an adequate gender perspective and building it into the entire educational system would also require the implementation of women's programmes such as legal literacy, awareness building etc., as also suggested in the POA (Para 10). For this purpose, special measures are needed in both universities and colleges.

Representation of Women in the Educational Hierarchy

4.1.35 The available data show that there are fewer women teachers at all levels of education, compared to men. Also, the number of women teachers declines as the level of education increases. The POA recommends that women may be given preference in 'recruitment of teachers up to school level' (Para 5f), but it does not look into the problems of accommodation, security, child-care etc. which constraint women teachers, particularly in rural areas. The experience of Operation Blackboard shows that the emphasis on posting at least one woman teacher often sought transfer out of the rural areas due to lack of accommodation, security and creche facilities.

4.1.36 While much has been said of the need to empower women through awareness programmes in the POA, little attention has been given to the fact that few women are represented in educational decision-making bodies.

Empowerment of Women

4.1.37 The parameters for the empowerment of women, outlined in the POA (Para 4), acknowledge some of the factors that lie outside the education sector, and have a critical bearing on women's status. Here, the POA appears to have taken cognizance of the patriarchal system which continues to constraint the role of women in society and their participation in education. However, the POA seems to be guided by the policy statement that education can be used as an agent of basic change in the status of woman. Hence, it formulates a set of measures within the narrow framework of education (training, re-designing curriculum, preference in teacher recruitment etc.) to achieve the parameters for empowering women (Para 5) . It is to the credit of the Ministry, therefore, that, in April 1989 , it launched Mahila Samakhya, a programme for empowering rural poor women. This programme makes an attempt to address the factors that lie outside the education sector. It assumes that the empowered group of women in a village will try and seek solutions to their problems by initiating action, and pressuring (sic) the block and district structure to respond and thereby lead to, among other things, enhanced women's participation in education'.

4.1.38 It must be recognised, however, that the Mahila Samakhya programme is still in its infancy (i.e. still only in parts of Gujarat, U.P. and Karnataka). While reports from Karnataka are encouraging, the Gujarat and U.P. units need to be observed and evaluated objectively over a longer period of time.

4.1.39 What emerges from the Mahila Samakhya programme is the importance of local level initiative by the women's groups and the need to guard against centralised planning mode. In this context, it may be noted that, unlike in other Centrally-Sponsored Schemes, Mahila Samakhya has recently taken a step towards setting up an autonomous state-level board for management.

4.1.40 The POA concept of women's empowerment has the following two lacunae—

(a) It presents the concept of empowerment of women as a process confined to women only and to be organised in isolation of men in the same community; and

(b) It does not refer to the critical role of raising, through education, awareness regarding the issues of women's health, including reproductive health and sexuality in the larger dimension of empowerment of women.

Adult Education

4.1.41. The POA envisaged a mass-scale adult education programme to 'Eradicate illiteracy amongst women by 1995'. Even at the time of mounting the National Literacy Mission for the purpose, awareness clearly was there that literacy might not be felt as a priority need by the women, as reflected by para 14 of POA which says " As majority of women in this age-group (i.e. 15-35) are workers, literacy may not have any relevance for them". Therefore, adult education programme for women should be designed with specific reference to this ground truth.

Resources

4.1.42 Many of the measures suggested here to ensure the success of the policy for giving 'a well-conceived edge' to education in favour of women would require a significant increase in allocation of resources in both the Plan and Non-Plan sectors. While a detailed exercise would have to be undertaken, certain guiding principles may be enunciated here.

Management

4.1.43. Unlike what is claimed by POA in para 3, there is no evidence that any move has been envisaged to create dynamic managerial structure to cope with the 'targets' set out for women's education. The POA seemingly stresses centralisation of planning, co-ordination, monitoring and evaluation, as is evident from the following statements (Para 19):

— "Women's Cell in the NCERT will be revived and strengthened";
— "NIEPA and Directorate of Adult Education will have strong cells to plan and administer women's training programmes";and
— "Women's Cell in the UGC will be strengthened ......".

4.1.44 In line with this centralised modality of management, the POA assigns major role to the above-named and other central agencies in training of teachers and NFE/AE instructors (Para 5 b), preparation of core curriculum component relating to women's equality (Para 5g), sensitisation of educational planners and administrators (Para 5h), sensitisation of educational planners and services (Para 12), and vocational training (Para 18v) . For good measure, the POA makes a passing reference in the last paragraph to the setting up of a Women's Cell at the State-level too. Even this reference is left vague as no clear role is assigned to this State-level Cell in a management structure where all major initiatives have been concentrated in the central agencies. The POA does not even assign any special role in the training of teachers and NFE/AE instructors on women's issues to DIETs, a centrally-aided district-level network. In the framework of this centralised style of management, the Government of India have also introduced a number of Centrally-Sponsored Schemes which have vital relevance to women's education (as to education in general). In the context of this centralised planning and management style, reference to community involvement made in the POA (Para 11) seems incongruous.

Recommendations

1. There is a crucial link between the easy access to water, fuel and fodder and schooling of girls. This understanding needs to be explicitly reflected in the policy of Government and be concretised in operational designs.
2. 'Local Area Planning', as envisaged in the 'Approach to the Eighth Five Year Plan' document, must take into account the above linkage while planning for programmes relating to forestry, drinking water and greening of common lands.
3. The Department of Education should coordinate with the other concerned departments and secure adequate resource allocation for the above mentioned programmes based on parameters which indicate the status of girls' education in a given habitation/village. For instance, priority needs to be given to the habitations/Villages having enrolment and retention rates for girls in schools below the average rates of the States.
4. To achieve the above purpose, planning for educational development of any given region would have to be necessarily conducted at the Block or sub-Block level. This task would be facilitated if it is undertaken through the proposed Educational Complexes in which there will be Block-level representatives of the various agencies/ departments concerned with social welfare and development, along with teachers, *Anganwadi* workers, and representatives of poor women's groups and Panchayati Raj institutions.
5. Teachers, *Anganwadi* workers, village-level functionaries of other departments, and representatives of women's groups and community-level organisations should play an important role in making micro-level information available to the Educational Complexes for prioritisation of action in this regard.
6. The policy framework on women's education must bring out the

criticality of the link between ECCE and girls' accessibility to elementary education.

7. Comprehensive and effective ECCE services should be provided in proximity to every primary and middle school and be programmatically linked with elementary education.
8. Priority should be given to child-care programmes catering to the 0-3 age-group, particularly among the under-privileged sections of society.
9. The timings of the ECCE centres should include the school hours so that the girls in the 6-14 age-group are relieved from the responsibility of sibling care.
10. While the *Anganwadis* (ICDS) should continue to be given importance, other models which are sensitive to local needs should also be encouraged.
11. The management of *Anganwadis* and other ECCE programmes should be decentralised and be made participative, as recommended in the chapter on ECCE.
12. In order that child-care facilities and pre-school and primary education of girls are prioritised in the village and the community, the Anganwadi workers and poor women's groups should be represented on the Village Education Committees.
13. The issue of regional disparities needs to be incorporated into the operational design for universalising girls' access to elementary education .
14. Any effective strategy for raising the educational status of women in India would have to give priority to the educationally backward districts.
15. Educational planning at the level of Educational Complexes will depend on Block-level or sub-Block-level information collected from habitations/villages. Teachers, Anganwadi workers, other village-level functionaries and representatives of poor women and other community level organisations should be involved in making such information available.
16. Decentralised and participative mode of planning and management offers an effective basis for responding to the challenge of regional disparities in education, including girls' education. Diverse strategies and disaggregated time-frames, worked out locally, constitute the twin instrumentalities to achieve the goal of universalisation.
17. The Curriculum in schools should include:

— Increase in the visibility of women and projection of a positive image of the role of women in history, their contribution to society in general and the Indian context in particular. For instance, social history should project the contribution that women have made in the national movement, All such issues should be carefully incorporated in the training and orientation of teachers, educators and administrators.

— Special efforts should be made to strengthen mathematics and science education among girls. Girls' schools should give greater importance to mathematics and science than at present.
— Undifferentiated curriculum for boys and girls.
— Elimination of negative stereotypes and biological and social concepts which have a sexist bias. This has been dealt with in greater detail in the Section that follows.
— Outmoded traditions and myths that hinder positive development of women and their role in national life should be objectively discussed in the classroom in a gender perspective. Similarly, the portrayal of women in our epics and mythology needs to be critically examined in the classroom.
— Basic legal information including protective laws regarding women and children and extracts from the Constitution to make the children aware of the fundamental rights and other basic concepts therein.
— Specific measures to improve the participation of girls in physical training and sports should be undertaken.

18. It is recommended that all school text-books, both by NCERT/SCERTs and other publishers, be reviewed to eliminate the invisibility of women and gender stereotypes, and also for the proper incorporation of a women's perspective in the teaching of all subjects. This review should also cover all the supplementary reading material and library books being recommended for schools, particularly those supplied by Operation Blackboard.
19. As an immediate step such an exercise should seek the active participation of different groups and individuals, such as Women's Studies experts, Women's Studies Centres of the Universities and Research Institutes, and Women's organisations working at grass-root level, rather than exclusive dependence on NCERT/SCERTs.
20. A similar exercise should be undertaken for the university curriculum and text-books in all disciplines. This should be initiated by University-based Women's Studies Centres and individuals already working on these issues.
21. All media channels, both in the public and private sectors, should take serious note of the crucial role that the media can play in promoting

gender equality and empowerment of women as enunciated in NPE.

22. In the specific context of gender, advertisements displaying women as sex symbols and using them for sales promotion should be seriously dealt with.
23. Media should project positive images of women. Women should also be shown in professional roles, for instance as doctors, engineers and scientists, so that they can serve as role models.
24. An awareness of the need for women's education, especially elementary and vocational education, should also be spread.
25. The Information and Broadcasting Ministry should evolve a network to monitor the projection of women, and evolve a code of ethics with regard to the presentation of women in all types of media (similar recommendations are also made in the Shramshakti Report, 1988).
26. An Inter-Ministerial Committee, comprising representatives of the Departments of Education, Women and Child Development, Culture, and Information and Broadcasting, should be constituted to monitor and ensure that the policy guidelines emerging from NPE and POA are being supported, rather than being violated, by the media, particularly Radio and TV. Representatives of women's organisations and Women's Study Centres may also be included in this Committee.
27. A National Policy on Communication, giving a gender perspective to all forms and processes of mass communication, should be formulated urgently. The National Commission on Women should play an active role in this exercise.
28. Vocational Training for women should be planned and implemented at the State level, partly through the proposed Educational Complexes.
29. Vocational Training for women should be encouraged in non-traditional occupations, following an undifferentiated curriculum.
30. Concerted efforts should be made towards discouraging the existing biases in vocational courses for women.
31. Vocational training courses for girls at Plus Class VIII' level (i.e. secondary stage) in order to expand the social base of vocational education. Opportunities should be especially given to drop-outs after middle school.
32. Diversification of courses and trades to match with the job potential at local level is important. For encouraging access to technical or craft-and-skill-training institutions, increased stipends, fellowships, and a system of placement is recommended. There should be at least one Women's polytechnic in each District.
33. Teacher training programmes in general require a critical evaluation

and re-orientation within which the incorporation of the women's perspective should be a key dimension. This would include sensitivity to women's issues and awareness of the problems in the education of girls.

34. Teacher educators, Women's Studies researchers in universities and institutes including those in the Women's Cells, as well as representatives of women's organisations and development groups, and not just a handful of Central or State level agencies, should be involved in this process of evaluation and re-orientation of teacher training programmes.
35. The 'Core' elements of a restructured teachers' training programme should emerge from the above exercises. Subsequently at the level of the State (or region), the DIETs and Educational Complexes along with educational institutions, Women's Study Centres, educators and grass-root level organisations should participate in evolving the actual curriculum of the teachers' training programme. This kind of decentralisation in curriculum planning, and later even in its implementation, allows for greater flexibility and meaningfulness.
36. Teachers' trianing institutes should adopt the revised curriculum so that all teacher trainees, male and female, are exposed to the restructured training programme.
37. A separate training and sensitisation programme for the teacher educators would have to be undertaken on a priority basis.
38. Simultaneously in-service training programmes should be conducted to sensitize teachers who are already in schools. The DIETs in consultation with the Education Complexes should take the initiative in organising these in-service programmes.
39. The actual form that the in-service training programmes will take, should be left to the DIETs in consultation with the Education Complexes. For instance, one school can serve as the 'training school' where teachers' training will include practice teaching. The 'internship model' referred to elsewhere can be explored.
40. Administrators and planners in education (including Heads of institutions) can be sensitised to women's issues through the diffusion of information, holding of workshops and frequent interaction with resource persons in the area of Women's Studies. This is particularly crucial when exercises involving decision-making in education are undertaken.
41. Women's Study Centres should be organised in all the universities and recognised social science research institutions within the Eighth

Plan.

42. Women's Studies research findings should be incorporated into curriculum revision and development, and teacher training programmes at all levels of education. At the university level, representatives of the Women's Study Centres should be included in all official bodies concerned with curriculum and syllabus development in all disciplines.
43. A close linkage in the work of the university-based Women's Study Centres and Educational Complexes should be encouraged with a view to widen participation, decentralised and diversified training, sensitisation and curriculum evaluation. This will also enrich the work of the Women's Study Centres themselves through feedback from the field. The Women's Study Centres of a university should play a key role in introducing a gender perspective in school education within the Education Complexes of the region that they serve.
44. The foundation courses introduced by the UGC should be reviewed and revised to incorporate women's dimensions. This should be part of the students' overall assessment at the undergraduate level. The course should be carefully structured with the active involvement of Women's Studies research and development organisations and women's organisations working at the grass-root level. Adequate representation of women's issues, from all sections of society, their concerns and living conditions should be incorporated.
45. Existing courses should also incorporate the gender perspective, as suggested in the POA. This must apply to all courses, including science and technology, medicine, law, agriculture and veterinary sciences.
46. All issues related to curricular revision and development on Women's Studies should be extended to the orientation of teachers as well.
47. Women's Development Centres, such as the ones existing in some university colleges should be extended to all colleges and higher educational institutions.
48. These Centres should also be given funds to conduct awareness workshops/seminars etc. at both the school and community levels.
49. The proportion of women teachers in Primary, Middle and High Schools should be increased to at least 50 per cent. For the success of this measure it would be desirable if the women teacher is selected from within or near the habitation where she is to teach. In case a local woman teacher cannot be found, it would then be necessary to —

(a) provide living quarters with certain minimum amenities to women teachers on priority basis;
(b) locate the living quarters within the habitation in order to ensure security; and
(c) wherever possible, provide living quarters to all women functionaries, apart from women teachers, in close proximity to each other.

50. While an increasing number of women should be recruited at different levels of education, there should be promotional avenues also within the educational hierarchy. Special measures would have to be devised to ensure that women are fairly represented in decison-making bodies in teaching and educational administration.
51. Special provisions to take care of women's needs should be built into the recruitment and service procedures, evaluation criteria, guidelines for promotion, etc. An example of such procedures is association of women in Selection Committees and Departmental Promotions Committees. This will ensure that women are not prevented by socio-cultural factors from rising in educational hierarchy.
52. Women and men in positions of planning and decision-making within the educational hierarchy and public administration should be sensitised to women's issues so as to adequately discharge their leadership roles.
53. Develop Mahila Samakhya in a decentralised and participative mode of management, with the decision-making powers devolved to the district or block-level, and ultimately to the poor women's groups themselves.
54. Implement Mahila Samakhya in such a way as to establish organic linkages with the ECCE programme and the efforts towards universalisation of girls' elementary education.
55. Build a component of closely working with men in the community also, as part of the process of women's empowerment.
56. Along with the means for economic independence for women, the issues of women's health, including reproductive health and sexuality, should be included in the parameters for empowerment of women.
57. For imparting adult education to women and thereby empower them, the Mahila Samakhya model should be tried out. (In fact this is being suggested as the basic strategy for adult education programme as a whole).
58. Earmarking 50 per cent of the elementary sector allocation for measures to increase girls' participation and making this allocation

non-divertible.

59. Earmarking a share of all developmental allocations for secondary, vocational and higher education for measures to improve girls' access thereto and improving the quality of education in these sectors;
60. Special earmarking for girls within the special component plan for Scheduled Castes and Tribal sub-plan .
61. Continuance of all Centrally Sponsored Schemes relating, in part or in full, to women's education may be treated in terms of the detailed recommendation given by the Committee in regard to Centrally Sponsored Schemes as a whole in the chapter on Decentralisation and Participative Management.
62. The responsibility for planning, implementing and internal monitoring of all school-based programmes for women's education be handed over to the Educational Complexes in the Panchayati Raj framework. At the institutional level, the Head of the institution (Primary/Middle/Higher Secondary Schools) should be made fully responsible for micro-level planning and ensuring universalisation (not just enrolment) of girls' education and their access to high school or vocational education, according to disaggregated strategies and time-frames.

3

Education for All by 2000 (1990)*

Introduction

Universalisation of elementary education has been one of the most important goals of educational development in India since Independence. The goal of free and compulsory education for all children up to age of 14 years as stipulated in Article 45 of the Constitution should have been fulfilled within a period of 10 years i.e. by 1960. On account of various constraints it has been revised several times; first by 1970, then by 1976, and later to 1990. The present date according to the National Policy on Education, 1986 is 1995. The document under reference does not subscribe to the present target. It makes on analytical study of the various aspects of the problem and attempts to indicate possible direction and broad resource requirements

EXTRACTS

Goals and Targets

Unrealistic Targets in the Past

A review of the progress of basic education shows that goals and targets were fixed in the past on the basis of an inadequate understanding of the significance of education. These targets did not take into account the problem of availability of resources, and the conflicting claims of social and economic planning.

---

* *Education for All A by 2000: Indian Perspective,* National Institution of Educational Planning and Administration (NIEPA), New Delhi, 1990.

Note -1. Serial number and captions inserted. 2. Figures in the parentheses indicate Chapter number and Page number respectively.

Realistic Targets

If right from the beginning,it is apparent that goals are unrealistic and unachievable, they do not lead to the kind of motivation and resource mobilisation required. The right approach, therefore, is to set realistic targets—realistic not defined as easily achievable, but as achievable, with conceivable maximum input of meticulous planning and resources—financial as well as human.

We shall, therefore, proceed to propose realistic targets that we believe can be achieved by the year 2000, keeping in view the past trends, the contemporary situation, and the future prospects of availability of resources and other favourable environment, as also the constraints. The targets will be presented in more precise and specific terms. Although it is a plan for ten years, it would be useful to set separate targets for the first five and the second five years to enable mid-term appraisal and corrective action. This will also coincide with the Eighth and the Ninth Five Year Plan periods. (3.26-27)

Identification of Educational Inputs

For ideal planning, educational inputs provided by other sectors should also be taken into account.

Limited Specificity and Disaggregation in Target Fixing

Different targets for different States and areas could be attempted, but this would make the whole exercise too cumbersome to be meaningful. It is, therefore, proposed that the national targets may have limited specificity and disaggregation with the further requirement that more detailed disaggregated targets will be set for each state, each district, each development block and each unit of micro planning. In this disaggregated target-setting at various levels, the following important considerations will be kept in view:

(1) Separate targets for rural and urban areas should be fixed.

(2) Separate targets for the disadvantaged sections of the society will be fixed genderwise.

(3) The low participation in education of girls and women is the most significant factor to be taken into account. Any target for a group may be achieved with continued inequity between males and

females of that group, so long as the targets do not clearly indicate the levels to be achieved separately for both genders. That is why it has been suggested that the groupwise disaggregated target will also be genderwise.

(4) Access to educational facilities, participation in education, and achievement in education are distinct, though interrelated. These aspects should be separately considered for fixing targets and appropriate planning.

National Level Targets

The mechanism of micro-level planning will result in separate targets for each planning unit—state, district, block, and village. In a truly decentralised approach of planning, realistic targets fixed by all the villages of the block should lead to the target of the block, the targets of all the blocks in a district should lead to the target of the district and so on. However, such a process will not only be time-consuming, it would also lack a national goal reference. By expecting certain national level targets on the basic of disaggregation, we are also hoping to oblige the national and state-level planners to pay higher attention to areas and groups and within them to girls/women, receiving special attention,

A. Access

1. By the year 1995, primary schools or their alternatives will be provided to every child in the rural areas with a distance of one km.

2. By the year 2000, upper primary schools or their alternatives will be provided to every child in the rural area within a distance of three kms.

According to the All India Educational Survey (1986), conducted by the NCERT, 94 per cent of the rural population is being served by a primary school within one km and 85.39 per cent of the rural population is being served by an upper primary school within a distance of three kms. In view of this, it should not be difficult to provide a school or an alternative education centre the next 5 years to the remaining 6 per cent of the rural population for primary education, and the remaining 14.61 per cent for upper primary education in the next 10 years. In this we are assuming a growth rate of slightly above one per cent, which is not very high.

B. Participation

3. Primary education through schools or alternatives will be provided

to:

(a) 80 per cent of all children up to the age of 11 years by 1995, which will necessarily include at least 70 per cent belonging to every identified disadvantaged group; and

(b) 95 per cent of all children up to the age of 11 years by the year 2000, which will necessarily include 85 per cent girls belonging to every identified disadvantaged group.

Taking into account the current lower participation rate of the children of disadvantaged groups as compared to the total participation of children, different levels of participation are proposed for children of disadvantaged groups and for the overall participation.

4. Upper primary education through schools or alternatives will be provided to:

(a) 60 per cent of all children up to the age of 14 years by 1995, which will necessarily include at least 65 per cent of girls belonging to every identified disadvantaged group, and

(b) 75 per cent of all children up to the age of 14 years by 1995, which will necessarily include at least 65 per cent of girls belonging to every identified disadvantaged group. (3.28.29)

The dropout rate is extremely high in the early stages of primary education and is considerably less between the conclusion of primary and the start of the upper primary education. Of those who complete primary education roughly 75 per cent continue studies for upper primary education. Most of the children who continue studies for upper primary education usually complete that stage. Keeping this in view, the targets for participation in upper primary education have been kept at approximately 75 per cent, of those for primary education. An assumption implicit is that if the existing transfer rate for primary to upper primary is 75 per cent, it is likely to go up and similarly the dropout rate at the upper primary stage would also be reduced. The effect of the level achieved in 1995 at the end of the primary stage will usually be seen at the end of the upper primary stage after three years. However, in view of the improved environment for education, it has been visualised that improved transfer to and retention, in upper primary education will not be sequential but partly contemporaneous with improvement in primary education.

(3.29)

4

Central Advisory Board of Education Working Group on Education for Women and Other Disadvantaged Groups (1991)

Introduction

The Central Advisory Board of Education (CABE)* in its Forty-sixth meeting held on March 8-9, 1991 at New Delhi, discussed the reports of the various working groups formed by it on education. The Working Group on Education of Women and other Disadvantaged Groups like SC, ST, Minorities etc. was headed by Shri H.S. Lyngdoh, Education Minister, Meghalaya. Shri, Ashok Kumar Mishra, Education Secretary, Orissa was the Rapporteur

Recommendations/Proceedings

1. At the outset, the Group discussed the reasons for low literacy among women in the country and focussed on the problems which prevent young girls from attending schools. Among other reasons, special emphasis was laid on the social attitudes of people, responsibility shouldered by the girl-child-specially in collecting water, fuel and in looking after her siblings. The regional variations especially between areas like North East on one hand where the position of women is different from regions such as Uttar Pradesh and Bihar were noted. Therefore, the first recommendation of the Sub-Group was that special efforts should be made to understand the region's specific problems of women and girls in order to design special inputs. All recommendations should, thus, be seen in area and culture

---

* Central Advisory Board of Education, Forty-sixth meeting March 8-9, 1991, *Proceedings*, Government of India, Ministry of Human Resource Development. Department of Education. New Delhi, 1992.

specific context.

2. The position of women in minority communities was an important focus of the Group. It was noted that literacy rate among Scheduled Castes and Scheduled Tribes and other minorities was much lower than the literacy rate among forward areas/communities. In some areas, the literacy rate among Scheduled Castes women is lower than 1 per cent. The Group, therefore, recommended that the problems of girls' education among these communities should receive special attention and area/community specific strategies may have to be devised.

3. Most young girls, especially in poor families share a very large burden of household responsibilities. In this context, the need to provide child-care facilities and ECCE centres along with primary schools was emphasised.

4. Focussing on problem of high drop-out rates among girls and their non-participation in the formal school system, the Group was of the opinion that the formal system needs to be non-formalised. Possibility for operating different shifts for girls and working children could be explored, along with reduction of school hours, wherever necessary. In order to achieve universal elementary education a special Action Plan may have to be prepared for addressing the problem of girls' education. If necessary, special funds could be earmarked for such an initiative.

5. The Group strongly recommended the need to evaluate the impact of special provisions, schemes and projects made for women over the last 40 years. An understanding of the impact of the Scheme could help policy-makers to make specific recommendations. Area specific special programmes will have to be devised after a thorough study of those regions where female literacy is extremely low.

6. The Group was of the opinion that a Council to monitor women's education should be set up under the Chairmanship of the Chief Minister with senior officers as members. This Council should have a Chief Executive who could systematically monitor progress of different schemes, ensure target is achieved and above all ensure resources are allocated for women's education.

7. The Group recommended the need to have awareness generation programmes which could create a demand for education for women and also encourage parents to send their girls to schools. Additional facilities or infrastructure alone cannot ensure increased participation. In this context, the Group took note of the pilot programme initiated by the Department of Education, Ministry of Human Resource Development and Mahila Samakhya.

8. The Group endorsed the recommendations made in agenda Item No. 18 on Women's Education. The Group noted that the specific recommendations of the NPE-1986 are still relevant. Special mention was made on the following items:—

- — Increased women's access to vocational, technical and professional education.
- — Preference for women in recruitment of teachers.
- — Special Polytechnics for women.
- — Special hostel facilities for women.
- — 100 per cent assistance for NFE centres for girls.
- — Schemes of freeships and scholarships.
- — Special focus on the campaign approach to encourage women's participation in adult literacy programmes.
- — Mahila Samakhya Programme as an important pilot programme.

9. The Group also took note of the main recommendations of the Report of the Committee for Review of National Policy on Education, 1986. Special mention was made to the following recommendations of that Committee:-

- — Need to link girls' access to elementary education with ECCE facilities.
- — Decentralised and participative mode of planning to address policy measures to region and community specific problems.
- — Need to encourage vocational and technical education.
- — Increase the number of women teachers in schools to at least 50 per cent and provide necessary facilities to them.
- — Awareness generation programmes as an important input in the Adult Education.
- — Earmarking funds for girls education.

10. Rounding off the discussion, the Group reiterated the need to focus on areas and region specific problems especially to encourage women's education. Culture attitudes and practices vary from region to region. Therefore, planning for education should be sensitive to the above context.

5

Programme of Action of National Policy on Education (1992)

Introduction

The Revised Formulations which set forth the modifications to the National Policy on Education, 1986 (NPE, 1986), were placed in both Houses of Parliament on 7th May, 1992. The revised NPE necessitated certain modifications in the Programme of Action, 1986, formed immediately after the announcement of NPE, 1986. The Programme of Action (1992) was evolved by constituting twenty-two task forces on different subject areas. These task forces included educationists and officials of the Union and State Governments. The draft Programme of Action was discussed at a conference of State Secretaries and Directors of Education held on 3-4 August, 1992. Suggestions received during this meeting were considered and incorporated in the document. The Central Advisory Board of Education (CABE) met on 8th August, 1992 and endorsed the document after the detailed consideration.

The Programme of Action 1992, entitled its first chapter 'Education for Women's Equality'. The text of the chapter is reproduced here.

EDUCATION FOR WOMEN'S EQUALITY

1 Preface

1.1.1 Education for Women's Equality is a vital component of the overall strategy of securing equity and social justice in education. Paras 4.2 and 4.3 of the National Policy on Education (NPE), 1986 are very strong and

* *Programme of Action 1992, National Policy on Education, 1986.* Ministry of Human Resource Development, Department of Education, Government of India , New Delhi, 1992.

forthright statements on the intervening and empowering role of education. *Inter alia,* they emphasize the provision of special support services and removal of factors which result in discrimination against women at all levels of education. The POA clearly spells out the actions which need to be taken to promote education for women's equality; it can hardly be improved upon. What is sought to be done is to modify the contents of the POA wherever appropriate. What comes out clearly is the need for will to implement and to devise institutional mechanisms to ensure that gender sensitivity is reflected in the implementation of educational programmes across the board. Education for Women's Equality is too important to be left to the individual commitments or proclivities of persons in charge of implementing programmes. It should be incumbent on all actors, agencies and institutions in the field of education at all levels to be gender sensitive and ensure that women have their rightful share in all educational programmes and activities.

2. Present Situation

1.2.1 According to the 1991 Census female literacy rate is 39.42 per cent compared to 63.86 per cent for males. The number of female illiterates at 197 million is more than male illiterates by 70 million even though the female population is less than the male population by 32 million. There are significant rural-urban disparities among women, rural female literacy is about half of urban female literacy. A striking finding is that for every 100 girls in class I in rural areas, there are only 40 in class V, 18 in class VIII, 9 in class IX and only one in class XII — the corresponding figures for urban areas being 82, 62, 32 and 14. If ten to twelve years of general education is the basic requirement for entrance into technical and professional education, rural girls would, therefore, stand excluded. An overwhelming proportion of vocational, higher and technical educational facilities are located in urban or semi-urban areas. Participation of girls in this sector continues to be low and gender stereotyped. Similarly, proportion of women and girls in engineering and agriculture-based courses is woefully low.

1.2.2 This is compounded by the fact that the proportion of women teachers in the low literacy States is extremely poor. The percentage of women teachers at the primary and middle schools is 21 per cent and 23 per cent in rural areas and 56 per cent and 57 per cent in urban areas.

Notes : 1. Paras refer to para numbers of chapter 1 of Programme of Action.

2. Paras 4.2 and 4.3 of the NPE, 1986 are reproduced at the end of this chapter.

1.2.3 It is, therefore, imperative that the entire educational system is made alive to the gender and regional dimensions of educational disparities.

3. Policy Parameters and Strategies

1.3.1 In pursuance of NPE the main features of the implementation strategy will consist of the following:-

(i) to gear the entire education system to play a positive interventionist role in the empowerment of women;
(ii) to encourage educational institutions to take up active programmes to enhance women's status and further women's development in all sectors;
(iii) to widen women's access to vocational, technical and professional education at all levels, breaking gender stereotypes; and
(iv) to create a dynamic management structure that will be able to respond to the challenge posed by this mandate.

4. Plan of Action

1.4.1 Strategies outlined below deal primarily with operational details regarding implementation of the POA:

(i) All the Bureaus of the Department of Education will prepare a concrete action plan addressing gender related concerns in their specific area of work by August, 1993. Relevant nodal institutions like the UGC, AICTE ICSSR, ICHR, CBSE, ICAR, ICMR, IAMR, State Boards, Vocational Education Bureaus, etc. will also prepare similar action plans. Part IV, para 4.1 to 4.3 of the NPE and Chapter XII of the POA will form the guiding principles for the action plan;

UGC	=	University Grants Commission
AICTE	=	All India Council for Technical Education
ICSSR	=	Indian Council of Social Science Research
ICHR	=	Indian Council of Historical Research
CBSE	=	Central Board of Secondary Education
ICAR	=	Indian Council of Agricultural Research
ICMR	=	Indian Council of Medical Research
IAMR	=	Institute of Applied Manpower Research

(ii) A monitoring unit will be created in the Planning Division of the Department of Education to ensure integration of gender issues into policies, programmes and schemes. This unit will develop indicators for monitoring implementation, ensure effective dissemination of information and coordinate action. This will be done by August, 1993.

(iii) Similar monitoring units/bureaus will be set up at the State level; and

(iv) Annual reports of all the bureaus and institutions will clearly spell out the steps they have taken to enhance women's and girls' access to education, ensuring that the content and process of education is sensitive to gender concerns and equal access is assured for science and technical education at all levels.

5. Empowerment of Women

1.5.1 Education can be an effective tool for women's empowerment, the parameters of which are :-

— enhancing self-esteem and self confidence of women;
— building a positive image of women by recognizing their contribution to the society, polity and the economy;
— developing ability to think critically;
— fostering decision-making and action through collective processes;
— enabling women to make informed choices in areas like education, employment and health (especially reproductive health) ;
— ensuring equal participation in developmental processes;
— providing information, knowledge and skill for economic independence;
— enhancing access to legal literacy and information relating to their rights and entitlements in society with a view to enhance their participation on an equal footing in all areas;

1.5.2 The following measures will be taken for achievement of the above parameters and the concerned bureaus and institutions will report on progress as stated in Para 4.1 above :

(i) Every educational institution will take up active programmes of women's development;

(ii) All teachers and instructors will be trained as agents of women's empowerment. Training programmes will be developed by NCERT, NIEPA, DAE, SRCs, DIETs, SCERTs and the University System. Innovative training programmes will be designed with the assistance of concerned organizations and women's groups;

(iii) Gender and poverty sensitization programmes will be developed for teacher educators and administrators. An environment will be created whereby all the sections of the education sector will become alive and sensitive to the role of education in eliminating gender disparities;

(iv) In order to create a greater confidence and to motivate parents to send girls to school, preference will be given to recruitment of women teachers;

(v) The common core curriculum is a potentially powerful instrument to promote a positive image of women. The Department of Women's Studies, NCERT will intensify activities already initiated in the area of developing gender sensitive curriculum, removing sex bias from textbooks and training of trainers/ teachers. SCERT and the concerned State-level boards and institutions will initiate similar work; and

(vi) Funds would require to be earmarked in all education budgets for such awareness and advocacy of related activities.

6. Research and Women's Studies

1.6.1 Women's Studies is a critical input to promote better understanding of women's contribution to social processes within social, technological and environmental change, their struggles and aspirations, conceptual obstacles that make them "invisible" in many areas of scientific enquiry. The programme aims to investigate and remove structural, cultural or attitudinal causes of gender discrimination, and thus empower women to achieve effective participation in all areas of national or international development. The four dimensions to be supported are :

(i) Research to advance the frontiers of knowledge, develop human resources and produce teaching/learning material in pursuit of the above aims;

(ii) Teaching to change present attitudes and values of men and women to one of concern for gender equality. Existing biases and deficiencies in curriculum will be addressed;

(iii) Training of teachers, decision-makers, administrators and planners to enable them to play a positive inter-ventionist role for gender equality; and

(iv) Extension or direct involvement of institutions in women's development activities among the community.

1.6.2 Special efforts will be made to make the Women's Studies Centres set up in 20 universities and 11 colleges to become more effective through intensive training of their staff. Eminent institutions and well known women's organizations will be involved in the process of revitalizing existing centres/units and helping in the establishment of new ones.

1.6.3 Networking between different institutions for research, extension and information dissemination has demonstrated high cost-effectiveness as well as potential for coordinated growth. Such networks will be initiated to increase output of quality teaching materials, especially in regional languages, training and curriculum design, and decentralized area-specific models of intervention.

1.6.4 Foundation course should be designed and introduced for undergraduates with a view to promote the objectives of empowerment of women. This will be done within the Eighth Plan period.

7. Universalization of Elementary Education and Adult Education

1.7.1 It is impossible to achieve Universal Elementary Education (UEE) unless concerted efforts are made to reach out to the girl-child. Girls who cannot attend formal schools or have had to drop out will be provided educational opportunities through Non-Formal Education (NFE). Efforts will be made to design special NFE programmes for out-of-school and adolescent girls with a view to get them back into the formal stream or qualify for technical or vocational education. The Open School, distance education systems and other innovative educational programmes will reach out to girls in rural/remote areas and urban slums. Voluntary and community-based efforts will be encouraged in this sector. The above tasks acquire a greater significance in the SAARC decade of the girl-child.

1.7.2 The rural girls are doubly disadvantaged by non-availability of educational facilities and by the work they have to do related with fuel, fodder, water, sibling care and paid and unpaid work. Coordinated efforts, albeit with other Departments/Ministries, need to be made to provide the necessary support services to enhance their participation and performance. Provision of support services and child-care facilities should be seen as a necessary and integral adjunct of UEE.

1.7.3 An important constraining factor for female education is the lack of women teachers in rural areas. The Revised Policy Formulations postulate that at least 50 per cent of teachers recruited in future would be women. Therefore special efforts would be made to recruit women teachers and to augment teacher-training facilities for women so that adequate number of qualified women teachers are available in different subjects, including Mathematics and Science.

1.7.4 Total Literacy Campaigns (TLCs) being taken up should pay special attention to women in the 15 to 35 age-group as it has been done with very positive impact in many districts. NFE should be dovetailed to TLCs in order to reach out to girls in the 10 to 20 age-group.

1.7.5 Programmes for continuing education should be designed to ensure that neo-literates and school going girls have access to reading materials. If necessary, books and magazines should be made available to women in their hamlets. The medium of radio will be utilised to sustain enthusiasm and motivation.

1.7.6 Efforts should be made to coordinate the different vocational schemes both within the formal system and those initiated by other Departments/Ministries.

8. Women's Access to Vocational, Technical and Professional Education and Existing and Emergent Technologies

1.8.1 Improvement of girls' access to technical, vocational and professional education requires a national programme to introduce and strengthen Science and Mathematics teaching in all girls schools. A special scheme will be designed to meet the shortfall of Science and Mathematics teachers in girls schools. Serious efforts should be made by the Centre and State planners, curriculum developers and administrators to consciously encourage participation of girls in non-traditional and emergent technologies at all levels. Guidance and counselling for girls should be undertaken as a necessary precondition to encourage participation.

1.8.2 Women's access to technical education will be improved qualitatively and quantitatively especially in rural areas. Women's ITIs will be revamped with a view to diversify disciplines, trades and courses to encourage participation in new and emerging technologies.

1.8.3 Information about credit, banking, entrepreneurial abilities will be developed in technical and vocational institutions. The apprenticeship scheme will be strengthened to increase the coverage of women.

9. Media

1.9.1 The electronic, print and traditional media will be used to create a climate for equal opportunities for women and girls. It will thus play a complementary and supportive role in awareness generation, dissemination of information and communication. Given the fact that almost all rural areas are covered by radio, special efforts will be made to utilize this medium to reach out to women.

10. Management Structure at Centre and State Level

1.10.1. Women's cells should be set-up forthwith in all Central and State agencies concerned with curriculum development, training and research.

1.10.2. A Monitoring cell will be set-up within the Planning Bureau of the Department of Education, Ministry of Human Resource Development. Similar units in the States should take responsibility for monitoring and evaluating progress.

1.10.3 A high-level Inter-Ministerial Committee will be constituted by the Department of Education, MHRD to :

(i) review implementation of POA on a continuing basis;
(ii) advise the government on policies and programmes related to girls education;
(iii) activate planning mechanism in consultation with each other to ensure provision of essential support services that will enhance girls' and women's participation in education; and
(iv) Similar committees will be constituted at the State-Level.

Para 4.2 and 4.3 of the National Policy on Education (1992)

4.2 Education will be used as an agent of basic changes in the status of women. In order to neutralise the accumulated distortions of the past, there will be a well-conceived edge in favour of women. The National Education System will play a positive interventionist role in the empowerment of women. It will foster the development of new values through redisgned curricula, textbooks, the training and orientation of teachers, decision-makers and administrators, and the active involvement of educational institutions. This will be an act of faith and social engineering. Women's studies will be promoted as a part of various courses and educational institutions encouraged to take up active programmes to further women's development.

4.3 The removal of women's illiteracy and obstacles inhibiting their access to and retention in, elementary education will receive overriding priority, through provision of special support services, setting of time targets, and effective monitoring. Major emphasis will be laid on women's participation in vocational, technical and professional education at different levels. The policy of non-discrimination will be at different levels. The policy of non-discrimination will be pursued vigorously to eliminate sex stereotyping in vocational and professional courses and to promote women's participation in non-traditional occupations, as well as in existing and emergent technologies.

6

Janardhan Committee to Review Implementation of NPE (1992)

Introduction

The National Policy on Education (NPE) was adopted by Parliament in May, 1986. The Policy was followed up by an elaboration through the Programme of Action (POA) which was adopted by Parliament in August, 1986. NPE envisages a review of the implementation of various parameters of the Policy every five years. The Central Government had, in May 1990, appointed a Committee to review NPE, 1986 (NPERC), under the chairmanship of Acharya Ramamurti. The Committee submitted its report on 26th December, 1990. The report was tabled in both the Houses of Parliament on 9th January, 1991. The Central Advisory Board of Education (CABE) in its meeting held on 8-9 March, 1991 examined the procedure to be adopted for consideration of the report of the NPERC and decided that a CABE Committee be constituted by the Chairman, viz., Union Minister of Human Resource Development, National Policy on Education Review Committee to consider the recommendations of the NPERC. In pursuance of the above decision, the Chairman of the CABE appointed a Committee on 31st July, 1991, to review the implementation of various parameters of NPE taking into consideration the report of the NPERC and other relevant developments since the Policy was formulated and to recommend modifications to be made in NPE.

Shri N. Janardhana Reddy, Chief Minister and Minister of Education, Andhra Pradesh was the Chairman of the Committee. The Committee gave its recommendations on women education in Chapter three of its report and the same are reproduced here.

Report of the CABE Committee on Policy, Government of India, Ministry of Human Resource Development, Department of Education, New Delhi, 1992.

Education and Women's Equality (Chapter 3)

3.1 The NPERC considered women's education to be a vital component of the overall strategy of securing equity and social justice in education. It rightly addressed the issue of women's education with reference to the special existential problems of women — such as the prevailing cultural norms of gender behaviour and the perceived domestic and reproductive roles of women which restrict the access of women to education. The NPERC strongly advocated intervention on behalf of women by the State in all its manifestations — the Central Government, the State Governments and the Local Bodies. The NPERC sought to differentiate its perspective from that of NPE by contending that the NPE seemingly construed that education alone was an agent of basic change in the status of women, the thrust of NPE lay in the intervention within the education system and that NPE did not adequately address socio-economic and cultural constraints that were outside the school system and had a direct bearing on education. In essence, the NPERC's perspective is very much in tune with what NPE envisaged in regard to women's education. Paras 4.2 and 4.3 of NPE are very strong statements on the interventionist and empowering role of education. Inter alia, they emphasise the provision of special support services and removal of factors which result in discrimination against women at all levels of education. There is nothing in them to be susceptible of the interpretation which NPERC had made.

3.2 The recommendations of the NPERC mainly relate to the logistics of implementation. Most of them, such as those relating to ECCE, availability of schooling, regional disparities, content of education and adult education are also reflected in the recommendations contained in the other chapters of the NPERC's Report dealing with these subjects. Our views on such recommendations are presented in the corresponding chapters. We present here our views only on those of the recommendations which are not treated elsewhere in the report of the NPERC.

3.3 R.Nos 1 to 5 bring out the nexus between girls' schooling and access to water, fuel and fodder. The suggestion is that this nexus should inform educational planning and that the Department of Education should co-ordinate with other departments with a view to bringing about an improvement in the access of women to education. The criticality of the nexus highlighted by the NPERC cannot be exaggerated; however, the co-ordinating role is better discharged by the Department of Women and Child Development and the Planning Commission at the Centre, the corresponding agencies at the State-level, and the agencies responsible for integrated planning and development at the district and sub-district level. It would not be realistic to expect the education department alone, whether at the Centre or in the States, to play the lead role for ensuring that women's development occurs in a holistic manner. The NPERC's recommendations in regard to the gender bias in curriculum and textbooks (R.Nos. 17 to 20), media (R. Nos. 21 to 27), women's studies (R.Nos.41 to 48) and representation of women in educational hierarchy (R.Nos.49 to 52) are very much in keeping with the spirit of the NPE/POA. R.Nos. 53 to 57 endorse the Mahila Samakhya approach which is a product of the NPE.

3.4 R.Nos. 58 to 62 call for earmarking of resources for women's education not only in the allocations of elementary, secondary, vocational and higher education but also in the Special Component Plan (SCP) for SCs and the Tribal Sub-Plan (TSP) for STs. However, there is a fundamental difference between SC/ST problems and the women's question. The problem of women's education cuts across caste and regional barriers. Therefore, while women's participation in education should be closely monitored and particular attention paid to remove the barriers impeding such participation, the earmarking of funds may not be administratively feasible.

3.5 To sum up, we are of the view that while the NPERC had rightly reiterated the importance of women's education, the NPE policy frame is adequate and the POA should be revised to take into account the recommendations of the NPERC.

Notes: 1. Paras refer to the Para Numbers of chapter 3

2. NPERC is also referred to Ramamurti Review Committee on Education.

7

Workshop on the Need of Women's Education in the Teacher Education Curriculum (1992)

Introduction

An NCERT sponsored workshop on developing inputs for teacher education on equality between sexes and promoting status of women was held at Institute of Education, Devi Ahilya Vishwavidyalaya, Indore, from 27th to 29th February, 1992. Main objectives of the workshop were as under:

(i) To review the curricula of teacher education of different universities of Madhya Pradesh (MP) at pre-primary, primary, secondary and post-secondary levels, from the point of view of equality of status of women and solution of problems of women's education;
(ii) To develop curriculum outlines on women's education in teacher training programmes meant for pre-primary and primary education, and secondary education;
(iii) To develop curriculum outlines on women's education at M.Ed. and M.Phil. stages; and
(iv) To chalk down the major research areas and topics concerning women's education in the country.

The workshop was participated by a number of teacher educators.

The Workshop recommended that there should be a special paper of women's education in teacher education programme at the B.Ed. and M.Ed. levels.

---

* NCERT, *Report on Developing Inputs for Teacher Education in MP on Equality between Sexes and Promoting Status of Women*, NCERT, New Delhi, 1993

Special Paper on Women Studies at B.Ed. Level

Objectives

1. To acquaint student teachers with the concept of women's education and its relationship with national development.
2. To make student teachers aware about various programmes of women's education.
3. To acquaint pupil teachers with barriers of women's education.
4. To train the teacher trainess in action based programs related with different problems of women.
5. To make student teachers familiar with different agencies working for women's education.
6. To develop understanding in pupil-teachers that community participation is necessary in women development.

Content

UNIT 1 Concept of women's education: Meaning, Need, Importance, Objectives and Constraints of Women's education, Efforts in promoting women education.

UNIT 2 Status of Women's Education: Historical overview, Brief Situational analysis of the status of women after independence. Role of state, Committees, Commissions and Policies, Constitutional rights, Different women movements-national and international, Role of media in women development.

UNIT 3 Community participation in women development: Role of parents, teachers schools and society in developing self-image in women. Role of volunteer agencies—UNICEF, Women world university, local clubs and organizations.

UNIT 4 Programmes for Women's education at Government Level: Special facilities for Girl Child Education, Vocational Institutions, Vocational guidance, Integrated child development scheme, other existing schemes.

UNIT 5 Evaluation: Measurement of women's status through demographic criteria (sex ratio, mortality, morbidity and fertility rate); Economic participation activities; Social—child marriage, crimes against women, sexual harassment, dowry deaths, etc.

Assignment

Project on any one of the following areas — Individual/Group:

1. Literacy programme for women.
2. Vocational Guidance or training for women.
3. Development of instructional material for women.
4. Health education programmes for women.
5. Any other programmes which facilitates women's education.

Special Paper on Women's Studies: M.Ed/M.A. Education

Objectives

1. To understand the historical perspective of women.
2. To make the students aware of the present status and position of women in Indian context with special reference to Madhya Pradesh.
3. To make the students aware about the perceptions of women regarding future status.
4. To create the competencies and sensitivity amongst the students in understanding the problems of girls' education and in development.

Contents

1. Status of women with respect to social, economic, political and legal aspects in:

   (i) Vedic, Buddhist, and Jain period.
   (ii) Medieval period.
   (iii) British period.

PART-II

STATISTICAL INDICATORS

INDIA (as a whole)

Scheduled Castes and Scheduled Tribes

Districtwise Women's Literacy (1991)

8

INDIA (AS A WHOLE)

TABLE 8.1: Women Literacy Rates in India 1951 to 1991

Year	Persons	Males	Females
1951	18.33	27.16	8.86
1961	28.31	40.40	15.34
1971	34.45	45.95	21.97
1981	43.56 (41.42)	56.37 (53.45)	29.75 (28.46)
1991	52.11	63.86	39.42

Notes : 1. Literacy rate for 1951, 1961 and 1971 relate to population aged five years and above. The rates for the years 1981 and 1991 relate to the population aged seven years and above. The literacy rates for the population aged five years and above in 1981 have been shown in brackets.

2. The 1981 rates exclude Assam where the 1981 Census could not be conducted. The 1991 Census rates exclude Jammu and Kashmir where the 1991 Census was not conducted.

TABLE 8.2: Sexwise and Statewise of Literates to Estimated: Percentage of Population Aged Seven Years and Above

State/Union Territory	1981			1991		
	Persons	Females	Males	Persons	Females	Males
1	2	3	4	5	6	7
India	43.56	29.75	56.37	52.11	39.42	63.86
1. Andhra Pradesh	35.66	24.16	46.83	45.11	33.71	56.24
2. Arunachal Pradesh	25.54	14.01	35.11	41.22	29.31	51.10
3. Assam	NA	NA	NA	53.42	43.70	62.34
4. Bihar	32.03	61.51	46.58	38.54	23.10	52.63

Table 8.2 (Contd.)

State/Union Tessitory	1981 Persons	1981 Females	1981 Males	1991 Persons	1991 Females	1991 Males
5. Goa	65.71	55.17	76.01	76.96	68.20	65.48
6. Gujarat	52.21	38.46	65.14	60.91	48.50	72.54
7. Haryana	43.85	26.89	58.49	55.33	40.94	67.85
8. Himachal Pradesh	51.17	37.72	64.27	63.54	52.46	74.57
9. Jammu and Kashmir	32.68	19.55	44.18	NA	NA	NA
10. Karnataka	46.20	33.16	58.72	55.98	44.34	67.25
11. Kerala	81.56	75.65	87.74	90.59	86.93	94.45
12 Madhya Pradesh	34.22	18.99	48.41	43.45	28.39	57.43
13. Maharashtra	55.83	41.01	69.66	63.05	50.51	74.84
14. Manipur	49.61	34.61	64.12	60.96	48.64	72.98
15. Meghalaya	42.02	37.15	46.62	48.26	44.78	51.57
16. Mizoram	74.26	68.60	79.37	81.23	78.09	84.08
17. Nagaland	50.20	40.28	58.52	61.30	55.72	66.09
18. Orissa	40.96	25.14	56.45	48.55	34.40	62.37
19. Punjab	48.12	39.64	55.52	57.14	49.72	63.68
20. Rajasthan	30.09	13.99	44.76	38.81	20.84	55.07
21. Sikkim	41.57	27.35	52.98	56.53	47.23	64.34
22. Tamil Nadu	54.38	40.43	68.05	63.72	52.29	74.88
23. Tripura	50.10	38.01	61.49	60.39	50.01	70.08
24. Uttar Pradesh	33.33	17.18	47.43	41.71	26.02	55.35
25. West Bengal	48.64	36.07	59.93	57.72	47.15	67.24
26. A and N Island	63.16	53.15	70.28	73.74	66.22	79.68
27. Chandigarh	74.81	69.31	78.89	78.73	73.61	82.67
28. Dadra and Nagar Naveli	32.70	20.38	44.69	39.45	26.10	52.07
29. Daman and Diu	59.91	46.51	74.45	73.58	61.38	85.67
30. Delhi	71.93	62.57	79.28	76.09	68.01	82.63
31. Lakshdweep	68.42	55.32	81.24	79.23	70.88	87.06
32. Pondicheery	65.14	53.03	77.09	74.91	65.79	83.91

NA = stands for not available.

Note: Literacy rates for 1981 excludes Assam where the 1981 census could not be held and the literacy rates for 1991 exclude Jammu and Kashmir where the 1991 Census was not conducted. The literacy rates for India for 1981 and 1991 excluding Assam and Jammu and Kashmir works out as under :

	Persons	Females	Males
1981	43.66	29.84	56.49
1991	52.07	39.31	63.90

TABLE 8.3: Sex-wise Enrolment by Stages/Classes since 1951 : School Level

Year	Primary			Upper Primary			High/Hr.Sec		
	Girls	Boys	Total	Girls	Boys	Total	Girls	Boys	Total
1950-51	54	138	192	5	26	31	2	13	15
1960-61	114	236	350	16	51	67	7	27	34
1970-71	213	357	570	39	94	133	19	57	76
1980-81	285	453	738	68	139	207	35	84	119
1990-91	410	581	991	124	209	333	69	140	209
1991-92	424	592	1016	130	214	344	70	142	212

TABLE 8.4: Girls Enrolment, 1950-51 to 1991-92

(In Lakhs)

Enrolment in Classes / Age-Group	1950-51	1991-92	Increase
1. Classes I to V			
(Age-group, (6 to 11)			
(a) Total Enrolment	191.5	1015.8	5.3 Times
(b) Girls Enrolment	53.8	423.6	7.8
(c) Boys Enrolment	137.7	592.2	4.3
2. Classes VI to VIII			
(Age-group 11-14)			
(a) Total Enrolment	31.3	344.5	11.0
(b) Girls Enrolment	5.4	130.0	24.0
(c) Boys Enrolment	25.9	214.3	8.3
3. Classes, I to VIII			
(Age-group 6-14)			
(a) Total Enrolment	222.8	1360.3	6.0
(b) Girls Enrolment	59.2	553.6	9.3
(c) Boys Enrolment	163.6	806.7	5.0

TABLE 8.5: Percentage of Girls Enrolment to Total Enrolment at the Primary Stages (Classes I to V), 1950-51 to 1991-92

Year	Girls Enrolment (In Lakhs)	Total Enrolment (In Lakhs)	% of Girls Enrolment to Total Enrolment
1950-51	54	192	28.12
1960-61	114	350	32.57
1970-71	213	570	37.36
1980-81	285	738	38.61
1990-91	410	991	41.37
1991-92	424	1016	41.73

TABLE 8.6: Percentage of Girls Enrolment to Total Enrolment at the Middle / Upper Stage: Classes. VI to VIII , 1950-51 to 1991-92.

Year	Girls Enrolment (In Lakhs)	Total Enrolment (In Lakhs)	% of Girls Enrolment to Total Enrolment
1950-51	05	31	16.12
1960-61	16	67	23.88
1970-71	39	133	29.32
1980-81	68	207	32.85
1990-91	124	333	37.23
1991-92	130	344	37.79

TABLE 8.7: Percentage of Girls Enrolment to Total Enrolment at the High / Hr. Sec. Stages (Classes IX to XII), (1950-51 to 92)

Year	Girls Enrolment (In Lakhs)	Total Enrolment (In Lakhs)	% of Girls Enrolment to Total Enrolment
1950-51	02	15	13.33
1960-61	07	34	20.58
1970-71	19	76	25.00
1980-81	35	119	29.41
1990-91	69	209	33.01
1991-92	70	212	33.01

TABLE 8.8: Percentage of Girls Enrolment to Total Population in the Age-Group 6 to 14,1950-51 and 1991-92

(Percentages)

Classes	1950-51	1991-92
Classes I to V		
(a) Girls	24.9	88.09
(b) Boys	60.8	116.61
(c) Total	42.8	102.74
Classes VI to VIII		
(a) Girls	4.3	47.40
(b) Boys	20.8	74.19
(c) Total	12.9	61.15

TABLE 8.9: Percentage of Sexwise Enrolment in the Respective Age-Group Population in Classes I to VIII Since 1987-1988

	Classes I to V Age 6 to 11 years			Classes VI to VIII Age 11 to 14 years		
Year	Girls	Boys	Total	Girls	Boys	Total
1987-88	81.7	113.1	97.9	40.6	68.9	55.1
1988-89	82.5	115.7	99.6	42.3	70.8	56.9
1989-90	83.6	115.5	99.9	44.6	73.0	59.1
1990-91	85.97	115.29	101.03	46.13	73.38	60.11
1991-92	88.09	116.61	102.74	47.40	74.19	61.15

TABLE 8.10: **Students Flow in School, Classes I-VIII and Retention Rate, 1960-61 to 1986-87.**

Years	Class I		Class V		Class VIII	
	Total	Girls	Total	Girls	Total	Girls
1	2	3	4	5	6	7
1960-61	1,33,91,347 (100.0)	46,80909 (100.0)	— —	— —	— —	— —
1961-62	1,57,46,164 (100.0)	57,05,962 (100.0)	— —	— —	— —	— —
1962-63	1,64,04,417 (100.0)	60,23,285 (100.0)	— —	— —	— —	— —
1963-64	1,69,05,528 (100.0)	62,83,003 (100.0)	— —	— —	— —	— —
1964-65	1,82,40,602 (100.0)	69,48,612 (100.0)	49,64,247 -(37.1) (27.2)	15,24,406 (32.6) (22.0)	— — —	— — —
1965-66	1,88,83,970 (100.0)	73,09,790 (100.0)	53,81,366 (34.2) (28.5)	16,83,795 (29.5) (23.0)	— — —	— — —
1966-67	1,95,33,259 (100.0)	75,11,283 (100.0)	57,10,325 (34.8) (29.2)	18,27,741 (30.3) (24.3)	— — —	— — —
1967-68	1,97,50,974 (100.0)	76,37,372 (100.0)	59,20,639 (35.0) (30.0)	19,46,193 (31.0) (25.5)	32,44,645 (24.2) (16.4)	8,63,384 (18.4) (11.3)
1968-69	1,98,35,890 (100.0)	76,95,708 (100.0)	60,42,209 (33.1) (30.5)	20,11,469 (28.9) (26.5)	34,59,461 (22.0) (18.1)	9,36,647 (16.4) (12.2)
1969-70	1,99,42,055 (100.0)	77,78,779 (100.0)	62,49,417 (33.1) (31.3)	21,00,326 (28.7) (27.0)	36,16,774 (22.0) (18.1)	9,89,776 (16.4) (13.4)
1970-71	2,04,38,788 (100.0)	79,24,508 (100.0)	64,55,109 (33.0) (31.6)	21,84,437 (29.1) (27.6)	37,43,951 (22.1) (18.3)	10,42,492 (16.6) (13.2)
1971-72	2,11,18,992 (100.0)	82,13,094 (100.0)	66,23,731 (33.5) (31.4)	22,65,014 (29.7) (27.6)	38,35,751 (21.0) (18.2)	10,90,540 (15.7) (13.3)
1972-73	2,17,51,947 (100.0)	87,10,611 (100.0)	69,49,504 (35.0) (31.3)	24,06,786 (31.3) (27.0)	39,55,524 (20.9) (17.8)	11,51,880 (15.7) (13.2)
1973-74	2,15,50,516 (100.0)	85,04,478 (100.0)	71,79,048 (36.0) (33.3)	25,54,553 (32.8) (30.0)	40,40,378 (20.7) (18.7)	11,76,798 (15.7) (13.8)
1974-75	2,19,75,542 (100.0)	86,69,345 (100.0)	75,15,743 (36.8) (34.2)	26,36,002 (33.3) (30.4)	42,14,680 (21.3) (19.2)	12,45,816 (16.3) (14.4)
1975-76	2,19,87,533 (100.0)	87,12,804 (100.0)	78,48,656 (37.2) (35.7)	27,71,442 (33.8) (31.9)	44,35,764 (22.8) (20.0)	13,20,559 (17.2) (15.9)
1976-77	2,27,24,536 (100.0)	91,85,204 (100.0)	81,87,777 (36.9)	28,91,726 (33.2)	45,54,847 (22.8)	13,85,322 (17.8)

Year	Class I		Class V		Class VIII	
	Total	Girls	Total	Girls	Total	Girls
1	2	3	4	5	6	7
			(36.0)	(31.5)	(20.0)	(15.1)
1977-78	2,11,27,331	84,28,795	83,74,954	29,52,175	47,21,813	14,53,672
	(100.0)	(100.0)	(38.9)	(34.7)	(23.1)	(18.3)
			(39.6)	(35.0)	(22.3)	(17.2)
1978-79	2,25,20,818	91,28,945	82,12,356	29,26,603	49,94,515	15,41,961
Fourth AIE	(100.0)	(100.0)	(37.4)	(33.8)	(24.4)	(19.4)
Survey	;	;	(36.5)	(32.1)	(22.2)	(18.3)
1978-79	2,16,39,468	87,21,757	84,78,011	30,11,600	50,12,525	15,83,564
	(100.0)	(100.0)	(38.6)	(34.7)	(23.7)	(19.3)
			(39.2)	(34.5)	(23.2)	(18.2)
1979-80	2,15,93,833	86,88,807	88,93,290	31,79,541	53,58,703	16,66,368
	(100.0)	(100.0)	(40.4)	(36.5)	(24.2)	(19.1)
			(41.3)	(36.5)	(24.0)	(19.2)
*1980-81	2,30,52,579	90,75,675	96,85,712	35,19,509	58,42,756	18,34,774
	(100.0)	(100.0)	(42.6)	(38.3)	(27.1)	(21.5)
			(42.0)	(38.8)	(25.2)	(20.1)
1981-82E	2,21,65,341	90,06,206	1,01,60,185	36,80,911	62,08,509	19,54,233
	(100.0)	(100.0)	(48.1)	(43.7)	(28.3)	(22.5)
			(45.8)	(40.1)	(28.0)	(21.7)
1982-83	2,27,10,608	92,87,200	1,05,72,688	40,66,244	65,36,939	20,92,984
	(100.0)	(100.0)	(48.9)	(46.6)	(29.7)	(24.2)
			(46.6)	(43.8)	(28.8)	(22.5)
	@2.46%	@3.20%	@4.20%	@5.57%	@5.29%	@7.10%
1986-87	2,48,90,467	1,04,46,305	1,22,96,768	47,06,771	8,52,098	26,48,310
Fifth AIE	(100.0)	(100.0)	(54.1)	(50.7)	(36.36)	(29.2)
			(49.4)	(45.1)	(31.5)	(25.4)

Notes: (i) Figures in the first bracket indicate the retention of children in Classes V and VII over those enrolled five/eight years before. These may be construed as cohort data.

(ii) Figures in the second bracket indicate percentage of children in Classes V and VIII over those enrolled in Class I during the same academic year.

* The figures in the rows are apparently doubtful . Since they are from an authentic source, they have been kept intact.

Sources: (i) Selected Educational and Allied Statistics, Ministry of Human Resource Development, Government of India, 1987.

(ii) 'Fourth and Fifth All India Educational Surveys', NCERT, 1980,1990.

(E) As the figures for 1982-83 were not readily available, the average percentage growth given under each column at @ was calculated on the basis of the increases of 1986-87 over 1981-82. This average percentage growth was used to estimate each of the figures shown against 1982-83.

(School Education in the 1990.

Problems and Perspecteives (Report of the National Seminar Held on 18-19 September 1991 at NIE Campus, NCERT, New Delhi, NCERT, 1992,

TABLE 8.11 : Girls Retention Rate up to Classes V and Classes VIII, 1964-65 to 1988-89

Years	Total Retention Rate		Girls Retention Rate	
	Class V	Class VIII	Class V	Class VIII
1964-65	27.2	N. A.	22.0	N. A.
1965-66	28.2	N.A.	23.0	N.A.
1966-67	29.2	N.A.	24.3	N.A.
1967-68	30.0	16.4	25.5	11.3
1968-69	30.5	18.1	26.5	12.2
1969-70	31.3	18.1	27.7	13.4
1970-71	31.6	18.3	27.6	13.2
1971-72	31.4	18.2	27.6	13.3
1972-73	31.3	17.8	27.6	13.2
1973-74	33.3	18.7	30.0	13.8
1974-75	34.2	19.2	30.4	14.4
1975-76	35.7	20.0	31.9	15.9
1976-77	36.0	20.0	31.5	15.1
1977-78	39.6	22.3	35.0	17.2
1978-79	36.5	22.2	32.1	18.3
1979-80	41.2	24.0	36.6	19.2
1980-81	42.0	25.3	38.8	20.1
1981-82	48.1	28.3	43.7	22.5
1982-83	48.9	29.7	46.6	24.2
1985-86	49.4	25.4	45.1	25.4
1988-89	52.07	24.64	50.31	20.54

TABLE 8.12 : Enrolment of Women and Their Number Per Hundred Men in Higher Education

Years	Total Women Enrolment (In Thousands)	Number of Women Per Hundred Men
1950-51	40	14
1955-56	84	17
1960-61	150	23
1965-66	271	24
1975-76	595	33
1981-82	817	38
1982-83	880	39
1983-84	940	40
1984-85	992	41
1985-86	1067	42
1986-87	1149	44
1987-88	1224	.46
1988-89	1292	46
1989-90	1367	47
1990-91	1437	48
1991-92	1510	49

TABLE 8.13: Enrolment of Women and its Percentage to Total Enrolment in Different Classes (1986-87).

Classes	Women Enrolment	Total Enrolment	% of Women Enrolment to Total
1. Ph.D./D.SC./M.Phill	10,465	31,533	33.18
2. M.A.	71,777	191,086	37.66
3. M.Sc	26,315	79,131	33.25
4. M. Com.	9,100	61,982	14.68
5. B.A./B.A (Hons)	5,47,997	14.05,396	38.99
6. B.Sc./B.Sc. (Hons)	2,07,551	6.71,888	30.93
7. B.Com./B.Com. (Hons)	1.69,269	7.70,242	21.97
8. BE./BSc. /Engg./B. Arch	22.792	1.82,421	12.49
9 B.Ed./ B.T	38,744	89,152	43.45
10. M.B.B.S	25,327	78,767	32.15
11. Teacher Traning Schools	45,901	92,885	49.41
12. Polytechnic Institutes	34,088	1,98,542	17.16
13. Technical, Industrial Arts and Crafts Schools	74,639	3.08,279	24.21
14. Intermediate/Junior Colleges	3,97,662	16.78,368	23.69
15. Pre-Degree/Pre-University (Two-Year Course)	1,37,112	3.11,658	43.99
16. Pre-University (One-Year Course)	26,630	50,841	52.37
17. Hr. Secondary (10+2) New Pattern	9,40,500	19.26,885	18.80
18. Hr. Secondary (Old Pattern)	32,708	1.60,882	20.33
19. High/Post Basic (IX-X)	38,51,420	1.24.72.932	30.87
20. Middle/Senior Basic (Classes VI to VIII)	1,02,36,646	2,87.80,099	35.56
21. Primary Stage/ Junior Basic (Classes I-IV)	3.61/43.018	8,99.93,046	40.16

TABLE 8.14: Enrolment of Women and its Percentage to Total Enrolment in Different Classes (1987-88)

	Classes	Women Enrolment	Total Enrolment	Women Enrolment
1.	Ph.D. /D.Sc / M.Phill	10,396	30,987	33.54
2.	M.A	75,113	1,97,812	37.97
3.	M.Sc.	23,459	72,143	32.51
4.	M.Com	10,354	65,027	15.92
5.	B.A./ B.A. (Hons)	5,22,272	13,20,586	39.54
6.	B.Sc./B.Sc. (Hons)	1,99,474	6,54,090	30.49
7.	B.E. / B.Sc./Engg./ B. Arch.	15,161	1,90,779	7.9
8.	B.Com/B.Com. (Hons)	1,69,675	7,58,378	22.37
9.	B. Ed./ B.T	39,253	92,820	42.28
10.	M.B.B.S.	26,522	81,367	32.59
11.	Teacher Training Schools	44,861	92,105	48.70
12.	Polytechnic Institutes	36,173	2,43,389	14.86
13.	Technical-Industrial Arts and Crafts Schools	—	—	—
14.	Intermediate / Jr. Collages	4,79,126	19,56,639	24.48
15.	Pre - Degree / Pre-University (Two Years Course)	1,66,243	3,93,275	42.27
16.	Pre - University (One Year Course)	3,164	11,253	28.11
17.	Hr. Secondary (10+2) New Pattern	9,96,849	29,15,231	34.19
18.	High /Post Basic (IX -X)	39,12,585	1,24,52,283	31.42
19.	Middle / Senior Basic (VI to VIII)	1,07, 06,054	2,99,14,499	35.78
20.	Primary/Junior Basic (Classes I - V)	3,77,74,671	9,29,43,556	40.64

TABLE 8.15: Enrolment of Women and Its Percentage to Total Enrolment in Different Classes 1988-89

	Classes	Women Enrolment	Total Enrolment	% to Total Enrolment
1.	Ph. D./ D. Sc./ M. Phill	10,439	31,386	33.26
2.	M.A.	77,796	2,017,33	37.00
3.	M.Sc.	24,410	73,347	33.28
4.	M.Com.	13,983	75,870	18.43
5.	B.A. / B.A. (Hons)	5,68,913	14,51,919	39.18
6.	B. Sc. /B.Sc (Hons)	2,12,432	6,66,405	31.87
7.	B. Com./B. Com. (Hons)	2,15,530	9,59,780	22.45
8.	BE/. BSc./ Engg. / B. Arch.	16,390	2,05,282	7.98
9.	B.Ed. / B.T.	40,435	91,017	44.42
10.	M.B.B.S.	26,261	80,237	32,72
11.	Teacher Training Schools	48,850	10,05,45	48.58
12.	Polytechnic Institutes	32,137	2,86,394	11.22
13.	Technical, Industrial Arts and Crafts Schools	84,647	3,68,205	22.98
14.	Intermediate / Junior Colleges	5,09,423	19,81,783	25.70
15.	Pre-Degree / Pre. University (Two - Year Course)	1,33,717	3,05,851	43.71
16.	Pre-University (One - Year Course)	894	3,716	24.05
17.	Hr. Secondary (10+2) New Pattern	10,51,564	30,80,591	34.13
18.	Hr. Secondary (Old Pattern)	—	—	—
19.	High / Post Basic (IX -X)	42,43,497	1,31,49,351	32.27
20	Middle / Sr. Basic (Classes VI - VIII)	1,11,87,784	3,09,40,062	36.15
21	Primary / Jr. Basic (Classes I - V)	3,95,97,94,251	9,57,39,776	41.35

TABLE 8.16: Enrolment of Women and Its Percentage to Total Enrolment in Different Classes, 1989-90

Classes	Women Enrolment	Total Enrolment	% to Total Enrolment
1. Ph.D./ D.Sc./ M.Phill.	9,129	27,815	32.82
2. M.A	78,227	206,113	37.95
3. M.Sc.	23,517	70,420	33.39
4. M . Com.	15,252	83,301	18.30
5. B.A /B.A.(Hons)	5,99,419	15,37,400	38,98
6. B.Sc. / B.Sc . (Hons)	2,69,983	7,39,467	36.51
7. B. Com. / B. Com. (Hons)	2,30,531	9,70,780	23.74
8. B.E. / BSc ./ Engg./ B. Arch.	18,424	2,22,775	8.27
9. B.Ed. /B.T	40,563	92.655	43.77
10. M.B.B.S.	29,051	84,264	34.47
11. Teacher Training Schools	64,793	1,37,323	47.18
12. Polytechnic Institutes	33,152	2,84,245	11.66
13. Technical / Industrial Arts and Crafts Schools	84,503	3,99,341	21.16
14. Intermediate / Jr. Colleges	6,41,421	24,39,957	26.28
15. Pre- Degree / Pre - University (Two - Year Course)	1,45,651	3,15,265	46.19
16. Pre-University (One-year course)	897	3,724	24.08
17. Hr. Secondary (10+2) (New Pattern)	11,72,678	34,31,931	34.26
18. Higher Secondary (Old Pattern)	—	—	—
19. High / Post Basic (IX - X)	44,86,497	1,37,89,333	32,53
20. Middle / Sr. Basic (Classes VI - VIII)	1,18,19,845	3,21,87,676	36.72
21. Primary / Jr. Basic (Classes I - V)	3,95,86,580	9,93,18,114	40.67

TABLE 8.17: Enrolment of Women and Its Percentage to Total Enrolment in Different Classes , 1990-91

	Classes	Women Enrolment	Total Enrolment	% to Total Enrolment
1.	Ph.D./ D.Sc./ M.Phill	8,499	32,968	26.17
2.	M.A	76,896	2,02,831	37.91
3	M.Sc.	24,349	71,891	33.86
4.	M . Com.	15,043	79,494	18.92
5.	B.A /B.A.(Hons)	6,15,393	15,34,348	40.10
6.	B.Sc. / B.Sc . (Hons)	2,81,035	7,56,876	37.12
7.	B. Com. / B. Com. (Hons)	2,42,936	9,94,532	24.42
8.	B.E. / BSc./ Engg./ B. Arch.	26,287	2,41368	10.89
9.	B.Ed. /B.T	40,764	92,17	44.20
10.	M.B.B.S.	28,911	84,373	34.25
11.	Teacher Training Schools	57,917	1,17,630	49.23
12.	Polytechnic Institutes	31,501	2,72,650	11.55
13.	Technical / Industrial Arts and Craft Schools	86,324	4,06,406	21.24
14.	Intermediate / Jr. Colleges	6,60,872	24,81,195	26.63
15.	Pre- Degree / Pre - University (Two - Years Course)	1,45,653	3,14,295	46.34
16.	Pre. University (one-year course)	903	3,815	23.66
17.	Hr. Secondary (10+2) New Pattern	12,24,799	35,58,615	34.41
18.	Higher Secondary (Old Pattern)			
19.	High / Post Basic (IX - X Class)	48,61,604	145,39,982	33.43
20.	Middle / Sr. Basic (Classes VI - VIII)	1,24,38,708	3,32,82,999	37.37
21.	Primary / Jr. Basic (Classes I - V)	4 ,10,23,604	9,91,18,320	41.38

TABLE 8.18: Percentage of Women Enrolment to Total Enrolment in Different Classes, 1986 -87 to 1990 - 91

Class	1956-57	1987-88	1988-89	1989-90	1990-91
1. Ph.D./ D.Sc./ M.Phill	33.18	33.14	33.26	32.82	26.17
2. M.A.	37.56	37.97	37.00	37.95	37.91
3. M.Sc.	33.25	32.51	33.28	33.39	33.86
4. M.Com.	14.68	15.52	18.43	18.30	18.92
5. B.A / B.A (Hons)	38.99	3954	39.18	33.48	40.10
6. B.Sc./ BSc. (Hons)	30.93	30.99	31.87	36.51	37.12
7. B. Com. B.Com. Hons)	21.97	22.37	22.45	23.74	24.12
8. B.E. / B.R / Eng / B.Arch	12.49	7.9	7.98	8.27	10.89
9. B.Ed /B.T.	43.45	49.28	44.42	43.77	44.20
10. M.B.B.S.	32.15	32.59	32.72	34.17	54.25
11. Teacher Training Schools	49.41	48.70	48.58	47.18	49.23
12. Polytechnic Institutes	17.16	14.86	11.22	11.66	11.55
13. Technical, Industrial Arts and Craft Schools	24.21	—	22.98	21.16	21.24
14. Intermediate/Junior Colleges	23.69	24.48	25.70	26.28	26.63
15. Pre-Degree	43.99	42.27	43.71	46.19	46.34
16. Pre-University (Two -Year Cource)	52.37	28.11	24.5	24.03	23.66
17. Hr. Secondary (10+2) (New-Pattern)	48.80	34.19	34.13	34.26	34.41
18. Hr. Secondary (Old Pattern)	20.33	—	—	—	—
19. Post Basic (IX -X)	3.87	31.42	32.27	32.53	33.43
20. Middle Senior Basic/ Junior Basic (Classes IX - VII)	35.56	35.78	36.15	36.72	37.37
21. Primary (Classes I - IV)	40.16	40.64	41.35	40.67	41.38

TABLE 8.19: Distribution of Teachers by Sex and Type of School Since 1951

(In Thousands)

Year	Primary			Upper Primary			High/Hr. Sec.		
	Female	Male	Total	Female	Male	Total	Female	Male	Total
1950-51	456	82	538	73	13	86	107	20	127
1960-61	615	127	742	262	83	345	234	62	296
1970-71	835	225	1060	463	175	638	474	155	629
1980-81	1020	343	1363	598	253	851	658	254	912
1990-91	1167	470	1637	706	353	1059	857	416	1273
1991-92	1194	499	1693	718	354	1072	880	430	1310

TABLE 8.20: Number of Women Teachers Employed in Various Types of Schools 1950-51-1980-81

(In Thousands)

Year	Primary Schools			Middle Schools			High/Hr. Sec.Schools		
	Number of Women teachers	% to total	No. of trained teachers	No. of Women teachers	% to total	% of trained teachers	No.of Women teachers	% of total	% to trained teachers
1950-51	82,281	18.0	69.1	12,887	18.0	58.1	19,982	19.0	66.2
1955-56	1,17,067	20.0	73.7	23,844	19.0	63.2	35,085	23.2	72.9
1960-61	1,26,788	21.0	73.4	83,532	32.0	73.4	62.347	22.0	73.9
1965-66	1,80,315	24.0	73.1	1,38,539	36.0	79.0	1.10,703	30.0	76.3
1970-71	2,24,610	20.7	79.8	1,74,506	27.0	85.8	1,55,424	24.3	80.8
1975-76	2,83,242	22.7	83.5	2,23,885	28.8	86.7	1,99,994	26.4	83.5
1979-80	3,21,283	24.5	86.8	2,50,206	30.0	88.9	2,39,429	27.9	82.2
1980-81*	3,30,793	25.0	87.6	2.56.786	30.3	89.5	2,49,288	28.3	89.4

* Estimated.

Source : *Educational Development of Women in India*, Ministry of Education and Culture, New Delhi, 1982.

TABLE 8.21: Number of Women Teachers Employed in Various types of Schools, 1986-87 to 1990-91

Year	Primary/Jr. Basic		Middle/Sr.Basic		High/Post Basic		Hr. Sec. Old Pattern		Hr. Secondary/Jr. Colleges New Pattern/ Total	
	Female	Total	Female	Total	Female	Total	Female	Total	Female	Total
1986-87	4,16,585	15,22,108	3,13,863	9,79,073	2,37,669	7,16,997	6,745	28,832	1,25,502	4,53,538
1987-88	4,25,539	16,16,685	3,27,111	10,14,162	2,52,082	7,55,519	6,034	26,944	1,30,249	4,60,360
1988-89	4,47,215	16,30,58	3,43,355	10,32,534	2,61,161	7,87,974	—	—	—	—
1989-90	4,52,765	16,01,717	3,44,630	10,47,588	2,71,421	8,01,630	—	—	1,39,291	4,62,619
1990-91	4,70,414	16,36,898	3,52,812	10,59,295	2,71,276	8,06,326	—	—	1,44,227	4,66,176

Source: *Selected Education Statistics* 1986-87, 1987-88, 1988-89, 1989-90 and 1990-91, Goverment of India, Ministry of Human Resource Development, Department of Education, New Delhi, 1988, 1989, 1990, 1991 and 1992.

TABLE 8.22 : Percentage of Female Teachers to Male Teachers at Different Levels of Education, 1950-51 - 1985-86

Year	Primary School	Middle School	High/Hr Sec.	College and University
1950-51	18	18	18	8
1955-56	19	19	22	12
1960-61	21	32	22	14
1965-66	24	36	30	16
1970-71	26	37	26	18
1975-76	29	40	36	21
1976-77	30	46	37	22
1977-78	31	41	38	22
1978-79	34	42	37	23
1979-80	33	42	38	24
1980-81	33	42	39@	23
1981-82	34	44	40@	24
1982-83*	34	45	41@	—
1983-84*	35	45	42@	—
1984-85*	35	46	42@	—
1985-86*	38	46	44@	—

Source : India. Ministry of Human Resource Development. Department of Education.

@ Data relates to Higher Secondary (old pattern and new pattern 10+2) and high/ post-basic schools.

— Not available.

* Provisional.

TABLE 23 : Students Going Abroad by Sex-wise, 1970-71 to 1985-86

Year	Female	Male	Total	% of female total	% of female to male
1970-71	281	4,666	4,947	5.68	6.02
1978-79	241	1,833	2,074	11,62	13.14
1981-82	201	1,899	2,100	9.57	10.58
1982-83	216	1,898	2,114	10.21	11.38
1983-84	263	1,918	2,181	12.05	13.71
1984-85	381	2,291	2.672	14.25	16.63
1985-86	467	2,750	3,217	14.51	16.98

Sources : (1) *A Handbook of Educational and Allied Statistics.* Department of Education. Ministry of Education and Culture : New Delhi, 1983.

(2) *Indian Students/Trainees Going Abroad,* 1981-82 and 1982-83, Ministry of Human Resource Development.

(3) Do, 1983-84 , 1984-85 and 1985-86, 1988.

TABLE 8.24: Female Students Going Abroad by Fields of Study, 1981-82-1985-86

Year	Arts	Science	Education	Engineering	Architecture	Tech. and Industry	Medicine	Vet. Sc.	Agriculture and Forestry	Law	Commerce	Banking and Insurance	Fine Arts	Nursing	Library Sc.	Other Subjects
1981-82	48	46	4	27	2	3	3	0	4	3	17	1	0	0	0	43
1982-83	53	45	5	17	2	2	11	0	1	2	14	0	1	0	0	65
1983-84	47	57	10	13	4	4	6	0	0	2	29	2	2	0	0	89
1984-85	146	76	7	31	13	2	9	2	0	4	31	0	2	0	0	58
1985-86	137	86	3	62	25	6	23	0	3	2	8	1	8	1	0	69

Source : (1) *Indian Students/Trainees Going Abroad, 1981-82 and 1982-83.* Ministry of Human Resource Development, New Delhi, 1987.

(2) *Indian Students/Trainers Going Abroad, 1983-84, 1984-85 and 1985-86,* Manager, Goverment of India Press; Ministry of Human Resource Development, New Delhi, 1988

9

States

TABLE 9.1: Distribution of Population, Sex Ratio, Density and Growth Rate of Population

Sl. No.	India/State/ Union Territory	Population 1991			Sex Ratio		Density		Growth Rate	
		Persons	Males	Females	1981	1991	1981	1991	1971-81	1981-91
1	2	3	4	5	6	7	8	9	10	11
	INDIA	843,930,861	437,597,929	406,332,932	934	929	216	267	+24.66	+23.50
	States									
1.	Andhra Pradesh	66,304,854	33,623,738	32,681,116	975	972	195	241	+23.10	+23.82
2.	Arunachal Pradesh	858,392	461,242	397,150	862	861	8	10	+23.36	+23.58
3.	Assam	22,294,562	11,579,693	10,714,869	910	925	230	284	+23.36	+23.58
4.	Bihar	86,338,853	45,147,280	41,191,573	946	912	402	497	+24.06	+23.49
5.	Goa	1,168,622	593,563	575,059	975	969	272	316	+26.74	+15.96
6.	Gujarat	41,174,060	21,272,388	19,901,672	942	936	174	210	+27.67	+20.80
7.	Haryana	16,317,715	8,705,379	7,612,336	870	874	292	369	+28.75	+26.28
8.	Himachal Pradesh	5,111,079	2,560,894	2,550,185	973	996	77	92	+23.71	+19.39
9.	Jammu and Kashmir	7,716,700	4,014,100	3,704,600	892	923	59	76	+29.69	+28.92

TABLE 9.1: *(Contd.)*

Sl. No.	India/State/ Union Territory	Population 1991			Sex Ratio		Density		Growth rate	
		Persons	Males	Females	1981	1991	1981	1991	1971-81	1981-91
1	2	3	4	5	6	7	8	9	10	11
10	Karnataka	44,817,398	22,861,409	21,955,989	963	960	194	234	+26.75	+20.69
11.	Kerala	29,011,237	14,18,167	14,793,070	1,032	1,040	655	747	+19.24	+13.98
12.	Madhya Pradesh	66,135,862	34,232,048	31,903,814	941	932	118	149	+25.27	+26.75
13.	Maharashtra	78,706,719	40,652,056	38,054,663	937	936	204	256	+24.54	+25.36
14.	Manipur	1,826,714	931,511	895,203	971	961	64	82	+32.46	+28.56
15.	Meghalaya	1,760,626	904,308	856,318	954	947	60	78	+32.04	+31.80
16.	Mizoram	686,217	356,672	329,545	919	924	23	33	+48.55	+38.98
17.	Nagaland	1,215,573	643,273	572,300	863	890	47	73	+50.05	+56.86
18.	Orissa	31,512,070	15,979,904	15,532,166	981	972	169	202	+20.17	+19.50
19.	Punjab	20,190,795	10,695,136	9,495,659	879	838	333	401	+23.89	+20.26
20.	Rajasthan	43,880,640	22,935,895	20,944,745	919	913	100	128	+32.97	+28.07
21.	Sikkim	403,612	214,723	188,889	835	880	45	57	+50.77	+27.57
22.	Tamil Nadu	55,638,318	28,217,947	27,420,371	977	972	372	428	+17.50	+14.94
23.	Tripura	2,744,827	1,410,545	1,334,282	946	946	196	262	+31.92	+ 33.69
24.	Uttar Pradesh	138,760,417	73,745,994	65,014,423	885	882	377	471	+25.49	+25.16
25.	West Bangal	67.982,732	35,461,898	32,520,834	911	917	615	766	+23.17	+24.55

TABLE 9.1: *(Contd.)*

Sl. No.	India/State/ Union Territory	Population 1991			Sex Ratio		Density		Growth rate	
		Persons	Males	Females	1981	1991	1981	1991	1971-81	1981-91
1	2	3	4	5	6	7	8	9	10	11
	Union Territories									
1.	A and N Isands	277,989	152.737	125,252	760	820	23	34	+63.93	+47.29
2.	Chandigarh	640,725	357,411	283,314	769	793	3,961	5,620	+75.55	+41.88
3.	Dadra and Nagar Haveli	138,542,	70,927	67,615	974	953	211	282	+39.78	+33.63
4.	Daman and Diu	101,439	51,452	49,987	1,062	972	705	906	+26.07	+28.43
5.	Delhi	9,370,475	5,120,733	4,249,742	808	830	4,194	6,319	+53.00	+50.64
6.	Lakshadweep	51,681	26,582	25,099	975	944	1,258	1,615	+26.53	+28.40
7.	Pondicherry	789,416	398,324	391,092	985	982	1,229	1,605	+28.15	+30.60

Notes: 1. In 1981 Census was not conducted in Assam. Based on the 1971 Census population and the 1991 provisional results the population of Assam for 1981 has been interpolated.

2. As a consequence of the revised estimates for Assam for the year 1981, the total population of India as of 1981 has been estimated as 683,329,097 as against earlier published figures of 685,184,692.

3. As a consequence of the revised figures, the decadel growth rate for India during 1971-81 has been estimated as 24.66 per cent.

4. The 1991 Census has not yet been conducted in Jammu and Kashmir. The figures are as per projections prepared by the Standing Committee of Experts on Population Projections, October, 1989.

5. Sex ratio is defined as number of females per 1,000 males.

TABLE 9.2: Sex Ratio: Females per 1,000, Males, 1901-1991

Sl. No.	India/State/ Union Territory	1901	1911	1921	1931	1941	1951	1961	1971	1981	1991
1	2	3	4	5	6	7	8	9	10	11	12
	India	972	964	955	950	945	946	941	930	934	929
	States										
1.	Andhra Pradesh	985	992	993	987	980	986	981	977	975	972
2	Arunachal Pradesh	*	*	*	*	*	*	894	861	862	861
3.	Assam	919	915	896	874	875	868	869	896	910	925
4.	Bihar	1,091	1,044	1,016	994	996	990	994	954	946	912
5.	Goa	1,091	1,108	1,120	1,088	1,064	1,128	1,066	981	975	969
6.	Gujarat	954	946	944	945	941	952	940	934	942	936
7.	Haryana	867	835	844	844	869	871	868	867	870	874
8.	Himachal Pradesh	884	889	890	897	890	912	938	958	973	996
9.	Jammu and Kashmir	882	876	870	865	869	873	878	878	892	923**
10.	Karnataka	983	981	969	965	960	966	959	957	963	960
11.	Kerala	1,004	1,008	1,011	1,022	1,027	1,028	1,022	1,016	1,032	1,040
12.	Madhya Pradesh	990	986	974	973	970	967	953	941	941	932
13.	Maharashtra	978	966	950	947	949	941	936	930	937	936
14.	Manipur	1,037	1,029	1,041	1,065	1,055	1,036	1,015	980	971	961
15.	Meghalaya	1,036	1,013	1.000	971	966	949	937	942	954	947
16.	Mizoram	1,113	1,120	1,109	1,102	1,069	1,041	1,009	946	919	924
17.	Nagaland	973	993	992	997	1.021	999	933	871	863	890

TABLE 9.2: *(Contd.)*

Sl. Nos.	India/State/ Union Territory	1901	1911	1921	1931	1941	1951	1961	1971	1981	1991
1	2	3	4	5	6	7	8	9	10	11	12
18.	Orissa	1,037	1,056	1,086	1,067	1,053	1,022	1,001	988	981	972
19.	Punjab	832	780	799	815	836	844	854	865	879	888
20.	Rajasthan	905	908	896	907	906	921	908	911	919	913
21.	Sikkim	916	951	970	967	920	907	904	863	835	880
22.	Tamil Nadu	1,044	1,042	1,029	1,027	1,012	1,007	992	978	977	972
23.	Tripura	874	885	885	885	886	904	932	943	946	946
24.	Uttar Pradesh	937	915	909	904	907	910	909	879	885	882
25.	West Bengal	945	925	905	890	852	865	878	891	911	917
	Union Territories										
1.	A and N Islands	318	352	303	495	574	625	617	644	760	820
2.	Chandigarh	771	720	743	751	763	781	682	749	769	793
3.	Dadra and Nagar Haveli	960	967	940	911	925	946	963	1,007	974	953
4.	Daman and Diu	995	1,040	1,143	1,088	1,080	1,125	1,169	1,099	1,062	972
5.	Delhi	862	793	733	722	715	768	785	801	808	830
7.	Lakshadweep	1,063	987	1,027	994	1,018	1,043	1,020	978	975	944
8.	Pondicherry	NA	1,058	1,053	NA	NA	1,030	1,013	989	985	982

NA = not available

* In Arunachal Pradesh the Census was conducted for the first time in 1961. Hence sex ratio for the earlier censuses is not available.

** The sex ratio for Jammu and Kashmir is based on projected population.

TABLE 9.3: Female Literacy : Six Top States/Union Territories

State / Union Territories		Female Literacy Rate
1.	Kerala	86.93
2.	Mizoram	78.09
3.	Chandigarh	73.61
4.	Lakshadweep	70.88
5.	Goa	68.20
6.	Delhi	68.01

TABLE 9.4: Female Literacy: Six Most Backward States/Union Territories

State /Union Territories		Female Literacy Rate
1.	Rajasthan	20.84
2.	Bihar	23.10
3.	Uttar Pradesh	26.02
4.	Dadra and Nagar Haveli	26.10
5.	Madhya Pradesh	28.39
6.	Arunachal Pradesh	29.37

TABLE 9.5 : States and Union Territories arranged in descending order of literacy rate among persons, Females and Males

Rank	Persons		Males		Females	
	State Union Territories	Literacy Rate	State Union Territory	Literacy Rate	State Union Territory	Literacy Rate
1.	Kerala	90.59	Kerla	94.45	Kerla	86.93
2.	Mizoram	81.23	Lakshadweep	87.06	Mizoram	78.09
3.	Lakshadweep	79.23	Daman and Diu	85.67	Chandigarh	73.61
4.	Chandigarh	78.73	Goa	85.48	Lakshadweep	70.88
5.	Goa	76.96	Mizoram	84.06	Goa	68.20
6.	Delhi	76.09	Pondicherry	83.91	Delhi	68.01
7.	Pondicherry	74.91	Chandigarh	82.67	A and N Islands	66.22
8.	A and N Islands	73.74	Delhi	82.63	Pondicherry	65.79
9.	Daman and Diu	73.58	A and N Islands	79.68	Daman and Diu	61.38
10.	Tamil Nadu	63.72	Tamil Nadu	74.88	Nagaland	55.72
11.	Himachal Pradesh	63.54	Maharashtra	74.84	Himachal Pradesh	52.46
12.	Maharashtra	63.05	Himachal Pradesh	74.57	Tamil Nadu	52.29
13.	Nagaland	61.30	Manipur	72.98	Maharashtra	50.51
14.	Manipur	60.96	Gujarat	72.54	Tripura	50.01
15.	Gujarat	60.91	Tripura	70.08	Punjab	49.72
16.	Tripura	60.39	Haryana	67.85	Manipur	48.64
17.	West Bengal	57.72	Karnataka	67.25	Gujarat	48.50
18.	Punjab	57.14	West Bengal	67.24	Sikkim	47.23

TABLE 9.5 : *(Contd.)*

Rank	Persons		Males		Females	
	State Union Territory	Literacy Rate	State Union Territory	Literacy Rate	State Union Territory	Literacy Rate
19.	Sikkim	56.53	Nagaland	66.09	West Bengal	47.15
20.	Karanataka	55.98	Sikkim	64.34	Meghalaya	44.78
21.	Haryana	55.33	India	63.86	Karnataka	44.34
22.	Assam	53.42	Punjab	63.68	Assam	43.70
	India	52.11	Orissa	62.37	Haryana	40.94
23.	Orissa	48.55	Assam	62.34	India	39.42
24.	Meghalaya	48.26	Madhya Pradesh	57.43	Orissa	34.40
25.	Andhra Pradesh	45.11	Andhra Pradesh	56.24	Andhra Pradesh	33.71
26.	Madhya Pradesh	43.45	Uttar Pradesh	55.35	Arunachal Pradesh	29.37
27.	Uttar Pradesh	41.71	Rajasthan	55.07	Madhya Pradesh	28.39
28.	Arunachal Pradesh	41.22	Bihar	52.63	Dadra and Nagar Haveli	26.10
29.	Dadra and Nagar Haveli	39.45	Dadra and Nagar Haveli	52.07	Uttar Pradesh	26.02
30.	Rajasthan	38.81	Meghalaya	51.57	Bihar	23.10
31.	Bihar	38.54	Arunachal Pradesh	51.10	Rajasthan	20.84

Note : Excluded Jammu & Kashmir where the 1991 Census was not held.

TABLE 9.6 : Sexwise and Statewise Enrolment Ratio in Primary and Middle Classes in 1991-92

State/Union Terrirory	Primary			Middle		
	Girls	Boys	Total	Girls	Boys	Total
1	2	3	4	5	6	7
Andhra Pradesh	**94.81**	123.16	109.16	**43.28**	70.80	57.17
Arunachal Pradesh	**91.11**	127.84	109.43	**37.35**	56.45	47.00
Assam	**108.59**	116.79	112.80	**54.64**	69.44	62.27
Bihar	**55.55**	104.60	80.47	**20.67**	53.17	37.02
Delhi	**88.15**	86.61	87.32	**80.26**	82.92	81.71
Goa	**96.65**	106.18	101.41	**96.19**	112.13	104.16
Gujarat	**110.64**	141.79	126.52	**58.64**	84.58	71.86
Haryana	**78.72**	93.59	86.27	**51.26**	74.78	63.59
Himachal Pradesh	**108.66**	125.30	116.99	**96.02**	124.71	110.47
Jammu and Kashmir	**71.20**	101.82	86.88	**46.70**	75.82	61.70
Karnataka	**106.54**	115.45	111.10	**47.11**	65.62	56.50
Kerala	**98.09**	100.02	99.07	**104.42**	106.17	105.31
Madhya Pradesh	**88.79**	119.20	104.54	**35.68**	74.22	55.53
Maharashtra	**119.31**	132.35	125.96	**66.83**	91.53	79.50
Manipur	**104.28**	116.58	110.61	**58.93**	66.78	62.91
Meghalaya	**62.38**	66.59	64.48	**53.67**	63.52	58.53
Mizoram	**132.95**	139.73	136.44	**72.83**	75.82	74.36
Nagaland	**104.22**	114.40	109.40	**67.76**	69.50	68.64

TABLE 9.6 : *(Contd.)*

State/Union Terrirory	Primary			Middle		
	Girls	Boys	Total	Girls	Boys	Total
1	2	3	4	5	6	7
Orissa	**86.53**	119.47	103.42	**37.74**	65.07	51.57
Punjab	**9.51**	101.97	98.40	**65.62**	79.34	72.84
Rajasthan	**50.05**	106.67	79.16	**22.61**	65.93	44.93
Sikkim	**112.68**	127.17	120.01	**47.63**	48.71	48.19
Tamil Nadu	**127.86**	142.28	135.24	**86.00**	109.43	97.95
Tripura	**121.48**	143.46	132.62	**70.61**	90.32	80.68
Uttar Pradesh	**66.88**	104.88	86.86	**33.42**	67.94	51.64
West Bengal	**107.93**	139.78	124.13	**55.49**	74.27	64.94
A. and N. Islands	**84.83**	100.39	92.37	**75.94**	87.73	81.96
Chandigarh	**59.40**	61.24	60.37	**57.04**	57.33	57.19
Dadra and Nagar Haveli	**87.04**	115.49	101.94	**34.70**	56.16	45.87
Daman and Diu	**0.00**	0.00	0.00	**0.00**	0.00	0.00
Delhi	**88.15**	86.61	87.32	**80.26**	82.92	81.71
Lakshadweep	**134.50**	157.27	145.88	**96.87**	118.12	107.84
Pondicherry	**136.38**	147.54	142.01	**117.40**	135.38	126.47
India	**88.09**	116.61	102.74	**47.40**	74.19	61.15

Source : Selected Education Statistics, 1991-92

TABLE 9.7: Sex-wise and State-wise Enrolment in Pre-Basic/Pre-Primary, 1990-91

State/Union Territory	Pre-Primary/Pre-Basic Stage		
	Girls	Boys	Total
1	2	3	4
Andhra Pradesh	10,255	15,125	25,380
Arunachal Pradesh	5,546	7,328	12,874
Assam	7,594	8,726	16,320
Bihar*	10,256	28,047	38,303
Delhi	34,710	30,180	64,890
Goa	—	—	—
Gujarat	67,000	87,000	1,54,000
Haryana	2,848	3,807	6,655
Himachal Pradesh*	2,500	2,800	5,300
Jammu and Kashmir*	7,100	3,900	16,000
Krranataka	1,53,000	1,77,480	3,30,480
Kerala	7,112	7,861	14,973
Madhya Pradesh	54,907	67,531	1,22,438
Maharashtra	72,640	92,101	1,64,741
Manipur	246	335	581
Meghalaya	29,579	30,359	59,938
Mizoram	—	—	—
Nagaland	30,747	34,850	65,597
Orissa	—	—	—
Punjab*	5,094	6,274	11,368
Rajasthan	56,642	69,291	1,25,933
Sikkim	6,595	8,198	14,793
Tamil Nadu	2,425	2,166	4,591
Tripura	78,061	79,734	1,57,795
Uttar Pradesh	14,156	21,224	35,380
West Bengal+	16,310	19,672	35,982
A. and N. Islands	1,770	1,913	3,683
Chandigarh	4,485	5,840	10,325
Dadra and Nagar Haveli	—	—	—
Daman and Diu	94	127	221
Lakshadweep	477	443	920
Pondicherry	5,129	5,500	10,629
India	6,87,278	8,22,812	15,10,090

* Figures relate to 1989-90.

\+ Figures relate to 1988-89.

TABLE 9.8: Sexwise and Statewise Enrolment Ratio in Classes I-IV and Classes VI -VIII of Schools for General Education (1990-91)

State/Union Territory	Classes I-V-(6-11 Years)			Classes VI-VIII-(11-14 Years)		
	Girls	Boys	Total	Girls	Boys	Total
1	2	3	4	5	6	7
Andhra Pradesh	**93.16**	121.02	107.25	**39.85**	67.49	53.79
Arunachal Pradesh	**88.14**	121.58	104.86	**35.43**	54.64	45.14
Assam	**107.27**	116.00	111.75	**48.73**	67.00	58.17
Bihar	**55.05**	107.55	81.70	**19.37**	53.54	36.51
Delhi	**91.09**	89.43	90.20	**82.52**	85.73	84.27
Goa	**97.53**	108.31	102.92	**98.55**	113.78	106.19
Gujarat	**108.37**	136.62	122.77	**57.27**	83.68	70.72
Haryana	**73.09**	93.99	83.59	**47.36**	75.38	62.03
Himachal Pradesh	**108.69**	125.67	117.21	**86.21**	109.06	7.75
Jammu and Kashmir	**68.19**	101.21	85.12	**42.34**	75.21	59.30
Karanataka	**101.70**	113.92	107.95	**47.15**	67.14	57.25
Kerala	**101.28**	103.58	102.45	**104.05**	107.29	105.69
Madhya Pradesh	**84.34**	122.03	103.85	**42.88**	80.54	62.23
Maharashtra	**116.52**	129.46	123.15	**68.26**	93.18	81.01
Manipur	**105.10**	119.20	112.30	**62.15**	70.68	66.47

Contd.

TABLE 9.8: *(Contd.)*

Meghalaya	**103.03**	109.02	106.02	**50.78**	59.53	55.09
Mizoram	**146.08**	153.36	149.81	**81.29**	78.27	79.75
Nagaland	**99.11**	113.23	106.29	**67.43**	69.79	68.12
Orissa	**83.87**	120.29	102.51	**41.88**	53.05	47.50
Punjab	**92.22**	99.00	95.76	**61.77**	73.77	68.11
Rajasthan	**48.79**	105.00	77.96	**19.17**	65.14	42.88
Sikkim	**115.15**	130.01	122.67	**45.12**	46.84	46.01
Tamil Nadu	**126.48**	141.08	133.95	**83.09**	107.95	95.75
Tripura	**126.02**	148.88	137.63	**67.05**	84.62	76.01
Uttar Pradesh	**62.27**	98.59	81.39	**27.61**	64.89	47.31
West Bengal	**108.73**	141.37	125.31	**56.31**	76.07	66.20
A. and N. Islands	**85.71**	101.16	93.24	**77.13**	89.87	83.68
Chandigarh	**60.07**	61.07	60.60	**57.50**	53.90	55.56
Dadra and Nagar Haveli	**84.89**	111.60	98.88	**34.00**	55.29	45.08
Daman and diu	—	—	—	—	—	—
Lakshadweep	**127.67**	150.00	139.13	**93.93**	108.94	101.68
Pondicherry	**136.14**	147.32	141.79	**112.94**	134.00	123.56
India	**85.97**	115.29	101.03	**46.13**	73.38	60.11

TABLE 9.9: Sexwise and Statewise Enrolment Ratio in Classes I-V and Classes VI -VIII of Schools for General (1990-91)

State/Union Territory	Middle/Senior Basic Stage Classes VI-VIII			Primary Stage Classes I-V		
	Girls	Boys	Total	Girls	Boys	Total
1	2	3	4	5	6	7
Andhra Pradesh	**32,34,834**	43,01,744	75,36,578	**7,80,407**	13,43,686	21,24,093
Arunachal Pradesh	**47,154**	65,043	1,12,197	**10,133**	15,956	26,089
Assam	**16,56,888**	18,93,197	35,50,085	**4,35,770**	6,40,427	10,76,197
Bihar	**28,41,810**	57,23,453	85,65,263	**5,60,989**	15,59,587	21,20,576
Delhi	**4,29,868**	4,90,965	9,20,833	**2,25,354**	2,80,346	5,05,700
Goa	**64,373**	71,483	1,35,856	**37,449**	43,464	80,913
Gujaraat	**24,58,000**	32,22,000	56,80,000	**7,50,000**	11,38,000	18,88,000
Haryana	**7,34,917**	9,54,490	16,89,407	**2,51,214**	4,39,601	6,90,815
Himachal Pradesh*	**3,19,123**	3,71,102	6,90,225	**1,46,131**	1,88,667	3,34,798
Jammu & Kashmir+	**2,88,386**	4,50,374	7,38,760	**1,00,860**	1,90,878	2,91,738
Karnataka	**26,17,318**	30,64,914	56,82,232	**6,97,952**	10,15,914	17,13,866
Kerala	**15,32,817**	16,23,059	31,55,876	**9,08,187**	9,61,533	18,69,660
Madhya Pradesh	**31,31,075**	48,63,414	79,94,489	**8,89,261**	17,64,639	2653,900
Maharashtra	**46,24,412**	53,97,629	1,00,22,041	**16,02,467**	22,92,177	38,94,644
Manipur	**1,21,074**	1,43,515	2,64,589	**36,360**	42,340	78,700
Meghalaya	**1,18,177**	1,24,393	2,42,570	**32,451**	36,909	69,360

(Contd.)

Mizoram	**57,117**	63,183	1,20,300	**19,509**	19,568	39,077
Nagaland	**66,600**	78,810	1,45,410	**26,904**	28,617	55,521
Orissa	**14,46,000**	21,74,000	36,20,000	**4,27,300**	5,48,500	9,75,800
Punjab*	**9,47,026**	11,08,729	20,55,755	**3,64,470**	4,87,970	8,52,440
Rajasthan	**13,71,810**	31,41,437	45,13,247	**2,85,398**	10,33,336	13,18,734
Sikkim	**33,625**	38,873	72,498	**7,038**	7,776	14,814
Tamil Nadu	**35,81,414**	41,82,459	77,63,873	**13,44,281**	18,14,266	31,58,547
Tripura	**1,81,220**	2,21,084	4,02,304	**52,502**	68,964	1,21,466
Uttar Pradesh	**50,50,215**	88,89,785	1,39,40,000	**12,29,582**	32,40,428	44,70,010
West Bengal+	**39,60,689**	53,13,432	9,27,412	**11,64,672**	15,78,095	2,74,27,671
A and N. Islands	**18,770**	21,042	39,812	**8,022**	9,886	17,908
Chandigarh	**23,248**	26,382	49,630	**12,362**	13,584	25,946
Dadra and Nagar Haveli	**6,791**	9,821	1,662	**1,598**	2,820	44,182
Daman and Diu	**4,787**	4,992	9,779	**3,438**	4,063	7,501
Lakshadweep	**3,850**	4,518	8,348	**1,409**	1,743	3,152
Pondicherry	**50,236**	55,394	1,05,630	**25,298**	30,551	55,849
India	**4,10,23,604**	5,80,94,716	9,91,18,320	**1,24,38,708**	2,08,44,291	3,32,82,999

* Figures relate to 1989-90 + Figures relate to 1988-89

TABLE 9.10: Sexwise and Statewise Girls Enrolment in High/Post-Basic Classes IX-X

States/Union Territory	High/Post Basic (IX-X Classes)		
	Girls	Boys	Total
1	2	3	4
Andhra Pradesh	**3,48,785**	6,25,830	9,74,575
Arunachal Pradesh	**3,717**	7,054	10,771
Assam	**1,76,752**	2,28,976	40,728
Bihar*	**1,82,887**	6,95,218	8,78,105
Delhi	**1,03,655**	1,36,817	2,43,472
Goa	**18,769**	22,251	41,020
Gujarat	**3,01,000**	5,00,000	8,01,000
Haryana	**92,441**	2,00,265	2,92,706
Himachal Pradesh*	**75,697**	1,10,796	1,86,493
Jammu and Kashmir+	**37,000**	71,583	1,08,583
Karnataka	**2,86,616**	4,92,749	7,79,365
Kerla	**4,68,474**	4,59,693	9,28,167
Madhya Pradesh	**1,68,855**	5,42,973	7,11,828
Maharashtra	**6,50,167**	11,36,029	17,86,196
Manipur	**19,827**	26,873	46,700
Meghalaya	**22,041**	25,592	47,633
Mizoram	**7,940**	8,289	16,229
Nagaland	**9,450**	11,413	20,863
Orissa	**2,70,000**	5,07,000	7,77,000
Punjab*	**1,80,094**	2,55,465	4,35,559
Rajasthan	**1,07,529**	4,64,113	5,71,642
Sikkim	**2,921**	3,732	6,653
Tamil Nadu	**4,49,505**	7,08,230	11,57,735
Tripura	**20,775**	29,249	50,024
Uttar Pradesh	**4,40,647**	15,95,461	20,36,108
West Bengal+	**3,92,927**	7,81,273	11,74,200
A. and N. Islands	**3,774**	4,419	8,193
Chandigarh	**7,413**	7,996	75,409
Dadra and Nagar Haveli	**614**	1,058	1,672
Daman and Diu	**2,096**	3,010	5,106
Lakshadweep	**470**	,775	1,245
Pondicherry	**8,806**	10,696	19,502
INDIA	**48,61,604**	96,77,878	1,45,39,482

*Figures relate to 1989-90.

+Figures relate to 1988-89.

TABLE 9.11: Sexwise and Statewise Enrolment in Pre-University and Hr. Secondary Classes 10+2, 1990-91

State/Union Territory	Pre-University. (One-Year Course)			Hr. Secondary (10+2 New Pattern)		
	Girls	Boys	Total	Girls	Boys	Total
1	2	3	4	5	6	7
Andhra Pradesh*	—	—	—	**1,574**	2,887	4,461
Arunchal Pradesh	—	—	—	**1,291**	3,634	4,925
Assam@	—	—	—	**57,688**	1,11,129	1,68,817
Bihar*	—	—	—	**6,871**	18,038	24,909
Delhi	—	—	—	**66,750**	75,580	1,42,330
Goa	—	—	—	**8,042**	9,983	18,025
Gujarat	—	—	—	**1,27,000**	2,01,000	3,28,000
Haryana	—	—	—	**15,964**	41,750	57,714
Himachal Pradesh*	—	—	—	**29,481**	60,409	89,890
Jammu and Kashmir+	—	—	—	**21,410**	51,320	72,730
Karnataka	—	—	—	**58,621**	1,22,718	1,81,339
Kerla	—	—	—	**1,344**	1,682	3,026
Madhya Pradesh	—	—	—	**79,805**	2,15,169	2,95,001
Maharashtra	—	—	—	**2,68,000**	5,41,000	8,06,000
Manipur	—	—	—	**1,160**	2,750	3,910
Meghalaya	—	—	—	—	—	—
Mizoram	—	—	—	—	—	—

Contd.

TABLE 9.11 *(Contd.)*

1	2	3	4	5	6	7
Nagaland	—	—	—	—	—	—
Orissa	—	—	—	**2,125**	4,373	6,498
Punjab*	—	—	—	**71,521**	1,07,239	1,78,760
Rajasthan	—	—	—	**45,360**	1,78,170	2,23,530
Sikkim	—	—	—	**667**	1,392	2,059
Tamil Nadu	—	—	—	**1,98,633**	2,79,919	4,78,552
Tripura	—	—	—	**5,248**	10,548	15,796
Uttar pradesh	**903**	2,912	3,815	—	—	—
West Bengal+	—	—	—	**1,47,173**	2,77,243	4,24,416
A and N Islands	—	—	—	**1,809**	2,212	4,021
Chandigarh*	—	—	—	**6,087**	8,212	14,299
Dadra and Nagar Haveli	—	—	—	**291**	468	759
Daman and Diu	—	—	—	**408**	781	1,189
Lakshadweep	—	—	—	—	—	—
Pondicherry	—	—	—	**3,479**	4,183	7,659
INDIA	**903**	2,912	3,815	**12,24,799**	23,33,816	35,58,615

@ Includes enrolment of 10+2 classes in colleges also.

* Figures relate to 1989-90.

+Figures relate to 1988-89.

TABLE 9.12: Sexwise and Statewise Enrolment in Intermediate /Junior Colleges and Pre-Degree / Pre-University Classes 1991-92

State/Union Territory	Intermediate/Junior Colleges			(Pre-Degree/Pre-University (Two-Year Course)		
	Girls	Boys	Total	Girls	Boys	Total
1	2	3	4	5	6	7
Andhra Pradesh	**1,16,057**	2,86,458	4,02,515	—	—	—
Arunachal Pradesh	—	—	—	—	—	—
Assam	**1,018**	1,208	2,226	—	—	—
Bihar*	**62,984**	3,30,714	3,93,698	—	—	—
Delhi	—	—	—	—	—	—
Goa	—	—	—	—	—	—
Gujarat	—	—	—	—	—	—
Haryana	—	—	—	**17,699**	41,891	59,590
Himachal Pradesh*	—	—	—	—	—	—
Jammu and Kashmir	—	—	—	—	—	—
Karnataka	**32,625**	1,22,900	1,55,525	—	—	—
Kerala	**10,958**	12,259	23,217	**1,08,290**	99,427	207,717
Madhya Pradesh	—	—	—	—	—	—
Maharashtra	**1,36,416**	2,91,043	4,27,459	—	—	—
Manipur	**2,150**	1,200	3,350	**5,900**	8,720	14,620
Meghalaya	—	—	—	**5,126**	5,845	10,971
Mizoram	**95**	121	216	**2,132**	3,030	5,162

(Contd.)

TABLE 9.12 : *(Contd.)*

1	2	3	4	5	6	7
Nagaland	**15**	29	44	**1,509**	2,199	3,708
Orissa	**41,090**	1,03,613	1,44,703	—	—	—
Punjab*	—	—	—	—	—	—
Rajasthan	—	—	—	—	—	—
Sikkim	—	—	—	—	—	—
Tamil Nadu	—	—	—	—	—	—
Tripura	—	—	—	—	—	—
Uttar Pradesh	**2,57,353**	6,70,539	9,27,892	—	—	—
West Bengal	—	—	—	—	—	—
A and N Islands	—	—	—	—	—	—
Chandigarh*	—	—	—	**4,524**	6,924	11,448
Dadra and Nagar Haveli	—	—	—	—	—	—
Daman and Diu	—	—	—	—	—	—
Lakshadweep	—	—	—	**183**	306	489
Pondicherry	**111**	239	350	**290**	300	590
INDIA	**6,60,872**	18,20,323	24,81,195	**1,45,653**	1,68,642	3,14,295

*Figures relate to 1989-90.

TABLE 9.13: Sexwise and Statewise Enrolment in Polytechnic Institutes and Technical, Industrial Arts and Crafts Schools, 1990-91

State/Union Territory	Polytechnic Institutes			Technical Industrial Arts and Crafts School		
	Girls	Boys	Total	Girls	Boys	Total
1	2	3	4	5	6	7
Andhra Pradesh	**5,312**	22,858	28,170*	**26,222**	2,782	29,004*
Arunachal Pradesh	—	—	—	**164**	90	254
Assam	**215**	2,745	2,960	**3,373**	345	3,718
Bihar*	**91**	4,093	4,184	**10,272**	1,076	11,348
Delhi	**1,399**	2,399	3,798	**6,481**	1,841	8,322
Goa	**180**	1,280	1,460	**2,531**	370	2,901
Gujarat	**1,700**	14,100	15,800	**31,000**	21,500	52,500
Haryana	**613**	4,619	5,232	**14,893**	3,290	18,183
Himachal Pradesh*	**88**	766	854	**2,083**	1,291	3,374
Jammu and Kashmir+	**50**	1,307	1,357	**1,109**	980	2,089
Karnataka	**4,400**	34,600	39,000	**3,163**	455	3,618
Kerala	**2,691**	8,785	11,476	**20,798**	9,385	27,183
Madhya Pradesh	**89**	4,176	4,265	**11,739**	1,682	13,421
Maharashtra	**2,551**	39,364	41;915	**87,413**	24,334	1,11,747
Manipur	**39**	285	324	**150**	520	670
Meghalaya	**21**	244	265	**154**	110	264
Mizoram	**58**	167	225	**142**	90	232
Nagaland	**4**	297	301	**291**	132	423

TABLE 9.13: *(Contd.)*

State/Union Territory	Polytechnic Institutes			Technical Industrial Arts and Crafts School		
	Girls	Boys	Total	Girls	Boys	Total
1	2	3	4	5	6	7
Orissa	**325**	235	560	**5,775**	25	5,800
Punjab*	**415**	4,081	4496	**12,078**	4,368	16,446
Rajasthan	**1,829**	3,316	5145	**7,537**	1,752	9,289
Sikkim	—	—	—	**40**	3	43
Tamil Nadu	**7,275**	48,946	56221	**21,240**	3,016	24,256
Tripura	—	90	90	**154**	19	173
Uttar Pradesh	**1,028**	22,257	23285	**44,494**	2,275	46,769
West Bengal+	**418**	18,925	19343	**5,503**	7,052	12,555
A. and N. Islands	**64**	128	192	**150**	48	198
Chandigarh	**283**	586	869	**632**	470	1,102
Dadra and Nagar Haveli	—	—	—	—	—	—
Daman and Diu	**13**	42	55	**222**	14	236
Lakshadweep	—	—	—	—	—	—
Pondicherry	**354**	454	808	**279**	9	288
INDIA	**31,505**	241,145	272650	**3,20,082**	86,324	4,06,406

*Figures relate to 1989-90.

+Figures relate to 1988-89.

TABLE 9.14: Sexwise and Statewise Enrolment in Teacher Training Schools, 1990-91

State/Union Territory	Teacher Training Schools		
	Girls	Boys	Total
1	2	3	4
ndhra Pradesh	**1,967**	3,341	5,308
runachal Pradesh	**—**	—	—
ssam	**483**	1,751	2,234
ihar*	**5,785**	4,977	10,762
elhi	**1,500**	125	1,625
oa	**67**	7	74
ujarat	**5,000**	4,700	9,700
aryana	**79**	214	293
imachal Pradesh*	**414**	596	1,010
mmu and Kashmir+	**270**	460	730
arnataka	**7,327**	7,558	14,885
erala	**5,804**	1,838	7,642
adhya Pradesh	**1,307**	5,692	6,999
aharashtra	**11,331**	12,083	23,414
anipur	**—**	—	—
eghalaya	**310**	335	645
izoram	**30**	395	325
agaland	**7**	34	41
rissa	**173**	120	293
njab*	**1,288**	192	1,480
ajasthan	**1,809**	5,528	7,337
kkim	**29**	49	78
amil Nadu	**4,805**	2,125	6,930
ipura	**—**	171	171
ttar Pradesh	**2,058**	3,237	5,295
est Bengal+	**6,005**	4,225	10,230
and N. Islands	**69**	60	129
handigarh	**—**	—	—
adra and Nagar Haveli	**—**	—	—
aman and Diu	**—**	—	—
kshadweep	**—**	—	—
ndicherry	**—**	—	—
DIA	**57,917**	59,713	1,17,630

* Figures relate to 1989-90.

\+ Figures relate to 1988-89.

TABLE 9.15: Sexwise and Statewise Enrolment in B.Ed./B.T. and M.B.B.S.

State/Union Territory	B.Ed./B.T.			M.B.B.S.		
	Girls	Boys	Total	Girls	Boys	Total
1	2	3	4	5	6	7
Andhra Pradesh	**3,062**	4,293	7,355	**2,817**	4,892	7,709*
Arunachal pradesh	**8**	18	23	—	—	—
Assam	**355**	824	1,179	**566**	1,430	1,996
Bihar*	**897**	1,324	2,221	**899**	3,160	4,089
Delhi	**531**	271	802	**1,848**	2,238	4,086
Goa	**85**	27	112	**144**	161	305
Gujarat	**2,000**	3,000	5,000	**2,000**	4,000	6,000
Haryana	**1,924**	2,104	4,028	**276**	399	675
Himachal Pradesh*	**33**	146	179	**261**	81	342
Jammu and Kashmir+	**610**	530	1,140	**925**	403	1,328
Karnataka	**2,729**	4,350	7,079	**1,964**	5,324	7,288
Kerala	**3,113**	1,178	4,291	**1,832**	2,486	4,018
Madhya Pradesh	**2,412**	3,026	5,438	**1,370**	3,105	4,475
Maharashtra	**4,077**	8,539	12,616	**5,996**	8,789	14,785
Manipur	—	—	—	**100**	308	408
Meghalaya	**195**	272	467	—	—	—

TABLE 9.15: *(Contd.)*

State/Union Territory	B.Ed./B.T. Girls	Boys	Total	M.B.B.S. Girls	Boys	Total
1	2	3	4	5	6	7
Nagaland	**21**	48	69	—	—	—
Orissa	**380**	985	1,365	**528**	1,290	1,818
Punjab*	**2,328**	793	3,121	**944**	1,363	2,307
Rajasthan	**2,287**	3,744	6,031	**1,410**	2,607	4,017
Sikkim	—	—	—	—	—	—
Tamil Nadu	**1,650**	1,214	2,864	**3,312**	4,223	7,535
Tripura	**60**	144	204	—	—	—
Uttar Pradesh	**7,280**	9,432	16,712	**1,589**	5,310	6.899
West Bengal+	**4,213**	5,020	9,233	**958**	2,812	3,770
A. and N. Islands	**50**	25	75	—	—	—
Chandigarh	**437**	44	481	—	—	—
Dadra and Nagar Haveli	—	—	—	—	—	—
Daman and Diu	—	—	—	—	—	—
Lakshadweep	—	—	—	—	—	—
Pondicherry	—	—	—	**174**	369	543
INDIA	**40,764**	51,453	92,217	**28,911**	55,482	84,393

Figures relate to 1989-90 + Figures relate to 1988-89

TABLE 9.16: Sexwise and Statewise Enrolment B. Com/ B.Com (Hons.) and B.E./B.Sc. (Engg.) /B. Arch., 1990-91

State/Union Territory	B.Com/B. Com (Hons.)			B.E./B..Sc. (Engg.) /B. Arch.		
	Girls	Boys	Total	Girls	Boys	Total
1	2	3	4	5	6	7
Andhra Pradesh*	**19,664**	52,598	72,262	**1,608**	20,630	22,238
Arunachal Pradesh	**7**	83	90	—	—	—
Assam	**1,024**	7,498	8,522	**164**	2,561	2,725
Bihar*	**43,424**	1,97,952	2,41,376	**326**	5,937	6,263
Delhi	**8,270**	25,263	33,533	**399**	3,509	3,908
Goa	**2,256**	3,017	5273	**158**	524	682
Gujarat	**32,000**	57,500	89,500	**1,300**	12,000	13,300
Haryana	**2,425**	6,549	8,974	**158**	1,680	1,838
Himachal Pradesh*	**63**	388	451	**18**	188	206
Jammu and Kashmir+	**400**	1,340	1,740	**205**	1,960	2,165
Karnataka	**19,294**	31,945	51,239	**3,150**	46,050	49,200
Kerala	**6,898**	12,135	19,033	**8,898**	11,955	20,853
Madhya Pradesh	**4,081**	42,160	46,241	**220**	2,391	2,611
Maharashtra	**75,386**	153,096	2,28,482	**3,515**	50,514	54,029
Manipur	**180**	500	680	—	—	—
Meghalaya	**81**	432	513	—	—	—
Mizoram	**22**	90	112	—	—	—
Nagaland	**42**	366	408	—	—	—

Orissa	**464**	6,501	6,965	**93**	2,460	2,553
Punjab*	**1,738**	4,873	6,611	**108**	1,623	1,731
Rajasthan	**3,230**	22,168	25,398	**126**	4,425	4,551
Sikkim	—	—	—	—	—	—
Tamil Nadu	**12,863**	22,554	35,417	**3,890**	23,530	27,420
Tripura	**61**	1,689	1,750	**40**	460	500
Uttar Pradesh	**1,656**	36,754	38,410	**514**	13,702	14,216
West Bengal+	**6,712**	62,915	69,627	**395**	7,292	7,687
A. and N. Islands	**25**	88	113	—	—	—
Chandigarh	**324**	724	1048	**854**	1,260	2,114
Dadra and Nagar Haveli	—	—	—	—	—	—
Daman and Diu	**67**	38	105	—	—	—
Delhi	**8270**	25263	33533	**399**	3509	3908
Lakshadweep	—	—	—	—	—	—
Pondicherry	**659**	279	380	**148**	430	578
INDIA	**2,42,936**	7,51,596	9,94,532	**26,287**	215081	241368

*Figures relate to 1989-90.

+ Figures relate to 1988-89.

TABLE 9.17: Sexwise and Statewise Enrolment in B.A./B.A. (Hons.) / B.Sc./ (Hons) 1990-91

State/Union Territory	B.A/B.A. (Hons.)			B.Sc./B.Sc. (Hons)		
	Girls	Boys	Total	Girls	Boys	Total
1	2	3	4	5	6	7
Andhra Pradesh*	**26,749**	53,568	80,317	**19,635**	39,207	58,842
Arunachal Pradesh	**282**	1,093	1,375	**9**	49	58
Assam	**26,483**	44,886	17,369	**2,840**	18,401	21,241
Bihar*	**34,648**	1,21,672	1,56,320	**7,137**	50,089	57,226
Delhi	**32,428**	30,335	62,763	**6,283**	7,858	14,241
Goa	**1,973**	940	2,913	**822**	702	1,524
Gujarat	**55,000**	49,500	1,04,500	**42,675**	19,325	32,000
Haryana	**18,222**	24,851	43,073	**4,096**	5,796	9,863
Himachal Pradesh*	**2,040**	3,876	5,916	**591**	1,542	2,133
Jammu and Kashmir+	**5,700**	4,460	10,160	**2,520**	5,610	8,130
Karnataka	**33,220**	60,026	93,246	**12,815**	20,881	33,696
Kerala	**29,282**	22,929	52,211	**32,261**	22,021	54,282
Madhya Pradesh	**37,207**	54,201	91,408	**13,772**	35,563	49,335
Maharashtra	**64,658**	91,792	1,56,450	**79,528**	56,098	1,35,626
Manipur	**5,700**	7,560	13,260	**1,820**	3,620	5,440
Meghalaya	**1,937**	2,344	4,281	**340**	820	1,160
Mizoram	**768**	965	1,733	**79**	107	186

Nagaland	**871**	1,436	2,307	**57**	194	**251**
Orissa	**11,040**	23,045	34,085	**2,028**	9,185	11,213
Punjab*	**24,090**	24,042	48,132	**3,749**	5,322	9,071
Rajasthan	**11,007**	19,402	30,409	**4,027**	13,900	17,927
Sikkim	—	—	—	—	—	—
Tamil Nadu	**24,842**	31,337	56,179	**35,946**	55,134	91,080
Tripura	**2,801**	3,405	6,206	**376**	1,372	1,748
Uttar Pradesh	**67,525**	1,76,634	2,44,159	**12,692**	52,473	65,165
West Bengal+	**92,204**	60,033	1,52,237	**23,306**	48,203	71,409
A. and N. Islands	**549**	665	1,214	**122**	142	264
Chandigarh*	**3,285**	3,009	6,294	**854**	1,260	2,114
Dadra and Nagar Haveli	—	—	—	—	—	—
Daman and Diu	**92**	148	240	**9**	16	25
Lakshadweep	—	—	—	—	—	—
Pondicherry	**790**	801	1,591	**775**	871	1,646
INDIA	**6,15,393**	9,18,955	15,34,348	**2,81,035**	4,75,861	7,56,896

*Figures relate to 1989-90.

+Figures relate to 1988-89.

TABLE 9.18: Sexwise and Statewise Enrolment in M.Sc / M. Com. 1990-91

State/Union Territory	M.Sc			M.Com		
	Girls	Boys	Total	Girls	Boys	Total
1	2	3	4	5	6	7
Andhra Pradesh*	**1,442**	3,871	5,313	**393**	2,442	2,835
Arunachal Pradesh	—	—	—	—	—	—
Assam	**396**	818	4,214	**15**	517	532
Bihar*	**567**	2,254	2,821	**3,372**	10,826	14,198
Delhi	**928**	947	1,872	**785**	765	1,550
Goa	**113**	121	234	**100**	145	245
Gujarat	**1,200**	2,800	4,000	**2,500**	4,500	7,000
Haryana	**504**	879	1,383	**145**	216	361
Himachal Pradesh*	**104**	155	259	**27**	105	132
Jammu and Kashmir+	**220**	550	770	**60**	230	290
Karnataka	**378**	2,053	2,431	**117**	851	968
Kerala	**3,162**	1,551	4,713	**608**	825	1,433
Madhya Pradesh	**2,799**	5,762	8,561	**1,499**	8,307	9,806
Maharashtra	**1,657**	2,298	3,955	**3,493**	17,618	21,111
Manipur	**163**	290	453	**31**	45	76
Meghalaya	**58**	99	157	**6**	18	24
Mizoram	—	—	—	—	—	—
Nagaland	**4**	14	18	**1**	5	6

Orissa	**750**	1,701	2,451	**95**	1,191	1,286
Punjab*	**661**	573	1,234	**90**	63	153
Rajasthan	**602**	1,230	1,832	**326**	2,360	2,686
Sikkim	—	—	—	—	—	—
Tamil Nadu	**3,529**	5,093	8,622	**841**	2,354	3,195
Tripura	**31**	63	94	—	96	96
Uttar Pradesh	**3,498**	11,597	15,095	**296**	8,785	9,081
West Bengal+	**1,302**	2,612	3,914	**205**	2,145	2,350
A. and N. Islands	**3**	8	11	—	—	—
Chandigarh	**186**	136	322	**25**	29	54
Dadra and Nagar Haveli	—	—	—	—	—	—
Daman and Diu	—	—	—	—	—	—
Lakshadweep	—	—	—	—	—	—
Pondicherry	**95**	67	162	**13**	13	26
INDIA	**24,349**	47,542	71,891	**15,043**	64,451	79,494

*Figures relate to 1989-90.

+Figures relate to 1988-89.

TABLE 9.19: Sexwise and Statewise Enrolment Ph. D/D.Sc//D.Phill and M.A. in 1990-91

State/Union Territory	Ph.D. / D.Sc./D. Phill			M.A.		
	Girls	Boys	Total	Girls	Boys	Total
1	2	3	4	5	6	7
Andhra Pradesh*	**366**	1,330	1,696	**2,074**	6,222	8,296
Arunachal Pradesh	—	—	—	**9**	50	59
Assam	**81**	145	226	**1,369**	1,311	2,680
Bihar*	**153**	578	731	**2,771**	7,910	10,681
Delhi	**1,795**	3,119	4,914	**3,165**	3,063	6,228
Goa	**78**	93	171	**164**	98	262
Gujarat	**350**	700	1,050	**5,300**	5,700	11,000
Haryana	**271**	708	979	**1,483**	2,469	3,952
Himachal Pradesh*	**304**	475	779	**400**	608	1,008
Jammu and Kashmir+	**180**	225	405	**840**	790	4,630
Karnataka	**120**	400	520	**3,191**	6,979	10,170
Kerala	**546**	773	1,319	**3,017**	2,205	5,222
Madhya Pradesh	**885**	7,372	8,257	**7,672**	9,802	17,474
Maharashtra	**193**	340	533	**5,768**	10,764	16,232
Manipur	**20**	58	78	**325**	319	644
Meghalaya	**32**	46	78	**242**	354	596
Mizoram	—	—	—	**17**	19	36
Nagaland	—	—	—	**11**	9	20

Orissa	**70**	260	330	**2,045**	3,870	5,915
Punjab*	**418**	314	732	**4,784**	3,583	8,367
Rajasthan	**65**	90	155	**1,943**	4,420	6,363
Sikkim	—	—	—	—	—	—
Tamil Nadu	**59**	125	184	**3,104**	4,348	7,452
Tripura	—	—	—	**136**	101	237
Uttar Pradesh	**2,102**	5,946	8,048	**20,746**	45,114	65,860
West Bengal+	**411**	872	1,283	**5,642**	5,125	10,767
A. and N. Islands	—	—	—	**29**	34	63
Chandigarh	—	—	—	**900**	637	1,537
Dadra and Nagar Haveli	—	—	—	—	—	—
Daman and Diu	—	—	—	—	—	—
Lakshadweep	—	—	—	—	—	—
Pondicherry	—	—	—	**47**	33	80
INDIA	**8,499**	23,969	32,468	**76,896**	1,25,935	2,02,831

*Figures relate to 1989-90

+Figures relate to 1988-89

TABLE 9.20: Sexwise and Statewise Drop-out Rates up to Class X (1988-89)

State/Union Territory	Class I-V			Class I-VII			Class I-X		
	Girls	Boys	Total	Girls	Boys	Total	Girls	Boys	Total
1	2	3	4	5	6	7	8	9	10
Andhra Pradesh	**57.54**	51.45	54.08	**77.90**	68.58	72.54	**83.94**	75.33	79.02
Arunachal Pradesh	**61.49**	62.32	62.00	**76.68**	74.98	75.57	**84.29**	82.76	83.25
Assam	**59.64**	52.20	55.12	**75.74**	71.94	73.59	**82.01**	78.29	79.91
Bihar*	**70.26**	64.39	66.34	**84.90**	77.39	79.76	**90.87**	82.66	85.17
Delhi	**22.73**	6.34	18.30	**22.62**	8.54	15.26	**38.77**	2.25	29.13
Goa	—	—	—	—	—	—	—	—	—
Gujarat	**78.30**	70.27	43.84	**66.93**	55.66	60.46	**77.04**	71.35	73.74
Haryana	**30.99**	26.11	28.13	**51.11**	39.27	43.77	**62.30**	50.79	54.89
Himachal Pradesh*	**27.99**	26.38	27.12	**33.49**	18.76	25.33	**59.43**	45.15	51.30
Jammu and Kashmir+	**38.16**	50.03	45.30	**70.36**	47.00	56.11	**76.19**	64.44	68.91
Karnataka	**55.61**	44.40	59.70	**74.98**	61.10	67.83	**72.17**	60.29	65.80
Kerala	**3.00**	1.00	-2.00	**16.99**	18.37	17.70	**38.14**	43.79	41.04
Madhya Pradesh	**42.64**	39.32	40.62	**66.65**	49.88	55.78	**84.41**	72.35	76.47
Maharashtra	**44.25**	34.24	38.91	**66.07**	51.27	58.67	**80.23**	68.16	73.68
Manipur	**70.82**	70.00	70.37	**79.50**	76.72	78.01	**79.38**	75.57	77.34
Meghalaya	**29.53**	28.60	29.03	**61.84**	66.94	64.59	**89.93**	59.48	89.70

Mizoram	**38.72**	37.28	37.98	**43.59**	49.91	45.34	**82.84**	80.06	81.42
Nagaland	**33.01**	34.81	33.96	**54.02**	56.19	55.28	**83.61**	81.87	82.64
Orissa	**37.32**	40.05	38.97	**73.28**	59.92	65.46	**78.83**	68.39	72.74
Punjab*	**29.62**	29.20	29.39	**63.83**	58.42	60.91	77.75	73.23	75.33
Rajasthan	**60.75**	53.12	56.35	**73.20**	63.06	65.69	**84.19**	77.31	79.02
Sikkim	**58.29**	64.12	61.61	**60.11**	63.83	62.51	**59.79**	86.52	87.91
Tamil Nadu	**24.01**	19.16	21.41	**51.34**	41.33	45.91	**73.93**	65.92	69.62
Tripura	**56.14**	55.11	55.58	**77.58**	74.84	76.06	**83.17**	82.23	82.62
Uttar Pradesh	**48.96**	50.30	40.89	**65.00**	51.82	56.06	**80.02**	59.5.	60.10
West Bengal+	**66.89**	62.57	64.45	**77.34**	75.35	76.18	**85.87**	85.60	85.71
A. and N. Islands	**18.69**	13.72	16.13	**40.03**	35.27	37.53	**57.43**	49.72	53.43
Chandigarh	**7.80**	–6.00	–5.40	**3.74**	11.88	8.78	**30.85**	25.15	27.82
Dadra and Nagar Haveli	**47.75**	14.13	40.68	**69.93**	62.54	65.70	**83.50**	79.54	81.24
Daman and Diu	**–.40**	–13.13	–3.63	**23.14**	15.34	19.02	**59.64**	54.73	87.06
Lakshadweep	**7.88**	11.55	–26.71	**47.86**	26.57	36.79	**73.98**	69.18	71.41
Pondicherry	**–1.05**	71.35	–3.81	**21.07**	4.79	12.55	**52.36**	45.91	48.96
Total	**49.69**	46.74	47.93	**68.31**	89.38	68.40	**79.46**	72.68	75.36

(Contd.)

TABLE 9.20: *(Contd.)*

Drop-out rate is calculated as follows:

Drop-out rate from classes I to V for the year 1987-88

$$\frac{\text{(No. of students enrolled in Class I in 1984-85)} \quad \text{(No - of students enrolled in Class V in 1988-89)}}{\text{No. of students enrolled in Class I in 1984-85}} \times 100$$

Drop-out rate from Classes I to VIII for the year 1988-89

$$\frac{\text{(No. students entrolled in Class I in 1981-82)} \quad \text{(No. of stuents enrolled in Class VIII in 1988-89)}}{\text{No. of students entrolled in Class I in 1981-82}} \times 100$$

Drop-out rate from Classes I to X for the year 1988-89

$$\frac{\text{(No. of students enrolled in Class I in 1979-80)-} \quad \text{(No. of students enrolled in Class VIII in 1988-89)}}{\text{No. of students entrolled in Class I in 1979-80}} \times 100$$

This ratio does not take into account: (1) Repeaters; and (ii) Children who enter the system after Class 1.

TABLE 9.21: Sexwise and Statewise Number of Teachers 1991-92

State/Union Territory	Primary School			Middle School			Sec./Hr. Secondary Schools		
	Female	Male	Total	Female	Male	Total	Female	Male	Total
1	2	3	4	5	6	7	8	9	10
Andhra Pradesh	**32,838**	80,286	1,13,124	**14,094**	28,847	42,941	**29,354**	60,628	89,982
Arunachal Pradesh	**584**	1,913	2,497	**369**	1,406	1,775	**470**	1,859	2,329
Assam	**17,055**	58,232	75,287	**6,554**	31,992	38,546	**9,326**	33,990	43310
Bihar*	**22,493**	93,665	1,16,158	**20,251**	79,763	1,00,014	**6,739**	40,822	4,756
Delhi	**14,280**	8,340	22,620'	**3,492**	2,367	5,859	**24,066**	17,750	41,814
Goa	**1,819**	1,100	2,919	**462**	349	811	**4,081**	3,206	7,287
Gujarat	**14,715**	22,070	36,785	**54,305**	81,460	1,35,765	**14,621**	45,579	60,200
Haryana	**19,170**	23,736	42,906	**4,694**	7,183	11,877	**19,380**	28,780	48,160
Himachal Pradesh*	**7,325**	12,890	20,215	**1,205**	4,200	5,405	**4,030**	6,999	13,729
Jammu and Kashmir+	**6,605**	9,841	16,446	**6,484**	11,515	17,999	**6,622**	14,928	21,550
Karnataka	**11,676**	30,101	41,777	**39,043**	56,779	92,822	**12,416**	41,025	53,441
Kerala	**31,240**	16,742	47,982	**32,272**	18,788	51,060	**57,849**	34,500	92,349
Madhya Pradesh	**43,416**	1,40,537	1,83,953	**21,592**	61,466	83,059	**14,771**	43918	58,659
Maharashtra	**50,031**	72,860	1,22,891	**57,327**	94,649	1,51,976	**60,859**	1,40,054	200,911
Manipur	**2,397**	8,187	10,584	**1,168**	1,487	5,355	**2,184**	5,130	7,314
Meghalaya	**2,488**	4,245	6,733	**1,120**	1,901	3,021	**1,494**	1,541	3,055
Mizoram	**1,773**	1,978	3,751	**648**	2,508	3,156	**275**	1,361	1,636

(Contd.)

TABLE 9.21: *(Contd.)*

State/Union Territory	Primary School			Middle School			Sec./Hr. Secondary Schools		
	Female	Male	Total	Female	Male	Total	Female	Male	Total
1	2	3	4	5	6	7	8	9	10
Nagaland	**1,766**	4.659	6,425	**790**	2,861	3,651	**443**	2,527	2,970
Orissa	**26,265**	78,675	1,04,940	**6,475**	32,040	38,515	**8,951**	33,886	42,837
Punjab*	**26,041**	21,933	47,974	**4,855**	5,549	10,404	**22,429**	27,390	49,819
Rajasthan	**21,343**	59,039	80,382	**18,139**	53,005	71,144	**14,291**	50,593	64,884
Sikkim	**642**	1,731	2,373	**498**	1,063	1,561	**922**	1162	2,084
Tamil Nadu	**49,496**	71,225	1,20,721	**31,707**	33,960	65,667	**48,173**	68,382	11,655
Tripura	**2,003**	7,888	9,891	**935**	3,656	4,591	**2,994**	7,491	10,484
Uttar Pradesh	**48,662**	2,15,051	2,64,713	**18,968**	76,556	95,524	**16,469**	81,201	94,070
West Bengal+	**40,636**	1,44,112	1,84,748	**7,139**	18,092	28,231	**41,691**	78,326	1,20,017
A. and N. Islands	**265**	467	732	**357**	262	719	**994**	1,215	2,209
Chandigarh	**713**	84	797	**534**	84	618	**2,403**	700	3,103
Dadra and Nagar Haveli	**51**	110	161	**214**	161	375	**46**	116	162
Daman and Diu	**181**	301	482	**91**	139	230	**57**	166	223
Lakshadweep	**70**	159	229	**56**	71	127	**68**	287	355
Pondicherry	**895**	923	1,818	**892**	919	1,811	**1,318**	1,801	3,119
INDIA	**4,98,934**	11,94,080	16,93,014	**3,53,731**	7,17,878	10,71,609	**4,29,786**	8,80,013	13,09,799

Source : Selected Educational Statistics, 1991-92.

TABLE 9.22: Sexwise and Statewise number of Teachers in Primary/Junior Basic School and percentage of Trained Teachers (1990-91)

State/Union Territory	Number of Teachers			Percentage of Trained Teachers
	Women	Men	Total	
1	2	3	4	5
Andhra Pradesh	**31,638**	79,219	1,10,857	97.00
Arunachal pradesh	**470**	1,869	2,366	35.12
Assam	**14,586**	57,732	72,318	64.00
Bihar*	**22,286**	95,355	1,17,641	87.93
Delhi	**13,943**	8,243	22,186	100.00
Goa	**1,759**	1,123	2,912	94.00
Gujarat	**13,800**	22,500	36,300	100.00
Haryana	**6,449**	9,012	15,461	99.99
Himachal Pradesh*	**6,020**	10,980	17,000	94.17
Jammu and Kashmir+	**5,565**	8,159	13,724	85.00
Karnataka	**11,599**	29,903	41,502	93.69
Kerala	**31,542**	18,231	49,773	69.00
Madhya Pradesh	**40,043**	1,36,161	176,204	N.A.
Maharashtra	**48,485**	72,626	1,21,111	93.00
Manipur	**2,397**	8,187	10,584	53.00
Meghalaya	**2,486**	4,243	6,729	42.00
Mizoram	**1,689**	2,058	3,747	49.31
Nagaland	**1,701**	4,531	6,232	50.07
Orissa	**26,265**	78,155	1,04,420	100.00
Punjab*	**25,702**	22,139	47,841	99.40
Rajasthan	**18,768**	55,440	74,208	98.00
Sikkim	**637**	1,608	2,245	50.42
Tamil Nadu	**49,921**	70,452	1,20,373	100.00
Tripura	**1,755**	6,847	8,602	29.50
Uttar Pradesh	**48,176**	2,15,553	2,63,729	98.00
West Bengal+	**40,636**	1,44,112	1,84,748	68.00
A. and N. Islands	**251**	473	724	95.00
Chandigarh	**686**	78	764	100.00
Dadra and Nagar Haveli	**50**	110	160	92.00
Daman and Diu	**159**	119	278	97.00
Lakshadweep	**71**	153	224	96.00
Pondicherry	**849**	1,086	1935	94.00
INDIA	**4,70,414**	11,66,484	16,36,898	89.81

* Figures relate to 1989-90.

+ Figures relate to 1988-89.

TABLE 9.23: Sexwise and Statewise Number of Teachers in Middle/Senior Basic Schools and Percentage of Trained Teachers, 1990-91

State/Union Territory	Number of Teachers			Percentage of Trained Teachers
	Women	Men	Total	
1	2	3	4	5
Andhra Pradesh	**13,567**	28.270	41,837	98.51
Arunachal Pradesh	**316**	1,355	1,671	35.90
Assam	**6,304**	31,742	35,046	27.00
Bihar*	**49,447**	78,914	98,364	88.13
Delhi	**3,369**	2.269	5,665	98.00
Goa	**476**	364	840	97.00
Gujarat	**61,750**	73,500	1,35,250	100.00
Haryana	**4,648**	7,167	11,815	99.50
Himachal Pradesh*	**1,300**	5,700	7,000	98.27
Jammu and Kashmir+	**5,807**	11,822	17,629	83.00
Karnataka	**35,620**	56,112	91,732	95.43
Kerala	**31,755**	19.875	51,630	93.00
Madhya Pradesh	**19,956**	60,932	80,888	N.A.
Maharashtra	**55,555**	93,365	148,920	95.00
Manipur	**1,168**	4.187	5,355	31.00
Meghalaya	**1,114**	1,895	3,009	35.00
Mizoram	**636**	2,626	3,262	68.27
Nagaland	**791**	2,807	3,598	29.02
Orissa	**6,375**	31,026	37,401	95.00
Punjab*	**4,205**	5.267	9,472	97.09
Rajasthan	**17,456**	52,897	7,035	99.00
Sikkim	**487**	1,078	1,565	41.02
Tamil Nadu	**31,928**	33,608	65,536	100.00
Tripura	**840**	3,286	4,126	33.37
Uttar Pradesh	**18,837**	76,442	95,279	95.00
West Bengal+	**7,139**	18,092	25,231	71.00
A. and N. Islands	**349**	351	700	97.00
Chandigarh	**506**	85	591	100.00
Dadra and Nagar Haveli	**215**	169	384	93.00
Daman and Diu	**91**	139	230	98.00
Lakshadweep	**49**	75	124	100.00
Pondicherry	**729**	1,063	1,792	98.00
INDIA	**3,52,812**	7,06,483	10,59,295	91.04

*Figures relate to 1989-90..
+Figures relate to 1988-89.
N.A. = Not available

TABLE 9.24: Sexwise and Statewise High/Post-Basic School percentage of Trained Teachers, 1990-91

State/Union Territory	Number of Teachers			Percentage of Trained Teachers
	Women	Men	Total	
1	2	3	4	5
Andhra Pradesh	**22,990**	51,761	74,751	99.25
Arunachal Pradesh	**199**	751	950	40.94
Assam	**6,548**	23,675	30,223	31.00
Bihar*	**4,856**	36,505	41,361	87.50
Delhi	**4,126**	3,235	7,361	99.00
Goa	**3,446**	2,707	6,153	86.00
Gujarat	**4,960**	18,423	23,383	100.00
Haryana	**15,637**	23,715	39,352	99.54
Himachal Pradesh*	**2,400**	6,300	8,700	97.13
Jammu and Kashmir+	**4,638**	9,494	14,132	82.00
Karnataka	**8,834**	25,514	34,348	96.39
Kerala	**54,852**	34,899	89,751	99.00
Madhya Pradesh	**3,534**	13,907	17,441	N.A.
Maharashtra	**39,233**	84,975	1,24,208	95.00
Manipur	**1,716**	4,237	5,953	32.00
Meghalaya	**1,446**	1,495	2,941	32.00
Mizoram	**242**	1,244	1,486	76.72
Nagaland	**1,029**	2,159	3,188	32.80
Orissa	**7,455**	32,547	40,002	95.00
Punjab*	**14,754**	49,116	33,870	99.39
Rajasthan	**6,727**	25,988	32,715	98.00
Sikkim	**532**	790	1,322	43.27
Tamil Nadu	**17,979**	24,400	42,379	99.70
Tripura	**1,204**	3,527	4,731	36.20
Uttar Pradesh	**6,578**	32,102	38,680	97.00

(Contd.)

TABLE 9.24: *(Contd.)*

State/Union Territory	Number of Teachers			Percentage of Trained Teachers
	Women	Men	Total	
1	2	3	4	5
West Bengal+	**32,798**	49,339	82,137	73.00
A. and N. Islands	**314**	346	660	97.00
Chandigarh	**1,293**	518	1,811	100.00
Dadra and Nagar Haveli	**15**	40	55	96.00
Daman and Diu	**51**	145	196	98.00
Lakshadweep	**66**	236	302	98.00
Pondicherry	**824**	960	1,784	100.00
INDIA	**2,71,276**	5,35,050	8,06,326	90.10

*Figures relate to 1989-90

+Figures relate to 1988-89

TABLE 9.25: Sexwise and Statewise Number of Teachers in Higher Secondary/ Junior Colleges (10+2 New Pattern and Percentage of Trained Teachers (1990-91)

State/Union Territory	Number of Teachers			Percentage of Trained Teachers
	Women	Men	Total	
1	2	3	4	5
Andhra Pradesh	**2,866**	5,232	8,098	95.37
Arunachal Pradesh	**186**	1,037	1,223	53.14
Assam	**2,602**	9,626	12,228	25.00
Bihar@	**1,665**	4,118	5,783 *	89.90
Delhi	**19,455**	13,845	33,300	99.00
Goa	**386**	584	970	59.00
Gujarat	**9,023**	25,385	34,408	100.00
Haryana	**3,531**	4,332	7,863	99.21
Himachal Pradesh@	**1,400**	2,800	4,200	94.09
Jammu and Kashmir+	**1,377**	3,493	4,870	88.00
Karnataka	**3,354**	14,851	18,205	100.00
Kerala	**2,120**	1,226	3,346	99.00
Madhya Pradesh	**7,939**	25,375	33,314	N.A.
Maharashtra	**19,448**	50,302	69,750	97.00
Manipur	**468**	893	1,361	47.00
Meghalaya	—	—	—	—
Mizoram	—	—	—	—
Nagaland	**2**	2	4	50.00
Orissa	**350**	1,250	1,600	100.00
Punjab@	**7,202**	8,655	15,857	99.03
Rajasthan	**6,994**	22,413	29,407	99.00
Sikkim	**306**	453	759	40.71
Tamil Nadu	**31,178**	43,260	74,438	98.23
Tripura	**1,664**	3,591	5,255	59.42
Uttar Pradesh	**9,861**	48,154	58,015	97.00
West Bengal+	**8,893**	28,987	37,880	70.00

(Contd.)

TABLE 9.25: *(Contd.)*

State/Union Territory	Number of Teachers			Percentage of Trained Teachers
	Women	Men	Total	
1	2	3	4	5
A. and N. Islands	**617**	833	1,450	99.00
Chandigarh	**940**	368	1,308	100.00
Dadra and Nagar Haveli	**29**	74	103	98.00
Daman and Diu	**6**	21	27	90.00
Lakshadweep	**1**	32	33	—
Pondicherry	**364**	757	1,121	100.00
INDIA	**1,44,227**	3,21,949	4,66,176	92.39

*Data relate to Hr. Sec. only.

@Figures relate to 1989-90

+Figures relate to 1988-89

TABLE 9.26: Indian Female Students Gone Abroad by State/UT, 1970-71 to 1985-86

	1970-71	1978-79	1981-82	1982-83	1983-84	1984-85	1985-86
Andhra Pradesh	7	11	13	18	18	36	31
Assam	1	0	0	0	0	4	4
Bihar	6	0	2	2	2	4	1
Delhi	67	45	35	40	71	68	99
Gujarat	47	8	6	2	4	25	24
Haryana	1	1	1	0	0	2	1
Himachal Pradesh	1	0	0	0	0	0	0
J. and K.	0	0	0	1	0	0	0
Karnataka	14	16	22	9	19	24	57
Kerala	1	2	2	0	2	2	1
Madhya Pradesh	4	2	0	1	1	1	3
Maharashtra	93	84	67	90	87	119	146
Manipur	0	0	0	0	0	0	0
Meghalaya	0	0	0	0	0	0	0
Nagaland	0	0	0	0	0	0	0
Orissa	0	1	0	0	0	1	1
Punjab	3	3	6	1	4	3	5
Rajasthan	1	2	0	0	0	1	0

(Contd.)

TABLE 9.27: *(Contd.)*

	1970-71	1978-79	1981-82	1982-83	1983-84	1984-85	1985-86
Sikkim	0	0	0	0	0	0	3
Tamil Nadu	11	22	30	30	30	59	38
Tripura	0	0	0	0	0	0	0
Uttar Pradesh	5	8	4	4	8	9	11
West Bangel	15	14	9	16	15	20	39
Arunachal Pradesh	0	0	0	0	0	0	0
A. and N. Islands	0	0	0	0	0	0	0
Chandigarh	3	2	4	2	1	0	1
Dadra and Nagar Haveli	0	0	0	0	0	0	0
Goa, Daman and Diu	1	0	0	0	1	2	2
Lakshadweep	0	0	0	0	0	0	0
Mizoram	0	0	0	0	0	0	0
Pondichery	0	0	0	0	0	1	0
ALL INDIA	281	241	201	216	263	381	467

Sources : (1) *A Hand Book of Educational and Allied Statistics,* New Delhi, Department of Education, 1983.

(2) *Indian Students Trainess Going Abroad 1983-84 to 1985-86.* Manager, Government of India Press, Delhi; Ministry of Human Resource Development, New Delhi, 1988,

(3) Do. 1981-82, 1982-83, 1987.

10

Scheduled Castes and Scheduled Tribes

TABLE 10.1: Sexwise Rural/Urban SC and ST Literates and Illiterates in India 1981-1991

Illiterates and literates in India

1981		Females	Males
All	Illiterates	**181.10**	120.96
Areas	Literates	**77.07**	157.08
RURAL	Illiterates	**154.79**	104.80
AREAS	Literates	**43.09**	103.51
URBAN	Literates	**26.31**	16.16
AREAS	Literates	**33.98**	53.57
SCs	Literates(%)	**10.93**	31.12
STs	Literates(%)	**80.4**	21.52
1991			
ALL	Illiterates	**195.64**	124.77
AREAS	Literates	**126.06**	223.70
RURAL	Illiterates	**165.12**	106.69
AREAS	Literates	**71.94**	146.38
URBAN	Illiterates	**30.52**	18.08
AREAS	Literates	**54.12**	77.32
SCs	Literates(%)	**23.76**	49.91
STs	Literates(%)	**18.19**	40.65

Note : Distribution of literates and Illiterates among Population Aged 7 years and above by Sex and Area 1981-1991 in Millions.

TABLE 10.2: Percentage of Sexwise SC Enrolment in respect of Scheduled Castes

Year	Classes Girls	I Boys	V Total	Classes Girls	VI Boys	VIII Total
1987-88	**76.86**	818.25	98.11	**28.73**	57.88	**43.72**
1988-89	**78.33**	121.26	100.37	**30.18**	58.81	**44.88**
1989-90	**78.81**	120.93	100.44	**31.08**	59.70	**45.75**
1990-91	**80.60**	122.68	102.21	**33.28**	61.40	**47.71**
1991-92	**83.56**	121.38	102.99	**36.03**	68.89	**52.89**

TABLE 10.3: Percentage of Sexwise Enrolment in Classes I-V and Classes VI-VIII

Year	Classes I	V		Classes VI	VIII	
	Girls	Boys	Total	Girls	Boys	Total
1987-88	**73.16**	121.71	98.09	**21.85**	96.56	34.55
1988-89	**76.00**	126.23	101.79	**22.73**	47.90	35.65
1989-90	**77.55**	127.53	103.22	**24.02**	49.63	37.15
1990-91	**78.60**	126.78	103.35	**27.50**	51.33	39.72
1991-92	**82.59**	125.63	104.70	**27.28**	54.11	41.05

TABLE 10.4: Percentage of Sexwise Enrolment: General SC and ST in Classes I to V and Classes VI to VIII 1991-92

Category	Classes I—V			Classes VI—VIII		
	Girls	Boys	Total	Girls	Boys	Total
General	**88.09**	116.61	102.74	**47.40**	74.19	61.15
Scheduled Castes	**83.56**	121.38	102.99	**36.03**	68.89	52.89
Scheduled Tribes	**82.59**	125.63	104.70	**27.28**	54.11	91.05

TABLE 10.5: Enrolment of SC Women and Its Percentage to Total SC Enrolment in Different Classes 1986-87

	Classes	SC Women Enrolment	Total SC Enrolment	% of Women to Total Enrolment
1.	Ph.D./D.Sc./M.Phill	**121**	644	18.78
2.	M.A.	**2,342**	16,157	14.49
3.	M.Sc	**538**	2,320	23.18
4.	M.Com.	**189**	2,180	8.08
5.	B.Sc./B.Sc.(Horns.)	**8,995**	31,694	28.38
6.	B.A./B.A.(Horns.)	**22,430**	1,02,975	21.78
7.	B.Com/B.Com.(Horns.)	**3,423**	29,262	11.69
8.	B.E/B.Sc.(Engg.)/B.Arch.	**391**	6,764	5.78
9.	B.Ed/B.T.	**1,197**	5,152	23.23
10.	M.B.B.S.	**1,135**	5,313	28.89
11.	Teacher Training Schools	**2,891**	7603	38.00
12.	Polytechnic Institutes	**1,850**	2,891	51.80
13.	Technical, Industrial Arts and Crafts Schools	**5,873**	22,890	38.80
14.	Intermediate/Jr. Colleges	**14,692**	54,312	27.05
15.	Pre-Degree/Pre-University (Two-Year Course)	**480**	6,019	7.97
16.	Pre-University (One-Year Course)	**1,588**	5,590	28.40
17.	Hr. Secondary (10+2) (New Pattern)	**25,407**	95,645	26.56
18.	Hr. Secondary (Old Pattern)	**594**	11,433	0.05
19.	High/Post Basic (IX, X)	**3,32,799**	12,92,939	25.73
20.	Middle/Senior Basic Classes (VI to VIII)	**10,98,777**	34,14,053	32.18
21.	Primary/Jr. Basic Classes (I to V)	**46,54,886**	1,25,25,770	37.16

TABLE 10.6: Enrolment of S.C. Women and Its Percentage to Total Enrolment of SC in Different Classes (1987-88)

	Classes	SC Women Enrolment	Total SC Enrolment	% of S.C Women to total Enrolment
1.	Ph.D./D.SC./M.Phill	**148**	812	18.22
2.	M.A	**3,159**	19,859	15.90
3.	M.Sc.	**705**	3,113	22.64
4.	M.Com	**478**	4,758	10.04
5.	B.A/B.A.(Hons.)	**30,693**	1,37,981	22.24
6.	B.SC./BS.(Hons.)	**10,013**	37,085	27.00
7.	B.Com./B.Com.(Hons.)	**6,029**	42,811	14.08
8.	B.E/B.SC(Engg.)/B.Arch	**640**	11,075	41.89
9	B.Ed/B.T	**1,474**	6,234	23.64
10.	M.B.B.S.	**1,954**	6,870	28.44
11.	Teacher Traning Schools	**2,994**	8,310	36.02
12.	Polytechnic Institutes	**2,404**	23,079	10.41
13.	Technical, Industrial Arts and Crafts Schools	**7,603**	30,485	24.94
14.	Intermediate/Jr. Colleges	**37,686**	1,80,776	20.84
15.	Pre-Degree/Pre-University (Two-Year Course)	**3,256**	16,575	19.64
16.	Pre-University (Two-Year Course)	**166**	813	20.41
17.	Hr. Secondary (10+2) XI-XII Classes (New Pattern)	**74,200**	2,94,412	25.20
18.	Hr. Secondary (Old Pattern)	**619**	13,060	4.73
19.	High School/Post Basic IX, X Classes	**3,90,952**	15,21,655	25.64
20.	Middle Stage Classes VI to VIII	**11,92,672**	37,35,231	31.93
21.	Primary Stage Classes I to V	**55,93,219**	1,46,76,132	33.11

TABLE 10.7: Enrolment of SC Women and its Percentage to Total Enrolment SC of (1988-89)

	Classes	S.C Women Enrolment	Total S.C Enrolment	% of SC Women Enrolment
1.	Ph.D./D.Sc./M.Phil	**182**	914	19.91
2.	M.A.	**3,332**	20,356	16.36
3.	M.Sc.	**873**	3,628	24.06
4.	M.Com	**540**	4,902	11.01
5.	B.A./B.A.(Hons.)	**31,962**	1,42,856	22.37
6.	B.Sc./B.Sc.(Hons.)	**11,041**	38,587	28.61
7.	B.Com./B.Com.(Hons.)	**6,375**	42,248	15.04
8.	B.E./B.Sc. (Engg.)/B.Arch	**797**	12,080	6.59
9.	B.Ed./B.T	**2,196**	6,979	31.46
10	M.B.B.S.	**2,529**	7,170	35.27
11.	Teacher Training Schools	**3,598**	10,099	35.62
12.	Polytechnic Institutes	**2,673**	25,525	10.47
13.	Technical, Industrial Arts and Crafts Schools	**7,853**	30,858	25.44
14.	Intermediate/Jr.Colleges	**27,207**	1,70,695	15.93
15.	Pre-Degree/Pre University (Two-Year Course)	**12,035**	28,499	42.22
16.	Pre. University (One-Year Course)	**73**	254	28.74
17.	Hr. Secondary (10+2) Classes XI-XII	**82,390**	3,27,773	25.13
18.	High School-IX and X Classes	**4,35,410**	15,75,198	27.64
19.	Middle Stage- VI to VIII classes	**12,56,604**	38,40,477	32.71
20.	Primary Stage I to V Classes	**57,71,002**	1,52,02,234	37.96

TABLE 10.8: Enrolment of SC Women and Its Percentage to Total S.C Enrolment in Different Classes (1989-90)

	Classes	SC Women Enrolment	Total SC Enrolment	% of SC Women Enrolment
1.	Ph.D./D.Sc./M.Phil	**151**	751	20.10
2.	M.A	**4,152**	22,976	18.07
3.	M.Sc.	**940**	3,682	25.52
4.	M.Com	**840**	6,313	13.30
5.	B.A/B.A(Hons.)	**34,498**	1,59,167	21.67
6.	B.Sc.(Hons.)	**12,845**	44,456	28.89
7.	B.Com/B.Com.(Hons.)	**8,673**	52,297	16.58
8.	B.E/B.Sc (Engg.)/B.Arch	**1,443**	13,796	10.45
9.	B.Ed./B.T.	**2,020**	7,704	26.22
10.	M.B.B.S.	**2,349**	7,283	32.25
11.	Teacher Training Schools	**5,570**	14,100	39.50
12.	Polytechnic Institutes	**2,681**	23,557	11.38
13.	Technical, Industrial Arts and Craft Schools	**10,774**	49,064	21.95
14.	Intormediate and Jr.Colleges	**43,706**	2,48,887	17.56
15.	Pre-Degree/Pre-University (Two-Year Course)	**14,630**	30,762	47.55
16.	Pre-University (Two-Year Course)	**74**	259	28.57
17.	Hr. Secondary (10+2) Classes XI-XII	**88,559**	3,33,808	26.52
18.	High School Classes IX-X	**4,88,045**	17,24,121	28.30
19.	Middle stage: Classes VI-VIII	**14,13,416**	41,60,516	33.97
20.	Primary stage Classes I to VI	**60,57,503**	1,57,94,427	38.35

TABLE 10.9: Enrolment of SC Women and Its Percentage to Total Enrolment of Different Classes (1990-91)

	Classes	S.C Women Enrolment	Total S.C Enrolment	% of Women Enrolment
1.	Ph.D/D.Sc./M.Phil.	**151**	751	20.10
2.	M.A.	**4,152**	22,976	18.07
3.	M.Sc.	**940**	3,682	25.52
4.	M.Com	**840**	6,313	13.30
5.	B.A./B.A.(Hons.)	**34,498**	1,59,167	21.61
6.	B.SC./B.SC.(Hons)	**12,845**	44,456	28.89
7.	B.Com/B.Com.(Hons)	**8,673**	52,297	16.58
8.	B.E./B.Sc. (Engg.)/B.Arch	**1,443**	13,796	10.45
9.	B.Ed./B.T.	**2,030**	7,704	26.34
10.	M.B.B.S.	**2,349**	7,283	32.25
11.	Teacher Training Schools	**5,570**	14,100	39.50
12.	Polytechnic Instituites	**2,681**	23,557	11.38
13.	Technical, Industrial Arts and Crafts Schools	**10,774**	49,064	21.45
14.	Intermediate Jr. Colleges	**43,706**	2,48,887	17.56
15.	Pre-Degree/Pre-University (Two-Year Course)	**14,630**	30,762	47.55
16.	Pre-University (One-Year Course)	**74**	259	28.57
17.	Hr.Secondary (10+2)-Classes XI,XII	**88,559**	3,33,808	26.52
18.	High School Classes IX, XI	**4,88,045**	17,24,121	28.30
19.	Middle Stage Classes VI to VIII	**14,13,416**	41,60,516	33.97
20.	Primary Stage Classes I to V	**60,57,503**	1,57,94,427	38.35

TABLE 10.10: Sexwise and Statewise Enrolment Ratio of SC Students in Primary and Middle Classes, 1991-92.

State/Union Territory	Primary			Middle		
	Girls	Boys	Total	Girls	Boys	Total
1	2	3	4	5	6	7
Andhra Pradesh	**123.70**	163.42	143.81	**45.71**	80.56	63.29
Arunachal Pradesh	**14.27**	30.04	22.13	**0.83**	1.63	1.24
Assam	**205.95**	213.92	210.04	**82.72**	111.67	97.64
Bihar	**40.00**	100.43	70.70	**10.09**	37.10	23.68
Delhi	**103.34**	116.85	110.60	**59.24**	77.74	69.32
Goa	**68.22**	75.21	71.71	**50.47**	72.31	61.39
Gujarat	**147.61**	202.42	175.55	**71.00**	118.13	95.01
Haryana	**91.51**	112.02	101.92	**39.26**	66.53	53.54
Himachal Pradesh	**110.34**	133.42	121.89	**78.48**	110.22	94.40
Jammu and Kashmir	**79.89**	106.00	93.26	**60.24**	79.11	69.96
Karnataka	**111.21**	130.96	121.31	**42.37**	66.09	54.41
Kerala	**113.04**	115.76	114.42	**115.03**	117.98	116.52
Madhya Pradesh	**89.83**	123.14	107.08	**28.08**	94.45	62.26
Maharashtra	**237.70**	277.16	257.83	**123.38**	181.22	153.05
Manipur	**136.38**	126.88	131.49	**64.57**	66.11	67.60
Meghalaya	**181.98**	221.74	201.82	**196.16**	295.74	245.26
Mizoram	**0.00**	0.00	0.00	**0.00**	0.00	0.00
Nagaland	**0.00**	0.00	0.00	**0.00**	0.00	0.00
Orissa	**105.84**	157.38	132.27	**20.12**	70.49	55.49
Punjab	**117.37**	137.26	127.72	**48.21**	67.56	58.39
Rajasthan	**41.05**	103.88	73.35	**13.29**	64.08	39.47
Sikkim	**117.15**	127.22	122.24	**36.30**	37.00	36.66
Tamil Nadu	**134.44**	155.43	145.18	**78.97**	106.60	93.07
Tripura	**147.72**	171.68	159.86	**71.64**	97.42	84.82
Uttar Pradesh	**39.09**	83.12	62.24	**15.05**	50.92	33.98
West Bengal	**72.28**	104.79	88.82	**18.30**	35.34	26.87
A. and N. Islands	**0.00**	0.00	0.00	**0.00**	0.00	0.00
Chandigarh	**112.26**	119.72	116.19	**76.12**	75.92	76.01
Dadra and Nagar Haveli	**81.98**	84.19	83.14	**68.05**	83.35	76.01
Daman and Diu	**0.00**	0.00	0.00	**0.00**	0.00	0.00
Lakshadweep	**0.00**	0.00	0.00	**0.00**	0.00	0.00
Pondicherry	**181.55**	174.93	178.21	**124.02**	134.16	129.13
INDIA	**83.56**	121.38	102.99	**36.03**	68.89	52.89

TABLE 10.11: Sexwise and Statewise Enrolment Ratio of ST Students in Primary and Middle Classes, 1991-92

States/Union Territory	Primary			Middle		
	Girls	Boys	Total	Girls	Boys	Total
1	2	3	4	5	6	7
Andhra Pradesh	**160.52**	102.60	131.93	**52.36**	24.67	38.64
Arunachal Pradesh	**133.04**	94.71	113.82	**54.76**	33.85	44.41
Assam	**175.43**	154.68	165.33	**71.14**	51.97	61.86
Bihar	**90.65**	52.10	71.69	**34.05**	16.08	25.12
Delhi	**0.00**	0.00	0.00	**0.00**	0.00	0.00
Goa	**19.42**	11.70	15.55	**12.03**	6.29	9.16
Gujarat	**160.83**	112.70	137.23	**66.91**	39.06	53.25
Haryana	**0.00**	0.00	0.00	**0.00**	0.00	0.00
Himachal Pradesh	**125.15**	95.96	110.58	**100.41**	63.64	82.15
Jammu and Kashmir	**0.00**	0.00	0.00	**0.00**	0.00	0.00
Karnataka	**121.00**	98.22	109.87	**55.52**	35.42	45.67
Kerala	**133.15**	126.46	129.86	**93.54**	90.15	91.87
Madhya Pradesh	**94.40**	60.11	77.87	**45.42**	15.42	30.87
Maharashtra	**137.27**	111.44	124.62	**67.27**	39.24	53.62
Manipur	**151.26**	133.18	142.49	**53.26**	43.37	48.38
Meghalaya	**73.04**	68.58	70.81	**59.89**	52.56	56.18
Mizoram	**141.78**	149.11	145.54	**80.54**	77.46	79.03
Nagaland	**107.32**	97.73	102.61	**63.17**	61.59	62.08
Orissa	**128.27**	63.78	96.85	**40.10**	17.92	29.14
Punjab	**0.00**	0.00	0.00	**0.00**	0.00	0.00
Rajasthan	**108.42**	39.01	74.69	**63.64**	8.25	36.80
Sikkim	**116.18**	104.29	110.31	**42.35**	47.23	44.73
Tamil Nadu	**124.01**	98.60	111.60	**66.64**	42.94	55.03
Tripura	**175.59**	131.41	153.79	**75.57**	49.50	62.82
Uttar Pradesh	**94.45**	58.42	77.36	**55.41**	22.12	39.69
West Bengal	**147.95**	65.28	107.34	**36.03**	12.55	24.36
A. and N. Islands	**68.90**	59.59	64.10	**64.90**	56.09	60.59
Chandigarh	**0.00**	0.00	0.00	**0.00**	0.00	0.00
Dadra and Nagar Haveli	**124.38**	89.38	107.71	**51.60**	27.41	40.00
Daman and Diu	**0.00**	0.00	0.00	**0.00**	0.00	0.00
Lakshadweep	**170.84**	146.44	158.64	**127.93**	103.09	115.91
Pondicherry	**0.00**	0.00	0.00	**0.00**	0.00	0.00
INDIA	**125.63**	82.59	104.70	**54.11**	27.28	41.05

TABLE 10.12: Sexwise and Statewise Enrolment Ratio of SC and ST at the Pre-primary Stage (1990-91)

State/Union Territory	Number of Students belonging to: Scheduled Castes			Scheduled Tribes		
	Girls	Boys	Total	Girls	Boys	Total
1	2	3	4	5	6	7
Andhra Pradesh	**1,776**	1,073	2,849	**385**	302	687
Arunachal Pradesh	**49**	29	78	**4,689**	3,548	8,237
Assam	**1,071**	663	1,734	**1,148**	689	1,837
Bihar*	**1,212**	562	1,774	**7,469**	4,253	11,722
Delhi	**4,537**	4,398	8,935	**29**	38	67
Goa	—	—	—	—	—	—
Gujarat	**7,850**	6,050	13,900	**4,000**	3,100	7,100
Hyaryana	**315**	194	509	—	—	—
Himachal Pradesh*	**156**	136	292	**34**	31	65
Jammu and Kashmir	**805**	403	1,208	—	—	—
Karnataka	**12,975**	10,608	23,583	**2,199**	1,740	3,939
Kerala	**1,110**	1,013	2,123	**172**	130	302
Madhya Pradesh	**3,411**	2,304	5,715	**3,130**	1,872	5,002
Maharashtra	**8,379**	6,496	14,875	**8,019**	6,950	14,969
Manipur	—	—	—	**90**	40	130
Meghalaya	**367**	428	795	**22,616**	22,943	45,559
Mizoram	—	—	—	—	—	—
Nagaland	—	—	—	—	—	—
Orissa	—	—	—	—	—	—
Punjab*	**173**	110	283	—	—	—
Rajasthan	**8,467**	5,656	14,123	**2,057**	1,692	3,749
Sikkim	**485**	424	909	**1,692**	1,339	2,958
Tamil Nadu	**82**	41	123	**18**	9	27
Tripura	**18,053**	18,598	36,651	**28,982**	27,503	56,485
Uttar Pradesh	**482**	221	703	—	—	—
West Bengal*	—	—	—	—	—	—
A. and N. Islands	—	—	—	**58**	53	111
Chandigarh	**572**	448	1,020	—	—	—
Dadra and Nagar Haveli	—	—	—	—	—	—
Daman and Diu	**8**	3	11	**5**	9	9
Lakshadweep	**1**	2	3	**425**	466	891
Pondicherry	**480**	389	869	—	—	—
INDIA	**60,249**	72,816	1,33,065	**76,702**	87,144	1,63,846

TABLE 10.13: Sexwise and Statewise Enrolment Ratio of SC Students in Primary and Middle Classes (1990-91)

State/Union Territory	Girls	Boys	Total	Girls	Boys	Total
1	2	3	4	5	6	7
Andhra Pradesh	**161.88**	122.02	142.18	**76.62**	42.35	59.63
Arunachal Pradesh	**28.72**	16.87	22.79	**7.52**	5.12	6.33
Assam	**194.15**	187.84	191.08	**108.33**	84.16	96.65
Bihar	**102.23**	39.36	71.27	**37.91**	9.70	23.85
Delhi	**120.43**	106.71	144.08	**80.27**	62.24	72.12
Goa	**116.16**	100.32	108.24	**71.24**	50.11	60.70
Gujarat	**184.18**	144.71	164.83	**117.79**	68.26	93.49
Haryana	**109.27**	86.85	98.12	**62.72**	31.19	47.70
Himachal Pradesh	**126.91**	104.38	115.68	**92.50**	58.88	75.86
Jammu and Kashmir	**97.89**	67.72	83.19	**74.44**	42.59	59.02
karnataka	**120.67**	102.86	111.96	**63.53**	41.56	52.67
Kerala	**119.92**	116.66	118.32	**116.74**	112.28	114.54
Madhya Pradesh	**138.14**	71.92	106.20	**71.08**	36.94	54.48
Maharashtra	**269.83**	231.38	251.08	**179.47**	118.01	149.46
Manipur	**129.73**	137.44	133.50	**71.55**	68.10	69.85
Meghalaya	**303.06**	293.67	298.35	**227.08**	158.55	192.30
Mizoram	—	—	—	—	—	—
Nagaland	—	—	—	—	—	—
Orissa	**158.52**	106.04	132.90	**69.34**	27.48	48.55
Punjab	**130.82**	112.05	121.84	**65.51**	48.03	57.27
Rajasthan	**101.28**	34.95	69.07	**56.27**	7.72	32.77
Sikkim	**130.95**	117.80	124.45	**35.63**	36.03	35.82
Tamil Nadu	**154.12**	133.00	143.80	**105.16**	76.30	91.00
Tripura	**178.42**	153.35	166.09	**94.24**	68.66	81.70
Uttar Pradesh	**91.88**	39.40	67.03	**31.94**	8.76	21.01
West Bengal	**105.99**	72.82	89.66	**36.19**	18.57	27.39
A. and N. Islands	—	—	—	—	—	—
Chandigarh	**122.88**	117.16	120.17	**83.19**	77.82	80.72
Dadra and Nagar Haveli	**74.99**	76.42	75.67	**86.53**	64.61	76.01
Daman and Diu	—	—	—	—	—	—
Lakshadweep	—	—	—	—	—	—
Pondicherry	**174.93**	181.55	178.21	**134.16**	124.02	129.13
INDIA	**122.68**	80.60	102.21	**61.40**	33.28	47.71

TABLE 10.14: Sexwise and Statewise Enrolment Ratio of ST Students in Classes I to VIII (190-91)

	Classes I-V (6 to 11 years)			Classes VI-VIII (11 to 14 Years)		
	Girls	Boys	Total	Girls	Boys	Total
1	2	3	4	5	6	7
Andhra Pradesh	**9,690**	15,346	12,551	**2,091**	4,995	3,555
Arunachal Pradesh	**9,089**	12,900	10,995	**3,238**	5,337	4,299
Assam	**13,708**	15,424	14,590	**4,364**	6,069	5,245
Bihar	**5,769**	10,669	8,257	**1,681**	4,126	2,907
Delhi	—	—	—	—	—	—
Goa	**1,983**	3,191	2,587	**336**	975	656
Gujarat	**11,332**	15,306	13,358	**3,700**	6,403	5,077
Haryana	—	—	—	—	—	—
Himachal Pradesh	**89,93**	11,515	10,258	**4,257**	8,536	6,418
Jammu and Kashmir	—	—	—	—	—	—
Karnataka	**7,992**	9,256	8,638	**3,283**	4,741	4,020
Kerala	**12,837**	13,631	13,241	**8,658**	8,820	8,740
Madhya Pradesh	**4,612**	10,276	7,545	**2,336**	4,282	3,336
Maharashtra	**10,635**	13,290	11,995	**3,630**	6,435	5,066
Manipur	**13,422**	15,465	14,466	**4,575**	5,637	5,112
Meghalaya	**10,702**	11,356	11,028	**5,528**	6,084	5,802
Mizoram	**15,405**	16,262	15,845	**8,597**	8,283	8,437
Nagaland	**12,631**	13,177	12,909	**5,382**	6,075	5,736
Orissa	**6,362**	12,877	9,662	**1,665**	4,015	2,847
Punjab	—	—	—	—	—	—
Rajasthan	**3,258**	10,268	6,863	**573**	4,919	2,815
Sikkim	**10,655**	11,893	11,281	**4,578**	4,487	4,531
Tamil Nadu	**9,754**	12,296	11,054	**4,149**	6,574	5,385
Tripura	**13,604**	18,211	15,944	**4,512**	6,983	5,772
Uttar Pradesh	**7,412**	11,399	9,511	**1,747**	5,104	3,521
West Bengal	**6,577**	14,964	10,836	**1,273**	3,690	2,483
A. and N. Islands	**6,097**	6,982	6,528	**7,081**	7,773	7,437
Chandigarh	—	—	—	—	—	—
Dadra and Nagar Haveli	**8,813**	12,097	10,533	**2,644**	5,170	3,958
Daman and Diu	—	—	—	—	—	—
Lakshadweep	**13,888**	16,361	15,125	**9,952**	11,746	10,878
Pondicherry	—	—	—	—	—	—
INDIA	**7,860**	12,678	10,335	**2,750**	5,133	3,972

TABLE 10.15: Sexwise and Statewise Enrolment Ratio of SC and ST Students at Primary Stage—Classes I-V (190-91)

State/Union Territory	Number of Students belonging to					
	Scheduled Castes			Scheduled Tribes		
	Girls	Boys	Total	Girls	Boys	Total
1	2	3	4	5	6	7
Andhra Pradesh	**8,55,619**	6,30,067	14,85,686	**3,23,476**	1,99,536	5,23,012
Arunachal Pradesh	**63**	37	100	**48,200**	33,962	82,162
Assam	**1,93,290**	1,76,980	3,70,270	**3,22,216**	2,71,020	5,93,236
Bihar	**7,89,358**	2,94,802	10,24,160	**4,71,823**	2,47,489	7,19,312
Delhi	**1,19,137**	9,07,739	2,09,876	**298**	274	572
Goa	**1,679**	1,450	3,129	**198**	123	321
Gujarat	**3,11,000**	2,35,000	5,46,000	**5,14,000**	3,66,000	8,80,000
Haryana	**2,11,603**	1,66,541	3,78,144	—	—	—
HimachalPradesh	**92,265**	75,450	1,67,715	**15,642**	12,146	27,788
Jammu and Kashmir	**36,200**	23,800	60,000	—	—	—
Karnataka	**4,89,228**	3,98,934	8,88,162	**1,22,261**	1,00,988	2,23,249
Kerala	**1,88,287**	1,76,914	3,65,201	**22,000**	20,012	42,012
Madhya Pradesh	**7,76,251**	3,76,471	11,52,722	**9,40,731**	3,93,331	13,34,062
Maharashtra	**8,03,284**	6,55,676	14,58,960	**5,09,215**	3,87,919	8,97,134
Manipur	**1,968**	1,995	3,963	**50,666**	42,074	92,740
Meghalaya	**1,314**	1,280	2,594	**1,04,420**	98,926	2,03,346
Mizoram	—	—	—	**62,666**	56,336	1,19,002
Nagaland	—	—	—	**77,039**	71,301	1,48,340
Orissa	**4,20,000**	2,68,000	6,88,000	**5,22,000**	2,46,000	7,68,000
Punjab	**3,93,526**	3,09,068	7,02,594	—	—	—
Rajasthan	**5,24,720**	1,70,993	6,95,713	**37,32,292**	1,11,834	4,85,126
Sikkim	**2,271**	1,995	4,266	**8,250**	7,218	15,468
Tamil Nadu	**8,38,389**	6,91,023	15,29,412	**39,003**	29,552	68,555
Tripura	**40,114**	33,387	73,501	**76,830**	55,577	1,32,407
Uttar Pradesh	**17,53,066**	6,76,224	24,29,290	**21,584**	12,625	34,209
West Bengal	**8,75,964**	5,83,280	14,59,244	**3,16,631**	1,34,878	4,51,509
A. and N. Islands	—	—	—	**1,763**	1,621	3,384
Chandigarh	**7,437**	6,352	13,789	—	—	—
Dadra and Nagar Haveli	**163**	151	314	**8,345**	5,527	13,872
Daman and Diu	**194**	168	362	**669**	578	1,247
Lakshadweep	**10**	7	17	**4,393**	3,729	8,122
Pondicherry	**10,719**	10,524	21,243	—	—	—
INDIA	97,36,924	60,57,503	1,57,94,427	**49,57,611**	29,10,576	78,68,187

Note : Figures relate to 1989-90.
*Figures relate to 1988-89.

TABLE 10.16: Sexwise and Statewise Enrolment of SC/ST Students of Middle Stage—Classes VI-VIII (1990-1991)

	Number of students belonging to					
	Scheduled Castes			Scheduled Tribes		
	Girls	Boys	Total	Girls	Boys	Total
1	2	3	4	5	6	7
Andhra Pradesh	**1,23,318**	2,26,832	3,50,150	**24,287**	58,966	83,253
Arunachal Pradesh	**6**	9	15	**5,468**	10,884	17,352
Assam	**45,912**	63,160	1,09,072	**49,960**	74,245	1,24,205
Bihar	**40,776**	1,60,231	2,01,007	**40,445**	99,885	1,40,330
Delhi	**30,631**	47,361	77,992	**247**	148	395
Goa	**471**	596	1,031	**12**	35	47
Gujarat	**64,000**	1,14,700	1,78,700	**69,000**	1,24,000	1,93,000
Haryana	**31,549**	69,753	1,01,302	—	—	—
Himachal Pradesh	**24,570**	39,397	63,967	**3,319**	6,793	10,112
Jammu and Kashmir	**8,430**	15,700	24,130	—	—	—
Karnataka	**92,720**	1,44,875	2,37,595	**23,860**	35,223	59,083
Kerala	**98,190**	1,04,829	2,03,019	**7,783**	8,142	15,925
Madhya Pradesh	**1,08,008**	2,19,579	3,27,587	**1,11,288**	2,15,472	3,26,760
Maharashtra	**1,97,792**	3,15,224	5,13,016	**78,313**	1,45,486	2,23,799
Manipur	**502**	540	1,042	**7,282**	9,188	16,470
Meghalaya	**385**	535	920	**28,470**	30,401	58,871
Mizoram	—	—	—	**19,298**	19,368	38,666
Nagaland	—	—	—	**18,039**	21,227	39,266
Orissa	**41,100**	1,05,100	1,46,200	**38,100**	93,100	1,31,200
Punjab	**76,109**	1,16,390	1,92,499	—	—	—
Rajasthan	**20,001**	1,55,320	1,75,321	**10,410**	95,273	105,683
Sikkim	**326**	343	669	**1,657**	1,728	3,385
Tamil Nadu	**2,26,534**	3,24,308	5,50,842	**7,183**	11,823	19,006
Tripura	**8,139**	11,628	19,767	**10,036**	16,169	26,205
Uttar Pradesh	**82,523**	3,37,523	4,20,046	**1,634**	5,353	6,987
West Bengal	**84,470**	1,65,098	2,49,568	**14,830**	43,094	57,924
A. and N. Islands	—	—	—	**894**	1,038	1,932
Chandigarh	**2,344**	2,937	5,281	—	—	—
Dadra and Nagar Haveli	**75**	109	184	**974**	2,067	3,041
Daman and Diu	**138**	122	260	**492**	499	991
Lakshadweep	**6**	7	13	**1,336**	1,682	3,018
Pondicherry	**4,445**	4,894	9,339	—	—	—
INDIA	41,13,416	27,47,100	41,60,516	5,75,518	11,31,388	17,06,906

TABLE 10.17: Sexwise and Statewise Drop-Out Rates of SC up to Class X (1988-89)

Sl.N.	State/Union Territory	I-V			I-VIII			I-X		
		Girls	Boys	Total	Girls	Boys	Total	Girls	Boys	Total
1	2	3	4	5	6	7	8	9	10	11
1.	Andhra Pradesh	**63.72**	58.48	60.72	**85.69**	77.33	80.95	**88.57**	83.85	85.90
2.	Arunchal Pradesh	—	—	—	—	—	—	—	—	—
3.	Assam	**66.43**	64.00	65.07	**54.72**	57.73	56.49	**66.43**	62.44	64.13
4.	Bihar	**76.27**	67.82	70.20	**89.61**	83.05	84.71	**94.31**	88.03	89.48
5.	Delhi	**10.25**	18.50	15.18	**54.16**	52.13	54.80	**75.19**	—	65.86
6.	Goa	**53.63**	44.01	48.69	**76.12**	61.51	68.71	**94.31**	88.03	89.48
7.	Gujarat	**43.61**	23.16	32.33	**69.01**	47.76	56.97	**80.82**	67.32	72.92
8.	Haryana	**38.09**	34.87	36.14	**72.97**	54.62	61.43	**82.12**	65.52	70.32
9.	Himachal Pradesh	**35.00**	32.40	33.55	**52.88**	40.74	45.97	**73.68**	61.00	66.08
10.	Jammu and Kashmir	**31.84**	41.15	37.55	**60.82**	61.42	61.21	**78.16**	76.47	77.04
11.	Karnataka	**64.66**	58.45	61.14	**76.22**	64.48	69.51	**85.38**	73.38	78.69
12.	Kerala	**1.81**	0.00	0.0	**25.36**	27.56	26.49	**47.60**	54.72	51.26
13.	Madhya Pradesh	**51.04**	33.87	40.11	**72.96**	53.36	59.06	**90.52**	77.09	88.99
14.	Maharashtra	**53.38**	39.70	446.02	**71.23**	54.00	61.78	**83.96**	70.51	76.50
15.	Manipur	**82.31**	79.48	80.88	**84.69**	83.47	84.26	**82.83**	81.50	82.29
16.	Meghalaya	**77.11**	75.67	76.34	**55.38**	31.11	43.02	**87.71**	77.16	81.93
17.	Mizoram	—	—	—	—	—	—	—	—	—
18.	Nagaland	—	—	—	—	—	—	—	—	—
19.	Orissa	**54.54**	50.53	52.10	**80.25**	72.30	75.35	**86.34**	78.16	81.33
20.	Punjab	**39.94**	32.69	35.92	**79.80**	79.99	75.49	**89.62**	83.89	86.52
21.	Rajasthan	**72.71**	59.27	2.47	**83.91**	67.27	70.32	**96.04**	82.81	85.93
22.	Sikkim	**70.86**	75.44	73.42	**79.96**	83.05	81.65	**94.83**	92.38	93.48
23.	Tamil Nadu	**29.83**	22.46	25.94	**60.77**	51.77	55.66	**83.71**	74.06	78.47
24.	Tripura	**63.26**	58.17	60.52	**84.34**	77.86	80.80	**89.71**	86.94	88.15
25.	Uttar Pradesh	**46.84**	46.97	46.94	**57.82**	57.83	60.26	**62.97**	85.79	72.91
26.	West Bengal	**66.5**	153.94	59.45	**82.46**	76.68	78.94	**91.30**	89.28	90.01
27.	A. and N. Islands	—	—	—	—	—	—	—	—	—
28.	Chandigarh	**7.33**	0.0	0.0	**0.0**	0:0	0.0	**48.26**		48.39
29.	Dadra and Nagar Haveli	—	—	—	—	—	—	—	—	—
30.	Daman and Diu	—	—	—	—	—	—	—	—	—
31.	Lakshadweep	—	—	—	—	—	—	—	—	—
32.	Pondicherry	—	—	—	**26.92**	12.49	19.	**69.67**	—	64.00

TABLE 10.18: Sexwise and Statewise Drop-out Rates of ST up to Class X (1988-89)

Sl. No.	State/U.T	I-V			I-VIII			I-X		
		Girls	Boys	Total	Girls	Boys	Total	Girls	Boys	Total
1	2	3	4	5	6	7	8	9	10	11
1.	Andhra Pradesh	**68.87**	63.70	65.66	**90.14**	84.21	86.42	**92.77**	88.83	90.34
2.	Arunachal Pradesh	**59.92**	64.77	63.01	**79.35**	75.60	76.95	**89.30**	80.49	83.37
3.	Assam	**70.71**	71.90	71.40	**68.17**	66.06	66.95	**77.21**	56.15	68.18
4.	Bihar	**77.14**	69.51	72.19	**88.65**	84.53	85.94	**93.64**	90.30	91.42
5.	Delhi	—	—	—	—	—	—	—	—	—
6.	Goa	**95.36**	83.79	89.91	**97.21**	96.63	96.89	—	—	—
7.	Gujarat	**68.50**	55.61	61.21	**84.03**	77.70	80.34	**90.10**	85.68	87.50
8.	Haryana	—	—	—	—	—	—	—	—	—
9.	Himachal Pradesh	**28.16**	24.39	25.89	**46.97**	33.97	38.65	**65.33**	55.88	59.27
10.	Jammu and Kashmir	—	—	—	—	—	—	—	—	—
11.	Karnataka	**45.77**	35.80	40.18	**70.07**	59.61	64.03	**80.52**	69.06	73.97
12.	Kerala	**16.37**	21.19	18.94	**37.94**	45.30	41.82	**67.39**	72.94	70.43
13.	Madhya Pradesh	**59.69**	47.12	51.80	**80.85**	70.75	73.79	**93.18**	83.26	86.20
14.	Maharashtra	**68.83**	57.89	62.60	**83.04**	73.00	77.10	**90.49**	83.34	86.18
15.	Manipur	**78.09**	77.20	77.61	**85.92**	84.87	85.30	**86.79**	85.12	85.88
16.	Meghalaya	**81.76**	73.21	77.40	**73.09**	72.85	72.96	**93.37**	91.63	92.47
17.	Mizoram	**62.70**	61.88	62.28	**24.66**	31.17	28.08	**78.49**	75.91	77.17
18.	Nagaland	**35.70**	34.94	35.29	**58.67**	64.41	61.99	**83.86**	79.64	81.53
19.	Orissa	**77.74**	75.41	76.19	**85.72**	83.99	84.59	**92.69**	87.34	89.23
20.	Punjab	—	—	—	—	—	—	—	—	84.72
21.	Rajasthan	**79.07**	66.77	69.63	**86.07**	72.34	74.44	**94.33**	83.09	87.64
22.	Sikkim	**57.19**	66.99	62.87	**62.25**	70.89	67.19	**88.83**	86.78	76.15
23.	Tamil Nadu	**54.31**	42.61	47.95	**59.72**	51.45	54.90	**77.13**	75.47	91.81
24.	Tripura	**78.41**	73.96	75.86	**88.17**	84.75	86.17	**93.44**	90.83	80.68
25.	Uttar Pradesh	**51.60**	41.73	45.14	**63.67**	55.83	53.10	**83.88**	70.30	92.47
26.	West Bengal	**67.55**	63.76	65.03	**87.03**	83.27	84.39	**92.74**	92.35	52.47
27.	A. and N. Islands	**13.33**	8.95	11.00	**38.13**	35.20	63.50	**64.31**	42.76	52.97
28.	Chandigarh	—	—	—	—	—	—	—	—	—
29.	Dadra and Nagar Haveli	**57.58**	41.26	47.60	**79.94**	69.67	74.04	**93.01**	87.62	89.94
30.	Daman and Diu	—	—	—	—	—	—	—	—	—
31.	Lakshadweep	**10.94**	—	—	**50.41**	29.72	39.61	**73.78**	71.11	72.34
32.	Pondicherry	—	—	—	—	—	—	—	—	—
	INDIA	**68.73**	61.94	64.53	**81.45**	76.21	78.08	**89.91**	84.87	86.72

* Includes Daman and Diu

TABLE 10.19: Sexwise and Statewise Enrolment of SC and ST Students in Classes IX and X (1990-91)

	State/Union Territory	Number of students belonging to					
		Scheduled Castes			Scheduled Tribes		
		Girls	Boys	Total	Girls	Boys	Total
	1	2	3	4	5	6	7
1.	Andhra Pradesh @	**1,00,941**	49,854	1,50,795	**23,833**	9,079	32,912
2.	Arunachal Pradesh	**3**	3	6	**4,995**	2,167	7,162
3.	Assam	**25,779**	18,208	43,987	**33,546**	23,729	57,275
4.	Bihar *	**65,612**	10,694	76,306	**42,346**	15,178	57,524
5.	Delhi	**24,239**	9,997	34,236	**149**	90	239
6.	Goa	**235**	178	413	**3**	—	3
7.	Gujarat	**53,000**	23,500	76,500	**43,500**	22,600	66,100
8.	Haryana	**26,343**	7,000	33,343	—	—	—
9.	Himachal Pradesh	**12,390**	5,556	17,946	**2,367**	923	3,290
10.	Jammu and Kashmir	**6,420**	2,340	8,760	—	—	—
11.	Karnataka	**64,290**	30,480	94,770	**14,328**	7,808	22,136
12.	Kerala	**46,121**	48,358	94,479	**3,070**	3,090	6,160
13.	Madhya Pradesh	**49,133**	10,274	59,407	**49,767**	10,448	60,215
14.	Maharashtra	**1,62,044**	80,599	2,42,643	**60,181**	25,425	85,606
15.	Manipur	**352**	333	685	**5,096**	4,014	9,110
16.	Meghalaya	**590**	315	905	**21,148**	18,065	39,213
17.	Mizoram	—	—	—	**7,427**	6,259	13,686
18.	Nagaland	—	—	—	**7,427**	6,259	13,686
19.	Orissa	**47,400**	15,100	62,500	**30,200**	12,100	42,300
20.	Punjab*	**50,757**	28,959	79,716	—	—	—
21.	Rajasthan	**65,301**	5,095	70,396	**42,153**	2,679	44,832
22.	Sikkim	**151**	127	278	**746**	716	1,462
23.	Tamil Nadu	**1,18,899**	62,090	1,80,989	**4,071**	2,527	6,598
24.	Tripura	**4,582**	2,789	7,371	**6,142**	2,942	9,084
25.	Uttar Pradesh	**2,14,908**	33,397	2,48,305	**4,072**	1,047	5,119
26.	West Bengal+	94,254	40,875	1,35,129	**7,937**	1,51,710	2,36,147
27.	A. and N. Islands	—	—	—	**406**	347	753
28.	Chandigarh	**936**	892	1,828	—	—	—
29.	Dadra and Nagar Haveli	**59**	44	103	**631**	292	923
30.	Daman and Diu	**155**	99	254	**206**	129	335
31.	Lakshadweep	**3**	2	5	**751**	430	1,145
32.	Pondicherry	**1,179**	887	2,066	—	—	—
	INDIA	12,36,076	4,88,045	17,24,121	4,25,002	1,87,912	6,12,914

@ Previous Year Enrolment pertained to the Classes VIII-X, whereas this Year it pertains to IX-X Classes, Hence Decrease

*Figures relate to 1989-90,

+Figures relate to 1988-89.

TBALE 10.20: Sexwise and Statewise Enrolment of SC/ST Students in Classes IX and X, (1990-91)

State/Union Territory	Number of students belonging to					
	Scheduled Castes			Scheduled Tribes		
	Girls	Boys	Total	Girls	Boys	Total
1	2	3	4	5	6	7
Andhra Pradesh	**66**	104	170	**10**	34	44
Arunachal Pradesh	**2**	4	6	**692**	2,677	3,369
Assam	**5,229**	10,576	15,805	**7,521**	15,799	23,320
Bihar	**413**	1,742	2,155	**254**	470	724
Delhi	**3,725**	7,628	11,353	**68**	76	144
Goa	**33**	52	85	—	—	—
Gujarat	**8,400**	19,200	27,600	**9,000**	17,800	26,800
Haryana	**546**	3,858	4,404	—	—	—
Himachal Pradesh*	**4,299**	11,038	15,337	**766**	1,876	2,643
Jammu and Kashmir	N.A.	N.A.	N.A.	—	—	—
Karnataka	**5,734**	16,500	22,234	**1,698**	2,772	4,470
Kerala	**17**	37	54	**3**	1	4
Madhya Pradesh	**8,815**	39,554	48,369	**36,324**	6,105	42,429
Maharashtra	**13,393**	29,596	42,989	**4,470**	11,585	16,055
Manipur	**20**	40	60	**180**	470	650
Meghalaya	—	—	—	—	—	—
Mizoram	—	—	—	—	—	—
Nagaland	—	—	—	—	—	—
Orissa	**120**	230	350	**50**	150	200
Punjab*	7,706	15,932	23,638	—	—	—
Rajasthan	**1,095**	19,628	20,723	**409**	11,345	11,754
Sikkim	**26**	40	66	**176**	292	468
Tamil Nadu	**17,368**	41,100	58,468	**979**	1,523	2,502
Tripura	**543**	1,344	1,887	**252**	809	1,061
Uttar Pradesh	—	—	—	—	—	—
West Bengal+	**9,969**	26,000	35,969	**2,623**	4,382	7,005
A. and N. Islands	—	—	—	**935**	997	1,932
Chandigarh	**801**	600	1,401	—	—	—
Dadra and Nagar Haveli	**14**	26	40	**98**	222	320
Daman and Diu	**12**	38	50	**13**	53	66
Lakshadweep	—	—	—	—	—	—
Pondicherry	**213**	382	595	—	—	—
INDIA	**88,559**	2,45,249	3,33,808	**36,302**	1,09,658	1,45,960

* Figures relate to 1989-90

\+ Figures relate to 1988-89.

TABLE 10.21: Sexwise and Statewise Enrolment of SC/ST Students at Pre-University One Year Course (1990-91)

State/Union Territory	Number of students belonging to					
	Scheduled Castes			Scheduled Tribes		
	Girls	Boys	Total	Girls	Boys	Total
1	2	3	4	5	6	7
Andhra Pradesh	—	—	—	—	—	—
Arunachal Pradesh	—	—	—	—	—	—
Assam	—	—	—	—	—	—
Bihar	—	—	—	—	—	—
Delhi	—	—	—	—	—	—
Goa	—	—	—	—	—	—
Gujarat	—	—	—	—	—	—
Haryana	—	—	—	—	—	—
Himachal Pradesh	—	—	—	—	—	—
Jammu and Kashmir	—	—	—	—	—	—
Karnataka	—	—	—	—	—	—
Kerala	—	—	—	—	—	—
Madhya Pradesh	—	—	—	—	—	—
Maharashtra	—	—	—	—	—	—
Manipur	—	—	—	—	—	—
Meghalaya	—	—	—	—	—	—
Mizoram	—	—	—	—	—	—
Nagaland	—	—	—	—	—	—
Orissa	—	—	—	—	—	—
Punjab	—	—	—	—	—	—
Rajasthan	—	—	—	—	—	—
Sikkim	—	—	—	—	—	—
Tamil Nadu	—	—	—	—	—	—
Tripura	—	—	—	—	—	—
Uttar Pradesh	74	185	259	7	16	23
West Bengal	—	—	—	—	—	—
A. and N. Islands	—	—	—	—	—	—
Chandigarh	—	—	—	—	—	—
Dadra and Nagar Haveli	—	—	—	—	—	—
Daman and Diu	—	—	—	—	—	—
Lakshadweep	—	—	—	—	—	—
Pondicherry	—	—	—	—	—	—
INDIA	74	185	259	7	16	23

TABLE 10.22: Sexwise and Statewise Enrolment of SC/ST Students at Pre-Degree/ Pre-University (Two-Year Course) 1990-91.

State/Union Territory	Number of Students belonging to					
	Scheduled Castes			Scheduled Tribes		
	Girls	Boys	Total	Girls	Boys	Total
1	2	3	4	5	6	7
Andhra Pradesh	—	—	—	—	—	—
Arunachal Pradesh	—	—	—	—	—	—
Assam	—	—	—	—	—	—
Bihar	—	—	—	—	—	—
Delhi	—	—	—	—	—	—
Goa	—	—	—	—	—	—
Gujarat	—	—	—	—	—	—
Haryana	**378**	3,678	4,056	—	—	—
Himachal Pradesh	—	—	—	—	—	—
Jammu and Kashmir	—	—	—	—	—	—
Karnataka	—	—	—	—	—	—
Kerala	**13,778**	11,672	25,450	**546**	790	1,336
Madhya Pradesh	—	—	—	—	—	—
Maharashtra	—	—	—	—	—	—
Manipur	**170**	175	345	**920**	1,400	2,320
Meghalaya	**127**	285	412	**3,937**	4,145	8,082
Mizoram	—	—	—	**1,808**	2,653	4,461
Nagaland	—	—	—	**1,418**	2,065	3,483
Orissa	—	—	—	—	—	—
Punjab	—	—	—	—	—	—
Rajasthan	—	—	—	—	—	—
Sikkim	—	—	—	—	—	—
Tamil Nadu	—	—	—	—	—	—
Tripura	—	—	—	—	—	—
Uttar Pradesh	—	—	—	—	—	—
West Bengal	—	—	—	—	—	—
A. & N. Islands	—	—	—	—	—	—
Chandigarh*	**173**	314	487	**32**	68	100
Dadra and Nagar Haveli	—	—	—	—	—	—
Daman and Diu	—	—	—	—	—	—
Lakshadweep	**3**	4	7	**135**	261	396
Pondicherry	**1**	4	5	—	—	—
INDIA	**14,630**	16,132	30,762	**8,796**	11,382	20,178

* Figures relate to 1989-90.

TABLE 10.23: Sexwise and Statewise Enrolment of SC/ST Students in Intermediate/Junior Colleges, (1990-91)

State/Union Territory	Number of Students belonging to					
	Scheduled Castes			Scheduled Tribes		
	Girls	Boys	Total	Girls	Boys	Total
1	2	3	4	5	6	7
Andhra Pradesh*	**11,309**	34,915	46,224	**1,013**	5,574	6,587
Arunachal Pradesh	—	—	—	—	—	—
Assam	**255**	337	592	**142**	214	356
Bihar	**N.A.**	N.A.	N.A.	**N.A.**	N.A.	N.A.
Delhi	—	—	—	—	—	—
Goa	—	—	—	—	—	—
Gujarat	—	—	—	—	—	—
Harayana	—	—	—	—	—	—
Himachal Pradesh	—	—	—	—	—	—
Jammu and Kashmir	—	—	—	—	—	—
Karnataka	**4,192**	17,044	21,236	**676**	2,754	3,430
Kerala	**221**	288	509	**13**	28	41
Madhya Pradesh	—	—	—	—	—	—
Maharashtra	**11,436**	39,263	50,699	**1,635**	6,533	8,168
Manipur	**45**	60	105	**65**	70	135
Meghalaya	—	—	—	—	—	—
Mizoram	—	—	—	—	—	—
Nagaland	—	—	—	**10**	24	34
Orissa	**1,854**	8,285	10,139	**1,022**	3,698	4,720
Punjab	—	—	—	—	—	—
Rajasthan	—	—	—	—	—	—
Sikkim	—	—	—	—	—	—
Tamil Nadu	—	—	—	—	—	—
Tripura	—	—	—	—	—	—
Uttar Pradesh	**14,377**	1,04,953	1,19,330	**468**	1,845	2,313
West Bengal	—	—	—	—	—	—
A. and N. Islands	—	—	—	—	—	—
Chandigarh	—	—	—	—	—	—
Dadra and Nagar Haveli	—	—	—	—	—	—
Daman and Diu	—	—	—	—	—	—
Lakshadweep	—	—	—	—	—	—
Pondicherry	**17**	36	53	—	—	—
INDIA	**43,707**	2,05,181	2,48,887	**5,044**	20,740	25,784

* Figures relate to 1989-90.

TABLE 10.24: Sexwise and Statewise Enrolment of SC/ST Students in M.B.B.S. (1990-91)

State/Union Territory	Number of Students belonging to					
	Scheduled Castes			Scheduled Tribes		
	Girls	Boys	Total	Girls	Boys	Total
1	2	3	4	5	6	7
Andhra Pradesh*	**311**	668	979	**96**	232	328
Arunachal Pradesh	—	—	—	—	—	—
Assam	**30**	85	115	**50**	180	230
Bihar	**N.A.**	N.A.	N.A.	**N.A.**	N.A.	N.A.
Delhi	**224**	246	470	**27**	13	40
Goa	**6**	11	17	—	—	—
Gujarat	**130**	370	500	**55**	210	265
Haryana	**36**	88	124	—	—	—
Himachal Pradesh*	**8**	38	46	**2**	19	21
Jammu and Kashmir	**N.A.**	N.A.	N.A.	—	—	—
Karnataka	**44**	94	138	**7**	22	29
Kerala	**149**	171	320	**43**	42	85
Madhya Pradesh	**107**	361	468	**87**	230	317
Maharashtra	**549**	1065	1614	**116**	305	421
Manipur	—	12	12	**65**	166	231
Meghalaya	—	—	—	—	—	—
Mizoram	—	—	—	—	—	—
Nagaland	—	—	—	—	—	—
Orissa	**48**	126	174	**56**	110	166
Punjab*	**130**	374	504	—	—	—
Rajasthan	**N.A.**	N.A.	N.A.	**N.A.**	N.A.	N.A.
Sikkim	—	—	—	—		—
Tamil Nadu	**492**	692	1,184	**18**	38	56
Tripura	—	—	—	—	—	—
Uttar Pradesh	**23**	181	181	**1**	41	42
West Bengal	**35**	313	348	**3**	12	15
A. and N. Islands	—	—	—	—	—	—
Chandigarh*	—	—	—	—	—	—
Dadra and Nagar Haveli	—	—	—	—	—	—
Daman and Diu	—	—	—	—	—	—
Lakshadweep	—	—	—	—	—	—
Pondicherry	**27**	62	89	—	—	—
INDIA	**2,349**	4,934	7,283	**626**	1,620	2,246

*Figures relate to 1989-90.

+Figures relate to 1988-89.

TABLE 10.25: Sexwise and Statewise Enrolment of SC/ST Students in M.B.B.S. (190-91)

State/Union Territory	Number of Students belonging to					
	Scheduled Castes			Scheduled Tribes		
	Girls	Boys	Total	Girls	Boys	Total
1	2	3	4	5	6	7
Andhra Pradesh*	**76**	492	568	**111**	646	757
Arunachal Pradesh	—	—	—	—	—	—
Assam	**42**	191	233	**33**	90	123
Bihar	**769**	687	1456	**984**	657	1,611
Delhi	**120**	37	157	**5**	—	5
Goa	—	—	—	—	—	—
Gujarat	**450**	440	890	**600**	740	1,340
Haryana	**5**	31	36	—	—	—
Himachal Pradesh*	**72**	169	241	**46**	85	131
Jammu and Kashmir	**N.A.**	N.A.	N.A.	—	—	—
Karnataka	**574**	663	1,237	**80**	85	165
Kerala	**324**	147	471	**28**	52	80
Madhya Pradesh	**116**	902	1,018	**301**	1,097	1,398
Maharashtra	**1,211**	1,805	3,016	**538**	767	1,305
Manipur	—	—	—	—	—	—
Meghalaya	—	—	—	**310**	335	645
Mizoram	—	—	—	**30**	289	319
Nagaland	—	—	—	**7**	34	41
Orissa	**3**	10	13	**2**	13	15
Punjab*	**269**	43	312	—	—	—
Rajasthan	**220**	1,606	1,826	**85**	836	821
Sikkim	—	1	1	**10**	7	17
Tamil Nadu	**851**	382	1,233	**10**	1	11
Tripura	—	16	16	—	86	86
Uttar Pradesh	**217**	406	623	**12**	24	36
West Bengal+	**251**	502	753	**74**	175	249
A. and N. Islands	—	—	—	**22**	8	30
Chandigarh	—	—	—	—	—	—
Dadra and Nagar Haveli	—	—	—	—	—	—
Daman and Diu	—	—	—	—	—	—
Lakshadweep	—	—	—	—	—	—
Pondicherry	—	—	—	—	—	—
INDIA	**5,570**	8,530	14,100	**3,312**	6,003	9,315

* Figures relate to 1989-90.

\+ Figures relate to 1988-89.

TABLE 10.26: Sexwise and Statewise Enrolment of SC/ST Students in Technical Industrial Arts and Crafts Schools (1990-91)

State/Union Territory	Number of Students belonging to					
	Scheduled Castes			Scheduled Tribes		
	Girls	Boys	Total	Girls	Boys	Total
1	2	3	4	5	6	7
Andhra Pradesh*	**283**	3,525	3,808	**25**	1,037	1,062
Arunachal Pradesh	—	9	9	**2**	51	53
Assam	**73**	279	352	**196**	383	579
Bihar	**30**	1,565	1,595	**720**	1,304	2,024
Delhi	**315**	1,389	1,704	**9**	26	35
Goa	**1**	19	20	—	1	1
Gujarat	**3,150**	5,700	8,850	**1,650**	5,150	6,800
Haryana	**359**	2,776	3,135	—	—	—
Himachal Pradesh*	**233**	526	759	**51**	96	148
Jammu and Kashmir	**N.A.**	N.A.	N.A.	—	—	—
Karnataka	—	119	119	**2**	27	29
Kerala	**1,270**	1,815	3,085	**70**	145	215
Madhya Pradesh	**76**	1,279	1,355	**71**	1,719	1,790
Maharashtra	**3,170**	10,288	13,458	**931**	3,336	4,267
Manipur	**9**	—	9	**320**	40	360
Meghalaya	**5**	13	18	**43**	21	66
Mizoram	—	—	—	**90**	142	290
Nagaland	—	—	—	**129**	270	399
Orissa	**14**	371	385	**13**	95	207
Punjab*	**843**	3,067	3,910	—	—	—
Rajasthan	**102**	1,254	1,356	**40**	752	792
Sikkim	—	—	—	—	—	—
Tamil Nadu	**433**	3,066	3,499	**30**	266	296
Tripura	**4**	15	19	**5**	48	53
Uttar Pradesh	**34**	827	861	**9**	66	75
West Bengal+	**315**	242	557	**3**	34	37
A. and N. Islands	—	—	—	—	—	—
Chandigarh*	**55**	97	152	**7**	2	9
Dadra and Nagar Haveli	—	—	—	—	—	—
Daman and Diu	—	6	6	**2**	8	10
Lakshdweep	—	—	—	—	—	—
Pondicherry	—	43	43	—	—	—
INDIA	**10,774**	38,290	49,064	**4,396**	15,142	19,538

*Figures relate to 1989-90.

+ Figures relate to 1988-89.

TABLE 10.27: Sexwise and Statewise Enrolment of SC/ST Students in Polytechnic Institutes (1990-91)

State/Union Territory	Number of Students belonging to					
	Scheduled Castes			Scheduled Tribes		
	Girls	Boys	Total	Girls	Boys	Total
1	2	3	4	5	6	7
Andhra Pradesh*	**386**	2,705	3,091	**27**	741	768
Arunachal Pradesh	—	—	—	—	—	—
Assam	**19**	204	223	**23**	242	265
Bihar*	**11**	640	651	**13**	273	286
Delhi	**179**	297	476	**93039**	—	—
Goa	**1**	7	8	—	5	5
Gujarat	**65**	835	900	**50**	1,000	1,050
Haryana	**58**	686	744	—	—	—
Himachal Pradesh*	**20**	164	184	**5**	54	59
Jammu and Kashmir	**N.A.**	N.A.	N.A.	—	—	—
Karnataka	**243**	2,652	2,995	**59**	464	523
Kerala	**228**	478	706	**20**	47	67
Madhya Pradesh	**7**	435	442	**6**	236	242
Maharashtra	**107**	1,642	1,749	**37**	790	827
Manipur	—	4	4	**2**	75	77
Meghalaya	—	14	14	**10**	97	107
Mizoram	—	—	—	**58**	167	225
Nagaland	—	—	—	**4**	288	292
Orissa	**25**	12	37	**22**	16	38
Punjab*	**103**	941	1,044	—	—	—
Rajasthan	**5**	386	391	—	298	298
Sikkim	—	—	—	—	—	—
Tamil Nadu	**955**	5,013	5,968	**16**	129	145
Tripura	—	15	15	—	31	31
Uttar Pradesh	**45**	1,728	1,773	**2**	23	25
West Bengal+	**42**	1,820	1,862	**17**	136	153
A. and N. Islands	—	—	—	**1**	5	6
Chandigarh*	**36**	112	148	**15**	2	17
Dadra and Nagar Haveli	—	—	—	—	—	—
Daman and Diu	—	6	6	**2**	8	10
Lakshadweep	—	—	—	—	—	—
Pondicherry	**46**	79	125	—	—	—
INDIA	**2,681**	20,876	23,557	**396**	5,153	5,549

*Figures relate to 1989-90.

\+ Figures relate to 1988-89.

TABLE 10.28: Sexwise and Statewise Enrolment of SC/ST Students in B.E./B.Sc. (Engg./B. Tech.) (1990-91)

State/Union Territory	Number of Students belonging to					
	Scheduled Castes			Scheduled Tribes		
	Girls	Boys	Total	Girls	Boys	Total
1	2	3	4	5	6	7
Andhra Pradesh*	**120**	1,919	2,039	**18**	266	284
Arunachal Pradesh	—	—	—	—	—	—
Assam	**8**	135	143	**18**	180	198
Bihar	**N.A.**	N.A.	N.A.	**N.A.**	N.A.	N.A.
Delhi	**32**	399	431	**3**	73	76
Goa	—	4	4	—	—	—
Gujarat	**15**	500	515	**15**	230	245
Haryana	**5**	296	302	—	—	—
Himachal Pradesh*	—	27	27	**1**	13	14
Jammu and Kashmir	**N.A.**	N.A.	N.A.	—	—	—
Karnataka	**160**	1,940	2,100	**45**	455	500
Kerala	**669**	690	1,359	**4**	58	62
Madhya Pradesh	**15**	240	255	**6**	81	87
Maharashtra	**102**	2,227	2,329	**8**	400	408
Manipur	—	—	—	—	—	—
Meghalaya	—	—	—	—	—	—
Mizoram	—	—	—	—	—	—
Nagaland	—	—	—	—	—	—
Orissa	**5**	224	229	**11**	280	291
Punjab*	**3**	242	245	–	–	–
Rajasthan	**N.A.**	N.A.	N.A.	**N.A.**	N.A.	N.A.
Sikkim	—	—	—	—	—	—
Tamil Nadu	**275**	2,039	2,314	**29**	166	195
Tripura	**3**	76	79	**2**	74	76
Uttar Pradesh	**3**	830	833	—	63	63
West Bengal+	**12**	320	332	**3**	50	53
A. and N. Islands	—	—	—	—	—	—
Chandigarh*	**4**	192	196	**1**	38	39
Dadra and Nagar Haveli	—	—	—	—	—	—
Daman and Diu	—	—	—	—	—	—
Lakshadweep	—	—	—	—	—	—
Pondicherry	**12**	52	64	—	—	—
INDIA	**1,443**	12,353	13,796	**164**	2,427	2,591

*Figures relate to 1989-90.

+ Figures relate to 1988-89.

TABLE 10.29: Sexwise and Statewise Enrolment of SC/ST Students in B.Ed/B.T. (1990-91)

State/Union Territory	Number of Students belonging to					
	Scheduled Castes			Scheduled Tribes		
	Girls	Boys	Total	Girls	Boys	Total
1	2	3	4	5	6	7
Andhra Pradesh*	**228**	718	946	**88**	282	370
Arunachal Pradesh	—	—	—	**1**	15	16
Assam	**11**	140	151	**16**	65	81
Bihar	**N.A.**	N.A.	N.A.	**N.A.**	N.A.	N.A.
Delhi	**52**	16	68	**2**	8	10
Goa	—	—	—	—	—	—
Gujarat	**175**	300	475	**175**	270	445
Haryana	**41**	188	229	—	—	—
Himachal Pradesh*	**1**	5	6	**1**	13	14
Jammu and Kashmir	**N.A.**	N.A.	N.A.	—	—	—
Karnataka	**89**	305	394	**15**	36	51
Kerala	**227**	162	389	**3**	2	5
Madhya Pradesh	**71**	367	438	**42**	99	141
Maharashtra	**265**	1,075	1,340	**115**	232	347
Manipur	—	—	—	—	—	—
Meghalaya	—	—	—	**81**	75	156
Mizoram	—	—	—	**30**	96	126
Nagaland	—	—	—	**12**	27	39
Orissa	**55**	140	195	**38**	120	158
Punjab*	**215**	220	435	—	—	—
Rajasthan	**N.A.**	N.A.	N.A.	**N.A.**	N.A.	N.A.
Sikkim	—	—	—	—	—	—
Tamil Nadu	**228**	222	450	**2**	2	4
Tripura	**3**	31	34	**23**	49	72
Uttar Pradesh	**263**	1,286	1,549	**17**	23	40
West Bengal+	**42**	470	512	**9**	31	40
A. and N. Islands	—	—	—	—	—	—
Chandigarh*	**47**	21	68	**10**	9	10
Dadra and Nagar Haveli	—	—	—	—	—	—
Daman and Diu	—	—	—	—	—	—
Lakshadweep	—	—	—	—	—	—
Pondicherry	**17**	8	25	—	—	—
INDIA	**2,030**	5,674	7,704	**679**	1,441	2,120

*Figures relate to 1989-90.

+ Figures relate to 1988-89.

TABLE 10.30: Sexwise and Statewise Enrolment of SC/ST Students in B.Com/ B.Com (Hons) (1990-91)

State/Union Territory	Number of Students belonging to					
	Scheduled Castes			Scheduled Tribes		
	Girls	Boys	Total	Girls	Boys	Total
1	2	3	4	5	6	7
Andhra Pradesh*	**1,175**	4,664	5,839	**140**	630	770
Arunachal Pradesh	—	—	—	**3**	64	67
Assam	**41**	828	869	**40**	381	421
Bihar	**N.A.**	N.A.	N.A.	**N.A.**	N.A.	N.A.
Delhi	**279**	1,595	1,874	**18**	52	70
Goa	**16**	28	44	—	—	—
Gujarat	**1,100**	4,000	5,100	**1,000**	3,000	4,000
Haryana	**28**	228	248	—	—	—
Himachal Pradesh*	**2**	24	26	**6**	12	18
Jammu and Kashmir	**N.A.**	N.A.	N.A.	—	—	—
Karnataka	**N.A.**	N.A.	N.A.	**N.A.**	N.A.	N.A.
Kerala	**570**	690	1,260	**16**	10	26
Madhya Pradesh	**180**	2,572	2,752	**71**	1,423	1,494
Maharashtra	**3,651**	1,4720	18,371	**532**	2,871	3,403
Manipur	—	3	3	**15**	20	35
Meghalaya	**9**	15	24	**57**	288	345
Mizoram	—	—	—	**N.A.**	N.A.	N.A.
Nagaland	—	—	—	**12**	177	189
Orissa	**47**	318	365	**66**	297	363
Punjab*	**27**	239	266	—	—	—
Rajasthan	**42**	1,805	1,847	**10**	728	738
Sikkim	—	—	—	—	—	—
Tamil Nadu	**1,317**	3,075	4,392	**24**	52	76
Tripura	**9**	192	201	—	50	50
Uttar Pradesh	**26**	2,702	2,728	**2**	72	74
West Bengal+	**138**	5,892	6,030	**12**	218	230
A. and N. Islands	—	—	—	—	—	—
Chandigarh*	**2**	1	3	—	—	—
Dadra and Nagar Haveli	—	—	—	—	—	—
Daman and Diu	**1**	6	7	—	4	4
Lakshadweep	—	—	—	—	—	—
Pondicherry	**13**	35	48	—	—	—
INDIA	**8,673**	43,624	52,297	**2,024**	10,349	12,373

*Figures relate to 1989-90.

+ Figures relate to 1988-89.

TABLE 10.31: Sexwise and Statewise Enrolment of SC/ST Students in B.Sc./B.Sc. (Hons) (1990-91)

State/Union Territory	Number of Students belonging to					
	Scheduled Castes			Scheduled Tribes		
	Girls	Boys	Total	Girls	Boys	Total
1	2	3	4	5	6	7
Andhra Pradesh*	**1,426**	3,645	5071	**142**	462	605
Arunachal Pradesh	—	—	—	**5**	28	33.
Assam	**189**	852	1,041	**254**	827	1,081
Bihar	**N.A.**	N.A.	N.A.	**N.A.**	N.A.	N.A.
Delhi	**95**	313	408	**13**	12	25
Goa	**2**	2	4	—	—	—
Gujarat	**200**	450	650	**120**	250	370
Haryana	**49**	217	266	—	—	—
Himachal Pradesh*	**16**	112	128	**10**	35	45
Jammu and Kashmir	**N.A.**	N.A.	N.A.	—	—	—
Karnataka	**N.A.**	N.A.	N.A.	**N.A.**	N.A.	N.A.
Kerala	**1,812**	1,467	3,279	**65**	54	119
Madhya Pradesh	**381**	1,723	2,104	**200**	896	1,096
Maharashtra	**1,236**	4,693	5,929	**236**	730	966
Manipur	**35**	70	135	**70**	100	170
Meghalaya	**25**	28	53	**199**	362	561
Mizoram	—	—	—	**62**	99	161.
Nagaland	—	—	—	**38**	172	210
Orissa	**98**	439	537	**46**	462	508
Punjab*	**107**	448	555	—	—	—
Rajasthan	**45**	704	749	**11**	420	431
Sikkim	—	—	—	—	—	—
Tamil Nadu	**3,616**	7,622	11,238	**55**	111	166
Tripura	**41**	150	191	**5**	37	42
Uttar Pradesh	**268**	4,678	4,946	**39**	129	168
West Bengal+	**3,172**	3,895	7,067	**41**	111	152
A. and N. Islands	—	—	—	—	—	—
Chandigarh*	**4**	20	24	**3**	7	10
Dadra and Nagar Haveli	—	—	—	—	—	—
Daman and Diu	—	1	1	—	—	—
Lakshadweep	—	—	—	—	—	—
Pondicherry	**28**	82	110	—	—	—
INDIA	**12,845**	31,611	44,456	**5,305**	1,614	6,919

*Figures relate to 1989-90.

+ Figures relate to 1988-89.

TABLE 10.32: Sexwise and Statewise Enrolment of SC/ST Students in B.A/B.A (Hons) (1990-91)

State/Union Territory	Number of Students belonging to					
	Scheduled Castes			Scheduled Tribes		
	Girls	Boys	Total	Girls	Boys	Total
1	2	3	4	5	6	7
Andhra Pradesh*	**3,735**	9,615	13,350	**296**	1,077	1,373
Arunachal Pradesh	—	—	—	**189**	841	1,030
Assam	**1,899**	3,903	5,802	**2,090**	4,910	7,000
Bihar	**N.A.**	N.A.	N.A.	**N.A.**	N.A.	N.A.
Delhi	**1,825**	2,006	3,831	**135**	135	280
Goa	**14**	21	35	—	—	—
Gujarat	**3,500**	7,000	1,050	**5,200**	8,200	13,400
Haryana	**428**	2,373	2,801	—	—	—
Himachal Pradesh*	**86**	340	426	**29**	111	140
Jammu and Kashmir	**N.A.**	N.A.	N.A.	—	—	—
Karnataka	**4,576**	16,766	21,342	**765**	3,805	4,570
Kerala	**1,869**	1,700	3,569	**107**	120	227
Madhya Pradesh	**1,627**	8,202	9,829	**1,371**	6,072	7,443
Maharashtra	**2,184**	15,424	17,608	**1,013**	3,052	4,965
Manipur	**175**	180	355	**720**	1,260	1,980
Meghalaya	**78**	100	178	**1,374**	1,594	2,968
Mizoram	—	—	—	**N.A.**	N.A.	N.A.
Nagaland	—	—	—	**797**	1,298	2,095
Orissa	**402**	2,055	2,457	**349**	1,401	1,750
Punjab*	**1,989**	4,457	6,446	—	—	—
Rajasthan	**200**	2,833	3,033	**83**	2,790	2,883
Sikkim	—	—	—	—	—	—
Tamil Nadu	**2,791**	7,147	9,938	**25**	85	110
Tripura	**274**	450	724	**68**	152	220
Uttar Pradesh	**2,587**	33,891	36,478	**277**	510	787
West Bengal+	**4,161**	6,002	10,163	**332**	212	544
A. and N. Islands	—	—	—	**8**	18	26
Chandigarh*	**61**	128	189	**10**	37	47
Dadra and Nagar Haveli	—	—	—	—	—	—
Daman and Diu	**2**	5	7	**32**	71	103
Lakshadweep	—	—	—	—	—	—
Pondicherry	**35**	71	106	—	—	—
INDIA	**34,498**	1,24,669	1,59,167	**15,760**	37,881	53,041

*Figures relate to 1989-90.

+ Figures relate to 1988-89.

TABLE 10.33: Sexwise and Statewise Enrolment of SC/ST Students in M.Com. (1990-91)

State/Union Territory	Number of Students belonging to					
	Scheduled Castes			Scheduled Tribes		
	Girls	Boys	Total	Girls	Boys	Total
1	2	3	4	5	6	7
Andhra Pradesh*	50	324	374	3	67	70
Arunachal Pradesh	—	—	—	—	—	—
Assam	—	61	61	2	31	33
Bihar	N.A.	N.A.	N.A.	N.A.	N.A.	N.A.
Delhi	14	76	90	1	10	11
Goa	—	1	1	—	—	—
Gujarat	150	600	750	300	50	350
Haryana	3	18	21	—	—	—
Himachal Pradesh*	1	13	14	—	6	6
Jammu and Kashmir	N.A.	N.A.	N.A.	—	—	—
Karnataka	N.A.	N.A.	N.A.	N.A.	N.A.	N.A.
Kerala	42	59	101	2	3	5
Madhya Pradesh	29	523	552	26	263	289
Maharashtra	422	2,522	2,944	29	403	432
Manipur	1	1	2	3	1	4
Meghalaya	—	—	—	3	10	13
Mizoram	—	—	—	—	—	—
Nagaland	—	—	—	1	2	3
Orissa	2	12	14	2	7	9
Punjab*	1	13	14	—	—	—
Rajasthan	4	320	324	1	200	201
Sikkim	—	—	—	—	—	—
Tamil Nadu	73	313	386	—	4	4
Tripura	—	6	6	—	—	—
Uttar Pradesh	43	584	627	33	1	34
West Bengal+	3	22	25	—	1	1
A. and N. Islands	—	—	—	—	—	—
Chandigarh*	1	4	5	—	2	2
Dadra and Nagar Haveli	—	—	—	—	—	—
Daman and Diu	—	—	—	—	—	—
Lakshadweep	—	—	—	—	—	—
Pondicherry	1	1	2	—	—	—
INDIA	840	5,473	6,313	124	1,343	1,467

*Figures relate to 1989-90.

* Figures relate to 1988-89.

TABLE 10.34: Sexwise and Statewise Enrolment of SC/ST Students in M.A (1990-91)

State/Union Territory	Number of Students belonging to					
	Scheduled Castes			Scheduled Tribes		
	Girls	Boys	Total	Girls	Boys	Total
1	2	3	4	5	6	7
Andhra Pradesh*	**235**	1,210	1,445	**39**	203	242
Arunachal Pradesh	—	—	—	**9**	49	58
Assam	**67**	90	157	**73**	129	202
Bihar	**N.A.**	N.A.	N.A.	**N.A.**	N.A.	N.A.
Delhi	**185**	285	470	**38**	82	120
Goa	—	—	—	—	—	—
Gujarat	**500**	1,000	1,500	**500**	900	1,400
Haryana	**23**	242	265	—	—	—
Himachal Pradesh*	**18**	96	114	**7**	55	62
Jammu and Kashmir	**N.A.**	N.A.	N.A.	—	—	—
Karnataka	**N.A.**	N.A.	N.A.	**N.A.**	N.A.	N.A.
Kerala	**227**	210	437	**10**	16	26
Madhya Pradesh	**369**	1,265	1,634	**191**	871	1,062
Maharashtra	**686**	2,302	2,988	**92**	749	841
Manipur	**2**	3	5	**11**	18	29
Meghalaya	—	6	6	**172**	260	36
Mizoram	—	—	—	**18**	17	35
Nagaland	—	—	—	**8**	9	17
Orissa	**75**	292	367	**36**	133	169
Punjab*	**374**	814	1,188	—	—	—
Rajasthan	**37**	725	762	**26**	890	916
Sikkim	—	—	—	—	—	—
Tamil Nadu	**405**	1,066	1,471	**1**	11	12
Tripura	**5**	10	15	**1**	2	3
Uttar Pradesh	**726**	8,803	9,529	**156**	330	486
West Bengal+	**175**	302	477	**2**	13	15
A. and N. Islands	—	—	—	—	—	—
Chandigarh*	**39**	90	129	—	—	—
Dadra and Nagar Haveli	—	—	—	—	—	—
Daman and Diu	—	—	—	—	—	—
Lakshadweep	—	—	—	—	—	—
Pondicherry	**4**	13	17	—	—	—
INDIA	**4,152**	18,824	22,976	**1,390**	4,737	6,127

*Figures relate to 1989-90.

+ Figures relate to 1988-89.

TABLE 10.35: Sexwise and Statewise Enrolment of SC/ST Students in M.Sc. (1990-91)

State/Union Territory	Number of Students belonging to					
	Scheduled Castes			Scheduled Tribes		
	Girls	Boys	Total	Girls	Boys	Total
1	2	3	4	5	6	7
Andhra Pradesh*	151	470	621	8	54	62
Arunachal Pradesh	—	—	—	—	—	—
Assam	12	66	78	9	44	53
Bihar	N.A.	N.A.	N.A.	N.A.	N.A.	N.A.
Delhi	11	32	43	1	2	3
Goa	—	—	—	—	—	—
Gujarat	20	50	70	20	40	60
Haryana	12	46	58	—	—	—
Himachal Pradesh*	5	26	31	1	4	5
Jammu and Kashmir	N.A.	N.A.	N.A.	—	—	—
Karnataka	N.A.	N.A.	N.A.	N.A.	N.A.	N.A.
Kerala	167	137	304	8	10	18
Madhya Pradesh	87	185	272	43	123	166
Maharashtra	56	227	283	16	23	39
Manipur	1	1	2	8	9	17
Meghalaya	—	4	4	27	28	55
Mizoram	—	—	—	—	—	—
Nagaland	—	—	—	3	11	14
Orissa	36	92	128	8	32	40
Punjab*	13	31	44	—	—	—
Rajasthan	5	66	71	2	42	44
Sikkim	—	—	—	—	—	—
Tamil Nadu	248	506	754	4	4	8
Tripura	—	1	1	—	1	1
Uttar Pradesh	92	632	724	9	27	36
West Bengal+	15	148	163	2	7	9
A. and N. Islands	—	—	—	—	—	—
Chandigarh*	6	14	20	3	2	5
Dadra and Nagar Haveli	—	—	—	—	—	—
Daman and Diu	—	—	—	—	—	—
Lakshadweep	—	—	—	—	—	—
Pondicherry	3	8	11	—	—	—
INDIA	940	2,742	3,682	173	462	635

*Figures relate to 1989-90.

+ Figures relate to 1988-89.

TABLE 10.36: Sexwise and Statewise Enrolment of SC/ST Students in Ph.D/D.Sc./M.Phill (1990-91)

State/Union Territory	Number of Students belonging to					
	Scheduled Castes			Scheduled Tribes		
	Girls	Boys	Total	Girls	Boys	Total
1	2	3	4	5	6	7
Andhra Pradesh*	17	55	72	6	5	11
Arunachal Pradesh	—	—	—	—	—	—
Assam	—	1	1	3	5	8
Bihar	N.A.	N.A.	N.A.	N.A.	N.A.	N.A.
Delhi	29	99	128	22	30	52
Goa	—	—	—	—	—	—
Gujarat	—	10	10	10	15	25
Haryana	2	7	9	—	—	—
Himachal Pradesh*	9	28	37	4	11	15
Jammu and Kashmir	N.A.	N.A.	N.A.	—	—	—
Karnataka	N.A.	N.A.	N.A.	N.A.	N.A.	N.A.
Kerala	9	9	18	—	—	—
Madhya Pradesh	8	18	26	1	5	6
Maharashtra	5	16	21	1	9	10
Manipur	—	—	—	3	4	7
Meghalaya	—	—	—	18	33	51
Mizoram	—	—	—	—	—	—
Nagaland	—	—	—	—	—	—
Orissa	3	12	15	3	16	19
Punjab*	10	11	21	—	—	—
Rajasthan	1	5	6	—	3	3
Sikkim	—	—	—	—	—	—
Tamil Nadu	2	6	8	—	—	—
Tripura	—	—	—	—	—	—
Uttar Pradesh	37	287	324	1	8	9
West Bengal+	19	36	55	—	3	3
A. and N. Islands	—	—	—	—	—	—
Chandigarh*	—	—	—	—	—	—
Dadra and Nagar Haveli	—	—	—	—	—	—
Daman and Diu	—	—	—	—	—	—
Lakshadweep	—	—	—	—	—	—
Pondicherry	—	—	—	—	—	—
INDIA	151	600	751	72	147	219

* Figures relate to 1989-90.

\+ Figures relate to 1988-89.

11

Districtwise Women's Literacy

TABLE 11.1 Women Literacy Rates Districtwise 1991: Andhra Pradesh

Sl.	District Name	Literacy Rate			All India Rank *		
No.		Female	Male	Total	Female	Male	Total
1.	Adilabad	20.60	45.05	32.96	75	40	48
2.	Anantapur	27.61	52.92	42.18	145	138	129
3.	Chittoor	36.44	62.61	49.75	216	216	221
4.	Cuddapah	32.35	63.14	48.12	185	224	204
5.	East Godavari	42.26	55.32	48.79	277	131	214
6.	Guntur	35.85	56.54	46.35	211	145	184
7.	Hyderabad	63.56	78.90	71.52	395	383	386
8.	Karimnagar	23.37	50.79	37.17	106	85	79
9.	Khammam	30.53	50.04	40.50	172	79	112
10.	Krishna	45.54	60.55	53.16	296	194	248
11.	Kurnool	26.04	53.24	39.97	23	105	106
12.	Mahbubnagar	18.03	40.80	29.58	55	24	25
13.	Medak	19.25	45.15	31.41	62	41	44
14.	Nalgonda	24.92	50.53	38.00	118	82	85
15.	Nellore	36.99	58.40	47.76	222	166	198
16.	Nizamabad	21.35	47.33	34.18	85	56	54
17.	Prakasam	27.06	53.14	40.30	136	104	108
18.	Rangareddi	36.91	60.43	49.07	221	192	216
19.	Srikakulam	23.52	49.14	36.22	109	71	74
20.	Visakhapatnam	34.60	56.13	45.51	202	141	169
21.	Vizianagaram	22.47	45.93	34.19	95	47	55
22.	Warangal	26.08	51.98	39.30	124	96	99
23.	West Godavari	46.98	58.75	53.38	305	182	252

* Ranks in the ascending order of relevant literacy rates.

TABLE 11.2: Women Literacy Rates Districtwise (1991) - Arunachal Pradesh

Sl. No.	District Name	Literacy Rate			All India Rank *		
		Female	Male	Total	Female	Male	Total
1.	Changlang	29.64	54.44	43.20	166	116	138
2.	Dibang Valley	32.27	56.94	46.88	191	154	187
3.	East Kameng	14.02	37.69	26.20	17	12	12
4.	East Stang	34.43	52.49	44.30	199	99	151
5.	Lohit	36.21	59.02	49.21	214	171	217
6.	Lower Subansiri	30.70	51.10	41.57	173	87	122
7.	Tawang	16.83	40.41	29.80	40	22	27
8.	Tirap	18.52	43.44	32.06	57	36	39
9.	Upper Subansiri	27.24	47.58	38.31	139	61	87
10.	West Kameng	35.85	35.22	46.31	207	126	182
11.	West Siang	35.85	53.86	45.64	211	110	172

* Ranks in the ascending order of relevant literacy rates.

TABLE 11.3: Women's Literacy Rate—Assam

Sl. No.	District Name	Literacy Rate			All India Rank*		
		Female	Male	Total	Female	Male	Total
1.	Barpeta	33.20	52.61	43.24	190	101	139
2.	Bongaigaon	38.72	58.67	49.06	241	168	215
3.	Cachar	48.76	68.79	59.19	314	288	307
4.	Darrang	32.53	50.80	42.00	187	86	127
5.	Dhemaji	41.12	65.43	53.84	262	247	257
6.	Dhubri	28.75	47.32	38.31	158	55	87
7.	Dibrugarh	48.89	66.72	58.32	317	264	294
8.	Golapara	37.58	55.47	46.81	225	134	186
9.	Golaghat	49.75	66.50	58.54	324	260	296
10.	Hailakandi	41.04	64.08	53.07	261	230	247
11.	Jorhat	56.88	73.29	65.51	372	332	355
12.	Kamrup	55.01	73.67	65.04	358	335	351
13.	Karbi Englong	34.35	55.55	45.57	198	136	170
14.	Karimganj	44.76	64.05	54.71	290	229	262
15.	Kokrajhar	30.92	49.57	40.57	175	77	115
16.	Lakhimpur	48.85	68.28	58.96	316	278	302
17.	Marigaon	39.19	56.17	47.99	246	142	201
18.	Nagaon	46.30	62.49	54.74	301	214	263
19.	Nalbari	44.19	66.95	55.99	286	268	275
20.	North Cachar Hills	47.34	66.39	57.76	306	258	287
21.	Sibsagar	56.14	71.91	64.46	366	318	347
22.	Sonitpur	38.60	56.70	48.14	239	149	205
23.	Tinsukia	39.99	59.27	50.28	254	176	226

* Ranks in the ascending order of relevant literacy rates.

TABLE 11.4: Women Literacy Rate Districtwise—Bihar (1991)

Sl. No.	District Name	Literacy Rate			All India Rank *		
		Female	Male	Total	Female	Male	Total
1.	Arraria	14.01	36.99	26.19	16	11	11
2.	Aurangabad	26.67	61.80	45.14	131	207	164
3.	Begusarai	23.52	48.66	36.88	108	59	78
4.	Bhagalpur	24.38	51.32	38.89	116	89	92
5.	Bhojpur	27.12	65.05	47.18	137	242	191
6.	Darbhanga	20.09	48.31	34.94	72	65	62
7.	Deoghar	19.54	54.12	37.92	65	114	84
8.	Dhanbad	37.88	69.47	55.47	230	293	271
9.	Dumka	17.91	49.29	34.02	72	73	52
10.	Gaya	24.20	55.22	40.47	114	128	111
11.	Giridih	17.65	52.89	35.96	49	102	71
12.	Godda	18.00	48.56	34.02	54	68	53
13.	Gopalganj	17.75	51.62	34.96	50	91	63
14.	Gunla	27.48	51.70	39.67	144	94	102
15.	Hazaribag	21.24	53.37	38.00	82	107	85
16.	Jehanabad	26.81	63.11	45.83	132	222	174
17.	Katihar	16.88	39.24	28.70	41	16	21
18.	Khagaria	19.79	42.97	32.33	68	31	43
19.	Kishanganj	10.38	33.12	22.22	4	3	2
20.	Lohardaga	26.11	54.99	40.79	125	125	119
21.	Madhepura	14.41	39.31	27.72	18	18	17
22.	Madhubani	16.75	48.49	33.22	38	67	50
23.	Munger	25.34	55.62	41.58	119	137	123
24.	Muzaffarnagar	22.33	48.44	36.11	92	66	73
25.	Nalanda	29.95	61.94	46.94	168	208	188
26.	Nawada	22.44	54.85	38.92	86	122	94
27.	Palamu	16.15	44.80	31.10	31	38	33
28.	Paschim Champaran	14.41	39.62	27.99	18	19	18
29.	Paschimi Singhbhum	22.44	54.75	38.92	94	121	93
30.	Patna	41.35	69.07	56.33	265	290	277
31.	Purba Champaran	13.69	39.65	27.59	15	20	16
32.	Purbi Singhbhum	45.50	71.18	59.05	295	311	305
33.	Purnia	16.80	38.92	28.52	39	14	20
34.	Ranchi	36.57	65.12	51.52	218	245	234
35.	Rohtas	27.03	61.50	45.41	135	205	167
36.	Saharsa	14.70	41.61	28.97	21	26	23
37.	Sahibaganj	16.32	36.97	27.03	33	10	13
38.	Samastipur	21.17	50.39	36.37	81	80	77
39.	Saran	22.71	60.18	41.79	100	189	125
40.	Sitamarhi	15.31	50.39	28.12	25	17	19
41.	Siwan	21.33	57.51	39.13	84	162	95
42.	Vaishali	25.08	55.62	40.56	113	137	114

* Ranks in the ascending order of relevant literacy rates.

TABLE 11.5: Women Literacy Rates Districtwise (1991) : Delhi

Sl. No.	District Name	Literacy Rate			All India Rank *		
		Female	Male	Total	Female	Male	Total
1.	Delhi District	66.99	82.01	75.29	405	400	396

* Ranks in the ascending order of relevant literacy rates.

TABLE 11.6: Women Literacy Rates Districtwise—Goa (1991)

Sl. No.	District Name	Literacy Rate			All India Rank *		
		Female	Male	Total	Female	Male	Total
1.	North Goa	68.86	86.15	77.67	409	416	404
2.	South Goa	64.76	80.30	72.64	400	388	388
		67.09	83.84	73.37	27	27	27

* Ranks in the ascending order of relevant literacy rates.

TABLE 11.7: Women Literacy Rates Districtwise—Gujarat (1991)

Sl. No.	District Name	Literacy Rate			All India Rank *		
		Female	Male	Total	Female	Male	Total
1.	Ahmadabad	62.39	82.73	73.10	394	407	390
2.	Amreli	48.77	71.26	60.06	315	313	311
3.	Banas Kantha	22.56	54.89	39.29	97	123	98
4.	Bharuch	49.71	73.21	61.92	322	331	325
5.	Bhavnagar	44.33	70.83	57.89	287	308	289
6.	Gandhi Nagar	80.51	93.21	87.11	422	428	416
7.	Jamnagar	47.45	69.96	58.96	307	299	302
8.	Junagarh	47.83	72.41	60.33	308	323	312
9.	Kachchh	40.89	64.26	52.75	260	233	243
10.	Kheda	49.93	80.49	65.83	326	391	357
11.	Mahasana	51.60	78.15	65.14	343	379	353
12.	Panch Mahals	27.31	59.35	43.79	143	177	144
13.	Rajkot	56.66	76.76	66.96	370	364	368
14.	Sabar Kantha	43.08	74.53	59.03	279	340	304
15.	Surat	55.13	72.61	64.36	359	326	346
16.	Surendera Nagar	40.65	67.83	54.77	258	273	264
17.	The Danges	35.31	59.55	47.56	209	181	194
18.	Vadodara	52.02	74.14	63.61	347	338	338
19.	Valsad	54.79	73.48	64.35	357	334	345

* Ranks in the ascending order of relevant literacy rates.

TABLE 11.8: Women Literacy Rates Districtwise—Haryana (1991).

Sl. No.	District Name	Literacy Rate			All India Rank *		
		Female	Male	Total	Female	Male	Total
1.	Ambala	56.62	75.08	66.41	368	346	362
2.	Bhiwani	35.10	70.93	54.18	206	309	259
3.	Faridabad	42.12	74.15	59.77	276	339	309
4.	Gurgaon	34.94	67.87	52.61	205	2744	242
5.	Hisar	32.12	61.41	47.87	183	203	199
6.	Jind	30.12	61.07	47.00	170	200	189
7.	Kaithal	28.37	54.71	42.59	155	120	132
8.	Karnal	43.54	67.02	56.15	282	269	276
9.	Kurukshetra	46.94	69.23	58.78	304	292	301
10.	Mahendragarh	36.75	77.17	57.87	220	368	288
11.	Panipat	41.17	67.04	55.17	264	270	269
12.	Rewari	46.18	82.16	64.77	300	403	350
13.	Rohtak	45.74	76.19	62.24	297	357	326
14.	Sirsa	34.02	57.21	46.32	196	156	183
15.	Sonipat	48.27	77.20	64.06	311	369	347
16.	Yamunanagar	50.07	69.76	60.53	328	298	314

* Ranks in the ascending order of relevant literacy rates.

TABLE 11.9: Women Literacy Rate Districtwise Himanchal Pradesh (1991)

S.No	District Name	Literacy Rate			All India Rank*		
		Female	Male	Total	Female	Male	Total
1.	Bilaspur	56.55	77.97	67.17	367	376	369
2.	Chamba	28.57	59.96	44.70	156	186	157
3.	Hamirpur	65.90	85.11	74.88	401	413	395
4.	Kangra	61.39	80.12	70.57	390	387	382
5.	Kinnaur	42.04	72.04	58.36	275	319	295
6.	Kullu	38.53	69.64	54.82	238	295	265
7.	Lahul and Spiti	38.05	71.78	56.82	232	316	281
8.	Mandi	49.12	76.65	62.74	319	362	332
9.	Shimla	51.75	75.96	64.61	345	355	348
10.	Sirmaur	38.45	63.20	51.62	237	226	236
11.	Solan	50.69	74.67	63.30	336	341	336
12.	Una	61.01	81.15	70.91	384	395	384

* Ranks in the ascending order of relevant literacy rates.

TABLE 11.10: Women Literacy Rate Districtwise—Karnataka (1991).

Sl. No.	District Name	Literacy Rate Female	Male	Total	All India Rank * Female	Male	Total
1.	Bangalore	68.81	82.94	76.27	408	410	401
2.	Bangalore Rural	38.15	61.51	50.17	234	206	224
3.	Belgaum	38.69	66.65	53.00	240	262	246
4.	Bellary	31.97	58.71	45.57	182	169	170
5.	Bidar	30.53	58.97	45.11	172	170	163
6.	Bijapur	40.06	69.69	55.13	255	296	268
7.	Chikmangalur	51.31	70.56	61.05	338	304	317
8.	Chitradurga	43.36	66.88	55.48	281	267	272
9.	Dakshin Kannad	67.96	84.40	75.86	407	411	400
10.	Dharwad	45.20	71.37	58.68	294	315	299
11.	Gulbarga	24.49	52.08	38.54	117	97	88
12.	Hassan	44.90	68.87	56.85	292	289	282
13.	Kidagu	61.22	75.35	68.35	387	348	373
14.	Kolar	37.75	62.69	50.45	227	217	227
15.	Mandya	36.70	59.18	48.15	219	174	206
16.	Mysore	37.95	56.23	47.32	231	143	193
17.	Raichur	22.15	49.53	35.96	89	76	71
18.	Shimoga	51.42	71.24	61.53	340	312	320
19.	Tumkur	41.93	66.49	54.48	273	259	261
20.	Uttar Kannad	56.77	76.39	66.73	371	358	364

* Ranks in the ascending order of relevant literacy rates.

TABLE 11.11: Women Literacy Rate Districtwise—Kerala (1991)

Sl. No.	District Name	Literacy Rate Female	Male	Total	All India Rank * Female	Male	Total
1.	Alappuzha	91.12	96.79	93.87	432	435	425
2.	Ernakulam	89.27	95.46	92.35	431	431	424
3.	Idukki	82.96	90.82	86.94	423	425	415
4.	Kannur	87.65	95.54	91.48	430	432	423
5.	Kasaragod	76.29	88.97	82.51	419	422	413
6.	Kollam	87.00	94.09	90.47	429	430	421
7.	Kottayam	94.00	97.46	95.72	435	437	428
8.	Kozhikode	86.79	95.58	91.10	427	433	422
9.	Malappuram	84.09	92.08	87.94	424	426	417
10.	Palakkad	75.72	87.24	81.27	417	418	408
11.	Pathanamthitta	93.29	96.55	94.86	426	427	419
12.	Thiruvantha Puram	85.76	92.84	89.22	426	427	419
13.	Thrissur	89.94	93.77	90.18	428	429	420
14.	Wayanad	77.69	87.59	82.73	420	419	414

* Ranks in the ascending order of relevant literacy rates.

TABLE 11.12: Women Literacy Rate Districtwise—Madhya Pradesh (1991).

Sl. No.	District Name	Literacy Rate			All India Rank*		
		Female	Male	Total	Female	Male	Total
1.	Balaghat	38.95	67.63	53.23	244	272	250
2.	Bastar	15.30	34.51	24.89	24	7	8
3.	Betul	33.90	57.42	45.89	195	160	175
4.	Bhind	28.20	66.20	49.23	153	253	218
5.	Bhopal	54.17	73.14	64.27	353	330	343
6.	Bilaspur	27.26	62.87	45.26	141	219	166
7.	Chhatrapur	21.32	46.87	35.20	83	53	65
8.	Chhindwara	32.52	56.65	44.90	186	148	160
9.	Damoh	30.46	60.49	46.27	171	193	180
10.	Datia	23.69	60.18	43.57	112	189	143
11.	Dewas	25.57	61.15	44.08	122	201	148
12.	Dhar	20.71	47.62	37.54	76	62	59
13.	Durg	42.78	74.06	58.70	278	337	300
14.	East Nimar	31.53	58.53	45.49	180	167	168
15.	Guna	17.99	48.86	34.58	53	70	60
16.	Gwalior	41.72	70.81	57.70	271	307	286
17.	Hosangabad	37.63	65.83	52.54	226	250	241
18.	Indore	53.35	77.99	66.32	352	377	359
19.	Jabalpur	45.02	71.88	59.11	293	317	306
20.	Jharua	11.52	26.29	19.01	7	1	1
21.	Mandla	22.24	52.20	37.29	90	98	80
22.	Mandsaur	28.32	67.89	48.67	154	276	213
23.	Morena	20.81	57.99	41.33	77	163	121
24.	Narsimhapur	41.59	68.44	55.65	269	282	274
25.	Panna	19.41	46.29	33.68	63	50	52
26.	Raigarh	26.46	56.03	41.22	129	140	120
27.	Raipur	31.04	65.06	98.08	177	243	203
28.	Raisen	25.47	54.02	40.76	120	112	118
29.	Rajgarh	15.62	46.73	31.81	28	52	37
30.	Rajnandgaon	27.83	61.26	44.39	148	202	153
31.	Ratlam	29.13	58.36	44.15	162	165	149
32.	Rewa	26.88	60.67	44.38	133	196	152
33.	Sagar	37.78	67.02	53.44	228	269	253
34.	Sarguja	17.40	42.13	30.09	48	29	29
35.	Satna	27.80	60.03	44.65	146	187	155
36.	Sehore	21.99	56.90	40.43	88	152	110
37.	Seoni	31.14	57.50	44.49	178	161	154
38.	Shahdol	20.09	48.44	34.78	72	66	61
39.	Shajapur	19.77	56.99	39.20	67	155	96
40.	Shivpuri	15.64	47.50	33.03	29	58	49
41.	Sidhi	13.61	43.23	29.15	14	34	24
42.	Tikamgarh	19.96	47.52	34.78	71	59	61
43.	Ujjain	32.64	64.25	49.06	188	232	215
44.	Vidisha	27.81	58.04	44.08	147	164	148
45.	West Nimar	23.23	47.99	35.95	104	63	70

* Ranks in the ascending order of relevant literacy rates.

TABLE 11.13: Women Literacy Rate Districtwise—Maharashtra (1991)

Sl. No.	District Name	Literacy Rate Female	Male	Total	All India Rank* Female	Male	Total
1.	Ahmednagar	45.99	75.30	61.03	298	347	316
2.	Akola	53.28	77.63	65.83	350	373	357
3.	Amravati	61.13	78.40	70.06	386	381	381
4.	Aurangabad	39.64	72.93	56.98	249	327	283
5.	Bhadara	50.44	78.82	64.69	335	382	349
6.	Bid	32.34	66.34	49.82	184	256	222
7.	Buldana	46.13	76.53	61.69	299	360	322
8.	Chandrapur	46.81	59.41	71.30	302	314	308
9.	Dhule	38.78	63.13	51.22	242	223	231
10.	Gadchiroli	28.87	56.56	42.89	159	146	134
11.	Greater Bombay	75.80	87.87	82.50	418	421	412
12.	Jalgaon	50.34	77.46	64.30	333	371	344
13.	Jallna	27.30	64.43	46.25	142	236	179
14.	Kolhapur	53.08	80.33	66.94	349	390	367
15.	Latur	39.74	70.47	55.57	252	303	273
16.	Nagpur	64.74	81.79	73.64	399	398	392
17.	Nanded	30.96	64.38	48.17	176	235	207
18.	Nasik	49.59	73.98	62.33	325	336	327
19.	Osmanabad	39.16	68.39	54.27	245	281	260
20.	Parbhani	29.41	64.90	47.58	163	241	195
21.	Pune	59.77	81.56	71.05	382	397	385
22.	Raigarh	52.20	75.94	63.95	348	354	341
23.	Ratnagiri	51.61	76.64	62.70	344	361	331
14.	Sangli	49.94	74.83	62.61	327	344	330
15.	Satara	53.35	80.61	66.67	352	393	363
16.	Sindhudurg	66.87	86.23	75.81	404	417	399
17.	Solapur	41.73	70.08	56.39	272	301	278
18.	Thane	60.28	77.56	69.54	383	372	379
19.	Wardha	61.02	78.33	69.95	385	380	380
20.	Yavatmal	44.81	70.45	57.96	291	302	291

* Ranks in the ascending order of relevant literacy rates.

TABLE 11.14: Women Literacy Rate Districtwise—Manipur (1991)

Sl. No.	District Name	Literacy Rate Female	Male	Total	All India Rank * Female	Male	Total
1.	Bishnupur	41.13	68.59	54.94	263	284	266
2.	Chandel	34.80	57.39	46.68	203	159	185
3.	Churachandpur	49.30	66.38	58.17	320	257	293
4.	Imphal	58.32	82.80	70.74	378	409	383
5.	Senapati	36.13	55.26	46.04	213	129	177
6.	Tamenglong	39.68	59.92	50.16	250	185	221
7.	Thoubal	36.31	68.33	52.47	215	280	239
8.	Ukhrul	51.57	72.11	62.54	342	321	328

* Ranks in the ascending order of relevant literacy rates .

TABLE 11.15: Women Literacy Rates Districtwise—Meghalaya (1991)

Sl. No.	District Name	Literacy Rate			All India Rank *		
		Female	Male	Total	Female	Male	Total
1.	East Garo Hills	41.70	54.70	48.38	270	119	209
2.	East Khasi Hills	57.04	62.86	60.04	374	218	310
3.	Jaintia Hills	36.31	34.37	35.32	215	6	66
4.	West Garo Hills	31.32	46.93	36.32	179	54	100
5.	West Khasi Hills	47.94	52.98	50.52	310	103	228

* Ranks in the ascending order of relevant literacy rates.

TABLE 11.16: Women Literacy Rates Districtwise (1991)—Mizoram

Sl. No.	District Name	Literacy Rate			All India Rank *		
		Female	Male	Total	Female	Male	Total
1.	Aizawl	85.51	90.40	88.06	425	424	418
2.	Chhimtuipui	51.24	66.14	59.11	337	252	306
3.	Lunglei	72.58	82.37	77.73	413	404	405

* Ranks in the ascending order of relevant literacy rates.

TABLE 11.17: Women Literacy Rate Districtwise—Nagaland (1991).

Sl.	District Name	Literacy Rate			All India Rank *		
		Female	Male	Total	Female	Male	Total
1.	Kohima	61.41	75.58	69.16	391	349	376
2.	Mokokchung	74.88	80.52	77.85	416	392	407
3.	Mon	29.10	41.90	36.02	160	28	72
4.	Phek	51.34	72.28	62.59	339	322	329
5.	Tuensang	41.98	53.98	48.39	274	111	210
6.	Wokha	65.99	81.06	73.92	402	394	393
7.	Zunheboto	57.63	70.76	64.36	375	306	346

* Ranks in the ascending order of relevant literacy rates.

TABLE 11.18: Women Literacy Rate Districtwise—Orissa (1991)

Sl. No.	District Name	Literacy Rate			All India Rank *		
		Female	Male	Total	Female	Male	Total
1.	Balangir	21.88	57.26	39.74	87	157	104
2.	Baleshwar	44.57	72.55	58.78	289	325	301
3.	Cuttack	50.38	75.74	63.28	334	351	355
4.	Dhenkanal	37.34	68.23	53.22	224	277	249
5.	Ganjam	28.09	60.77	44.26	151	198	150
6.	Kalahandi	14.56	45.54	30.65	19	43	28
7.	Kendujhar	30.01	59.04	44.73	169	172	159
8.	Koraput	13.09	32.15	22.66	11	2	3
9.	Mayurbhanj	23.68	51.84	37.88	111	95	83
10.	Phulbani	20.26	56.92	38.64	73	153	89
11.	Puri	49.94	79.82	63.82	327	365	340
12.	Sambalpur	33.55	64.64	49.38	193	239	219
13.	Sundargarh	39.60	65.41	52.97	248	246	245

* Ranks in the ascending order of relevant literacy rates.

TABLE 11.19: Women Literacy Rate Districtwise—-Punjab (1991).

Sl. So.	District Name	Literacy Rate			All India Rank*		
		Female	Male	Total	Female	Male	Total
1.	Amritsar	50.10	65.07	58.09	329	244	292
2.	Bathinda	34.51	50.55	43.03	201	83	126
3.	Faridkot	41.50	56.43	49.42	267	144	220
4.	Firozpur	38.11	56.88	48.01	233	151	202
5.	Gurdaspur	53.33	69.56	61.84	351	294	323
6.	Hoshiarpur	61.48	79.31	70.74	393	384	383
7.	Jalandhar	61.33	74.87	68.45	389	345	374
8.	Kapurthala	55.83	70.03	63.31	365	300	337
9.	Ludhiana	61.23	72.47	67.35	388	324	370
10.	Patiala	50.33	65.93	58.62	332	251	297
11.	Rupnagar	58.84	76.45	68.14	379	359	372
12.	Sangrur	37.86	53.37	46.16	229	107	178

* Ranks in the ascending order of relevant literacy rates.

TABLE 11.20: Women Literacy Rates Districtwise—Rajasthan (1991).

Sl. No.	District Name	Literacy Rate			All India Rank *		
		Female	Male	Total	Female	Male	Total
1.	Ajmer	34.50	68.75	52.34	200	287	238
2.	Alwar	22.54	60.98	43.09	96	199	137
3.	Barmer	13.42	38.16	26.00	13	13	10
4.	Barmer	7.68	36.56	22.98	1	9	4
5.	Bharatpur	19.60	62.11	42.96	64	210	135
6.	Bhilwara	16.50	445.95	31.65	36	48	35
7.	Bikaner	27.03	54.63	41.73	135	118	124
8.	Bundi	16.13	47.40	32.75	30	57	45
9.	Chittorgarh	17.15	50.55	34.28	45	83	56
10.	Churu	17.32	51.30	34.78	47	88	61
11.	Dholpur	15.25	50.45	35.09	23	81	64
12.	Dungarpur	15.40	45.71	30.55	26	46	31
13.	Ganganagar	26.39	55.29	41.82	127	130	126
14.	Jaipur	28.69	64.83	47.88	157	240	200
15.	Jaisalmer	11.28	44.99	30.05	6	39	28
16.	Jalaur	7.75	38.97	23.76	2	15	05
17.	Jhalawar	16.18	48.22	32.94	32	64	47
18.	Jhunjhunu	25.54	68.32	47.60	121	279	196
19.	Jodhpur	22.58	56.74	40.69	98	150	116
20.	Kota	29.50	64.03	47.88	164	228	200
21.	Nagaur	13.29	49.35	31.80	42	74	36
22.	Pali	16.97	54.42	35.96	43	115	71
23.	Sawai Madhopur	14.64	54.60	36.27	20	117	75
24.	Sikar	19.88	64.13	42.49	70	231	131
25.	Sirohi	16.99	46.24	31.94	44	49	38
26.	Tonk	15.24	50.64	33.67	22	84	51
27.	Udaipur	19.00	49.27	34.38	61	72	57

* Ranks in the ascending order of relevant literacy rates.

TABLE 11.21: Women Literacy Rates Districtwise—Sikkam (1991).

Sl. No.	District Name	Literacy Rate			All India Rank *		
		Female	Male	Total	Female	Male	Total
1.	East District	55.66	73.10	65.13	363	329	352
2.	North District	40.69	63.64	53.47	259	227	254
3.	South District	43.70	63.18	54.08	284	225	258
4.	West District	35.26	54.92	45.62	208	124	171

* Ranks in the ascending order of literacy rates.

TABLE 11.22: Women Literacy Rates Districtwise—Tamil Nadu (1991).

Sl. No.	District Name	Literacy Rate			All India Rank *		
		Female	Male	Total	Female	Male	Total
1.	Chengalpattu-MGR	55.22	77.07	66.38	361	367	361
2.	Chidambaranar	64.57	82.02	73.02	398	401	389
3.	Coimbatore	55.73	76.45	66.35	364	359	360
4.	Dharmapuri	34.23	57.21	46.02	197	156	176
5.	Dindigul Anna	43.94	69.19	56.68	285	291	280
6.	Kamarajar	50.17	75.67	62.91	330	350	333
7.	Kanniyakumari	78.39	85.70	82.06	421	415	411
8.	Madras	74.87	87.86	81.60	415	420	409
9.	Madurai	54.74	77.74	66.41	355	374	362
10.	Nilgiri	61.47	81.79	71.70	392	398	387
11.	North Arcot-Ambedkar	48.58	72.94	60.87	312	328	315
12.	Pasumpon M Thevar	49.74	76.92	63.04	323	366	334
13.	Periyar	41.58	65.54	53.80	268	248	256
14.	Puddukkottai	43.62	71.78	57.63	283	316	285
15.	Ramanathipuram	48.70	74.76	61.59	313	343	321
16.	Salem	41.45	64.58	53.31	266	238	251
17.	South Arcot	39.70	65.59	52.86	251	249	244
18.	Thanjavur	54.77	77.24	66.02	356	370	358
19.	Tiruchirapalli	48.94	73.36	61.22	318	333	310
20.	Tirunelveli Kattabomman	54.23	77.46	65.58	354	371	356
21.	Tiruvannamala-Sambuvara	39.25	66.71	53.07	247	263	247

*Ranks in the ascending order of relevant literacy rates.

TABLE 11.23: Women Literacy Rates Districtwise—Tripura (1991)

Sl. No.	District Name	Literacy Rate			All India Rank*		
		Female	Male	Total	Female	Male	Total
1.	North Tripura	50.31	69.74	60.37	331	297	313
2.	South Tripura	39.75	62.34	51.35	253	213	233
3.	West Tripura	55.15	75.87	65.83	360	353	357

* Ranks in the ascending order of relevent literacy rates.

TABLE 11.24: Women Literacy Rates Districtwise—Uttar Pradesh (1991).

Sl. No.	District Name	Literacy Rate			All India Rank *		
		Female	Male	Total	Female	Male	Total
1.	Agra	30.83	63.09	48.58	174	221	212
2.	Aligarh	27.17	60.19	45.21	138	190	165
3.	Allahabad	23.45	59.14	42.66	107	173	133
4.	Almora	39.60	79.96	58.66	248	386	298
5.	Azamgarh	22.67	56.13	39.22	99	141	97
6.	Bahraich	10.73	35.57	24.39	5	8	6
7.	Ballia	26.13	60.49	43.89	126	197	146
8.	Banda	16.44	51.50	35.70	35	90	69
9.	Barabanki	15.41	43.00	30.42	27	32	30
10.	Bareilly	19.85	43.33	32.78	69	35	46
11.	Basti	17.82	51.68	35.54	51	93	67
12.	Bijnor	26.47	52.56	40.53	130	100	113
13.	Budaun	12.82	33.96	24.64	10	5	7
14.	Bulandshahr	24.30	61.96	44.71	115	209	158
15.	Chamoli	40.37	82.01	61.08	256	400	318
16.	Dehradun	59.26	77.95	69.50	381	375	378
17.	Deoria	18.75	55.34	37.30	60	132	81
18.	Etah	22.91	54.09	40.15	101	113	107
19.	Etawah	38.34	66.24	53.69	235	255	255
20.	Faizabad	22.97	55.49	39.90	102	135	105
21.	Farrukhabad	31.97	59.48	47.13	182	179	190
22.	Fatehpur	27.25	59.88	44.69	140	184	156
23.	Firozabad	29.85	59.76	46.30	167	183	181
24.	Garhwal	49.44	82.46	65.35	321	406	354
25.	Ghaziabad	38.81	68.64	55.22	243	285	270
26.	Ghazipur	24.38	61.48	43.27	116	204	270
27.	Gonda	12.58	40.00	27.34	9	21	15
28.	Gorakhpur	24.49	60.61	43.30	117	195	142
29.	Hamirpur	20.88	55.13	39.64	79	12	110
30.	Hardoi	19.75	49.45	36.30	66	75	76
31.	Hardwar	34.93	59.51	48.35	204	180	208
32.	Jalaun	31.60	66.21	50.72	181	254	230
33.	Jaunpur	22.39	62.24	42.22	93	212	130
34.	Jhansi	33.76	66.76	51.60	194	266	235
35.	Kanpur Dehat	35.92	62.88	50.71	212	220	229
36.	Kanpur Nagar	58.82	76.73	68.75	380	363	375
37.	Kheri	16.35	40.58	29.71	34	23	26
38.	Lalitpur	16.62	45.22	32.12	37	42	42
39.	Lucknow	46.88	66.51	57.49	303	261	284
40.	Maharajganj	10.28	45.67	28.90	3	45	22
41.	Mainpuri	33.05	64.26	50.21	189	233	225
42.	Mathura	23.04	62.55	45.03	103	215	161
43.	Mau	27.86	59.44	43.80	149	178	145
44.	Meerut	35.62	64.47	51.30	210	237	232
45.	Mirzapur	22.32	54.75	39.68	91	121	103

(Contd.)

TABLE 11.24: *(Contd.)*

Sl. No.	District Name	Literacy Rate			All India Rank *		
		Female	Male	Total	Female	Male	Total
46.	Moradabad	18.34	41.65	31.03	56	27	32
47.	Muzaffarnagar	29.12	56.63	44.00	161	147	147
48.	Nainital	43.19	47.88	56.52	280	275	279
49.	Pilibhit	17.22	44.37	32.10	46	37	41
50.	Pithoragarh	38.37	79.44	59.01	236	385	303
51.	Pratapgarh	20.48	60.29	40.40	74	191	109
52.	Rae Bareli	21.01	53.30	37.78	80	106	82
53.	Rampur	15.31	33.79	25.37	25	4	9
54.	Saharanpur	28.10	53.85	42.11	152	109	128
55.	Shahjehanpur	18.59	42.68	32.07	58	30	40
56.	Siddharth Nagar	11.84	40.91	27.09	8	25	14
57.	Sitapur	16.90	43.10	31.41	42	33	34
58.	Sonbhadra	18.65	47.56	34.40	59	60	58
59.	Sultanpur	20.84	55.36	38.69	78	133	90
60.	Tehri Garhwal	26.41	72.10	48.38	128	320	209
61.	Unnao	23.62	51.63	38.70	110	92	91
62.	Uttarkashi	23.57	68.74	47.23	109	286	192
63.	Varanashi	28.87	64.37	47.70	159	234	197

* Ranks in the ascending order of relevant literacy rates.

TABLE 11.25: Women literacy Rate Districtwise—West Bengal (1991)

Sl. No.	District Name	Literacy Rate			All India Rank *		
		Female	Male	Total	Female	Male	Total
1.	Bankura	36.55	66.75	52.04	217	265	237
2.	Barddhaman	51.46	71.12	61.88	341	310	324
3.	Birbhum	37.17	59.26	48.56	223	175	211
4.	Calcutta	72.09	81.94	77.61	411	399	403
5.	Darjiling	47.84	67.07	57.95	309	271	290
6.	Howrah	57.83	76.11	67.62	376	352	365
7.	Hugli	56.90	75.77	66.78	373	352	365
8.	Jalpaiguri	33.20	56.00	45.09	190	139	162
9.	Koch Bihar	33.31	57.35	45.78	192	158	173
10.	Maldah	24.92	45.61	35.62	118	44	68
11.	Medinapur	56.63	81.27	69.32	369	396	377
12.	Murshidabad	29.57	46.42	38.28	165	51	86
13.	Nadia	44.42	60.05	52.53	288	188	240
14.	North 24-Parganas	57.99	74.72	66.81	377	342	366
15.	Puruliya	23.24	62.17	43.29	105	211	141
16.	South 24-Parganas	40.57	68.45	55.10	257	283	267
17.	West Dinajpur	27.87	49.79	39.29	150	78	98

* Ranks in the ascending order of relevant literacy rates.

TABLE 11.26: Women Literacy Rates Districtwise—A. and N. Islands (1991).

Sl. No.	District Name	Literacy Rate			All India Rank *		
		Female	Male	Total	Female	Male	Total
1.	Andamans	67.15	80.31	74.52	406	389	394
2.	Nicobars	55.26	70.68	63.72	362	305	339

* Ranks in the ascending order of relevant literacy rates.

TABLE 11.27 Women Literacy Rates Districtwise—Chandigarh (1991).

Sl. No.	District Name	Literacy Rate			All India Rank *		
		Female	Male	Total	Female	Male	Total
1.	Chandigarh	72.34	77.81	82.04	412	402	406

* Ranks in the ascending order of relevant literacy rates.

TABLE 11.28 Women literacy Rates Districtwise—Dadra and Nagar Haveli (1991).

Sl. No.	District Name	Literacy Rate			All India Rank *		
		Female	Male	Total	Female	Male	Total
1.	Dadra and Nagar Haveli	26.98	53.56	40.71	134	108	117
2.	Dadra and Nagar Haveli	26.98	53.56	40.71	4	4	3

*Ranks in the ascending order of relevant literacy rates.

TABLE 11.29: Women Literacy Rates Districtwise—Daman and Diu (1991).

Sl. No.	District Name	Literacy Rate			All India Rank*		
		Female	Male	Total	Female	Male	Total
1.	Daman	64.39	85.24	75.34	397	414	397
2.	Diu	51.99	78.06	64.46	346	378	347

* Ranks in the ascending order of relevant literacy rates.

TABLE 11.30: Women Literacy Rates Districtwise—Lakshadweep (1991).

Sl. No.	District Name	Literacy Rate Female	Male	Total	All India Rank* Female	Male	Total
1.	Laskshadweep	90.18	72.89	81.78	423	414	419

* Ranks in the ascending order of relevant literacy rates.

TABLE 11.31: Women Literacy Rates Districtwise—Pondicherry (1991).

Sl. No.	District Name	Literacy Rate Female	Male	Total	All India Rank * Female	Male	Total
1.	KARAIKAL	66.65	85.05	75.78	403	412	398
2.	MANE	91.73	96.90	94.10	433	436	426
3.	PONDICHERRY	63.60	82.75	73.35	396	408	391
4.	YANAM	71.19	82.38	76.86	410	405	402

* Ranks in the ascending order of relevant literacy rates.

TABLE 11.32: Women Literacy Rate—10 Top Districts in India

Sl.No.	District	State	Female Literacy Rate
1.	Kottayam	Kerala	94.00
2.	Pathanamthitta	Kerala	93.29
3.	Alappuzha	Kerala	91.12
4.	Ernakulam	Kerala	89.27
5.	Kannur	Kerala	87.65
6.	Kollam	Kerala	87.65
7.	Thrissur	Kerala	87.00
8.	Kozhikode	Kerala	86.94
9.	Thiruvananthapuram	Kerala	85.79
10.	Aizawal	Mizoram	85.51

TABLE 11.33: Women Literacy Rate—10 Bottam Districts in India

Sl. No.	District	State	Female Literacy Rate
1.	Barmer	Rajasthan	7.68
2.	Jalaur	Rajasthan	7.75
3.	Gonda	U.P.	12.58
4.	Kishangang	Bihar	10.38
5.	Bahraich	U.P.	10.73
6.	Jhabua	Madhya Pradesh	11.52
7.	Jaisalmer	Rajasthan	11.28
8.	Siddharth Nagar	U.P.	11.84
9.	Maharajgang	U.P	10.28
10.	Budaun	U.P.	12.82

TABLE 11.34: Female Literacy : Top District in Each State (1991)

Sl. No.	State	District	Literacy Rate		
			Female	Male	Total
1.	Andhra Pradesh	Hyderabad	63.56	78.90	71.52
2.	Arunachal Pradesh	Lohit	59.02	59.02	49.21
3.	Assam	Jorhat	56.88	73.29	65.51
4.	Bihar	Purlia Singhbhum	45.50	71.18	59.05
5.	Goa	North Goa	68.86	86.15	77.6
6.	Gujarat	Gandhinagar	80.51	93.21	87.11
7.	Haryana	Ambala	56.62	75.08	66.41
8.	Himachal Pradesh	Hamirpur	65.90	85.11	74.88
9.	Karnataka	Bangalore	68.81	82.94	76.27
10.	Kerala	Kottayam	94.00	97.46	95.72
11.	Madhya Pradesh	Bhopal	54.17	73.14	64.27
12.	Maharashtra	Greater Bombay	75.80	87.87	82.50
13.	Manipur	Imphal	58.32	82.80	70.74
14.	Meghalaya	East Khasi Hills	57.04	62.86	60.04
15.	Mizoram	Aizawal	85.51	90.40	88.06
16.	Nagaland	Mokokchung	74.88	80.52	69.16
17.	Orissa	Cuttack	50.38	75.74	63.28
18.	Punjab	Hoshiarpur	61.48	79.31	70.74
19.	Rajasthan	Ajmer	34.50	75.74	63.28
20.	Sikkim	East District	55.66	73.10	65.13
21.	Tamil Nadu	Kanniya-Kumari	78.39	85.70	82.06
22.	Tripura	West Tripura	55.15	75.87	65.83
23.	Uttar pradesh	Dehradun	59.26	77.95	69.50
24.	West Bengal	Calcutta	72.09	81.94	77.61
25.	A. and N. Islands	Andaman	66.22	79.68	73.74
27.	Dadra and Nagar Haveli	Dadra & Nagar Haveli	26.10	52.07	39.45
28.	Delhi		68.01	82.63	76.96
29.	Daman and Diu	Daman	64.39	85.24	75.39
30.	Lakshadweep	Lakshadweep	70.88	87.06	79.23
31.	Pondicherry	Yanam	65.63	83.68	74.74
26.	Chandigarh	Chandigarh	73.61	82.67	78.73

Note : Figures for Jammu and Kashmir are not available as 1991 Census was not conducted there.

PART III

GLOBAL OVERVIEW

Select Documents

Women's Education: Comparative Indicators

12

Women: Challenges to the Year 2000

Women's Education: Key to Empowerment

If you educate a man, you educate one person; if you educate a woman, you educate an entire family.

Mythologies around the world have ascribed to women the supreme literary achievements of creating alphabets and inventing language. "Goddess of the Logos, Mother of the Gods, One with Creation, thou art Intelligence, the Mother of Science...." begins the Hindu prayer to the mother of Krishna. Queen Isis has been credited with conferring the alphabet on the Egyptians, as did Medusa on Hercules in Greece, while the Indian goddess-priestess Kali invented the Sanskrit alphabet. Even the world's first novel, *The Tale of Genji,* was written by Lady Murasaki in eleventh century Japan.

These scattered examples show that women were once at the centre of the world of learning before patriarchal dictates denied them the right to education, condemning them to centuries of intellectual obscurantism. Yet, even after education became a requirement for men—though it remained a forbidden fruit for women almost everywhere—a few unique women succeeded in circumventing formidable obstacles to excel in all fields of learning.

Illiteracy: A Lifelong Cul-De-Sac

According to the United Nations Educational, Scientific and Cultural Organization (UNESCO), in 1990, 26.5 per cent of the adult population of the world (948.1 million) were illiterate. Of that number, 346.5 million were men (i.e. 19.4 per cent of the male population) while 601.6 million were women (i.e. 33.6 per cent of the female population). The numbers were even more striking for developing countries, where the illiteracy rate for women stood at 45 per cent.

For these women, illiteracy compounds their other problems, contributing to their marginalization within the family, the workplace and public life. It accounts for the fact that women have often not benefited from socio-economic and technological progress. Illiterate women are invariably caught in a vicious circle of poverty, repeated child bearing, ill health and powerlessness, lacking the means to break out of their predicament: education.

The direct correlation between literacy, health, economic and political power and the exercise of informed choice, especially for women, cannot be emphasized enough. Education decisively determines a woman's access to paid employment, her earning capacity, her overall health, control over her fertility, family size and spacing, and the education and health of her family. For example, it has been found that women with seven years or more of education tend to marry on average four years later and have 2.2 fewer children statistically than women with no schooling.

Education also plays a crucial role in child survival. In Ghana, women with no education are twice as likely to lose children as mothers with primary schooling and four times as likely as mothers with secondary education. In Indonesia, mothers who have not received any education are three times more likely to lose children under five than mother with some schooling.

In addition, education helps women overcome social prejudice, take control of their lives and assume a status and identity beyond child bearing, thereby allowing them to participate more fully in the public life of their community. It opens up wider horizons, creates new opportunities and, most importantly, empowers women with choice. And, last but not the least, education is the single most important weapon to combat sexual stereotyping and discriminatory attitudes towards women.

The Education Avalanche

The dramatic global increase in school enrolment between 1950 and 1980, striking especially in developing countries, was tantamount to a revolution that promised to sweep away illiteracy, improve the quality of life of millions of the world's people and decisively change the course of women's lives. Massive investments in social services meant that education budgets increased seven-fold in the developing world and four-fold in industrialized countries, while all countries adopted universal primary education as a fundamental goal. Primary school swelled to include girls who had virtually been excluded until then in many developing countries, while modest but significant enrolment increases for girls in secondary schools and in higher education courses were also recorded.

The educational gains for girls and women at all levels were impressive. The world adult female illiteracy rate fell from 45 per cent in 1960 to 35 per cent in 1985. Female enrolment in primary schools in the developing world was as high as 44 per cent by 1980, up 7 per cent from 1950. Near universal primary school enrolment had been attained in Latin America and much of Asia. Girls' enrolment in secondary schools increased from 24 per cent 1950 to 40 per cent in 1980.

Throughout this entire period, women continued to close the gap with men, not only in secondary school enrolment but also in university. Today there are more women than men enrolled in higher education in several countries, according to UNESCO sources. For instance, in 1990 in Qatar, there were 202 women per 100 men in university, in Dominica, there were 200 women per 100 men; likewise, in Lesotho 172 per 100, in Mongolia 149 per 100, in Panama 136 per 100, in Bulgaria 124 per 100, and in Portugal 113 per 100. Yet, the gap between male and female literacy rates grew as illiteracy rates for men fell faster than for women, highlighting the fact that access to education continued to be easier for males than for females.

Women have also made great progress in the teaching profession and, after decades of improvement, half or more of first-level teachers around the world (excluding Africa) are women. In Asia and the Pacific, 49 per cent of first-level teachers are now women, compared to 38 per cent in 1970; in Africa, 39 per cent are now women, compared to 28 per cent in 1970.

The Effects of the Economic Crisis on Education

The economic crisis of the 1980s and the remedial structural adjustment programmes adopted by developing countries under the auspices of international financial institutions abruptly slowed and, in some instances, actually reversed the steady progress of preceding decades. Pre-existing inequalities experienced by women worsened during the economic crisis and women suffered disproportionately from the cuts in education. Rapid population growth also contributed to the rise in the total number of illiterate women—a trend which is expected to continue into the twenty-first century.

According to the United Nations Children's Fund (UNICEF), the world's least developed countries slashed their education budgets by 25 per cent per capita during the 1980s in order to deal with the debt crisis; Latin America and the Caribbean effected the largest cuts. In Jamaica, per capital real expenditure on education was cut by about one third from 1980 to 1985. Bolivia and Costa Rica cut their education expenditures by over 45 and 41 per cent respectively.

The deterioration of education programmes became most acute in many African nations which had made great strides after achieving independence. Some countries virtually eliminated education from their budgets: Zaire, one of the world's poorest countries with one of the highest illiteracy rates, slashed its education budget from 15.2 per cent of total government expenditure in 1972 to 0.8 per cent in 1986. As school buildings and equipment decayed, teachers' salaries were devalued up to 10 times as a result of spiralling inflation, and school fees were introduced in many countries. The dramatic fall in per capita income often meant that parents could not afford the transportation costs or the school supplies their children required. Reports of schools operating without desks, black-boards, slates or books became common; some African communities, in a desperate attempt to provide even minimum of learning for their children, created makeshift outdoor schools with volunteer teachers, most of whom were women.

The impact of the global economic crisis and subsequent efforts at adjustment on the availability and quality of education has yet to be fully assessed, but as Adebayo Adedeji, former Executive Secretary of the Economic Commission for Africa, recently warned, "If things continue like this, Africa will have more illiterate people as a proportion of the population than at independence" —a scenario which will have disastrous consequences for the continent's future, for, as Adedeji put it: "How can you develop an illiterate society?"

During the 1980s, as a result of the economic crisis:

— Some 16 low-income and 14 middle-income countries with ongoing structural adjustment programmes experienced falling ratios of primary school enrolment. In the first category, female enrolments were most severely affected in Somalia, Togo and Mali where rates fell 40, 18 and 15 per cent respectively. In the second category, Yemen,

Chile and Costa Rica were most affected;

— Improvements in secondary education enrolments slowed down in much of Asia and Africa, and in several countries there was a lower enrolment for girls than for boys among the poorer strata of society;
— In six Latin American countries, education deteriorated both in quantitative and qualitative terms; and
— Drop-out rates increased in several countries as a result of the introduction of school fees.

Girls are often the first to suffer from these set-backs since female education is not a priority among families, local communities and governments. If a family is to choose which child will continue its education, preference is invariably given to boys, in the belief that their chances for employment are better than girls'. Hard-pressed parents also tend to take their girls out of school to help them with domestic work and child-care, or else to marry them off. In addition, rapid population growth and shrinking education budgets in many developing countries mean that there are not enough schools to accommodate the school-age population, which expanded by a staggering 35 per cent between 1970 and 1985. Again, girls are the first to be excluded.

The introduction of school fees in developing countries already suffering from declining per capita incomes further undermined girls' access to education. Moreover, as social services available to women deteriorated during the 1980s, their workload increased along with their financial responsibilities, and education became an additional burden. In Uganda, for instance, about a third of mothers now pay school fees that were previously taken care of by their spouses. Even where education is free, however, the cost of basic school items can be prohibitively expensive for poor families: in 1985, Zambian parents had to allocate over one fifth of their per capita income per child for basic school supplies — an insurmountable financial burden considering that these families generally average six or seven children.

Rural Women: When Education Interferes with Survival

Rural societies, which depend heavily on women for their survival, are especially resistant to educating them. In Afghanistan, for instance, the illiteracy rate for women in rural areas is 93.8 per cent, versus 56.4 per cent in cities. In Benin, 92.1 per cent of rural women are illiterate compared to 59 per cent of urban women.

Rural women tend to have more children, be poorer, and, in their struggle to survive, have little or no time and energy to spare on adult literacy programmes. Children of female-headed households in rural areas are often put to work in order to ensure the survival of the family. According to a study published in 1984, in India, even though 60 per cent of rural children were enrolled in primary school, after five years only 16 per cent of the girls continued to attend classes, as opposed to 35 per cent of the boys. Survival needs aside, rural women are also more likely to encounter resistance from within the family to their pursuing an education: an educated woman might pose a threat to her husband and upset the family status quo.

Recession in the Developed World

In the industrialized world, following the education boom of previous decades, the economic recession of the late 1970s came as a shock. It was tackled with cut-backs which struck a severe blow at the quality of the entire educational system, from primary schools to universities.

Female enrolment in adult literacy and education programmes in industrialized countries also suffered, while university enrolments reportedly declined as fees skyrocketed and the availability of scholarships declined drastically. In the United Kingdom, educational grants which were previously the right of every national became restricted; in the United States, the cost of university education became prohibitively high for many middle-class families.

The Gender Gap

The gap between literacy rates for men and women has decreased significantly in developing countries, especially in Latin America over the past 20 years, and particularly for young women under 24 years of age. In some regions, illiteracy rates for young women have been cut in half. In Latin America and the Caribbean, the percentage of illiterate young women aged 20 to 24 in 1970 was 19.4; by 1990, it had fallen to 8 per cent. In sub-Saharan Africa (including the Sudan but excluding South Africa), the equivalent figures are 80.3 and 49.2 per cent; in Eastern and Western Asia, illiteracy among young women fell from 37.9 to 12.2 per cent.

Despite this progress, however, today there are considerably more illiterate women than men in most parts of the world, particularly in

Africa and Eastern and south-Eastern Asia where the ratio approaches 2 to 1 in certain regions. Furthermore, the gap between male and female literacy remains high in most of the developing world, especially for adult women living in rural areas. Even in Europe, where only 2 per cent of the population is illiterate, there are twice as many women as men who cannot read and write.

One of the primary reasons for the education gap is that girls are brought up and educated only for "traditional occupations". Social custom often accounts for the popular belief that girls do not need an education since they will marry and raise children rather than work at a job outside the home where educational qualifications are required. "A girls has the additional disadvantage of being born into a world that does not even expect her to succeed, a world that perhaps does not really want her to succeed, a world that has been systematically schooling her for failure", argued the 1985 *State of the World's Women.* Having always been excluded from education, many women have come to believe that their abilities are restricted to cooking, cleaning and minding children all of which are crucial, yet unpaid and undervalued tasks.

Such beliefs have been reinforced by sexist stereotypes which are pervasive in textbooks and curricula from elementary schools to universities. Consider the following Introductory Logic exercise:

"Exhibit the logical form for the following sentences by translating them into the notation of the predicate calculus;

(*a*) Susan is feather-brained;
(*b*) Janet is feather-brained;
(*c*) All women are feather-brained;
(*d*) No man is feather-brained;
(*e*) Some men are not feather-brained; and
(*f*) John is not feather-brained".

Girls' secondary school enrolment lags behind boys' in much of Asia and Africa, and in southern Asia the discrepancy is particularly striking, with only 40 girls per 100 boys enrolled at secondary level. In Afghanistan, only 9 per cent of girls are enrolled in secondary school, while in Pakistan the equivalent figure is 17 per cent. Girls' enrolment in vocational and technical training schools is also very low. As an increasing number of women around the world seek paid employment, vocational and technical training becomes all the more significant.

The gap in male/female university enrolment continues to be very wide in most countries. Furthermore, female enrolment in science, engineering, business and law is especially low. There has been little progress in the promotion of women in university-level teaching. For example, a recent investigation into the male to female ratio of tenured professors at Harvard University in the United States found that there were 161 tenured male professors as opposed to less than half a dozen women. Such examples of education-related discrimination point to the fact that education should not be dealt with in isolation but as part of the advancement of the status of women as a whole.

Educating Women for the Future

As a result of the set-backs that the economic crisis inflicted on education during the 1980s and the criticism of the devastating effects of adjustment and stabilization policies in much of the developing world, special measures to mitigate the adverse effect of structural adjustment programmes on education were adopted in the late 1980s. However, women have been largely absent from such programmes. Ghana's model Programme of Action to Mitigate the Social Costs of Adjustment (PAMSCAD), designed to cushion the impact of adjustment among the hardest hit the urban poor, retrenched civil servants and small-scale farmers-is no exception.

Tackling the current regression in education, particularly in the developing world, should be a component of sustainable development strategies in the 1990s, considering that:

— About 75 per cent of women aged 25 and over cannot read and write in much of Asia and Africa;
— In some countries, illiteracy is virtually pandemic. In Burkina Faso and Somalia, only 6 per cent of adult women are literate, while in Afgahistan and Nepal the figures are 8 and 12 per cent respectively; and
— In Africa, primary school enrolment was only 76 per cent in 1987 (84 per cent for boys and 68 per cent for girls).

Education Challenges to the Year 2000

Educating women is a high return investment in socio-economic development for society as a whole since, by educating a woman, one is in effect reaching an entire family. At present, however, this simple equation appears to go unrecognized by development planners and governments alike. If the recorded negative trend in female school enrolment is to be reversed and the gender gap closed over the next decade, it is imperative that governments, as well as the private sector.

— Make a concentrated world-wide effort to end illiteracy among females by the year 2000;
— Create incentives aimed at achieving equal literacy rates for males and females; measure progress towards the goal of universal literacy and numeracy by the year 2000;
— Intensify efforts towards universal primary education during the 1990s by making education a priority concern;
— Revise all textbooks to eliminate sex stereotyping and to include the contributions of women to civilization;
— Improve secondary education for girls, especially in rural areas, by introducing double shift or single-sex schools in regions where gender segregation discourages female education; provide incentives to families for girls to remain in school;
— Guarantee equal access to quality education and training in all subjects and at all levels; provide preferential treatment or financial subsidies which would facilitate female access to male-dominated universities;
— Promote more women teachers at secondary and university level, encouraging them to act as role models and mentors for female students;
— Increase the salary scale and status of the overall teaching profession, from kindergarten to university, in recognition of the fact that education is a vital key to the quality of life;
— Encourage women to select male-dominated occupations and desegregrate the curricula; improve training in the sciences and mathematics, as well as in vocational, technical and business subjects, for girls and young women;
— Provide convenient access to adult education for women, including child-care facilities and night classes; and
— Develop adult legal, economic and political literacy programmes to augment basic literacy and numeracy.

13

SAARC Decade of The Girl Child, 1991

Introduction

The Heads of State/Government of SAARC countries met at Male in November, 1990. They decided to observe the years 1991-2000 AD as "SAARC Decade of the Girl Child." They endorsed the recommendations made by the Second SAARC Ministerial Meeting of Women in Development held in Islamabad in June, 1990.

The successful observance of this programme spreading over a decade requires an insight into the fieldwork already done earlier in the National Workshop of 1987 and SAARC Workshop of 1988. The recommendations of both these workshops are given here so as to facilitate the planning of the programmes of the "SAARC Decade of the Girl Child."

The Main Observations and Recommendations of the Workshop

1. A holistic perspective approach be adopted for the overall development of the female child instead of the prevalent segmented approach.
2. A correlation has to be established between different policies such as the National Health Policy, National Children Policy, National Policy on Child Labour etc., with special emphasis on the needs of the female child.
3. Certain indices such as religion, caste, region, literacy, health, nutritional level, incidence of mortality, morbidity and poverty be identified and utilized at different levels for better coverage of disadvantaged girl children. Within this the priority should be to

---

Source : Naya Shikshak/Teacher Today, July-September 1991, Bikaner.

identify the most disadvantaged group, that is, a cluster of disadvantaged working girl children, so that immediate efforts can focus upon alleviating their status.

4. In programmes and policies, male/female stereotypes should be rejected. Content and curricula of programmes such as non-formal education be formulated in such a way that they portray positive images of women and girl children.
5. Age limit for training programmes such as TRYSEM be relaxed in order to encompass female children, i.e., adolescent girls. Protective discrimination be provided for girls in all existing government programmes. Reservations be made for girls in admissions to professional educational institutions.
6. Provision of support services such as provision of fuel, fodder, water-supply and child-care is essential to reduce the burden of the female child and at the same time to enable her to avail of education/training programmes.
7. Provision of child-care if made along with the government's training programmes would enable more women to participate in these programmes.
8. Alternative models of child-care to suit regional conditions and needs should be formulated.
9. Grass-root workers be sensitized to the dangers of stereotype roles. Functionaries, particularly at the lower levels, be sensitized to the need for communicating positive messages.
10. The media also should be geared to project positive images of women and girls but no derogatory or contradictory images.
11. Censor Board and other media monitoring agencies need to be oriented to issues regarding women and girl children.
12. It was observed that during the last two decades, there has been a complete shift towards female sterilization which became synonymous with laproscopic operations. This trend should be reversed.
13. Fertility awareness programmes be taken up on a large-scale for adolescent girls and boys.
14. It was found that virtually no data exist on girl-children, particularly on those between 6 to 14 years. There is negligible gender-based information collected on children in the ICDS programme. Research has to be taken up to build a data base on this group. The suggested areas were education, labour, household chores, socialization, age at marriage and effective marriage.

15. While formulating the national vocational training schemes for girls, local needs and conditions should be taken into consideration.

SAARC WORKSHOP ON THE GIRL-CHILD

Recommendations

The thrust of all recommendations made at the concluding session of the workshop was on formulating action plans for the girl-child at the national level, respecting the variety and divergent cultures of each country as well as at the level of regional cooperation between SAARC countries. The following recommendations were made by delegates representing their respective countries, addressing specific problems peculiar to their own culture and social conditions.

BHUTAN

Discrimination against the girl-child in Bhutan is not a part of the cultural or social ethos as in other countries. Problems, however, arise on account of the difficult geographical terrain and shortage of manpower which is responsible for limiting the access of girls to educational facilities, health-care and participation in public life. Areas requiring attention were identified as enrolment and drop-out at the middle school level, exploitation of young girls from villages working as domestic help in the homes of modern couples who both go out to work, access to health facilities and lack of infrastructural support.

Recommendations

1. Undertake research studies to find out reasons for low enrolment and drop-out of adolescent girls.
2. Reduce workload of parents so that girls are left free to attend school.
3. Encourage participation of girls in sports and cultural activities.
4. Create awareness of health through programmes of health education, especially with respect to hazards of early marriage and attendant problems.
5. Institute programmes for adult education, both formal and non-formal.
6. Train women volunteers as health workers oriented towards mother and child-care.

7. Orientation of school curricula according to skills.
8. Seek encouragement from government for greater participation of women in the National Assembly.
9. Adequate infrastructural development such as roads to facilitate women's access to school and health facilities.

INDIA

Discrimination against the girls in India exists in all sectors, particularly in education, health and employment. An adverse sex ratio, higher malnutrition, maternal morbidity and mortality, low school enrolment and high dropout rates, low skill levels with low value at work together with lack of legal protection are some of the priority areas that need redressal. Social problems such as a poor self-image, early marriages and dowry also need to be tackled simultaneously. It appears that the strong racial memory of women as Shakti which was prevalent in the older matriarchal cultures has been largely forgotten.

The general recommendations proposed were that the constitutional guarantees of equality for men and women must be implemented and programmes designed specially to reach the adolescent girl and the girl child. Additionally, all development programmes must have a strong focus on this target group and schemes which adversely affect even a small proportion of girl children should be modified or redesigned. Sectorwise recommendations were as follows:

Education

1. Compulsory education for boys and girls. It will be obligatory under law to send all children to school or non-formal courses upto at least primary level.
2. Analysis of reason for girl school drop-outs and innovative measures like non-formal education, change in school hours for girls, provision of creche facilities for girls, second shift for girls should be provided.
3. Non-monetary incentives to parents and communities for encouraging participation of girls in education at all levels.
4. Vocational training in economically viable skills to be integrated with education for older girls.
5. Empowerment of women in order to achieve self-reliance. The objectives of the National Policy on Education and National

Perspective Plan for Women to be examined in detail.

6. A determined percentage of GNP to be reserved for education up to school final levels and 50 per cent of this budget be reserved for education of girls.
7. The school curriculum and extra-curricular activities to be reviewed and special efforts made to reverse role models and sex stereotypes.
8. School enrolment should ask for either parents' name and specific attempts should be made at deletion of the concept of illegitimacy.

Health

1. Appropriate health education which includes fundamental information regarding physiology of reproduction and health facilities including abortion facilities, nutrition, balanced diet and special needs, especially for the adolescent age-group.
2. Education of parents regarding health and nutrition needs of the girls-child with emphasis during growth spurt.
3. Schools can provide iron-folic acid tablets to all adolescent girls. For girls not going to school, IFA tablets may be provided by ANM or any other worker at village level.
4. Many time-consuming and arduous chores are performed by mothers and hence automatically by their daughters. Special efforts to introduce low-cost time-saving scientific gadgets to reduce health hazards are needed.
5. Counselling services to cater specifically to the problems of growing girls and women. Existing family counselling centres should extend to children and special recreational facilities to be provided for girls.
6. Positive incentives to parents for health-care and timely interventions for children, particularly girls.
7. Use of medical technology to determine the sex of the foetus should be banned by law.

Resocialisation

1. Massive public awareness campaign to raise the value of the girl-child.
2. Listing of organisations, such as, the following:

   — Professional bodies, i.e., demographers, sociologists, doctors, scientists, educationists, lawyers;

- Academic training institutions;
- Community-level organisations, Panchayats;
- All educational institutions;
- Voluntary organisations involved in social development; and
- Government at all levels.

3. Reactive existing institutions at Central and State levels for situational analysis and implementation of the programme necessary for positive improvement in the status of the girl-child.
4. Mobilisation of media for raising awareness and projecting the right images. This would include the following:

- Press
- Radio
- TV
- Posters
- Street theatre.

In order to achieve this, a consistent approach reflecting the policy objective of equality has to be developed and monitored.

5. Public awareness campaign to raise the values of girls, and present alternatives other than marriage and motherhood.

- encourage employment of girls.
- enlist support of various levels.

6. Specific orientation programmes for sensitization towards issues related to girl-child with the following;

- Professional Groups
- Journalists and Media Persons
- School Teachers
- Administrators
- Panchayats
- Anganwadi Workers
- ANMS

7. Build upon women's organisations for community binding on women's issues.

Legislation

1. Awareness and information should be generated on the following:

   — Laws of Inheritance of property
   — Divorce/Maintenance and Child Custody
   — Equal Remuneration Act
   — Maternity Benefit Act.

2. Laws such as Anti-Rape Act, Antidowry Act, ITPA, Child Labour Laws be examined and positive attempts made to revise these laws in favour of the girl.
3. Formulate legislation regarding compulsory education and against exploitative situations such as domestic servants, bonded labour, child prostitution.

Information

1. In order to plan public awareness campaigns, systematic collection of information to highlight, local, regional, sex disparties in demographic data, education and health differentials, social attitudes and practices has to be undertaken through existing policy—making bodies.
2. Specific interventions including communication campaigns to be based on the above information.

MALDIVES

The girl-child has equal opportunities for education and self-development as the boy in Maldives, including the right to decide her career and marriage partner. Discrimination, however, comes at the point of adolescence, where without opportunities for further study or employment, she enters the cycle of early marriage, early and frequent pregnancies, divorce and remarriage. The consequences of this pattern of socialisation are a high maternal history rate, low birth weight babies and associated complications. The following recommendations were made with respect to the above:

1. Awarencess building through the media, health and education sectors on all the islands in the Maldives, for increasing age at marriage; delay of first pregnancy till 18 and subsequent pregnancies

for a further minimum of 2 years; improvement of maternal and child nutrition, and need for stability in marriage.
2. Improvement in accessibility of contraceptives to the rural population.
3. Inclusion of career or vocational guidance for school curricula in both urban and rural areas.
4. Formation of girls clubs to provide recreational activities for girls after leaving school.
5. Starting radio and TV programmes for girls in the age-group 14 to 20 years, to widen their scope of interest.
6. Stimulating income generating activities for girls in the same age-group, i.e. 14 to 20 years.
7. Training of health personnel towards improving antenatal care, and upgrade facilities at health centres and regional hospitals.
8. Encouraging the participation of NGO's in all government programmes for women's development, education, health and vocational training.

The Government of Maldives has certain ongoing national programmes such as the expanded programmes of immunisation for all by 1990, birth control for all the islands and eradication of illiteracy and universal primary education by 1995. Five population centres are planned with provision for higher education and health facilities, as well as centres for rural areas under the Integrated Rural Development Programme. The recommendations and plan of action could be linked to the above programmes, together with new programmes to specifically improve the situation of the girl-child.

NEPAL

In Nepal, the girl-child as a target group has received the attention of policy plannets and included in implementation strategies. Data needs to be collected to see how far ongoing programmes have reached the girl-child.

General Recommendations

1. The Eighth National Development Plan should incorporate the objectives of the ongoing Seventh Plan by specifying the girl-child as the target group in the action plan of the National Policy for Child Development.

2. The upper age limit for the girl-child should be defined as 20 years.
3. The already established *Bal Mandirs* in the 75 districts of Nepal should be strengthened into a nucleus which fully functions and acts as a watchdog to raise the social, economic and cultural status of the girl-child by the year 2000.
4. The successful model of the non-formal education programmes for girls, the *Cheli-beti* classes should be replicated fully throughout Nepal.
5. The equal access to girls' and women's education programmes should be extended to other remote areas of Nepal.
6. The ongoing legal literacy programme should spell out the girl-child as their target group while dealing with women's problems such as desertion, early marriage etc.
7. The legal age of marriage should be raised to 18 years with consent of parents, and 20 years without consent.
8. All Women-in-Development programmes should have a special focus on the girl-child in their programmes in terms of labour and time-saving schemes and income-generating programmes.
9. The girl-child should not be the focus of only child and maternal health programmes but should be specified in all immunisation and child health delivery programmes too.
10. All preventive health care programmes should include the sex ratio of children in growth monitoring and running family planning programmes.

Specific Recommendations

1. The ongoing free primary education should be raised to Class 7 or lower primary level.
2. Free text-books, scholarships for girls and national sponsor-ship programmes for all girl children should be vigorously encouraged.
3. The motivation programme for schools, teachers, parents who encourage girls' education should be encouraged by various means.
4. The ongoing child-care centres, home-based programmes and child to child programmes should be expanded by Government and NGOs.
5. The Media, i.e. TV, newspaper, radio, posters, charts should portray and be conscious about the girl child. Nepal urged the SAARC member countries to declare 1989-90 as the Year of the

Girl-Child, and include this in their action plan. It was felt that this would create immense public awareness and draw the attention of policy-planners to the need for remoulding their national plan by focussing on the girl-child. Since UNICEF works in the SAARC region, UNICEF should advocate the cause of the Girl-Child by supporting regional studies and media production which should reflect the status of the girl-child in the region so that integrated over-all plans and programmes could be chalked out.

PAKISTAN

The objectives of the Government with regard to improving the situation of the girl-child are firstly to create awareness among people, especially women, that the girl-child is an asset, not a liability, as she helps the family most and therefore, needs equal opportunities for survival and development, and secondly, to enrich the girl-child herself with knowledge of her rights as enjoined by religion, the Constitution and the law. Within this framework recommendations were made for a holistic approach to be adopted for ameliorating the status of the girl-child. This should include:

1. Creation of awareness at all levels and through all media.
2. Programmes for survival of children, provision of health coverage to rural women, food supplements to the poor.
3. Extension of school health programmes to all girls' schools upto high school level in phases.
4. Popularisation of girls' education and reorientation of the curriculum from primary to high school.

   These should include projects for destitute, neglected, working and exploited girls.

8. Laws concerning girls and women should be reviewed and enforced, the procedures being simplified and decentralised.
9. At least 50 per cent of the target groups should come into the fold of survival and development strategy through formal as well as alternate measures.
10. Voluntary action should be motivated to join hands with the Government.

SRI LANKA

In Sri Lanka, the concept of the girl-child as a specific target group is a new one. With the forthcoming census in 1991, the time is opportune for collection of data specific to women and the girl-child. For the first time, the census will include a one per cent sample on women.

Problems in major sectors were identified as low birth weight babies, due to malnutrition among women, iodine deficiency and malnutrition in adolescent girls, curriculum differentiation based on gender bias in secondary schools, drop-out among girls in school and special problems of young girls due to factors such as migration of mothers in search of work, and the prevailing armed and civil con-flicts. The following recommendations were made for the different sectors in view of these problems:

Health

1. Anaemia Intervention programmes in the field of anaemia control to be popularised.
2. More income generating activities specifically in rural areas for mothers and adolescent girls should be introduced to supplement the family income.
3. In isolated pockets where iodine defficiency is prevalent, iodinated salt to be distributed free, and an awareness campaign to make them realise that iodine deficiency is preventable.

Nutrition

1. Studies on its different aspects should be undertaken to ascertain why malnutrition among girls is on the increase.
2. Economic status of the women to be increased through self-employment programmes.
3. Increase nutritional awareness programmes.
4. Focus nutritional interventions on female children, particularly during the pre-school, pre-puberty and adolescent phases of their development as this involvement would lead to better health for pregnant mothers and their children.
5. Within the school health services and the educational system, tangible programmes for female children would be useful, specially in the more remote and rural schools where malnutrition levels

are high or in extreme climatic situations.

6. Non-governmental organisations to be closely associated in carrying out these intervention programmes.

General Awareness Programmes for the Society

1. Introducing inputs into the primary school curriculum that promote the concept of gender equality and the sharing of responsibility with the female in society as equal partners and improving the status of girls.
2. Awareness programmes through print and mass media, of employment opportunities open to girls after completing vocational courses.
3. Curriculum in the secondary schools to include vocational courses.
4. Study to be conducted to assertain the reasons and introduction of measures related to the drop-out rate.
5. Under employment—a survey to be conducted to ascertain percentage of girls engaged in domestic labour and their problems, and the present legislation regarding employment of young persons to be strictly enforced.
6. Vocational guidance centres to guide the girls to complete secondary school which would considerably increase their chances of gainful technical employment and self-employment.

Legislation

1. Vigorous legal literacy campaigns should be launched and legal aid centres for the rural women should be set up at every provincial district level. Three general recommendations have been identified as follows:

   (a) Adolescent girls/women migrating abroad for employment are made to act as mother substitutes which deprives them of childhood and the benefits that go with them. Therefore, special programmes to be designed to help them lead normal lives in the absence of their mother's protection;

   (b) Army and civil conflict in several parts of the country have affected the normal growing up process of the girls in the family. Therefore, special efforts to be taken to help them lead a normal life. Rehabilitation and counselling centres to be established to help them overcome this problem. Entrepreneur development skills for women to be instituted; and

(c) An action plan would be drafted keeping in mind that the girls should not be isolated from the boys, and allowed opportunity to grow up together, keeping in mind the principles of equality, human rights dignity.

Recommendations for Regional and International Co-operation

1. A SAARC forum for learning and adopting each other schemes and programmes, sharing information and location of materials.
2. A SAARC Media network on the girl-child which could form part of the existing SAARC Audio-Visual Exchange programmes.
3. Frequent exchange of information and experiences of successful achievements in survival, development and equality of the girl-child, including international experiences.
4. Establishment of a SAARC Institution for Training, Research and Development of the girl-child for equality. This could serve as a clearing house for information sharing.
5. A network for training of master trainers, planners, and policy makers to be established at the national level.
6. The international community should assist in development of forums for ensuring implementation of the UN Declaration of the Rights of the Child, as well as redressal of grievances. The United Nations may be persuaded to adopt the much awaited National Convention on the Rights of the Child.
7. International meets for sports and cultural activities, and scholarships for new types of vocations.

It was also proposed in conclusions that a meeting be held following year to review in the appropriate SAARC forum the action taken by each country under its Action Plan.

See also Appendix-12 "Council of Europe: Education of Women in Australia."

14

Literacy, Education and Women (1992)

Education is a powerful instrument of progress. Literacy is the most basic and necessary of learning skills. Women's literacy and education. is challenge of the decade. It is essential to development, which is impossible without the active participation of women and their participation depends, to a very large extent, upon their education. Now it is agreed by all development agencies that the education of women is important in order to promote and maintain family education, health and nutrition, general well-being and environmental care and protection etc.

Discrimination Against Women in Literacy and Education

Despite all efforts, in 1990 there were 948 million illiterates in the world—a figure which has not changed substantially since 1985. If efforts to deal with the problem are not intensified, projections for the year 2000 indicate at best only a very slight decrease.

Rapid population growth, poverty and certain political and economic mechanisms in society, all linked to incomplete coverage of primary education for school-age children, are at the root of the constant increase in the absolute numbers of illiterates in the world.

It is a fact that more women than men are illiterate, and there are many reasons for this. In most societies women have lower status than men. From childhood on they have less access to education, and sometimes to food and health-care. As adults, not only do they frequently receive less education, but work longer hours, have lower incomes and little or no access to ownership of property.

In all the developing countries, the percentage of literate women

---

Adapted from *Women and Literacy*, United Nations Non-Government Liaison Service (NGLS), 1992.

is lower than that of literate men. Socio-cultural factors and discrimination against women are the basis of this situation. Such discrimination can take different forms, as the following example shows.

Girls receive less health-care and food than boys. A study in Bangladesh showed that 14 per cent of girls, as against 5 per cent of boys, are malnourished. Women typically work about 25 per cent more hours than men, but their total remuneration is less. Women are usually concentrated either in the rural areas or in the informal sector of urban areas, where pay levels tend to be lower than in the formal sector of the economy. Gender-specific inequalities are reinforced by unequal access to education. Girls often are simply not sent to school, or drop out earlier, thereby increasing the level of illiteracy among women.

The Legacy of Female Illiteracy

In situation of extreme poverty it may well be necessary to resolve such problems as food shortages, poor health-care, housing, employment and agricultural production before any successful literacy action can be undertaken. In addition, many women living in semi-literate cultures do not feel any social pressure to acquire literacy and numeracy skills, unlike in the industrialized countries where the social pressure is strong.

Obstacles to Literacy

Even when the motivation is there, formidable obstacles remain. Foremost among them is probably lack of time. The traditional or new roles that women fill rarely leave them enough free time to devote to full-time or even part-time educational activities. Fatigue, frequent or early pregnancies, caring for children and families, agricultural and cultural activities, and formal or informal employment, are among the many reasons for lack of time. This heavy workload is reflected in the high rate of absenteeism and drop-out of women from literacy activities. The same reasons apply to girls' schooling.

Organizational problems—male instructors, mixed gender classes, considerable distances between home and the education centre, lack of transport, evening courses and cultural clashes between instructors and participants—are also constraints to women's full participation in educational activities.

Then again, there is the problem of cultural patterns and customs. Many parents believe that it is not worthwhile to invest in girls' education; instead they invest time and money to educate their sons, who will provide support for them when adult. Daughters are seen as additional sources of household labour who, once married, will become part of the (re)productive labour force of another household. Discrimination against women in the labour market, and in salaries, reinforces parents' negative attitudes towards educating girls.

Husbands, fathers and men in general have such attitudes towards women's education, especially when it results in the possibility of learning new skills which give women a new role in the family. Better earning prospects tend to give women more independence and change their economic status in the family, and this may give rise to family tensions, particularly if women's earnings are controlled by the husband.

Some religious traditions may restrict women's activities to domestic tasks, stressing their role as mothers, which limits their access to education. Lack of self-confidence, timidity, submissiveness to male authority, as well as isolation and age differences between participants are also limiting factors for women's participation in education. The main reason, however, is the poverty of most illiterate women, which oppresses them in their everyday lives and prevents them from taking an active part in educational activities.

Becoming Literate: The Question of Motivation

Whenever literacy programmes or projects are carried out in developing countries, there is a high level of female participation. Several studies have indicated that the reasons behind this are the changing social roles of women and men. The gradual increase in the number of female heads of households, due in part to the rising number of men leaving home in search of better job opportunities, gives women the responsibility of supporting the family including taking over agricultural production in rural areas, or by entering the informal or formal labour force. Literacy is seen as a tool that will help women carry out these tasks better, once their basic needs have been met. But whether it is a social pressure, or women's new roles, other personal motivations also play an important part when making decisions.

Child-care, Education and Family Income

These are common reasons given by women, living in industrialized and developing countries in both urban and rural areas, for seeking to become literate. The importance women give to schooling their children for a better future, to providing their children and family with better health-care and the acquisition of income-generating skills, motivate them to take a more active role in literacy activities.

Communicating with the Literate Community

It is not sufficient to be able to sign documents; women must also fill in forms, contracts and cheques, keep accounts, write letters and read those received from family members who have emigrated, send cheques, receive money, send telegrams, and read recipes and agricultrual instructions. In short, women use literacy and numeracy skills for everything that can provide them with greater autonomy in everyday life.

Religious Reasons

Many indigenous groups associate learning to read and write with Christianity, reading the holy scriptures and hymns in church. Some studies have found that religious reasons can play an important role in motivating adults to acquire literacy skills.

Social Change

In countries undergoing revolutionary changes that include widespread political mobilization in support of literacy, women see this as a way to become actors in the process of change their country is experiencing. Examples are to be found in Cuba, Mozambique, Nicaragua and Tanzania.

Even where these and other motivating factors exist, the obstacles already discussed in this chapter often prevent women benefiting from literacy and, in the case of school-age girls, from enrolling in primary education, a crucially important stage in preventing girls from becoming future illiterates.

Women's Role in Development

A number of studies have demonstrated the effect of women's literacy and education in both social and economic development. Women's literacy enables a better use of family planning and results in a fall in birth rate. While this relationship is not always constant, the results of the study carried out by the Demographic Health Survey (DHS) in 1990 in 28 countries in Africa, Latin America and the Caribbean, Asia and the Arab States, noted that the tendency for smaller families increased with the educational level of women. The average number of children fell to less than four among women with secondary education. Family planning methods are more widely used in countries such as Botswana, Kenya and Zimbabwe, where over 70 per cent of women have some education.

Women's education plays an important role in child-care, especially in relation to infant morality levels. A study carried out by the Research Triangle Institute (1990) in 80 developing countries indicated that an increase of 70 per cent in girls' enrolment in primary schools, together with a comparable growth in secondary education, would after 20 years result in a decrease in the infant mortality rate of 40 per 1,000 live-births. Such primary and secondary education for women would contribute to a continuation of this decrease, over and above other relevant development inputs such as increased per capita income, level of urbanization, medical facilities and male school enrolment. *The State of the World Population* (1990) reported that the results of studies carried out in 46 countries indicated that a one per cent increase in women's literacy rate is three times more effective in reducing infant mortality than a one per cent increase in the number of doctors.

As women's level of education rises, the number of malnourished children declines. DHS (March 1990) found that in Guatemala, where only 65 per cent of the women have had some level of education, the percentage of stunted infants aged 3 to 35 months is over 50 per cent, compared with fewer than 10 per cent in Trinidad and Tobago, where women have a higher level of education. While other factors are relevant, the educational levels of women are of paramount importance.

The same study indicated that pre-natal care and medical treatment at childbirth increases with the mother's level of education. It also has a strong bearing on whether or not children received treatment for diarrhea, one of the major causes of mortality among young children. Use of oral rehydration salts also increases with the mother's education.

Women's literacy has a positive effect on school enrolment and attendance. In Mexico, a study carried out by Munoz Izquierdo established that adults who completed literacy courses had more daughters with some formal education than those who had not finished their studies.

Women in the Labour Force

The number of women participating in the labour force in the formal sector is directly to their educational level. The Triangle Research Institute study showed that a 70 per cent increase in primary and secondary education will, after 20 years, lead to a 7.3. per cent increase in women's participation in the labour force. Many researchers have stressed the close association between the level of education and productivity increase in the modern sector of the economy. Nevertheless, the increasing trend towards reducing the number of jobs in the formal sector most directly affects disadvantaged groups such as women.

Women's literacy also increases productivity and self-employment in the informal sector. The trend towards an increase in the number of self-employed women, or of those who work on a sub-contract basis, opens up several possibilities, particulary for those women who are their family's only means of economic support. Examples of successful activities linking literacy with income-earning are found among projects aimed at setting up small enterprises to meet market needs and ensure the continuity of economic activities.

Increased productivity in the agricultural sector is also linked to the educational level of rural women. This is shown by a study on the effects of education on productivity in agriculture in a number of developing countries. This study concluded that four years of primary education (usually considered the minimum level for retaining literacy) increased productivity by 7.4 per cent, with additional benefits in the form of increased modernization of agriculture.

Literacy and Sustainable Development

The term 'sustainable development' refers to humanity's ability to survive by means of the rational use of renewable resources, by refraining from disrupting the eco-system or over-exploiting natural resources, and by refraining from activities that destroy cultures or societies and instead allow them to reach their potential.

Because women play an important role in the development process, radical measures to increase literacy will enhance their participation in development and at the same time improve their status. Action must be taken during the 1990s to increase efforts by the international community and by governments to provide women and girls with full access to education.

Women must be educated in terms of their crucial role in society, whether as producers or reproducers: they are mainly responsible for the care and well-being of their families; they play an important role as educators of future generations; they fulfil economic functions, in both urban and rural areas, that are vital for the survival of female heads of household is again noteworthy).

As part of an individual's personal development, literacy is a right to which everyone—women as well as men—should have access. Acquiring it enables women to increase their self-confidence, improve their self-esteem, become aware of their civil rights, improve their income-earning capabilities and to play an active role in family and community decision-making. Literacy is a means for women to participate on equal terms in the process of social development and change, for quantitative and qualitative progress in society: in short, for sustainable development.

While women's literacy promotes sustainable development, and plays a major role in socio-economic change, it must be supported by the necessary structural changes in society.

15

Women in Development (1992)

Introduction

A Seminar on the Integration of Women in Development held at Vienna (Austria) from 9 to 11 December 1991, was organised by the Division of the Advancement of Women, Centre for Social Development and Humanitarian Affairs of the United Nations at Vienna. The recommendations and the conclusions of the Seminar were submitted to the Commission on the Status of Women at its thirty-sixth Session held at Vienna from 11 to 20 March, 1992. A resolution was adopted by the Commission.

Conclusions and Recommendations of the Seminar on the Integration of Women-in-Development (WID)

The Seminar on the Integration of Women in Development was intended to review the efforts undertaken to integrate women into the process of development, to assess the strategies evolved to achieve that goal and to consider future prospects in this area. The conclusions and recommendations of the Seminar, which were appended to the Secretary-General's report (E/CN.6/1992/8), are quoted below.

1. The participants at the Seminar on the Integration of Women in Development reviewed the experience acquired in the implementation of different women-in-development (WID) strategies and then discussed emerging issues that needed to be tackled in the 1990s and proposals for future, in particular, proposals for the period

---

Seminar on the Integration of Women in Development, Advancement of Women Centre for Social and Humanitarian Affairs, Vienna, International Centre, Vienna, 1991.

leading up to the convening in 1995 of the Fourth World Conference on Women: Action for Equality, Development and Peace.

I. WOMEN IN DEVELOPMENT: EXPERIENCE AND LESSONS

2. WID was discussed from two perspectives: its conceptual framework and the experience acquired in its implementation.

A. Conceptual framework

Conclusions

Integration of Women into Development — What kind of Integration, what kind of Development?

3. A distinction was made between two possible approaches to WID: one was an attempt to add women's concerns to the development agenda already set by others; the other involved in attempt to transform development agendas on the basis of women's analysis of what would both meet their basic needs and empower them.
4. It was agreed that the implementation of all aspects of the Nairobi Forward-looking Strategies for the Advancement of Women* required that women be present to share the task of determining what type of development should take place. The objective should be to transform the whole range of public policy so that women would gain more control over their own lives through, for example, better health, better income, better education, better access to skills and technology, entitlements to capital and land, legal equality, and control over their own bodies. The extent to which indicators of women's development improved should be a measure of policy success. That would then place women in the position of bringing their perspectives to bear on a whole range of national and international issues.
5. It was noted that donors and development agencies had an important role to play in the implementation of WID policies. At the same time, it was acknowledged that they were intermediaries

---

* *Report of the World Conference to Review and Appraise the Achievements of the United Nations Decade for Women: Equality, Development and Peace*, Nairobi, 15-26 July 1985 (United Nations Publication, Sales No. E.85.IV.10), Chapter I, Section. A.

of social change and that little could be achieved without the full involvement of all concerned at all levels.

Women and Gender

6. The participants agreed that it was appropriate to use the concepts "women" and "gender" with an emphasis that would vary depending on different contexts. Gender referred to socially constructed and culturally variable roles that women and men played in their daily lives. It referred to a structural relationship of inequality between men and women and was manifested in labour markets and in political structures, as well as in the household. It was reinforced by custom, law and specific development policies. In order to meet the objective of the advancement of women it was necessary to develop gender-based analysis and to integrate it into macro-economic and micro-economic policies. It was recognized that gender-based training, both in terms of concepts and in terms of skills in gender-based analysis and planning, was an important strategy for advancing the WID agenda.

The Need to Rethink Development and Concurrently Refocus WID

7. It was agreed that there was a need to give the concept of WID a broader meaning and to refocus it within a new theoretical framework and a transformed development agenda.
8. Central to the refocusing of WID was an emphasis on the self-empowerment of women, a process in which women gained control over their own lives by knowing and claiming their rights at all levels of society: at the international, national and "household" levels. Self-empowerment meant that women gained autonomy, were able to set their own agendas, and were fully involved in economic, political and social decision-making processes. That would translate into everyday reality the principles of the Convention on the Elimination of All Forms of Discrimination against Women, adopted by the General Assembly in its resolution 34/180.
9. The new theoretical framework should recognize the importance of global economic and political issues for the advancement of women and should provide an analysis of the gender dimensions

of those issues. It should also incorporate a gender analysis that took into account race, ethnic origin and class and recognized the existence of gender-based hierarchies in the household, the community and other areas of society and their impact on women's access to power and resources. One central requirement for the self-empowerment of women was more time.

10. The participants saw the need to link democratization, human resource development and empowerment. Women could only participate in the process of democratization to the extent that their human rights were fully recognized, their human potential was developed and they were empowered. Those were necessary preconditions for women to create opportunities for themselves to participate. "Human development" and empowerment were essential for effective participation in democratic processes.
11. The participants redefined human resource development as "human development" in order to underline the fact that human development was a lifelong process that started at birth. It must focus on improving the quality of life and on enlarging people's choices by investing in programmes on the health of women and children, nutrition, housing, basic education etc.

Developing Statistics, Indicators and Analysis for a Fuller Understanding of Gender Inequality

12. The participants recognized the efforts to develop gender-disaggregated data. Further work was necessary to provide a basis on which to build more effective policies. Efforts were needed to demonstrate and illuminate:

    (a) The gender dimension in all areas of social, economic and political life; and
    (b) The complex interrelationship between different dimensions of gender inequality.

13. Particular effort was necessary to produce concepts and measures that reflected the value of all work, paid and unpaid, and the link between the productive and reproductive roles of women. The extent to which unpaid work, both in the home and in the community, supported and underpinned general social and economic development needed to be better understood in order for the burden to be shared more equally between men and women.
14. The kind of gender-based analysis advocated was central to *The*

*World's Women 1970-1990: Trends and Statistics,** second edition of which should be prepared prior to the Fourth World Conference on Women. National efforts at similar compilation and analysis should be developed further. Concepts and indicators developed to measure and illuminate gender inequality must be reflected in future editions of the Human Development Report, published by the United Nations Development Programme, the World Development Report, published by the World Bank, and other United Nations publications.

B. Implementation

Conclusions

National Capacity for Sustainability

15. The participants concluded that the experience of WID revealed the need for a two-level approach to implementing national WID strategies; at the public-policy level and at the grass-roots level. The power granted to WID offices and national machinery within national administrations reflected the importance attached to having women's advancement on national political agendas.
16. The power of WID offices and national machinery, together with their sense of strategy, technical competence and political skills, would determine their influence on the policy debate and, hence, the extent to which economic and social policies favourable to women's advancement would be adopted as well as the nature of such policies. In addition, there was a need for commitments at the national level to incorporate a gender perspective in the policies and programmes of all ministries and to elaborate well-targeted strategies to close the gap for women in key sectors.
17. There could be no effective WID policy at the grass-roots level without basic human rights such as freedom to associate, freedom of speech and freedom to criticize government policy directions. The will and ability to form strategic alliances between, on the one hand, groups outside Governments (including academic, private-sector and community groups) that wanted progress for women and, on the other, public policy-makers would significantly influence

---

* United Nations publication, Sales No.E.90.XVII.3.

the likelihood that policies and programmes would emerge that were favourable to women. That applied to donor agencies and Governments in both developed and developing countries.

18. At the grass-roots level, a larger constituency for advancing the concerns of women had to be built with other social movements, such as the peace movement and the environmental movement. It was also important for women's advocacy groups to internationalize their concerns and to become more knowledgeable about the economic and political consequences of changes currently occurring world-wide.

Accountability

19. The participants agreed that another important lesson was the need to pay more attention to accountability. Binding procedures needed to be developed by donors and development agencies, as well as recipients, to ensure that WID activities could be monitored and evaluated by the constituency they were meant to serve. The links between, on the one hand, specific organizational structure, goals and procedure and, on the other, the extent and forms of accountability also meant strengthening lobbying and advocacy skills among women's movements and non-governmental organizations in order to critically follow and question the work of institution responsible for WID policy and implementation, such as development agencies and Governments.

Training

20. Agencies involved in gender-based training had concluded that there was a need to incorporate personal and political analysis into such training and to improve coordination of those programmes at the international level. It was proposed that materials and modules analysing macro-economic trends from a gender perspective should be incorporated into gender-based training. It was vital to deal with the interface between the world economy, national development plans and the role of women. Gender-based analysis could also be usefully introduced at the level of project beneficiaries in order to increase awareness of women's roles and contributions to development and to serve

of women's roles and contributions to development and to serve as a basis for programme improvement. It was recognized that there was already a capacity in that area in some developing countries, both within and outside of Governments, and that it was important for bilateral and multilateral agencies, as well as non-governmental organizations, to help develop that capacity and the sharing of those experiences in building similar capacities in other developing countries.

21. In addition to consultants and local research staff, training efforts had to include the staff of non-governmental organizations, government counterparts of donor agencies, as well as donor and development agencies.

The Relationship between International Agencies and Local Women's Movements

22. It was important to recognize that over the preceding 10 years a number of women's organizations had launched programmes and networks at the national level in developing countries, as well as at the international level. There was a need for those initiatives to be recognized and for United Nations entities and bilateral organizations to involve them in project and programme development exercises where appropriate. Those organizations also needed to be supported and strengthened.

23. The limitations of working exclusively with women's bureaux needed to be recognized by bilateral organizations and United Nations specialized agencies, and efforts should be made where possible to encourage such bureaux to reach out and support the work of women's organizations in developing countries.

Coordination among Agencies

24. It was felt that there was a need for better coordination of WID programmes at the international, regional and national levels among agencies in order to avoid unnecessary duplication and overlapping, and to increase the impact of programmes.

25. There was a need for the work involved in efforts to integrate gender issues to be shared more equally between countries. That would entail more consultation and coordination among donor agencies and recipients, within and outside of Governments.

II. IDENTIFICATION OF EMERGING ISSUES

A. Global Trends

Conclusion

26. The participants agreed that little had been done to incorporate women into international strategies such as the International Development Strategies (IDS) and to analyse the gender dimensions of global economic and political restructuring and of emerging international environmental problems.

B. Democratization

Conclusion

27. Relationships between democratization, human rights, survival, violence and gender were important issues in their own right and in relation to linking global trends with local ones.

C. Marketization, Privatization and Deregulation

Conclusion

28. The participants, noting the widespread trends towards marketization, privatization and deregulation, agreed that it was important to recognize that markets and the private sector might be no less biased against women than the State or the public sector. It was also vital to recognize the complementarity between the provision of public sector services for women and women's ability to take advantage of new opportunities.

D. Human Resources and Development

Conclusion

29. Concern was expressed about the deterioration of social sector services and labour market conditions in many countries in periods in which structural adjustment programmes were being carried out. In designing and implementing macro-economic policies, both

donors and recipients should include positive measures to ensure that the needs of women were fully taken into account, especially in terms of their access to social and public services and to better income opportunities.

Health and Sanitation

30. Emerging issues in the area of health and sanitation included:

(a) The impact of structural adjustment programmes on the quantity and quality of health services;
(b) The Acquired Immune-Deficiency Syndrome (AIDS) pandemic and the resurgence of cholera and other epidemic diseases;
(c) The contamination of land, air and water;
(d) Concerns about the environment and population growth that were used to reduce women's reproductive rights; promoting equal opportunity and giving women choice and control over their own fertility provided a more sustainable development path; and
(e) The use of technology to undermine the survival of women (for example, to abort female fetuses), and other attitudes towards female children that discriminated against them.

Labour Markets and Employment

31. Deregulation policies, changes in ways of organizing production processes, changes in skill requirements, increased automation, and the relocation of production were threatening, in many countries, the quality of women's employment opportunities and working conditions. There was a need to design and introduce measures to improve the situation of women in home-based work.
32. The importance of over-coming barriers to the participation of disabled women in the process of development was emphasized.
33. Female education was perhaps the most important means of achieving the combined benefits of higher productivity (including access to and actual employment), lower infant mortality and lower fertility. It was, therefore, essential to increase female enrolment levels in primary and secondary education and to control the drop-out rates for girls and young women. There was a need to give special attention to training, from literacy to vocational training, in order to improve

women's access to employment and self-employment. There was also a need to promote female interest in scientific and technical education and training at the primary, secondary and higher levels and to encourage girls and young women to successfully complete such courses.

34. In the field of education and research, emphasis was placed on the importance of improving the quality of education and of paying attention to research methods involving participatory action. The introduction of gender-sensitive education in curricula already at the primary level was considered an important vehicle in breaking down existing cultural barriers to the advancement of women. Academic institutions and women's organizations in developing countries should be encouraged to undertake gender studies and research.

III. PROPOSALS FOR THE FUTURE

A. Making Governments Accountable

Recommendations

35. Governments must be held accountable for the effectiveness of WID programmes by actually committing adequate funds and resources to such programmes and by including WID personnel with sufficient authority in all policies and planning and programming priorities. Governments should identify quantitative and qualitative national targets (including timetables) that are appropriate to each national situation for the public and private sectors and should regularly report on that matter to the Commission on the Status of Women and to national forums. It is recommended that information on national WID programmes should be made available and accessible to groups and individuals and that people should be free to provide comments and inputs on the direction of those programmes.

B. Research for Policy Reformulation

Recommendations

36. The relationship between global trends and women's productive

and reproductive roles should be systematically researched. Comparative research on the effects of development strategies on women and on gender relations should be undertaken and the possibility of gender-aware alternative development strategies should be investigated. Such efforts should include the development of appropriate methodologies including modelling and country case studies in order to strengthen the arguments used in the WID debate. The priority areas for investigation are described below.

Human Development

37. There should be a critical evaluation of the emerging strategy, usually termed human resource development, paying particular attention to the treatment of the interrelationship of production and reproduction, and of paid and unpaid work. What are the implications of the "human capital" perspective for human development? What do women want from human development strategies? The needs of women in different age-groups and situations vary; for instance, poor, young or adolescent women workers may have a lot to gain from minimum wage legislation, while professional women gain more from policies in favour of equal opportunities. What are the implications of inequality within households for human development strategies? What is the object of human development, to promote growth or to enhance the capabilities of individual women and men as well?

Democratization of Development

38. A critical evaluation should be made of the emerging democratization of development, paying particualr attention to gender-bias in concepts of democratization. There should be research on the following:

(a) The kinds of democratization women want, and what is needed to facilitate their empowerment in the process of democratization;
(b) The way to extend democratization beyond periodic elections in order to give citizens real control over resource allocation in the public and private sectors; and
(c) The identification of the barriers to women exercising such

control and of ways in which the effectiveness of democratization could be increased once the barriers are reduced.

The International Economy

39. There should be a review of the implications of emerging trade and investment patterns for different categories of women, for instance, what implications the entry of formerly centrally planned economies into the international market would have for women's employment in labour-intensive manufacturing. There should also be an evaluation of gender-bias in the way that international trade and investment are organized; new ways of regulating international trade and investment in order to avoid this bias should be considered. The role that non-governmental organizations can play in constructing new types of international relations between women in different countries should be explored. There should be an evaluation of gender-bias which might improve the functioning of the international economy.
40. An international programme of work should be established to develop the recommendations made at the present Seminar for refocusing the conceptual framework of WID and their operationalization prior to the convening in 1995 of the Fourth World Conference on Women, in order to provide it with inputs to accelerate the implementation of the goals of the Nairobi Forward-looking Strategies. The programme of preparation should include input by practitioners, policy makers, community leaders, academics and project participants. International assistance will be indispensable if such an effort is to be completed in time for the Fourth World Conference on Women.

C. Strengthening Policy Capacity

Recommendations

41. Within national machineries and WID offices, whether in national or multilateral agencies, staff should have strong skills in policy analysis — particularly, but not only, in economics. They should have a good understanding of gender-bias in existing policies and

an ability to communicate this understanding to colleagues in the relevant policy sectors. Training could strengthen the skills but appropriate recruitment is probably even more important. It is also important that the policy function of WID units be recognized and respected by their Governments and organizations so that their views are sought in making decisions on policy.

D. Enhancing Strategic Alliances

Recommendations

42. Those responsible for women's programmes within Governments and development institutions should strengthen alliances with groups outside of the Government working for women's advancement:

(a) By funding joint meetings;
(b) By facilitating the establishment of women's support groups;
(c) By including women's support groups in the elaboration of policy; and
(d) By supporting international networking of women's advocacy groups, be they non-governmental organizations, academics, political and social movements or private sector associations.

43. The utilization of communications technology to facilitate such processes should be encouraged.

E. Programme Planning

Recommendations

44. Current development programmes should be examined and existing resources should be reallocated in order to more effectively enhance women's contribution to national development.

Closing the Gaps

45. The gaps between men's and women's development should be closed:

(a) By putting into broader practice what is known to work for women;

(b) By promoting technologies that have a proven record of meeting needs, and saving women's time and labour, by reviewing new technologies to ensure that those appropriate are also accessible, and by directing programmes to disseminate information on technologies to girls and women; and

(c) By ensuring that all education programmes have numerical targets for the enrolment of females at all levels and that they are reviewed from the point of view of the following:

(i) Appropriateness of curriculum;
(ii) Quality of teaching;
(iii) Stereotyping of sectors; and
(iv) Social incentives for families, teachers and communities to ensure that girls stay in school.

(d) By reviewing health and sanitation services for their accessibility and appropriateness to women. In particular, goals and targets should be set:

(i) To reduce maternal mortality;
(ii) To increase the access of women to information on and the treatment of AIDS, cholera and other epidemic diseases;
(iii) To improve sanitation;

(e) By encouraging:

(i) States that have not done so to ratify the Convention on the Elimination of All Forms of Discrimination against Women;
(ii) Governments to review their laws in order to identify continuing discrimination against women, to implement changes provided for by law and to establish a specific time-frame to complete this work; and
(iii) The exploration of means of transforming customary laws that put women at a disadvantage and of educating women on their rights.

Reshaping the Development Agenda

46. The development agenda must be reshaped based on an analysis of how the reduction of gender bias might improve the functioning of the international economy. At the national level, such an analysis should be carried out by departments of finance and Planning Commissions. In addition, the research capacity of international financial institutions should be brought to bear.
47. WID units and national machinery should argue for reallocating budgetary resources to sectors that have been identified as key sectors for women.
48. In addition, a network of experts on the gender dimension of macro-economic policy should be created and supported. Furthermore, mechanisms should be found to position experts with a gender perspective in forums crucial to reshaping the global agenda.

RESOLUTION ADOPTED BY THE COMMISSION ON THE STATUS OF WOMEN

At its thirty-sixth session, the Commission on the Status of Women adopted, by 42 votes to 1, the following resolution sponsored by the Group of 77 (i.e. the developing countries), the European Community, Australia, New Zealand and Turkey.

Women and Development

The Commission on the Status of Women,

Recalling Economic and Social Council resolution 1990/15, annex, of 24/May 1990 and Commission resolutions 34/3 of 8 March 1990 and 35/7 of 8 March 1991,

Reaffirming the principles contained in the Declaration on the Right to Development adopted by the General Assembly in its resolution 41/128, annex, of 4 December 1986,

Convinced that the effective mobilization of women is an essential element in achieving the objectives of the Nairobi Forward-looking Strategies for the Advancement of Women and the International Development Strategy for the Fourth United Nations Development Decade, adopted in General Assembly resolution 45/199, annex, of 21 December 1990,

Aware that the slow progress in the implementation of the Forward-looking Strategies as related to development necessitates urgent action to be taken by all parties concerned,

Aware also of the need to recognize the importance of gender in all areas of social, economic and political life in order to bridge the gap between the roles of men and women in development and to train planners, policy-makers, decision-makers and relevant staff in gender analysis,

Reaffirming that the full integration of women in development, both as agents and beneficiaries, should concern all sectors of society,

Convinced that improving the distribution between both sexes of the tasks related to productive and reproductive functions is an essential strategy for development and has to be reflected in the implementation of concrete economic and social policies,

Further convinced that international cooperation for development has a fundamental role in the creation of proper conditions that allow women to achieve full integration in development,

Deeply concerned about the worsening situation of women in developing countries, particularly in the least developed countries,

Expressing special concern about women living in extreme poverty, in rural as well as urban areas,

Expressing deep concern that, despite the fact that poor rural women contribute to all aspects of the well-being of rural families and account for more than half of the food production of developing countries, they are often the most vulnerable and disadvantaged group in society,

Aware of the need for women, as agents and beneficiaries of development, to be empowered to define their own means of development as well as of the need to guarantee them access to services, such as education, health, maternity and child-care and credit, among other, in order to fully integrate women into the development process,

Keeping in mind that the impact of structural adjustment policies, adverse terms of trade and the growing foreign debt on developing countries, particularly the least developed countries, has had a negative effect on efforts for the full integration of women in development,

(1) *Takes note* of the report of the Secretary-General on development: integration of women in the process of development (E/CN.6/1992/8), which contains the conclusion of the Seminar on the Integration of Women in Development;

(2) *Urges* Governments to foster women's full participation in the

elaboration, planning, execution and evaluation of development policies and projects so that they can be agents and beneficiaries of development;

(3) *Also urges* Governments to adopt policies to promote economic development that will ensure the full and explicit integration of women's needs and concerns;

(4) *Further urges* Governments to include gender perspectives in the major guidelines for economic and social policies and to increase their capacities and capabilities in gender-responsive and gender-sensitive planning of development programmes;

(5) *Urges* Governments to foster the access of women to income-generating activities as a means of stimulating economic independence, a basic requirement for women's self-sufficiency;

(6) *Urges* Governments to identify their own quantitative and qualitative national targets in such fields as education and training, employment, income generation, health and women in public life with regard to the full integration of women in development and to commit adequate resources to women and development programmes;

(7) *Recommends* that Governments create or strengthen national machinery for the advancement of women, placing it at the highest level, and ensure its greater involvement in the political, economic and social planning processes;

(8) *Further recommends* Governments, international donors and non-governmental organizations to develop gender-oriented research in all development areas, particularly by the involvement of national research institutes, as well as to promote specific measures in the field of training in gender analysis programmes for development of decision-makers and the relevant staff involved in the policy and programme areas, in addition to implementation processes;

(9) *Calls* upon Governments, international financial and other relevant institutions and non-governmental organizations to promote measures to stimulate the economies of developing countries and the full integration of women in the development process and to provide financial services on the basis of equal opportunity for women and men, while avoiding adverse effects on their well-being, particularly that of vulnerable groups;

(10) *Calls* upon donor Governments and international financial institutions to provide adequate and timely support for the efforts of the developing countries, particularly the least developed countries,

in reducing the negative effects of the external debt burden, structural adjustment policies and adverse terms of trade with a view to integrating women in mainstream development;

(11) *Appeals* to Governments, donor countries, international agencies and appropriate financial institutions to make greater efforts to support the establishment of co-operative rural banks and other development-related institutions to assist women, particularly those engaged in small-and medium-scale productive activities;

(12) *Requests* Member States to make provision for specific training programmes for women in rural and urban areas aimed at developing their technical and management skills and to give financial support, fellowships or both for training women, particularly those from developing countries, in science, technology, agriculture and management;

(13) *Calls* upon Governments, donor countries and the relevant international agencies to take further coordinated measures to facilitate the access of women, particularly rural and urban poor women to basic education, health and child-care facilities;

(14) *Requests* the Secretary-General in reporting on the implementation of the present resolution in his biennial monitoring report on the implementation of the Nairobi Forward-looking Strategies for the Advancement of Women to include policy and programme recommendations on the basis of gender analysis; and

(15) *Also requests* the Secretary-General to ensure that the issues of women and development and of the integration of women in development programmes are an integral part of the International Development Strategy for the Fourth United Nations Development Decade.

16

Women in a Literate World (1992)

Everyone has the right to education, or so it says in the Universal Declaration of Human Rights, proclaimed by the United Nations in December 1948. But by the year 2000 there will probably still be twenty-one African countries where 40 per cent of the population can not read. The problem is by no means confined to Africa. Illiteracy still exists in both Asia and Latin America. *On average, two out of every three illiterates are women.*

Illiteracy is not simply a question of reading and writing. For young people in Third World countries, the real-life problems are about survival. A man who is illiterate cannot participate fully in social and economic life. He is likely to be less healthy, poorer and die sooner than his literate brother.

Poor societies are usually less literate societies. Many developing countries are poverty-stricken through adverse terms of world trade for their products and heavy interest repayment on money borrowed from abroad. When governments are short of cash, schools and teachers do not get priority. In extreme cases, the education system is threatened with collapse. Developing countries should re-examine their priorities, particularly with regard to defence expenditure.

International measures are needed to reduce the amount of money flowing out of low-income countries and restore their trade balances so that they can rebuild their economies. Only then can the necessary human and financial resources be released to make their people literate.

Children without Schools

At present, according to UNESCO statistics, the world numbers approximately 950 million men and women who do not possess the most elementary tools to assume their own development: reading and writing. Another appalling figure: more than 135 million children do not go to school. *More than 60 per cent of these children are girls.*

As the world's population grows—which is the case at present and is likely to continue for the next fifty years—developing countries will have more and more difficulty in building enough schools for their children.

TABLE 16.1: Adult Literacy Rates by Sex 1990

	Both sexes	Females	Males
World Total	73.5	66.4	80.6
Developing countries of which:	65.1	55.0	74.9
Sub-Saharan Africa	47.3	36.1	59.0
Arab States	51.3	38.0	64.3
Latin America/Caribbean	84.7	83.0	86.4
Eastern Asia	76.2	66.4	85.7
Southern Asia	46.1	32.2	59.1
Least-developed countries	39.6	27.9	51.4
Developed countries	96.7	96.1	97.4
By Continent			
Africa	49.9	38.5	61.7
America	90.0	89.2	90.8
Asia	66.5	56.0	76.6
Europe/USSR	96.9	91.1	97.7
Oceania	92.5	91.1	93.9

* Sexwise percentage of literate adults in the population aged 15 years and over, 1990

Source: UNESCO, *World Education Report,* 1991, p.26.

Helping Women and Girls

As far as literacy is concerned, women are particularly underprivileged. In Africa and Southern and Eastern Asia, the literacy rate for females is on average 20per cent below that for men. In five of the least advanced countries, 90 per cent of women cannot read and write.

Girls are often not considered equal to boys and do not get the same education. The reasons for this situation are complex—cultural, economic and political. The content of education often forces women into traditional female roles. Furthermore, women who missed out on primary education may find it difficult to attend adult literacy classes because of their family commitments.

It is vital, however, to involve women since both as learners and as trainers they are particularly well motivated. Their role in educating the next generation is central—a mother who can read is more likely to have children who can read.

Literate mothers have healthier children and can help society to develop in other ways, such as improved child-care and community services. The success of family planning campaigns is closely linked to the number of women who have completed primary education, and even more so secondary education. In fact, women's role in society is so important that delegates at the Geneva conference on literacy said that nothing short of absolute priority for them would do!

Changing the status of women, however, depends on changing the attitude of men, particularly in their role as fathers and husbands. Here, there was one sign for optimism: the higher the literacy rate among men, the higher the literacy rate among women.

In some countries, high-level national commissions have been formed to make sure that women's education gets the attention it needs. Elsewhere, special programmes have mobilized educated women in the community to help other women become literate. This kind of positive action helps women to gain imagination, courage and confidence in themselves, so that they can understand the causes of injustice and find the strength to change their way of life.

What Stops Women Learning?

Women often face practical barriers to their participation in literacy programmes, such as:

— hostile family or community attitudes;
— local traditions and ancestral customs about their role in society;
— lack of time after family and household commitments;
— frequent pregnancies;
— irrelevant literacy programmes; and
— lack of child-care facilities.

Helping Girls Succeed at School

— Change attitudes in communities where (male) cultural traditions do not allow girls to go to school;

- Increase the number of female teachers by encouraging rural women to follow teaching careers by relaxing the qualifications for their recruitment;
- Run special condensed in-service courses for female teachers;
- Provide residential accommodation for female teachers;
- Stop girls being removed from school for early marriage;
- Set targets for increasing the number of girls enrolled in education; and
- Provide child-care services so as to free young girls from looking after their younger brothers and sisters.

Measures in Favour of Women

- Choose reading materials dealing with subjects of interest to female learners;
- Let illiterate women choose their own teachers;
- Provide child-care facilities;
- Run courses at times when women with young children are free to attend;
- Include course material emphasizing that men and women are equal;
- Form national commissions to concentrate on women's education;
- Recruit educated women as literacy volunteers; and
- In post-literacy activities, women should be encouraged to set up their own co-operatives and income-generating projects, particularly those saving them time and energy for other purposes.

17

UNICEF and Girls' Education (1994)

Introduction

For the past several years UNICEF has been publishing a yearly report on the state of children in the world which highlights the achievements made and the future action needed. Following extracts from *News Feature* of the Report are reproduced here.

Educating Girls

Where child health remains poor and death rates high, says the report, parents tend to ensure by having more children than they actually want. "Deploying all today's means to drastically lower child death rates would be a significant step towards slower population growth," says Grant.

Economic insecurity also makes large families attractive for support in illness or old age. Similarly, lack of labour-saving technologies, from water-pipes and handpumps to fuel-efficient stoves and mills for grinding grain, makes large numbers of children desirable as a source of help in fields and homes.

The education of girls, in particular, has been shown to be one of the most basic determinants of fertility decline. Educated women usually have more opportunities, more awareness of family planning possibilities, and are more likely to discuss and decide with their partners how many children to have and when. "They are also more likely to marry late, to postpone the first pregnancy, to leave more time between births, and to have fewer children in total," says the Report.

Not all the factors are quantifiable. "In very poor societies," says

---

The State of the World's Children, 1994, UNICEF, 1994

the UNICEF report, "children may be one of the few sources of joy and pride, of change and hope, in lives that are often monotonous, hard, and resigned."

Specifically, the UNICEF report calls for a major international effort to reach the year 2000 goals which were adopted by a majority of the world's political leaders at the 1990 World Summit for Children. The goals include the overcoming of major childhood diseases, a one-third reduction in child deaths, the provision of safe water to all communities, a basic education for all children, and family planning for all who need it. "Whether world population stabilizes at 10 billion or 20 billion will depend to a significant extent on action in this decade to achieve these goals," says Grant.

UNICEF Report 1994 on PPE Problem and Education of Girls

The Poverty, Population Growth, Environmental Stress (PPE) problem which is itself part of the transition to a sustainable future is largely the responsibility of the established industrialized countries. The path pioneered by a small group of nations over the last five centuries has brought to the rest of the world many benefits amid much pain. It has also pushed the tolerance of the biosphere close to breaking-point. Overwhelmingly, global environmental pressures arise from the already industrialized nations. Such a state of affairs cannot long continue, both because the industrialized world's levels of consumption and pollution are in themselves unjust and unsustainable, and because the other four fifths of the world cannot reasonably be expected to restrain or modify the course of its own development in order to protect the biosphere while the industrialized nations continue to monopolize the earth's capacity to provide and to absorb.

This challenge, which many are unwilling to think about today, will become more and more unavoidable as the 21st century begins.

For the industrialized world, the most difficult challenge will undoubtedly be the redefining of its own concepts of growth and progress. But if the great transition is to be made, then it is clear that the industrialized nations will also have to play a major part in resolving the PPE problem in the developing world.

In the face of all the immediate political and economic issues that command the attention of press, public, and politicians in all countries, it might be expected that the problems faced by the poorest people in the poorest countries would continue to occupy a lowly place on the international agenda. But sooner or later this too will have to change. For it will simply not be possible to negotiate the transitions that lie ahead without addressing the PPE problem in the poorest communities of the world. Within a very few years, failure to cope with the combined impact of the worst aspects of poverty, rapid population growth, and environmental decline will almost certainly translate itself into increasing social division, economic disruption, political unrest, and the gradual dwindling of the present opportunity for progress towards democracy and international stability. From the consequences of such a failure, no country—north or south, rich or poor—would be immune.

Action Now

Part 3 of the report unites the themes of progress for today's children with the longer-term PPE problem. Its central argument is that pursuing today's low-cost opportunities to protect the health, nutrition, and education of women and children in the developing world is one of the most immediately available and affordable ways of weakening the grip of poverty, population growth, and environmental deterioration.

In particular, it seeks to show that the PPE problem will not be resolved without a sustained national and international effort to overcome the very worst aspects of poverty in the remaining years of this century. For poverty is the root of the population and environment crisis in the developing world, and it is also the most accessible point at which to break into the powerful synergisms which form the downward spiral of PPE problems.

What is now required is a determined effort to protect millions of children from the very worst effects of the poverty into which they are born. Today's knowledge and outreach capacity make it possible, for the first time, to protect the mental and physical development of almost all the world's children. It has, therefore, become possible to interrupt one of the major processes by which poverty is perpetuated from one generation to the next.

An adequate response to the PPE problem must, therefore, include, among many other actions in many other fields, at least four basic kinds of investment in the lives of the world's poorest communities. They are:

— The prevention of common diseases and disabilities, and a steep reduction in both severe and moderate malnutrition;

— Rapid progress towards at least a primary education for all children, and especially for all girls;

— An unprecedented world-wide effort to improve the lives of women in poor communities — their health and education, their status and choices, their rights and opportunities. This is an important issue of principle; it is also the most important practical step that could be taken towards weakening the hold of the PPE problem; and

— Making available of family planning information and services to all who need them;

In sum, the central message of this year's report is that making further investments in the well-being of women and children—investments which are at risk of being neglected in the face of newer and seemingly more dramatic problems—is not only one of the most important humanitarian goals that the world could set for itself, but also one of the most incisive and cost-effective contributions that could be made towards coping with the broader problems of poverty, population growth, and environmental deterioration:

The cost of making such an investment in the 1990s would amount to not much more than one tenth of one per cent of the world's annual economic product.

It is a rare bargain. And one that the world cannot afford to miss.

18

International Responses to Women's Education and Allied Issues

Over the last few decades a number of actions have been taken to promote the equality of women in society. In 1967 the General Assembly of the United Nations adopted the Declaration on the Elimination of Discrimination against Women, as part of the Universal Declaration of Human Rights. In 1980 this measure was strengthened when the Assembly proclaimed the Convention on the Elimination of All Forms of Discrimination against Women.

Between 1975 and 1985 the United Nations adopted an Action Plan for the newly designated Decade for Women. Equality, development and peace were declared the basic principles for the implementation of women's programmes, with special reference to equality of opportunity in education. But in spite of all the efforts made, the Decade only partially achieved its aims.

The Nairobi Conferences

The results were thoroughly debated at an important meeting held in Nairobi in 1985 known as the World Conference to Review and Appraise the Achievements of the United Nations Decade for Women: Equality, Development and Peace. Since that Conference, which produced the Nairobi Forward-Looking Strategies for the Advancement of Women, new measures have been proposed to overcome the obstacles encountered during the UN Decade for Women, the aim being to ensure that they are implemented before the year 2000.

While progress towards ensuring gender equality has been achieved

---

Adapted from Marcella Ballara, *Women and Literacy*, United Nations Non-Governmental Liaison Service, 199.

in some countries, practical measures have yet to be taken. In many instances women's position is still far from satisfactory. Their lower status in both industrialized and developing countries is rooted in economic inequalities, discrimination with regard to access to power, society's reluctance to change attitudes and sexually discriminatory practices, customs and habits that negatively affect the education of women and girls, and ignorance of legal rights due to the influence of cultural models.

Within this context the Nairobi Conference highlighted three sub-themes—employment, health and education—as milestones in enhancing equality, development and peace, education being seen as the basis for the promotion and improvement of women's status and a tool to support their role as equal partners in society.

The UNESCO Programme

Already, at the beginning of the 1980s UNESCO had begun to implement plans and strategies in co-operation with Member States and international Non-Governmental Organizations (NGOs) in the field of women's education. A special programme, Equal Opportunities in Education for Women and Girls, was launched with the aim of reducing gender disparities among the various social programme groups, its main objectives being promotion of the equality of women and increasing their participation in development in the interests of justice and peace.

UNESCO proposed in 1985 that the United Nations declare a year for literacy. Education is one of the inalienable rights of every person and has been recognized as such in both the Universal Declaration of Human Rights and the Universal Covenant Rights. Economic, Social and Cultural Rights. Since in many developing countries illiteracy still constitutes a serious obstacle to the process of social and economic development, functional literacy and adequate education programmes assume even greater importance as indispensable elements for social development and progress. Recognizing this, the United Nations Assembly declared 1990 as International Literacy Year (ILY).

International Literacy Year (ILY) 1990

Launching a year dedicated to literacy provided a unique opportunity for mobilizing national, regional and international efforts in the struggle to extend literacy to the whole of the world's population. UNESCO undertook an awareness campaign in order to focus world public opinion on the need to achieve literacy for all by the year 2000, thereby embarking upon a decade devoted to this end.

Informing the public, mobilizing resources and laying the groundwork for educational activities over the new decade were among the various ILY goals, many of which have borne fruit. For example, at the initiative of the International Council for Adult Education (ICAE), based in Canada, more than 30 non-governmental organizations (NGOs) met in 1987 to set-up the International Task Force on Literacy (ITFL) to mobilize and promote actions during ILY and throughout the 1990s.

To reduce illiteracy during the 1990s is not an easy task. The economic crisis of the past decade has profoundly affected efforts made in favour of formal and non-formal education. UNICEF'S *State of the World's Children* (1990) points out that in the 1980s there was a significant decrease in public expenditure for education; in the 37 poorest countries such expenditures have fallen by approximately 25 per cent of Gross National Product (GNP), resulting in fewer children aged from 6 to 11 years enrolled in schools. It also states that, sadly, more than two-thirds of those children who never go to school or who drop out at an early stage are girls. As the 1990s begin, a girl born in South-East Asia or in the Middle East has less than one chance in three of completing primary education.

Most of these children will be illiterate for the rest of their lives unless they are given a second chance in formal or non-formal education; investment is therefore needed in both sectors.

The struggle to extend literacy to all is a challenge of such dimensions that it will require multi-sectoral collaboration from international, governmental and non-governmental organizations and national governments. A world movement has, therefore, been organized to unite all efforts towards the achievement of this goal, with the participation of the United Nations system.

This took the form of international actions carried out in 1990, such as UNESCO's Plan of Action for the Eradication of Illiteracy by the Year 2000, and the World Conference on Education for All: Meeting Basic Learning Needs, which took place in Jomtien, Thailand, in March 1990. Both have complementary proposals for countries and international organizations, using a two-track approach based on parallel measures for children and adults, a programme for the universalization of primary education, including literacy.

UNESCO'S Plan of Action

This identifies four major objectives upon which UNESCO shoud focus its efforts: (1) alerting world public opinion; (2) rallying the international community; (3) strengthening the regional literacy projects and programmes; and (4) reinforcing technical cooperation with Member States. Two priorities are proposed: (1) to improve the education of women and girls; and (2) to help countries confronting especially severe problems of illiteracy.

These objectives will be implemented through the regional literacy structures established by governments during the past decade, and with the assistance of UNESCO. These include the Major Project in the Field of Education in Latin America and the Caribbean (1981); the Regional Programme for the Eradication of Illiteracy in Africa (1984); the Regional Programme for Universal Provision and Renewal of Primary Education and Eradication of Illiteracy in Asia and the Pacific—APPEAL—(1987); and the Regional Programme for the Universalization and Renewal of Primary Education and the Eradication of Illiteracy in the Arab States by the Year 2000—ARABUPEAL—(1989).

Although these regional structures have their own programmes, objectives and modes of functioning, the plan of action in all of them is based on the two-track approach involving universal primary education and non-formal adult education, including literacy teaching.

The World Conference on Education for All

From 5 to 9 March 1990 the international community met in Jomtien, Thailand for the purpose of discussing illiteracy. With the participation of UNESCO, the United Nations Children's Fund (UNICEF), the United Nations Development Programme (UNDP), the World Bank, 20 inter-governmental agencies, delegates from 155 governments and 150 non-governmental organizations, the conference adopted the World Declaration on Education for All and endorsed the Framework of Action to Meet Basic Learning Needs, which propose specific educational actions for this decade.

The World Declaration on Education for All states that the

fundamental role played by basic education in the development of society is an inalienable right for all, in order to meet basic learning needs. These include: literacy, oral expression, knowledge, skills, values and attitudes, not as ends in themselves but as the first steps towards continuing education. The Declaration asserts that in order to meet these basic learning needs, a wider vision should be adopted that involves improving present resources, institutional structures, curricula and conventional delivery systems.

An appeal is made to all sectors of society to increase and mobilize financial and human resources from public, private and voluntary organizations. The need to strengthen international solidarity in order to implement the Declaration is emphasized, and it suggests that more equitable economic relations and reduced inequalities should be promoted.

The Framework for Action to Meet Basic Learning Needs constitutes guidelines for governments, international organizations, non-governmental organizations and others engaged in the struggle against illiteracy. The meeting suggested that countries might wish to set their own targets for the 1990s in terms of the following proposed dimensions:

1. Expansion of early childhood-care and developmental activities, including family and community interventions, especially for poor, disadvantaged and disabled children;
2. Universal access to, and completion of, primary education (or whatever higher level of education in considered as 'basic' by the year 2000);
3. Improvement in learning achievement such that an agreed percentage of an appropriate age cohort (for example, 80 per cent of 14-year-olds) attains or surpasses a defined level of necessary learning achievement;
4. Reduction of the adult illiteracy rate (the appropriate age-group to be determined in each country) to, say, one-half of its 1990 level by the year 2000, with sufficient emphasis on female literacy to reduce significantly the current disparity between male and female illiteracy rates;
5. Expansion of provisions of basic education and training in other essential skills required by youth and adults, with programme effectiveness assessed in terms of behavioural changes and impacts on health, employment and productivity;

and

6. Increased acquisition by individuals and families of the knowledge, skills and values required for better living and sound and sustainable development, made available through all education channels including the mass media, other forms of modern and traditional communication, and social action, with effectiveness assessed in terms of behavioural change.

The Role of Non-Governmental Organizations (NGOs)

Non-governmental organizations (NGOs) are independent groups with their own priorities and programmes. They are not at the service or disposition of government, multilateral or bilateral agencies. They are thus able to foster a new and innovative vision in education and take responsibility for preparing programmes and projects, including the identification, design, implementation and evaluation of basic education programmes. This independence means that NGOs can support parts or all of programmes initiated by governments, although their role in such collaborative efforts needs to be precisely defined in order to avoid duplication of effort.

NGOs have played an important role in educational action, both in industrialized and developing countries. Likewise, they can make a valuable contribution to future actions in the struggle against illiteracy. The close ties that NGOs have with communities make them well-placed to identify the population's needs and concerns, and to meet basic learning needs. This in turn puts them in an exceptionally good position to motivate and mobilize the public, as well as to extend their influence to areas of the community that state sectors do not reach.

NGOs can broaden their range of action concerning the education of women and girls in the following ways:

— *Functioning as Catalysts for Change* the regional networks of NGOs concerned with adult and women's education can serve as lobbies for international organizations in order to increase women's participation in development programmes. National NGOs can play a similar role with their governments to promote women's equal access to education.

— *Mobilizing public opinion* on the need to integrate women into education, and to recognize the obstacles they now face.

— *Motivating women* to take part in basic education programmes in order to improve their condition and position in society, to increase awareness of their rights and their self-confidence, to enhance their aspirations, to question gender stereotypes and relations of inequality that limit their individual development, and, lastly, to support everything that can help improve the quality of their lives, including participation in and equal access to development.

— *Conducting follow-up women's progress in basic education* by assessing the impact of education on women and supporting the introduction of measures and programmes that favour women's integration in literacy programmes and education in general.

— *Mobilizing funds and resources* to support educational programmes for women.

— *Making use of the mass media* to disseminate useful information addressed to women.

— *Helping to develop facilities* to reduce the excessive load of women's work and to enable them to take part in education programmes by providing such facilities as day-care centres, activities, incentives and transportation.

— *Providing services,* so that participants may increase their income and enter the informal sector of the economy, such as access to credit and assistance in quality control and marketing.

— *Encouraging the creation of, and women's participation in co-operative groups,* to defend their rights, as well as any organization that may help them to gain self-confidence and contribute to sustainable development.

Non-governmental organizations can make important contributions to the qualitative and quantitative improvement of basic education for all women and girls, especially through their participatory and integrated approach characterizing their actions.

19

United Nations and Women's Education Including Allied Issues: Retrospect and Prospect

Ever since its founding in 1945, the United Nations has been instrumental in improving the status of women by spearheading change and raising awareness of their situation throughout the world.

Even in the post-war world in which women enjoyed the right to vote in only 31 countries, "the equal rights of men and women" were enshrined in the Preamble of the United Nations Charter which legally established gender equality as a fundamental human right for the first time in history.

Yet discrimination against women, entrenched in deep-rooted cultural beliefs and traditional practices, persisted throughout much of the world. In order to draw attention to these obstacles and catalyse a swifter change in women's status, the United Nations declared 1975 as International Women's Year.

It also convened the 1975 World Conference of the International Women's Year in Mexico City, the first global conference ever held on women, which was attended by 133 States and more than 1,000 delegates.

The 1975 Conference produced the first World Plan of Action for the advancement of women, a blueprint for action by Governments and Non-Governmental Organizations (NCOs). It identified key areas for national action: international cooperation and peace; political participation; education and training; employment; health and nutrition; the family; population; housing; research; and the mass media.

Appreciating the growing global importance of women's issues.

Women: Challenges to the Year 2000, United Nations, New York, 1991.

the United Nations General Assembly then proclaimed 1976-1985 as the "United Nations Decade for Women: Equality, Development and Peace". Described as the "start of an international effort to right the wrongs of history", the combination of the Year and the Decade succeeded in putting women's concerns—in particular gender equality, full integration in the development process and the promotion of peace—firmly on the global agenda.

The Decade for Women had some far-reaching, concrete results. One was the creation of two UN bodies devoted exclusively to women: UNIFEM (the United Nations Development Fund for Women, originally called the United Nations Voluntary Fund for Women), which funds innovative development activities to benefit women, especially in rural regions of the developing world; and INSTRAW (International Research and Training Institute for the Advancement of Women) which supports the fuller participation of women in the economic, social and political spheres.

The next milestone on the road to women's equality was the adoption of the *Convention on the Elimination of All Forms of Discrimination against Women* by the United Nations General Assembly on 18 December 1979. Sometimes described as a Women's Bill of Rights, the Convention commits governments to take all "appropriate measures ... to ensure the full development and advancement of women, for the purpose of guaranteeing them the exercise and enjoyment of human rights and fundamental freedoms on a basis of equality with men". This Convention entered into force on 3 September 1981 and has now been ratified by over 100 nations, thereby legally binding them to implement its provisions.

The World Conference to Review and Appraise the Achievements of the United Nations Decade for Women, held in Nairobi, Kenya, in July 1985 , marked the end of the Decade. At the conclusion of Conference, which drew some 16,000 delegates and non-governmental organization representatives from all over the world, all participating Governments adopted by consensus the *Nairobi Forward-looking Strategies for the Advancement of Women to the Year 2000,* a blueprint for women's future in all realms of life. It identified specific areas for action by governments and the international community to improve the status of women over the 15 years until the year 2000.

In 1990 the Commission on the Status of Women undertook a five-year review and appraisal of the implementation of the *Nairobi Forward-looking Strategies.* The results were discouraging. The

Commission found that the situation of women had deteriorated in many parts of the world, especially in developing countries where economic stagnation or negative growth, continued population increases, the growing burden of debt and the reduction of public expenditures for social programmes had further constrained opportunities for women to improve their situation. There was also evidence of an alarming regression in the status of women in the spheres of education, employment and health. Too often the issue of the advancement of women had received only low priority.

Citing "entrenched resistance", exacerbated by the global economic crisis and the subsequent reduction in resources available for change, the Commission noted that there had been a "loss of impetus and even stagnation" in certain areas. Although there had been some progress at the grass-root level, the success had been largely invisible since it had not been translated into improvements in women's daily lives.

The Commission warned that the cost to societies of failure to achieve true gender equality in all realms of life would be high in terms of slowed economic and social development, misuse of human resources and reduced progress for society as a whole. It, therefore, urged that the pace of implementation be improved in the crucial last decade of the twentieth century. Many of the actions recommended to overcome entrenched obstacles to the advancement of women are contained in this book.

Women: Challenges to the Year 2000 has been prepared as part of a world-wide educational campaign to increase awareness of the obstacles encountered in implementing the *Nairobi Forward-looking Strategies for the Advancement of Women.* The major issues dealt with include:

— obstacles to de facto equality in political participation, and decision-making;
— obstacles to the advancement of women in education, employment and health, especially in developing countries, giving special attention to problems faced by women living in extreme poverty, rural women and women in the informal sector of the economy; and
— obstacles to the participation of women in the peace process.

The year 1995, the mid-point of this century's final decade, will mark the convening of the Fourth World Conference on Women. As part of the ongoing effort to overcome the obstacles cited above, this United Nations Conference will conduct a second review and appraisal of the implementation of the *Forward-looking :Strategies* and identify measures to achieve the stated objectives during the last five years of the century. Many United Nations activities will be geared to generation momentum for this event.

United Nations bodies devoted to the promotion of women's equality and their participation in development include the United Nation Children's Fund (UNICEF), the United Nations Population Fund (UNFPA), the United Nations Development Fund for Women (UNIFEM), the United Nations Division for the Advancement of Women, the International Research and Training Institute for the Advancement of Women (INSTRAW), and the United Nations Development Programme (UNDP).

Priority Themes for Women: 1991-1996

The General Assembly proclaimed 1975 as *International Women's Year* and stipulated that the year was to be devoted to intensified action to: promote equality between men and women, ensure the integration of women in the total development effort, and increase the contribution of women to the strengthening of world peace.

Thus, when the World Conference of the International Women's Year was convened in Mexico City in 1975, many participants associated themselves strongly with these 1975 themes of equality, development and peace. They stressed that these three basic international concerns were inextricably interrelated and that progress in one would be inseparable from progress in the other two.

The 1975 Conference in Mexico City was heralded by many as the "beginning of a new era" and in fact this single international year was followed by a United Nations Decade for Women (1976-1985) which incorporated into its title these themes of equality, development and peace.

It was decided that the Commission on the Status of Women would designate priority themes under each of these areas upon which activities for a given year would focus. Below is the enumeration of priority themes which have been designated by the Commission from 1991 through 1996.

1991

Equality : Vulnerable women, including migrant women.
Development : National, regional and international machinery for the effective integration of women in the development process, including non-governmental organizations.
Peace: Refugee and displaced women and children

1992

Equality: Elimination of de jure and de facto discrimination against women.
Development: Women and the environment; integration of women in the development process.
Peace: Equal participation in all efforts to promote international cooperation, peace and disarmament.

1993

Equality : Increased awareness by women of their rights, including legal literacy.
Development : Women in extreme poverty; integration of women's concerns in national development planning.
Place : Women and the peace process.

1994

Equality : Equal pay for work of equal value, including methodologies for measurement of pay inequities and work in the informal sector.
Development : Women in urban areas; population, nutrition and health factors for women in development, including migration, drug consumption and AIDS
Peace : Measures to eradicate violence against women in the family and society.

1995

Equality : Equality in economic decision-making.
Development : Promotion of literacy—education and training, including technological skills
Peace : Women in international decision-making

1996

Equality : Elimination of stereotyping of women in the mass media.
Development : Child and dependent care, including sharing of work and family responsibilities
Peace : Education for peace.

20

Women's Education : Comparative Indicators

TABLE 20.1: WOMEN'S EDUCATION WORLD COMPARISION

	Total Adult literacy rate 1990	Adult Literacy rate females as % of males 1990	Adult literacy rate 1990		Enrolment ratios females as a % of males 1986-91		Primary school enrolment ratio 1986-91 (gross)		1986-91 (net)		Secondary school enrolment ratio 1986-91 (gross)	
			Male	Female	Primary School	Secondary School	Male	Female	Male	Female	Male	Female
1. Niger	28	43	40	17	57	44	37	21	31	19	9	4
2. Angola	42	52	56	29	93	—	98	91	—	—	—	—
3. Mozambique	33	47	45	21	71	56	68	48	35	37	9	5
4. Afghanistan	29	32	44	14	52	45	31	16	25	13	11	5
5. Sierra Leone	21	35	31	11	70	57	56	39	—	—	21	12
6. Guinea-Bissau	37	48	50	24	55	44	76	42	58	32	9	4
7. Guinea	24	37	35	13	48	33	50	24	34	17	15	5
8. Malawi	..	..	..	..	83	50	77	64	55	52	6	3
9. Rwanda	50	58	64	37	99	67	69	68	65	65	9	6
10. Mali	32	59	41	24	57	44	30	17	24	14	9	4
11. Liberia	40	58	50	29	55x	39x	51x	28x	—	—	31x	12x
12. Somalia	24	39	36	14	50x	58x	20x	10x	14x	8x	12x	7x
13. Chad	30	43	42	18	44	25	79	-35	52	23	12	3
14. Eritrea	—	—	—	—	—	—	—	—	—	—	—	—
15. Ethiopia	24x	48x	33x	16x	65	71	46	30	32	24	17	12

Compiled from *The State of World's Childrens*, 1994, UNICEF *Contd.*

TABLE 20.1: *(Contd.)*

16. Mauritania	34	45	47	21	70	45	60	42	—	—	22	10
17. Zambia	73	80	81	65	92	56	99	91	81	79	25	14
18. Bhutan	38	49	51	25	65	29	31	20	—	—	7	2
19. Nigeria	51	65	62	40	77	77	82	63	—	—	22	17
20. Zaire	72	73	84	61	75	50	89	67	67	53	32	16
21. Uganda	48	56	62	35	83	50	76	63	57	50	16	8
22. Cambodia	35	46	48	22	—	—	—	—	—	—	—	—
23. Burundi	50	66	61	40	61	67	79	64	55	46	6	4
24. Central African Rep.	38	48	52	25	61	35	83	51	66	43	17	6
25. Yeman	39	49	53	26	39	21	111	43	—	—	47	10
26. Tanzania, U. Rep. of.	—	—	—	—	98	80	64	63	46	47	5	4
27. Ghana	60	73	70	51	82	65	82	67	—	—	48	31
28. Madagascar	80	83	88	73	96	90	94	90	64	63	20	18
29. Sudan	27	28	43	12	71x	74x	58x	41x	—	—	24x	17x
30. Gabon	61	66	74	49	—	—	—	—	—	—	—	—
31. Lesotho	—	—	—	—	116	148	99	115	64	76	21	31
32. Burkina Faso	18	32	28	9	62	56	45	28	36	23	9	5
33. Benin	23	50	32	16	51	38	87	44	69	36	16	6
34. Senegal	38	48	52	25	73	52	67	49	55	41	21	11
35. Laos, Peo. Dem. Rep.	84x	83x	92x	76x	78	68	116	91	—	—	31	21
36. Pakistan	35	45	47	21	55	45	47	26	—	—	29	13
37. Togo	43	55	56	31	63	30	126	180	85	58	33	10
38. Haiti	53	80	59	47	94	95	86	81	44	44	20	19
39. Nepal	26	34	38	13	51	40	112	57	84	43	42	17
40. Bangladesh	35	47	47	22	87	52	78	68	69	61	23	12
41. Cote d'Ivoire	54	60	67	40	70	44	88x	62x	—	—	27	12
42. India	48	55	62	34	76	61	109	83	—	—	54	33
43. Bolivia	78	84	85	71	90	87	78	78	83	75	37	31
44. Cameroon	54	64	67	43	86	68	108	93	80	69	31	21
45. Myanmar	81	81	89	72	94	92	106	100	—	—	25	23
46. Indonesia	82	85	88	75	96	84	119	114	100	96	49	41
47. Congo	57	63	70	44	—	38x	—	—	—	—	37	14
48. Libyan Arab Jamahiriya	64	67	75	50	—	—	—	—	—	—	—	—
49. Turkmenistan	—	—	—	—	—	—	—	—	—	—	—	—
50. Turkey	81	79	90	71	92	64	114	105	..	..	66	42

TABLE 20.1 *(contd.)*

51. Zimbabwe	67	81	74	60	98	85	118	116	—	—	54	46
52. Tajikistan	—	—	—	—	—	—	—	—	—	—	—	—
53. Iraq	60	70	70	49	84	64	104	87	90	78	58	37
54. Mongolia	—	—	—	—	104	110	96	100	—	—	87	96
55. Namibia	—	—	—	—	111	127	89	99	—	—	30	38
56. Papua New Guinea	52	58	65	38	84	67	77	65	79	67	15	10
57. Gautemala	55	75	63	47	85	85x	82	70	—	—	20x	17x
58. Nicaragua	—	—	—	—	107	142	94	101	74	77	31	44
59. Kenya	69	74	80	59	96	70	96	02	92x	89x	27	19
60. Algeria	57	66	70	46	85	80	103	88	94	83	66	53
61. South Africa	76x	96x	78x	75x	—	—	—	—	—	—	—	—
62. Uzbekistan	—	—	—	—	—	—	—	—	—	—	—	—
63. Brazi	81	96	83	80	96x	116x	101x	97x	—	—	31x	36x
64. Peru	85	87	91	79	96x	91x	125x	120x	—	—	66x	60x
65. El Salvador	73	82	76	70	101	100	77	78	69	71	26	26
66. Morocco	50	62	61	38	68	71	81	55	66	45	42	30
67. Kyrgyzstan	—	—	—	—	—	—	—	—	—	—	—	—
68. Philippines	90	99	90	89	99	104	111	110	100	98	72	15
69. Ecuador	86	95	88	84	99	104	118	117	—	—	55	57
70. Botswana	74	77	84	65	105	107	107	112	88	93	44	47
71. Honduras	73	95	75	71	101	103x	108	109	89	94	29x	30x
72. Iran, Islamic Rep. of	54	67	64	43	89	75	19	106	99	90	63	47
73. Egypt	48	54	63	34	86	77	105	90	—	—	92	71
74. Azerbaijan	—	—	—	—	—	—	—	—	—	—	—	—
75. Dominican Rep.	83	96	85	82	101	130x	95	96	73	73	44x	57x
76. Kazakhstan	—	—	—	—	—	—	—	—	—	—	—	—
77. Viet Nam	88	91	92	84	94x	93x	105x	99x	—	—	43x	40x
78. Lebanon	80	83	88	73	90x	98x	105x	95x	—	—	57x	56x
79. China	73	74	84	62	92	77	140	129	100	100	53	41
80. Saudi Arbia	62	66	73	48	87	75	83	72	69	56	55	41
81. Syrian Arab Rep.	65	65	78	51	89	72	114	102	100	93	60	43
82. Tunisia	65	76	74	56	89	80	122	109	100	91	50	40
83. Moldova	—	—	—	—	—	—	—	—	—	—	—	—
84. Albania	—	—	—	—	100	87	98	98	—	—	85	74
85. Armenia	—	—	—	—	—	—	—	—	—	—	—	—

TABLE 20.1 *(Contd.)*

86. Paraguay	90	96	92	88	97	107	109	106	95	94	29	31
87. Korea, Dem, Peo. Rep	—	—	—	—	94	—	110	103	—	—	—	—
88. Mexico	88	94	90	85	97	102	113	110	—	—	52	53
89. Thailand	93	94	96	90	99	97	86	85	—	—	33	32
90. Russian Federation	—	—	—	—	—	—	—	—	—	—	—	—
91. Oman	—	—	—	—	92	81	108	99	87	82	59	48
92. Jordan	80	79	89	70	97x	92x	105x	102x	94x	91x	79x	73x
93. Georgia	—	—	—	—	—	—	—	—	—	—	—	—
94. Romania	—	—	—	—	112	97	86	96	—	—	93	90
95. Latvia	—	—	—	—	—	—	—	—	—	—	—	—
96. Ukraine	—	—	—	—	—	—	—	—	—	—	—	—
97. Argentina	95	100	95	95	107	113	107	114	—	—	69	78
98. Estonia	100x	100x	100x	100x	—	—	—	—	—	—	—	—
99. Mauritius	—	89x	—	—	102	100	102	104	92	94	53	53
100. Venezuela	88	103	87	90	100	137	94	94	60	62	30	41
101. Belarus	—	—	—	—	—	—	—	—	—	—	—	—
102. Trinidad and Tobago	95x	96x	97x	93x	101	104	95	96	90	90	79	82
103. United Arab Emirates	—	66x	—	—	97	114	117	114	100	100	63	72
104. Uruguay	96	99	97	96	99	102x	107	106	—	—	61x	62x
105. Yugoslavia (former)	93	91	97	88	100	99	95	95	80	79	80	79
106. Columbia	87	99	87	86	102	119	109	111	—	—	48	57
107. Lithuania	98x	99	99x	98x	—	—	—	—	—	—	—	—
108. Panama	99	100	88	88	96	109	109	105	91	92	57	62
109. Bulgeria	—	—	—	—	98	014	97	95	85	84	72	75
110. Sri Lanka	88	90	93	84	97	107	108	105	100	100	72	77
111. Malaysia	78	81	86	70	100	105	93	93	—	—	55	58
112. Chile	93	100	93	93	98	108	99	97	—	—	71	77
113. Kuwait	73	87	77	67	98	94	101	99	84	86	93	87
114. Poland	—	—	—	—	99	105	99	98	97	97	80	84
115. Hungary	99x	100x	99x	99x	100	101	94	94	90	91	78	79
116. Costa Rica	93	100	93	93	99	105	102	101	87	87	41	43
117. Jamaica	98	101	98	99	101	111	104	105	98	100	57	43
118. Slovakia	—	—	—	—	—	—	—	—	—	—	—	—
119. Portugal	85	91	89	81	97	102	121	117	99	100	58	59
120. Czech Republic	—	—	—	—	—	—	—	—	—	—	—	—

TABLE 20.1: *(Contd.)*

121. Cuba	94	98	95	93	95	112	105	100	96	95	84	94
122. Israel	92x	94x	95x	89x	103	109	92	95	—	—	79	86
123. Belgium	—	—	—	—	101	101	102	103	98	99	103	104
124. USA	—	—	—	—	99	99	105	104	99	99	92	91
125. New Zealand	—	—	—	—	99	013	106	105	100	100	88	91
126. Italy	97	98	98	96	100	100	96	96	—	—	78	78
127. Spain	95	96	97	93	99	110	109	108	100	100	102	112
128. Greece	93	91	98	89	101	96	100	101	96	97	101	97
129. Korea, Rep.	96	95	99	94	103	97	106	109	100	100	89	86
130. Austria	—	—	—	—	99	104	103	102	93	93	82	85
131. France	—	—	—	—	98	108	112	110	100	100	93	100
132. United Kingdom	—	—	—	—	101	104	106	107	100	100	82	85
133. Australia	—	—	—	—	100	104	105	105	97	97	82	85
134. Switzerland	—	—	—	—	—	—	—	—	—	—	—	—
135. Germany	—	—	—	—	100	97	105	105	89	90	99	96
136. Canada	—	—	—	—	98	101	106	104	96	97	106	107
137. Denmark	—	—	—	—	101	102	97	98	—	—	108	107
138. Norway	—	—	—	—	100	104	99	99	99	98	98	102
139. Netherlands	—	—	—	—	103	97	115	118	100	100	104	101
140. Sweden	—	—	—	—	101	104	106	107	100	100	89	93
141. Hong Kong	—	—	—	—	99	106	105	104	95x	95x	71	75
142. Singapore	83x	80x	92x	74x	98	104	111	109	100	100	68	71
143. Finland	—	—	—	—	99	119	100	99	—	—	104	124
144. Japan	—	—	—	—	100	103	101	101	100	100	94	97
145. Ireland	—	—	—	—	101	110	100	101	87	89	93	102

TABLE 20.2: Regional Summaries: Women's Education

	Sub-Saharan Africa	Middle East and North Africa	South Asia	East Asia and Pacific	Latin America and Caribbean	Former USSR	Industrialized countries	Developing countries	Least developed countries
1. Adult literacy rate 1970, Female (%)	17	19	19	56	69	—	95	33	18
2. Adult literacy rate 1970, Male (%)	34	37	44	76	76	—	97	53	36
3. Adult literacy rate 1990, Female (%)	41	46	32	67	83	—	—	55	32
4. Adult literacy rate 1990, Male (%)	61	70	59	86	87	—	—	75	54
5. Life expectancy, Females as % of Males	107	104	101	106	109	—	109	105	104
6. Primary school enrolment ratio (%) 1960 (gross), Female	24	40	39	85	71	—	107	62	23
7. Primary school enrolment ratio (%) 1960 (gross), Male	46	72	77	120	75	—	109	93	48
8. Primary school enrolment ratio (%) 1986-91 (gross), Female	60	87	73	120	102	—	103	92	57
9. Primary school enrolment ratio (%) 1986-91 (gross), Male	76	103	97	128	105	—	103	107	74
10. Primary school enrolment ratio (%) 1986-91 (gross), Female	46	79	—	—	75	—	97	36	12
11. Primary school enrolment ratio (%) 1986-91 (gross), Male	54	90	—	—	74	—	97	82	45
12. Enrolment, Females as % of Males, primary school	80	84	75	93	98	—	100	87	78
13. Enrolment, Females as % of Males, secondary school	66	72	60	82	109	—	102	77	58
14. Secondary school enrolment ratio, Female (%)	14	45	28	43	48	—	92	36	12
15. Secondary school enrolment ratior, Male (%)	21	62	47	52	44	—	91	47	21

COUNTRY GROUPINGS

Sub-Saharan Africa

Angola	Eritrea	Malawi	Sierra Leone
Benin	Ethiopia	Mali	Somalia
Bostwana	Gabon	Mauritania	South Africa
Burkina Faso	Ghana	Mauritius	Tanzania, U.Rep. of

Burundi	Guinea	Mozambique	Togo
Cameroon	Guinea-Bissau	Namibia	Uganda
Central African Rep.	Kenya	Niger	Zaire
Chad	Lesotho	Nigeria	Zambia
Congo	Liberia	Rwanda	Zimbawe
Cote d'Ivoire	Madagascar	Senegal	

Middle East and North Africa

Algeria	Kuwait	Saudi Arabia	United Arab Emirates
Egypt	Lebanon	Sudan	Yemen
Iran, Islamic Rep. of	Libyan, Arab Jamahiriya		Syrian Arab Rep.
Iraq	Morocco	Tunisia	
Jordan	Oman	Turkey	

South Asia

Afghanistan	Bhutan	Nepal	Sri Lamka
Bangladesh	India	Pakistan	

East Asia and Pacific

Cambodia	Korea, Dem. Peo. Rep.	Mongolia	Singapore
China	Korea, Rep. of	Myanmar	Thailand
Hong Kong	Laos Peo. Dem. Rep.	Papua Guinea	Viet Nam
Indonesia	Malaysia	Philippines	

Latin America and Caribbean

Argentina	Cuba	Honduras	Peru
Bolivia	Dominican Rep.	Jamaica	Trinidad and Tobago
Brazil	Eduador	Mexico	Uruguay
Chile	El Salvador	Nicaragua	Venezuela
Colombia	Guatemala	Panama	
Costa Rica	Haiti	Paraguay	

Former USSR

Armenia	Georgia	Lithuania	Turkmenistan
Azerbaijan	Kazakhstan	Moldova	Ukraine
Belarus	Kyrgyzstan	Russian Federal	Uzbekistan
Estonia	Latvia	Tajikistan	

Industrialized Countries

Albania	Finland	Japan	Sapin
Australia	France	Netherlands	Sweden
Austria	Germany	New Zealand	Switzerland
Belgium	Greece	Norway	United Kingdom
Bulgeria	Hungary	Poland	USA
Canada	Ireland	Portugal	Yugoslavia (former)
Denmark	Italy	Slovakia	

Developing Countries

Afghanistan	Egypt	Liberia	Rwanda
Algeria	El Salvador	Libyan Arab Jamahiriya	Saudi Arabia
Angola	Eritrea	Madagascar	Senegal
Argentina	Ethiopia	Malawi	Sierra Leone
Bangladesh	Gabon	Malaysia	Singapore
Benin	Ghana	Mali	Somalia
Bhutan	Guatemala	Mauritania	South Africa
Bolivia	Guinea	Mauritius	Sri Lanka
Botswana	Guninea-Bissau	Mexico	Sudan
Brazil	Haiti	Mongolia	Syrian Arab Rep.
Burkina Faso	Honduras	Morocco	Tanzania, U.Rep.of
Burundi	Hong Kong	Mozambique	Thailand
Cambodia	India	Myanmar	Togo
Cameroon	Indonesia	Namibia	Trinidad and Tobago
Central African Rep.	Iran, Islamic Rep. of	Nepal	Tunisia
Chad	Iraq	Nicaragua	Turkey
Chile	Jamaica	Niger	Uganda
China	Jordan	Nigeria	United Arab Emirates
Colombia	Kenya	Oman	Uruguay
Congo	Korea, Dem. Peo, Rep.	Pakistan	Venezuela
Costa Rica	Korea, Rep. of	Panama	Viet Nam
Cote d'Ivoire	Kuwait	Papua New Guinea	Yemen
Cuba	Laos, Peo. Dem. Rep.	Paraguay	Zaire
Dominican Rep.	Lebanon	Peru	Zambia
Eduador	Lesotho	Philippines	Zimbabwe

Least Developed Countries

Afghanistan	Chad	Malawi	Somalia
Bangladesh	Ethiopia	Mali	Sudan
Benin	Guinea	Mauritania	Tanzania, U.Rep.of
Bhutan	Guinea-Bissau	Mozambique	Togo
Botswana	Haiti	Myanmar	Uganda
Burkina Faso	Laos Peo. Dem Rep.	Nepal	Yemen
Burundi	Lesotho	Niger	Zaire
Cambodia	Liberia	Rwanda	Zambia
Central African Rep.	Madagascar	Sierra Leone	

Defination

Adult Literacy Rate

Percentage of persons aged 15 and above, who can read and write.

Primary and Secondary Enrolment Ratios

The gross enrolment ratio is the total number of children enrolled in a schooling level—whether or not they belong in the relevant age group for that level—expressed as a percentage of the total number of children in the relevant age-group for that level. The net enrolment ratio is the total number of children enrolled in a schooling level who belong in the relevant age-group, expressed and a percentage of the total number in that age-group.

Children Reaching Final Grade of Primary School

Percentage of the children entering the first grade of primary school who eventually reach the final grade.

Exploitation of Symbols

Since the aim of the statistics section is to provide a broad picture of the situation of children and women worldwide, detailed data qualifications and footnotes are seen as more appropriate for inclusion elsewhere. Only two symbols are used in the tables.

Data not available

Indicates data that refer to years or periods other than those specified in the column heading, differ from the standard definition, or refer to only part of a country.

APPENDICES

APPENDIX-I

WOMEN'S EDUCATION IN ANCIENT INDIA

Introduction

The *Rigveda* and the *Yajurveda* speak of women's education in the following verses. "Mother should impart proper education to her children so as to broaden the horizon of their ideas. (*Rigveda* 5:47:6). So it is directed: O King and other nobles: make adequate arrangements to train lady teachers for imparting training to girl students who, on obtaining maturity, select for themselves their partners for marriage". (*Yajurveda* 10:6).

The *Rigveda* (3.55.16) mentions "An unmarried young learned daughter should be married to a bridegroom who like her is learned. Never think of giving in marriage a daughter of very young age." *The Yajurveda* (8.1) repeats the same thing and so it says, "A young daughter who has observed *brahmacharya* (i.e., finished her studies) should be married to a bridegroom who like her is learned". The *Atharva Veda* says clearly that; Brahmacharyena Kanya yuvanam vindate patim," which means a maiden wins a young husband through bramacharya or Vedic studentship.

The Vedas mention a number of *Rsikas* or learned ladies in their various verses: The foremost of these *Rsikas* is *Ghosa* (*Rig Veda* 10.39-40), the wife of the great seer, Kaksivan. She has been mentioned in the *Rig Veda* in two long hymns: 39 and 40 of the tenth mandala stand to her credit. This daughter of a king (*Rig Veda* 10:40:15) is equally important in her concept of divinity Lopamudra (*Rig Veda* 1:179:1-6), another lady, is credited with having composed a hymn jointly with her husband Agastya. Apala (*Rig Veda* 8:91:1-7) To Romasa (*Rig Veda* 1:126:6-7); (*Sama Veda* 550-51;1016:18; 1631:33), is ascribed a beautiful verse of fine imagery and tender feeling. The seer and speaker of the first verses of hymn 18 of the tenth book of the *Rig Veda* is Vasukara's wife, while the mother of the Gaupayanas along with her sons, Bandhu, Subandhu, Srutabandhu and Siprabandhu, is that of 10:60.

Indrani, the powerful consort of Indra, is the speaker of the verses 2:4-7;9;10;15;18;22; and 23 of the hymn 86 of the tenth book of

Rig Veda. She is also the independent *Risi* of a powerful hymn (*Rig Veda* 10:45). Yami, is the author of the hymn 10:10, jointly with her brother.

In the famous line of *Satapatha Brahmana* it is said: Mataman pitamanacharyavan puruso veda, which means that a child does not receive so much good from any other person as he does from his loving mother and father.

Prior to the Upanisadic period woman's education was very popular. Learned women were called rsikas and *Brahmavadinis.* The young unmarried daughters were qualified for marriage on the basis of their education.

R.D. Ranade has classified the women of the Upanisadic period into three different types: "Katayani, the woman of the world, mentioned in the Brahadaranyaka; Maitreyi, the type of a spiritual woman, a fit consort to the philosopher Yajnavalkya; and Gargi, fully equipped in the art of intellectual warfare who dares to wrangle with Yajnavalkya even at the court of King Janaka where a number of great philosophers are assembled."

The position of women in the entire Vedic-till-post-Upanisadic period was very high in the society. *Manu-Smrti,* one of the most ancient of all Smrtis, pays the greatest tribute to the women in a voice that cannot lose its rhythm in course of time:

Yatra naryastu pujyante ramante tatra devatah.
Yatraitastu na pujyante sarvastatraphalah kriyah.

Where women are honoured, there the gods are delighted, but where they are insulted, all sacred rites become futile.

(*Manu Smrti* 3:56; in *Mahabharata* 13:45:5) of Panini refers to female students as *Chhatri* and their hostels *chhatri-sala.* (Asta 6:2:86). The wife of an acarya is referred to as acaryani (Asta 4:1:49), but acarya was the title of female teachers corresponding in status to an acarya.

The *Ramayana* and *the Mahabharta* throw a flood of light on the education of Women.

APPENDIX- II

GIRLS: NCERT STATUS STUDY (1986)

Introduction

The enrolment of girls has traditionally lagged behind the enrolment of boys on account of several socio-economic and educational handicaps in the present social system. Consequently great emphasis has been laid on additional enrolment of girls both in formal and non-formal sectors. It is felt that Constitutional Commitment of universalising elementary education of girls cannot be realized only through formal system of education. Non-formal system of education has been devised as a viable means to bring the non-starters and drop-outs within the periphery of education. Efforts have been made to make it as flexible as possible to suit the convenience of the parents as well as the girls who are planned to be brought to the fold of educational system. All possible steps are taken to ensure that learners' activities in their world of work at home or outside home do not get intrupted. The ultimate purpose of running the Non-Formal Education Centres (NFECs) is to enrol, retain, guide and support them so as to put them in the main stream of national system of education. Keeping in view the importance of this scheme a project was taken up on this subject in the Department of Teacher Education, Special Education, and Extension Services, NCERT, New Delhi during the year 1985-86.

The purpose was to identify the extent of benefit it accrued to the girls in the age-group 6-14 years and then to design strategies for augmenting the benefit to them under this system.

While analysing the data it was felt that certain aspects needed further clarifications. As these clarifications were about the functioning of the programme, it was thought necessary to organize a seminar on the subject wherein the concerned officers may be requested to brief us about those aspects. It was also felt that this seminar will provide a forum for the mutual exchange of ideas to the participants and consequently some strategies may be worked out for strengthening

---

Source: *Non-Formal Education for Girls: A Status Study*, Department of Teacher Education. NCERT, 1986, New Delhi.

(Not included in the previous volume).

the programme. Some Delhi-based voluntary organisations and agencies, which have acquired rich experience in the field by working at the national level, were also consulted and their experiences and suggestions were noted down and transmitted to the participants during the seminar.

The seminar of a select group of the officials responsible for running the programme in their States was organized at State Institute of Education, Chandigarh on February 25-26, 1986. Some local experts in the area were also invited to gear discussion. After thorough discussion on the reports presented by the State representatives, the participants appreciated the efforts being made in these States for making the programme a success. It was felt that much more is needed to be done to achieve results through this system to the expected level. The participants were of the view that the weakest link in the programme is the instructor and there is an urgent need to formulate some guidelines to prepare Instructor as per local needs. It was felt that the instructional material for the preparation of Instructor should be such which may enable her to take up the role of dynamic change agent and enable her to motivate the non-starters to join formal or non-formal system of education and also save them from dropping out from the system.

Realising the importance of an Instructor as a key person in the non-formal education system, it was felt necessary to prepare guidelines for Instructor preparation which may prepare her to shoulder her expected task successfully. Hence a second seminar of educationists, sociologists and key persons working in the field was organized for this purpose on March 4-6, 1986 at C.R. Polytechnic, Rohtak. Participants of the seminar visited a few NFE Centres in the rural areas to have first hand information and to decide the lines on which such Instructors should be prepared. In the background of Instructor training package were suggested some items for Instructor preparation on which methods and materials were required to be developed.

As a follow up of this seminar a workshop to develop methods and materials for Instructor preparation was held on March 31 to 5th April, 1986 at C.R. Polytechnic, Rohtak. This workshop was attended by instructors and supervisors of NFE Centres along with educationists, social scientists, basic scientists and mathematicians. A few more items in the guidelines were added to make the same more comprehensive and broad-based. Illustrative moduls were drawn out on the suggested items and discussed in detail to analyse the same from different angles. To crystallize the ideas further the material thus developed was tried out in the field for a day before finalization. Details of the three programmes conducted in the area are given in Volume I and II of this report. Volume I covers the proceedings and outcomes of the first programme and Volume II consists of the details of the second and third programmes.

Methods for Non-Formal Education of Girls—Collection of Data

An exploratory study of the methods adopted for non-formal education of girls in the States was conducted in the year 1985-86, under the major programme of universalization of girls' education. The specific purposes of the programme were to find out:

(i) The provisional aspects of NFE of girls;
(ii) The functional aspects of NFE of girls: and
(iii) The methods of training female instructors.

The information was collected through a questionnaire. The questionnaire had two parts. The first part concerned the provisional, functional and training aspects of the NFE programme and the second part dealt with difficulties encountered and suggestions for improvement of the programme. The first part consisted of factual information concerning number of NFE Centres at State/District level, in rural/urban areas; centres started during the Sixth Five Year Plan, centres planned to be started during the Seventh Five Year Plan; organisational set-up of the centres; criteria for opening a NFEC; minimum requisites for opening a centre; expectations from local community; timings of the centres; steps taken to motivate parents and girls; approximate cost of educating a girl in a NEFC; corriculum adopted; evaluation system; details of the training programme for Instructors, their pay scales etc; In the second part they were to report the bottlenecks which are coming in the way of the successful running of the programme. They were also requested to give suggestions if any to overcome those problems.

After the analysis of the data it was felt that some details about the functioning of the programme needed further clarification. Hence a seminar of the representatives of the selected States was organized for the purpose on February 25-26, 1986 at State Institute of Education, Chandigarh. The participants who attended the seminar were from

Assam, Andhra Pradesh, Bihar, Union Territories of Chandigarh and Delhi, Gujarat, Haryana, Himachal Pradesh, Maharashtra, Rajasthan, Uttar Pradesh and West Bengal. Some local persons working in the field were also invited. After the inauguration session the State representatives presented briefs of their reports about functioning of the programme in their respective States. The presentation of individual reports was followed by general discussion seeking clarifications wherever required.

In the late afternoon some of the NFE Centres were visited by the group which observed the functioning of the same. The participants also discussed about the working of the centres with the instructors and tried to find out the difficulties encountered by them in bringing and retaining the children to the centres. Their suggestions were also sought in overcoming the problems and difficulties. Their difficulties and suggestions were kept in view by the participants while formulating strategies for strengthening the programme on the following day.

Next day a general discussion was held on the working of the centres and participants were asked to name the centre which they considered best. They were also requested to give reasons for adjudging a centre the best. This exercise helped in bringing to the surface what a good centre should have for effective functioning of the programme. This also proved beneficial for the participants to crystallize their thinking about the programme and consequently they put forward quite practical suggestions for strengthening the programme during the seminar.

Part of the afternoon session was devoted to penning down of difficulties faced in running the programme and strategies which can be adopted to overcome the same. Rest of the session was utilized in conducting a general session to discuss the suggested strategies.

Salient Features of the Non-formal Education Programme for Girls in States

The information on non-formal education programme was received through questionnaire from Andhra Pradesh, Andaman and Nicobar Islands, Assam, Bihar, Union Territory of Chandigarh, Gujarat, Haryana, Himachal Pradesh, Madhya Pradesh, Maharashtra, Punjab, Rajasthan and West Bengal. Analysis of the data and discussion with the representatives of the States invited to participate in the seminar held on February 25-26, 1986 at State Institute of Education, Chandigarh revealed the following salient features of the non-formal education programme being run at present in different States.

1. The programme has been introduced in most of the States with the financial assistance of Government of India with a purpose to bring non-enrolled and drop-out children in the age-group 6 to 14 into the fold of education.
2. Majority of centres have been started by the initiative of the State Education Department in their respective States. A few voluntary organizations are also working in this area. There is a provision of giving cent per cent grant in aid by the Central Government to the voluntary agencies for running this programme.
3. Some of the centres are running separately for girls and boys and some are co-educational.
4. Number of centres in the rural area is more in comparison to urban areas for both boys and girls. This is possible because the drop-out rate is higher in the rural areas than in the urban areas.
5. Number of centres meant for girls is higher than for boys. This indicates that States are recognising the importance of universalization of education among girls.
6. Majority of the centres have been opened during the Sixth Five Year Plan. Even in the Seventh Five Year Plan the scheme has been given great importance.
7. In some of the States these centres are being run upto primary standard and in others upto middle standard.
8. In most of the States NFE Centers have been opened in separate buildings having infrastructure of their own. But at certain places these have been tucked with infra-structure provided for formal schools. They are permitted to use the same building, play-grounds, furniture etc. Their timings are adjusted in a way that these start working when the timings of formal schools are over. Examples of Union Territory of Chandigarh and some places in Gujarat may be cited in this context.
9. The main criteria for opening a centre are the availability of the target population (number of non-starter and drop-out); percentage of disadvantaged population; parents' willingness to send the children to NFE Centre; non-availability of formal education facilities; demand from the community members;

report and recommendation of the District Education Officer; and suggestions/recommendations of the public representatives. On the basis of the above mentioned criteria the project officer recommends the opening of a centre through District Education Officer to the State Education Department. In some of the States District level committees are set up to examine the proposal in detail before recommending to the State Education Department. Central Government approves the opening of a centre on the recommendation of the respective State Government.

10. In most of the States accommodation for opening a Centre is provided by the community. It may be *Dharamshala, Chopal, Panchayat Ghar,* a temple or some person's personal house with no restriction for entry or building of a local voluntary organization etc. Sometimes Instructor of the centre provides accommodation in his/her residence. At some place a room in the local school building is used for running a centre. In such cases the furniture and equipment of the school is utilized for the NFE centres also. In other cases the furniture and equipment are provided by the government according to NFE pattern.
11. These centres are run mostly for 2 to 2-1/2 hours a day. In certain cases these are run for 3 hours also. In some cases these are run in the morning. In other cases the timings are in the afternoon or in the evening. Timings are fixed keeping in view the occupations of the guardians of the learners and convenience of the target group. As such timings differ from centre to centre.
12. Parents are motivated to send their daughters to the centres through periodical persuation through personal contacts by Project Officers, Supervisors and Instructors. Influence of the village leaders are also made use of in convincing parents of the utility of education for the girls. Public meetings and film shows are also arranged for the purpose.

    Free books and stationery are supplied to the learners in all the NFE Centres. Scheduled Caste girls are supplied free uniforms in most of the States and in some of the States all girls irrespective of caste are provided free uniforms (e.g. West Bengal). There are some NFE centres for example, in Chandigarh and West Bengal where free tiffin is also provided to the learners.
13. The core curriculum followed in the NFE centres and in the formal school system is the same. Keeping in view that the

children coming to these centres are comparatively older in age a condensed form of curriculum has been prepared in almost all the States to be completed in shortest possible period. While preparing the condensed course efforts have been made to relate the same to the local occupations, values, norms and interests of the learners.

Efforts are made to cover the curriculum meant for primary stage in the formal schools in two years and middle stage in 2 to 3 years in the NFE centres.

Curriculum is mostly divided into units and at the end of each unit exercises have been provided for simulataneous evaluation by the learners or instructors.

The learners in the NFE can join formal system of education after giving test in the school or appearing in the Board's examination. They can also take the test given by Project Officers for which they are issued certificate on getting success.

14. Proper record of the progress of the learners is maintained by the instructor. In this manner evaluation is a continuous process in these centres.
15. Average annual cost of educating a girl in a NFE Centre has been calculated by some of the States as follows:

State	Amount in Rs.
Assam	67.40
Bihar	37.00
Haryana	60.00
Maharashtra	75.00
Punjab	50.00
Rajasthan	65.00

As far as tuition cost is concerned, parents have no financial implications for sending their daughters in NFECs in any of the states.

16. The person-incharge of a centre is called an instructor. Then there are supervisors, Co-ordinators and District Education Officers to ensure proper functioning of the centres. At State-level there is usually a senior officer who looks after the non-formal education programme.
17. At the time of selection and posting of an instructor, preference is given to a local person. Prescribed qualifications for an

Instructor for primary-level is High School and for middle-level is Higher Secondary but these qualifications are relaxed in case of non-availability of suitable candidates. Aptitude for social work is considered as an added qualifications for an Instructor. In case of non-availability of good Instructor any local school teacher, ex-service man or retired person is employed as an Instructor.

18. Instructors are imparted in-service training in some of the States by co-ordinators of non-formal education programme. They are often drawn from Teacher Training Institutes, SIEs/ SCERTs or State Resource Centres. In most of the States there is no provision of in-service training for these Instructors. Efficient Instructors are issued merit certificates by some of the State Education Departments for motivating them to work vigorously.

In nutshell it appears that States have realized the importance of NFE programme for universalisation of elementary education of girls and are sincere in their efforts to implement the same. But there are certain genuine difficulties which are coming in the way of effective implementations of the programme. If something concrete may be done in the direction of overcoming these problems it is not difficult to achieve the set targets of universalisation of education of girls through this programme. Difficulties encountered by the persons working in this area and a few suggestions to overcome the same have been discussed in the following pages:

Difficulties Encountered in Running the Programme and Suggestions for Improvement

1. The girls in the age-group 6-14 who are neither attending formal schools nor coming to the NFE centres are mostly engaged in their own world of work either at home or outside home. Hence it is a genuine problem for an Instructor to motivative their parents to send them to the centre. In most of the cases where it is a question of survival, it is a hard task to make them understand the value of education for their life. Even personal visits of the Instructors to their homes; flexible curriculum, timetable; incentive in the form of free learning material etc. have also not resulted in expected outcomes.

This sort of situation discourages the organizers to put in more efforts. The participants felt that unless it is made obligatory on parents to send their daughters to school or NFE centres by law, social programme, economic sanctions or by some other viable method, mere persuasion will not bring fruit.

2. The remuneration of Rs.105 paid to an Instructor is too meagre an amount to attract a good worker to the programme. It was suggested that the same may be increased to attract qualified and dedicated persons to the programme.
3. Most of the States have found it difficult to get properly qualified Instructors from the local population. Hence the requisite qualifications have to be invariably relaxed in their case at the time of their selection. It was suggested that regular, systematic training programme may be taken up in each of the States to prepare Instructors for their special job. The participants were of the view that job of an Instructor is much more difficult than an ordinary school teacher mainly because she has to deal with girls who primarily are reluctant to come to the centre and are not willing students to learn. The Instructor has to create environment to make them interested in the studies and from time to time has to be very flexible in her approach to retain them in the centre. She has to mould her to appeal to the whims of individual child and parents. Secondly they have to cover the same curriculum within two years which a formal school teacher takes five years to complete. Moreover, she has only 2 to 2-1/2 hours per day at her disposal when she can make children learn vis-a-vis the formal school teacher who has 4 to 5 hours at her disposal. These limitations make the task of non-formal education pretty difficult for an Instructor. Hence there is an urgent need for preparing an Instructor to face these special work and day-to-day challenges to meet the situation successfully.

It was felt that in the whole programme of NFE, Instructor is the weakest link by both qualification and professional training-wise. The success of a centre hinges on this crucial link. She is the most important person who should be properly equipped if the nation feels concerned about making this programme a success. It was suggested that another workshop may be organized to pin-point the areas on which special emphasis may be laid in the instructor's preparation programme.

The group was also of the view that various training packages suiting target group in different situations may be prepared and Instructors should be trained according to the package suiting the conditions in which they have to work.

4. In most of the States there is no separate official cadre to plan, organize, implement, supervise and evaluate the NFE programme at the district and State levels. The officers made incharge of this programme are often not adequately and properly staffed to take exclusive interest in the management of the programme. It was suggested that a separate wing at the sub-divisional level may be created to improve functioning of NFECs. Non-formal wing of the Directorate of State Headquarters should also be strengthened to ensure better direction and supervision.
5. It was pointed out that remuneration of the Instructors is not paid regularly due to non-receipt of sanction in time. It was suggested that funds may be sanctioned at the beginning of the financial year to enable. State Government to pay the Instructors in time each month.
6. It was suggested by the participants that some useful crafts related to learners' world of work may be started in the centres besides providing some recreational-cum-educational material for the girls and their mothers. These may help them in the performance of their duties with competence at home and elsewhere and also work as hooking points to attract girls to these centres. Besides this all other incentives e.g. free uniform, attendance scholarships etc. which are provided in the formal schools should be made available for the learners in these centres. These incentives are rather much more needed in these centres in comparison to the girls going to the formal education schools.
7. In some of the States guardian-teacher associations have been started to solicit co-operation of the rural community. It was suggested that the possibility of constituting such type of association in the rural areas may be explored by other States.
8. The participants were of the opinion that non-formal system of education should work as a supportive system to the formal education and not as an alternative to the formal system. All efforts should be made to establish proper linkage with the formal system of education. Ultimate aim of NFE should be to bridge the gap and bring the non-starters or the drop-outs

back to the main stream of formal education.

9. It was also suggested that Instructor should be full time employee and available in the centre through out the day. Learners should be free to come to the centre any time during the day according to their convenience to get guidance from the Instructor to cover the prescribed curriculum.
10. The group was of opinion that frequent transfers of the Supervisory staff of NFE programme should be avoided. This will help the Supervisory staff to understand the local conditions thoroughly, plan the programmes with proper understanding and implement the same with interest, devotion and sincerity The good work done by them should be given recognition in the form of merit certificate, special increments or may be even the place of choicest posting.
11. It was pointed out that in hilly areas lack of vehicle facilities for the field officers is one of the main bottlenecks in the proper supervision of the NFE centres. Steps may be taken to overcome the same.
12. Periodical evaluation of the situation in which NFECs are working is a must for the purpose of understanding local problems and to bring about an improvement. Hence requisite research facilities may be provided at district-level to undertake such type of surveys from time to time. This will save the programme from stagnation.
13. The group felt that appointment of more and more women Instructors and supervisors may attract more girls to the programme of NFE.
14. Wide use of mass media may be made to motivate parents to send their daughters to NFECs. Catchy serials and captions on televisions, slogans on radio, meaningful posters and messages at public places, film shows and other such means can be helpful in popularizing the programme.
15. Development of competitive spirit among the different villege communities may also help the programme to grow at a faster speed. Funds for approach roads, water supply, sewerage schemes, subsidy in fertilizers, seeds etc. and other developmental amenities may be given to the villages in preference to those villages which may be lagging behind in the enrolement drive of girls in the target group.
16. Active co-operation of the public representatives may be sought

in the enrolement drive of the girls. Public opinion may be created to put pressure on the political parties so that they may make their representatives accountable to them for their contribution to the enrolement drive of girls in their area/ constituency.

17. Efforts may be made to motivate more and more voluntary organizations to take up non-formal education programme in a massive manner.
18. The centres run by state government or by voluntary organizations should be regularly evaluated to ascertain their performance. Criteria for evaluating a NFEC may be worked but to adjudge the same systematically. The centres which have come up to the standard may be ultimately converted into formal schools.
19. It was suggested that an explanatory study of the learners who drop out from the NFE programme may be taken up to ascertain the reason as to why they drop out, what is their world of work, how many join formal schools, can curriculum be related to their world of work etc.

The above mentioned points indicate that the basic problem in this programme is to motivate non-starters and drop-out girls to enrol and retain them in the NFECs. This objective can be achieved if parents are convinced of the utility of education as a value in the life of their daughters on the one hand and teaching-learning process made lively for the learners on the other hand. For the former, community co-operation and for the latter, competent and devoted Instructors are of vital importance. The possibilities of soliciting the co-operation of the community can be explored through regular periodical personal contacts by the Instructor or other supervisory staff; mass media; financial incentives, etc. The most crucial link in this programme is the Instructor. It was strongly felt during the seminar that steps may be taken to prepare Instructor for this special job which needs activists and continued workers.

APPENDIX-III

WOMEN'S EDUCATION AND FERTILITY BEHAVIOUR: A CASE-STUDY OF RURAL MAHARASHTRA, INDIA

Introduction

The enhancement of female education is currently accepted as the most promising agent of change in women's access to power and control over resources as well as in demographic condition. Female education is also viewed as an important determinant of fertility decline. However, to check the validity of this a study was planned by UNESCO to trace the pattern of the relationship between women's education and fertility in a rural setting in the State of Maharashtra, an area that is in the process of modernization and demographic transition. Date for the study came from a sample survey carried out in 1983-84, by United Nations, New York, 1993.

Summary and Conclusions

In the analysis of rural Maharashtrian women, the expected inverse relationship between women's education and fertility has been observed, but the overall effect is neither as strong nor as uniform as is often implied. It is shaped by a complex set of inter-relationship whose individual effects cancel each other out, thereby weakening the overall relationship. Four main conclusions emerge.

First, the evidence suggests that, although it is moderate, education does effect on fertility and the variables that intervene between education and fertility, even when such related factors as economic status, mass-media exposure and women's work status are controlled. To be sure, control for socio-economic variables does diminish the size of the education differentials, but even so the independent effect of education consistently exceeds that of any other socio-economic factor. This result is consistent with earlier findings supporting the role of female education as a determinant of fertility change.

In this connection, however, it is interesting to note that the level

United Nations, New York, 1993.

of female education appears to be more closely related to economic status (income, living conditions and ownership of consumer durables) and to mass-media exposure than to such other aspects of female status as work and domestic autonomy. This calls into question the usually accepted autonomy enhancing aspects of education. It appears that, rather than education, cultural and kinship norms continue to shape autonomy and decision-making among women.

Secondly, the results indicate that the effect of education is by no means uniform. On the contrary, a little education has only a marginal effect on fertility itself, or on factors affecting the supply of or demand for children. The threshold is quite unambiguously a middle school education (5-7 years), at which point the expected effects on fertility and the intervening variables become evident.

Thirdly, the evidence shows that the inverse effect of education on fertility is largely the result of inadvertent factors rather than volitional changes, whether they are factors related to the demand for children or to contraceptive use. It is noteworthy that age at marriage exhibits particularly pronounced differences by education. The mean age at marriage for women with a middle school education is almost two years higher than that for uneducated women, and women with eight or more years of education marry almost four years later than uneducated women. Hence, it is no surprise that most of the observed differentials in fertility by education result from delayed marriage.

Educational differences in such other supply factors as fecundability, duration of lactat on and post-partum amenorrhoea, to some extent, tend to counter the effect of age of marriage. Durations of breast-feeding and post-partum and amenorrhoea and the lengths of the first and second birth intervals decline considerably with increasing education. For example, women with no schooling were amenorrhoeic for about three months longer than the best educated group, and their first birth interval was on average six months longer. Although the custom of post-partum of abstinence is observed in this population, it lasts only about four to five months and there is little education-specific variation; in any case, since the period of abstinence overlaps with post-partum amenorrhoea, it would not be expected to have much effect on fertility.

The extent to which observed differentials in fertility reflect education-specific differences in the number of children desired and the values and expectactions attached to children is an important issue.

Although fertility desires are consistently associated negatively with educational attainment, even after other socio-economic factors are controlled , these differences are rather small. A woman with middle school education wants in all about half a child less than an uneducated woman, but she nevertheless wants about the same number of sons; this suggests that even education has not yet proved powerful enough to crack the cultural preference for sons in this society.

This point is reinforced when the factors that underlie family size preferences, notably the economic value of children and expectations of them, are examined. Education of women has certainly eroded some of the traditional values attached to children; better educated women are consistently less likely to rely on their children's (especially their sons') labour in childhood and they are consistently more likely to educate their children and expect them to attain a secondary school education. They are also consistently more likely to rely on their own savings and to expect to do so for old-age support. However, education has not yet succeeded in eroding the traditional reliance on sons for the future, including both economic and residential support. It is true that education has, to some extent, weakened dependence on sons and has opened up alternative sources of economic support. But even the most educated women continue to expect to rely at least partially on their sons for economic assistance in old age, and co-residential expectations are quite unaffected by education.

In other words, the evidence suggests that educated women are willing to incur heavier costs and obtain less labour support from their children than uneducated women, and they are more likely to anticipate meeting the need for economic security in old-age from savings and other economic resources. However, sons also continue to be an important source of old-age economic security and the focus of co-residential expectations. This dichotomy accounts for the relatively modest negative effect of education on both family size preferences and fertility.

Finally, it has been found that although contraception is relatively minor consideration in the relationship between education and children ever born, it is clearly important when it comes to the role of education in containing unwanted fertility. There is relatively little unmet need for contraception among better educated women, even after such important factors as economic status, age and duration of marriage are controlled. From this it is inferred that the influence of volitional factors on such women increases when desired family size has been achieved or surpassed.

In sum, this investigation emphasizes that, in the context on the population studied here, education-specific differentials in fertility cannot be attributed simply to volitional factors such as the demand for children or the practice of contraception. It suggests, rather,that the predominant effect of education in bringing about fertility decline continues to be through inadvertent behavioural changes, notably delayed age at marriage. Contraception emerges as important only after desired family size has been achieved thereby lowering the unmet need for family planning among the better educated

APPENDIX-IV

EDUCATION AND SEX-GAP

TABLE A-4.1: Percentage of Females to Total Enrolment

Zone/Region	First Level	Second Level.	Third Level
1. World	45	43	40
2. Developed Countries	49	51	49
3. Developing Countries	44	40	37
4. Africa	44	32	18
5. Asia	43	39	35
6. Arab States	42	40	34
7. Latin America and the Caribbean	48	51	45

(*Source*: *UNESCO Sources,* No.5, June, 1989)

Girls and women are well behind men and boys in terms of education, as is clearly shown in the above Table 4.1. The figures are based on the three globally recognized levels of education—primary, secondary and tertiary.

The percentage of female students only cracks the 50 per cent mark in two cases—in secondary education in the developed countries and in the region of Latin America and the Caribbean. The figures for these two zones show almost a parity between male and female students, and reflects the differences between the male and female populations. Tertiary education in Latin America and Caribbean is the only area where this parity drops off.

However, everywhere else girls and women are clearly worse off, and the higher the level of education, the greater the disparity. The situation for females in the Arab States and Asia is comparable, with only one student in three being a woman. The gap is most marked in Africa where less than one primary or secondary student in three and less than one tertiary student in five is female.

APPENDIX-V

SEXWISE DISTRIBUTION OF NOBEL LAUREATES

TABLE A-5.1: Sexwise Distribution of Nobel Laureates, 1901-1989

Year	Male	Female	Institution	Total
1	2	3	4	5
1901	6	0	0	6
1902	7	0	0	7
1903	6	1	0	7
1904	5	0	1	6
1905	4	1	0	5
1906	6	0	0	6
1907	6	0	0	6
1908	7	0	0	7
1909	7	1	0	8
1910	4	0	1	5
1911	5	1	0	6
1912	6	0	0	6
1913	5	0	0	5
1914	3	0	0	3
1915	4	0	1	4
1916	1	0	0	1
1917	3	0	1	4
1918	2	0	0	2
1919	4	0	0	4
1920	5	0	0	5
1921	5	0	0	5
1922	6	0	0	6
1923	7	0	0	7
1924	3	0	0	3
1925	6	0	0	6
1926	5	1	0	6
1927	7	0	0	7
1928	3	1	0	4
1929	7	0	0	7
1930	5	0	0	5
1931	5	1	0	6
1932	5	0	0	5
1933	5	0	0	5

(Contd.)

TABLE A-5-1: *(Contd.)*

Year	Male	Female	Institution	Total
1	2	3	4	5
1934	6	0	0	6
1935	4	1	0	5
1936	7	0	0	7
1937	7	0	0	7
1938	3	1	1	5
1939	5	0	0	5
1940, 1941, 1942 prize was not awarded due to Second World War.				
1943	4	0	0	4
1944	5	0	1	6
1945	6	1	0	7
1946	7	1	0	8
1947	5	1	1	7
1948	4	0	0	4
1949	6	0	0	6
1950	8	0	0	8
1951	7	0	0	7
1952	7	0	0	7
1953	6	0	0	6
1954	7	0	1	8
1955	5	0	0	5
1956	9	0	0	9
1957	6	0	0	6
1958	9	0	0	9
1959	7	0	0	7
1960	6	0	0	6
1961	6	0	0	6
1962	8	0	0	8
1963	8	1	1	10
1964	7	1	0	8
1965	8	0	1	9
1966	5	1	0	6
1967	8	0	0	8
1968	7	0	0	7
1969	9	0	1	10
1970	9	0	0	9
1971	6	0	0	6

(Contd.)

TABLE A-5-1: *(Contd.)*

Year	Male	Female	Institution	Total
1	2	3	4	5
1972	11	0	0	11
1973	12	0	0	12
1974	12	0	0	12
1975	12	0	0	12
1976	7	2	0	9
1977	9	1	1	11
1978	11	0	0	11
1979	10	1	0	11
1980	11	0	0	11
1981	10	0	1	11
1982	8	1	0	9
1983	6	1	0	7
1984	9	0	0	9
1985	7	0	1	8
1986	10	1	0	11
1987	9	0	0	9
1988	11	0	1	12
1989	10	0	0	10

Source: Bagchi, Ashok K., *Hinduja Foundation Encyclopaedia of Nobel Laureates, 1901-1987*, Delhi, Konark Publishers, 1988.

APPENDIX-VI

WOMEN'S DEVELOPMENT TASKS STRATEGIES AND INITIATIVES OF GOVERNMENT OF INDIA

Tasks

1. The equal sharing power by women.
2. The Social, Educational and Economic empowerment of women.
3. The mainstreaming of women's perspectives across all sectors and enusuring that the development process does not by-pass women.
4. Safeguarding and protection of women's basic human rights.
5. To develop gender sensitivity in Government and society.
6. Enabling the girl-child to attain her full potential.

Strategies and Initiatives of Government of India

Economic Empowerment of Women

Support to Training and Employment Programmeme for Women (STEP) to strengthen and improve women's work and employment. Under this scheme so far employment support has been provided to 92,000 women.

Employment-cum-Income Generating Production Units to extend training for women belonging to weaker sections in the non-traditional trades and employing them on a sustained basis. Under this scheme, training and employment support was given to 31,000 women.

Socio-Economic programmes to provide wage and work to needy women in a wide variety of income generating activities, both in traditional and non-traditional areas. Under this programme 85.707 women have been benefited since inception. (Implemented by CSWB).

Condensed Courses of Education for Adult Women and Vocational Training Programme to extend opportunities for adult women to continue their education and acquire vocational training and employment. Since inception, total of 4,15,000 women have been benefited. (Implemented by CSWB).

Rehabilitation of Women in Distress to provide vocational training-cum-employment and residential care to destitute women.

(Implemented by State Governments)

Rashtriya Mahilakosh (National Credit Fund for Women) set-up to extend credit to poor women both in rural and urban areas in the unorganised sector through voluntary organisations to assist such women for undertaking self-employment/income generating activities. Loan assistance amounting to Rs. 3.36 crores have so far been sanctioned for 14 projects benefiting nearly 29,000 poor women borrowers.

Mahila Samriddhi Yojana (MSY) to empower women to exercise greater controls over house-hold resources and to encourage thrift so that women can start their saving to assure themselves of security in times of need. Upto 31st January1994, 4.11 lakh MSY accounts with a deposit of Rs.5.06 crores have been opened.

Network of Support Services for Women

The Government of India runs a network of support services for women. These support services represent an important plan for the empowerment of women.

ICDS and Creches

In the sphere of child development and nutrition, the Government of India administers the world's largest integrated child development programme called the ICDS which at present covers over16.3 million children and 3.2 million mothers. It offers a package of services comprising supplementary nutrition immunization, health care, growth monitoring, pre-school education and nutrition and health education. Government also runs a network of creches through NGO's covering 3,11,000 children.

Short Stay Home and Working Women Hostels to promote greater mobility of women in the employment markets. The Government has sanctioned over 655 Working Womens Hostels throughout the country. The Government has also sanctioned over 220 Short Stay Homes to protect and rehabilitate women and girls who are facing social or moral danger for a variety of reasons.

Political enpowerment: Constitutional amendment for increasing

---

Source: Hindustan Times, March 8, 1994.

Department of Women and Child Development, Ministry of Human Resource Development, Government of India

political participation of women providing one-third reservation for women in all elected offices in local bodies in rural as well as urban areas and in posts of Chairpersons.

Generating Awaerness

To sensitise all sections of society and administration.

Awareness Generation Projects for Rural and Poor Women for identifying the needs of rural and poor women and generating awearness among them of their status in the family and society and to activate them to work for achieving their rights.

Information and Mass Educaton Activities to create awereness about issues which affect the developement of women and children.

Education Work for Prevention of Atrocities against Women by extending financial assistance to volountary organisations to work for prevention of atrocities against women.

Setting up of the National Commission for Women. A statutory body to study and moniter matters relating to the constitutional and legal safeguards provided for women and to review existing legislation to suggest amendments whereever necessary and to look into complaints involving deprivation of rights of women.

APPENDIX-VII

SEMINAR ON DECLINING SEX RATIO: IMPLICATIONS FOR EDUCATION AND MEDIA (1991)

Introduction

The 1991 Census of India registered a lower sex ratio. There were only 929 females per 100 males. It is observed that sex-ratio has continuously declined from 972 in 1901 to 929 in 1991 with the exception of 1981 census, when a small increase was noticed. A balanced sex ratio is considered reasonably good indicator of women's status. On account of negative trend it was felt to re-examine the policies and programmes. Accordingly the Department of Women's Studies of the National Council of Educational Research and Training (NCERT) organised on May 6, 1991, a one-day seminar on the declining Sex Ratio Implication for Education and Media participant represented by All India Institute of Medical Sciences, Indian Council of Child Welfare, Indira Gandhi Open University, Institute of Economic Growth, Jawaharlal Nehru University, Delhi University, ICMR, doctors and journalists.

Recommendations

1. Sensitization of social institutions.
2. Education of both women and men.
3. Coordination between different agencies to avoid overlapping of programmes.
4. Change in teaching methodology—avoiding sex stereotyping in teaching and transaction of curriculum, free books from sex stereotyping.
5. As far as 1950s, State Governments had decided to send messeges through intervention in culture. This has not been implemented. Culture remains untouched. It should be taken as a basic issue of education and life. A definite cultural policy is needed.
6. Media should project women in all the roles positively.

NCERT, New Delhi : 1991

7. Shift from win-lose to win-win situation—cooperation model needed where both women and men should work together for a healthy society minus social evils.
8. Opening of production centres for rural as well as urban girls to become wage earners.
9. The community or the village committees should ensure education and health-care.
10. Intervention programmes needed for minority communities to ensure that they send their daughters to schools. Bhils, for example, did not wish to educate their girls but wanted educated daughters-in-law for their educated sons. They were told that this could only be possible if they send all the girls to schools. Intervention must necessarily keep the regional disparities in view.
11. Create awearness about the effects of declining sex-ratio on our society. Action needed.
12. Need to change the attitude of people towards the girls/ women and to bring out the factors responsible for declining sex-ratio.
13. There should be Penal Strictures for families that do not educate girls to ensure that Parents/Communities educate their girls.
14. Amniocentesis/sex-selective abortions should be banned. Need for a central legislation.
15. Create awareness to save the girl-child through media, posters, street plays.
16. Increase the health-care services, improve their quality.
17. Need to study the morbidity rates and nutritional status of male/female utilisation pattern of health services.
18. Experts must study the declining sex-ratio and expose the society the consequences of declining sex-ratio.
19. Sympathy for girl-child must be translated into educational concrete programmes. The NCERT could think of such programmes.
20. Needs of all girls/women should be looked into.
21. Life cycle approach—Discrimination at every stage—media should highlight this aspect.
22. Geographical Approach—Area Specific Approach in Research studies.
23. Media Approach—Project girls as wage earners, report

bravery deeds, achievements of girls/women.

24. Studies should be taken up in Kerala as an example of State with highest sex-ratio and highest literacy rate. Background has to be prepared in other States to enable them to achieve what Kerala has achieved.
25. Physical survival and mental health of the society must be studied.

APPENDIX-VIII

SOURCES OF FINANCIAL SUPPORT FOR RESEARCH IN INDIA

All research organisations listed in this guide, more or less, provide either financial support, or research facilities in the form of providing library services, affiliation facility and consultancy services in data compilation and project execution. Following are the few major institutions, in India, which have various financial assistance schemes for undertaking research programmes. The researchers may contact these organisations for getting further details and also latest rules and regulations.

1. Indian Council of Social Science Research (ICSSR), New Delhi

The ICSSR, set up as an autonomous organisations in 1969, has been playing a supporting as well as catalytic role in the development of social-science research and its utilization. It considers for support for research proposals on any subject or any theme, which have a significant social science orientation. The proposals may fall within a discipline such as economics, education, geography, history, political science, psychology, public administration, sociology, social and cultural anthropology, international relations, etc. or inter-disciplinary in character. Programmes of ICSSR are detailed below:

Research Grants

The ICSSR provides research grants for the following purposes:

Research Projects/Programmes

Research projects are given financial Assistance of normally over Rs. one lakh, for a period from 3-5 years.

Sponsored Research

The Council has identified from time to time a number of areas of national significance for promoting research in a coordinated way.

These include: (i) women's studies; (ii) rural development; (iii) poverty and unemployment; (iv) governmental systems and development; (v) integrated area development; (vi) public distribution system; and (vii) studies in urbanisation, etc.

The ICSSR has also sponsored in the past a number of coordinated studies on the educational problems of scheduled castes and scheduled tribes, finances of universities and electoral behaviour.

Flowships

The ICSSR awards several types of fellowships to assist social scientists to engage in research on a whole-time basis or complete research already in progress. The following types of fellowships are available.

National Fellowships

National Fellowships have been instituted for eminent social scientists who have made outstanding contributions in their own areas of specialisation. They are offered by the ICSSR at its own initiative and purely on the basis of merit, irrespective of age and status of the scholar.

Senior Fellowships

Senoir Fellowships are awarded on request to senior social scientists who have made significant contributions to social science research. The award protects the existing emoluments of employed scholars to enable them to take leave of absence and work full-time on a piece of research; a consolidated salary is offered to other scholars. The award also carries an annual contingency grant.

General Fellowships

These fellowships are meant for relatively junior social scientists who have completed their Ph.D. or have done equivalent research work of merit and desire to work on approved research projects. The award protects the existing emoluments of employed scholars and offers a consolidated amount to others. It carries an annual contingency grant.

Doctoral Fellowships

Doctoral Fellowships are awarded to scholars who are registered candidates for a doctorate in any of the social sciences. A contingency grant is also attached to the fellowship. College teachers and members of professional staff in research institutions below the age of 35 years may be given the benefit of salary protection. These fellowships are administered as follows:

(i) Institutional fellowships are awarded to young scholars preferably below the age of 30 years who are enrolled for research leading to a doctoral degree preferably in any of the research institutions supported by the ICSSR;

(ii) Centrally administered fellowships are awarded directly by the ICSSR for the physicaliy handicaped scholars and for the two specific areas, namely: (i) Women's studies and (ii) medical sociology/health-care to encourage scholars to take up research work in these areas. An effort is also being made to revive a central pool of scholarships for university research students;

(iii) A certain number of such fellowships are awarded to scholars from foreign countries especially neighbouring countries desirous of undertaking research in India; and

(iv) Short-term Doctoral Fellowships, for a duration not exceeding 12 months, are meant for field work or for completing writing work already undertaken.

Contingency Grants

Contingency Grants not exceediing Rs.5,000 are awarded to doctoral students who are not in receipt of any fellowship or who receive a fellowship without an adequate contingency grant for meeting expenses on field work, computer fees, printing, purchase of books, etc.

Study Grants

Financial assistance to cover travel and maintenance costs is provided for scholars for visiting libraries/ documentation centres for collection of material pertaining to their research work.

International Collaboration

One of the important programmes of the ICSSR is collaboration with international bodies and academic institutions abroad for promotion of research in the field of social sciences. The Council is also an important implementing agency for social science activites under different Cultural Exchange Programmes signed from time to time between the Government of India and that of the other countries. The Council is a member of several international bodies, namely Association of Asian Social Science Research Councils (AASSREC), International Federation of Social Science Organisations (IFSSO), and International Social Science Council (ISSC). One of the important collaborative programmes recently undertaken by the ICSSR has been the Indo-Dutch Programme of Alternatives in Development. Besides, the Council has initiated and developed collaborative programmes with UK, France, USA, China, Japan, Thailand, Hungary and Czechoslovakia. The ICSSR also functions as the secretariat of the Indo-Soviet Commission for Cooperation in Social Sciences which has organised a number of symposia, exchange of scholars, publications, etc.The AASSREC secretariat is located in the ICSSR with the Member-Secretary as the Secretary General.

ICSSR provides financial Assistance to individual scholars for visits abroad for collection of data for their research and for attending seminars and conferences in selected countries of Asia and Africa. Distinguished foreign social scientists are also invited to visit India.

Publication Grants

The Publication Grants Scheme which was discontinued earlier has been revived in a modified form. Financial Assistance for publication to doctoral theses and research/seminar reports is considered under this scheme.

Other Programmes

Several other programmes are conducted by the ICSSR, among which the following may be mentioned:

(i) Grants for organisation of seminars;

(ii) Anual grants for maintenance and development of activities to professional organisations in the field of social sciences;
(iii) Annual grants, or funds for establishing endowments to professional organisations for conducting journals in social sciences; and
(iv) Guidence and consultancy services in data processing.

Forms of Application

Forms of Application for: (i) Research Project, (ii) Partial Assistance to Ph.D. Scholars, (iii) Contingency Grant, and (iv) Study Grant are in Annexures I, II, III and IV respectively.

APPENDIX VIII-I

INDIAN COUNCIL OF SOCIAL SCIENCE RESEARCH FORM OF APPLICATION FOR RESEARCH PROJECT

Bio-Data of the Project Directer

1. Name of the applicant
2. Position held
3. Department
4. Institution
5. (a) Mailing address with pin code (b) Telegraphic address (c) Telephone No. Office Residence
6. Permanent address
7. (a) Date of Birth (b) Place of birth
8. Nationality
9. Academic Qualifications

Degree	Subjects	University	Division/ grade obtained	Year of passing
B.A.				
M.A.				
Ph.D.				

Any other specialized courses (please list)

10. List of publications (in the past five years)
11. Experience
12. The number of projects completed by the applicant so far:

Sl. No.	Title of the project	Duration	Total costs	Source of budget support	Status of the project*

* Please indicate whether the report has been published, is to be published, or is still to be completed.

13. Research project(s) currently being conducted by the appllicant.

Sl. No	Title of project	Source of support	Budget of estimate	Date of commen-cement	Probable date of completion

14. Was this proposal submitted to any other funding agency?If so, what was the outcome?
15. Is this research currently being supported by any other agency or is this application being submitted elsewhere? If so, please give details. Decisions about application to other agencies (including those made after the award of ICSSR grant) should be reported to the ICSSR as soon as available.
16. Any other information that you think is relevant for the evaluation of the proposal.

(Signature)

Forwarding Form for Use of the Institution

Project proposed by
Status

I forward the proposal for financial support to the ICSSR.
The institution agrees to :

— Administer and manage the finances;
— Provide accommodation and furniture required for the project; Make available all its research facilities such as library, laboratory and other equipments; and
— Provide the material and managerial Assistance for the project.

If the scholar directing the project leaves our institution to join some other institution, after part of the sanctioned grant has been received, we would have no objection to the project being transferred to a new institution, if the Project Director/ICSSR so desires. The institution, however, shall continue to be responsible for submitting the audited statement of accounts and utilization certificate for the grant received by it, for this purpose.

Date:	Name and Designation (in block letters)	Signature (Official seal)

APPENDIX VIII-2

INDIAN COUNCIL OF SOCIAL SCIENCE RESEARCH

Application Form for Partial Assistance to Ph.D. Scholars

(Please note that the maximum period of partial Assistance to Ph.D. scholars is 8 months for unemployed scholars and six months for Salary Protection also.)

Note: Application will be considered from only such candidate as has completed the basic preliminary readings on the subjects of research. For survey type of research, there should be, at least a stage where the field work has been thought through the sampling plan and the questionnaire (where applicable). For other empirical studies, the basic plan for data processing should be ready. For conceptual/theoretical studies, the basic framework of the study should have been worked out.

1. Particulars of the Applicant:
   (a) Name (In Block Letters) Surname Family Name (Mr/Mrs/Miss)
   (b) Date of birth
   (c) Nationality
   (d) Postal Address
   (e) Home Town Address:
2. Do you belong to Scheduled Castes/Scheduled Tribes?
3. (a) Purticulars of academic qualifications:

Examinatons Passed	Year of Passing	Board University	Subjects/ Papers	Class/ Division	Percentage of Marks
Matric/Hr.Sec.					
B.A/B.Com					
M.A/M.Com					
M.Phil					
Other Qualifications					

(b) Detailed published work, if any, (Please attach separate list) Please also enclose copies of published papers.

(c) Details of papers published in seminars and conferences etc., if there (Please attach separate list).

(d) Have you attended any Research Methodology course either conducted by the ICSSR or any other Institution?

YES/NO

If Yes,

Name of the instituition	Year	How many weeks	Result

(e) Present status of work:

4. (a) Date of registration enrolement for Ph.D.(after M.Phil)

(b) Name of the University

(c) Name and Designation of Supervisor

(d) Theme of research

(e) Probable date of its completion

(f) Period for which Partial Assistance is required (*Note:* The maximum period for which a Partial Assistance to Ph.D Scholars is sanctioned is six months).

(g) Name and address of the Institution through which you want to draw the Partial Assistance:

5. *A brief note on the theme along with proposal in 3000 words*

   Every applicant is required to enclose with his/her application Ph.D proposal (two copies) in about 3,000 words. It should state the scope and objectives of the project and review of literature should be given in the proposal. Sources of information should be clearly indicated and the methods to be used for collection and analysis of data should be described clearly. In case work on a research theme has already started, please indicate the time required to complete the remaining part of the work.

6. Have you applied to ICSSR for financial assistance earlier and if so, when and with what results? Please give file number also.

7. Have you applied to any other organisation for financial assistance and if so, furnish the details?

8. Have you received a fellowship, study grant, contingency grant, field trip or any other assistance from any source?
   (a) From ICSSR YES/NO
   If yes, please specify the amount, nature and duration (Please give file number)
   (b) From any other organisation YES/NO
   (If yes, 1. Name of the organisation.
   2. Amount, nature and duration of assistance.
9. If already drawn/drawing a scholarship or a fellowship, please give purticulars below:

Source of Scholarship/ Fellowship	Value and Date of Commencement	Date upto which Tenable

10. Are you employed ? YES/NO
    If yes,

Name of the Institution	Date of Appoinment	Designation Are you on leave with pay/without pay?	Temporary/ Permanent	Scale, present allowances, date and amount of the next increment

11. Any other information relevant to the research work which you may like to give in support of your application
12. List of the enclosures sent alongwith application.

Essentials

(A) Two copies of detailed Ph.D. synopsis.
(B) Attested copies of mark-sheets of high school onward.
(C) Certificate of scheduled castes/scheduled tribes (for SC/ST candidates only).
(D) Supervisor's recommendation.
(E) Copy of the registration certificate for Ph.D. issued by the University after completion of M.Phil.

(f) Certificate from the employer stating:(i) that he/she is a permanent employee and that the Institution Certificate that it will maintain lien on the permanent post and will allow him /her to rejoin the same post after the tenure of the Partial Assistance. (ii) The present employment.(iii) The present scale of pay and the date and the amount of the next increment.

(G) A note on the present status of the study duly certified by the research supervisor.

(H) Two copies of interview schedules.

Others

(I) (M)
(J) (N)
(K) (O)
(L) (P)

13. Write in the space below why are you interested in conducting research in the theme mentioned (in ten lines).

I Hereby Declare

(i) That I have read the rules regarding the award of Partial Assistance to Ph.D. scholars of the Indian Council of Social Science Research and I agree to abide by these rules if Partial Assistance is awarded to me.
I further declare that entries made in the form above and the additional purticulars furnished by me are true to the best of my knowledge and belief and in the event of any wrong/false statement, the grant may be forfeited.

(ii) That if selected, I shall work on a whole-time basis for my financial Assistance to and I shall not accept any other employment without the prior approval of the ICSSR.

Place: (Sinature of Candidate)
Date :

(Name in block letters)

Notes : 1. Applications incomplete in any respect will not be considered.
2. Answer to each question should be given in words and not by DASHES AND CROSSES.

(FOR USE BY UNIVERSITY/COLLEGE)

Recommendation of the Forwarding Authority

(Views of the Supervisor/Head of the Department regarding the candidate's suitability for the award should be obtained separately and enclosed with application. Partial Assistance to Ph.D.scholars is not given to M. Phil students).

Place:

Date :

Signatures
Registrar/Principal
University/College

APPENDIX - VIII-3

INDIAN COUNCIL OF SOCIAL SCIENCE RESEARCH

Form of Application for Contingency Grant

1. (a) Name in full (in block letters)
   (b) Father's/Husband's name
2. (a) Postal address
   (b) Permanent address
3. Date of birth
4. (a) Academic Qualifications:

Examinations passed	Name of the University Board	Year	Division and percentage of marks	subjects
Matric/Hr.Sec				
B.A				
M.A				
Other qualifications				

   (b) Details of published work (if any)
   (c) papers presented in seminars and conferences
5. Do you belong to SC/ST? YES/NO
   (If yes, please attach a certificate from a competent authority.
6. If employed

Name of the Institution	Designation	Since when	Total	Emoluments

   (b) If not employed
      (i) Father/Guardian's profession
      (ii) Monthly income
7. Are you registered for Ph.D.?
   1. No
   2. Yes
   3. I am planning to be registered for Ph.D.
      If yes:
      (a) Date of registration
      (b) Name of the university

8. Have you applied to ICSSR for financial assistance earlier, and if so, when and with what result?
9. Have you applied to any other organisation for financial assistance, and if so, furnish the details?
10. Have you been in receipt of fellowship, study grant, contingency grant, field trip or any other assistance from any source?
    - (a) From ICSSR YES/NO
    - (b) From any other organisation YES/NO

      If yes: (1) Name of the organisation

      (2) Amount, nature and duration of assistance.
11. (i) Topic of Research
    - (ii) Name of the Supervisor
    - (iii) Progress of Research Work
      - (a) Preliminary reading and work
      - (b) Data collection
      - (c) Report writing
    - (iv) University affiliation
12. Enclosures essential for consideration of Application
    - (a) An attested copy of Ph.D. registration certificate.
    - (b) Supervisor's recommendations.
    - (c) A detailed research proposal (A detailed research proposal covering a note on the work done so far in the field, main objectives, perspectives and framework, chief hypotheses/ research questions, methodology of data collection—including size and type of sample and justification for the same and principal analytical variables and tools proposed to be used, should be enclosed).
    - (d) Detailed break up of estimated expenditure with suitable justification for each item.
13. Estimated Expenditure
    - I. Field work
      - (a) Location of the field
      - (b) Duration of field work
      - (c) Estimated Expenditure
      - — On travelling
      - — On daily allowance
    - II. Computer work
      - (a) Computer time
      - (b) Estimated computer charges
      - (c) Any other

III. Printing of schedules/questionnaires
   (a) No. of questionnaires/schedules to be printed
   (b) No. of pages in the questionnaire/schedule
   (c) No. of copies of questionnaires/schedules to be printed and total estimated printing/cyclostyling cost

IV. Cartographic work
   (a) Number of work
   (b) Types of maps
   (c) Estimated cost

V. Books and journals
   (kindly ensure that the list of books given below is not available in the nearby University/College library).

VI. Any other item (please specify).
   Total of all the items mentioned above.

13. Please indicate the name and address of the institution through which you would like to draw the Contingency Grant, if sanctioned (attach certificate from the institution).
14. Any other information which you wish to furnish in support of your application.

I hereby declare that the entries made here are true to the best of my knowledge and belief.

If awarded, I shall abide by the rules and regulations of the award and shall not accept any financial assistance for the purpose for which I have been sanctioned this grant by the ICSSR from any other source without the prior approval of the Council.

Date: (Signature)
Place:

(Name in block letters)

Supervisor's recommendations:

Views of the Head of the Department

Notes :

(a) The awardee will be eligible for the class of travel on railway and daily allowance in accordence with the rules of the affiliating institutions.

(b) The expenditure has to be incurred only on the sanctioned items of Contingency Grant to the extent laid down in the sanction letter. Deviation from the sanctioned items upto 10 per cent will be allowed with the approval of the Supervisor. Reappropriation beyond 10 per cent an expenditure on new items will need prior approval of the Council.

(c) Any expenditure incurred before the issue of sanction letter would normally be inadmissible.

(d) Non-empirical and theoretical research work can also be considered for support in terms of xeroxing of articles/ paper and other normally non-accessible type of research material and for purchasing a few selected books, publications, etc .

Enclosures :

1.
2.
3.
4.

APPENDIX -VIII-4

INDIAN COUNCIL OF SOCIAL SCIENCE RESEARCH

Application for Study Grant

(For Visiting Libraries to Collect Material for Research)

1. (a) Name
   (in block letters) (First Name) (Surname)
   (b) Address Pin code

2. Age (Years)

3. Educational Record (of all University Examinations)

Examination	Name of the University	Year	Class	Percentage of marks	Subjects studied	Rank if any

4. (a) Date of Registration for Ph.D.
   (b) University/Institution of Registration
   (c) Name and designation of Supervisor/Guide
5. Approved Research Theme
6. Centre(s)/Library(ies) to be visited
   (i)
   (ii)
   (iii)
7. Duration of the proposed visit days
   (with probable dates) from to
8. Whether the Centre(s)/Library(ies) has/have agreed to provide facilities for work: Yes/Not yet
9. In case, Study Grant has been awarded previously by any of the ICSSR Centres, please intimate:

Name of the Centre	Year(s) of Study Grant	Period of Study Grant during

10. Details of financial assistance applied for/being received/received from ICSSR under other Schemes such as Fellowships, Contingency Grants, etc.

Name of the Scheme	Amount Received	ICSSR Ref./File No. for correspondence

11. Details of Financial assistance applied for/being received/received *from agencies other than ICSSR*, such as University, U.G.C.etc, about this research proposal.

12. I hereby declare that :

    (i) I have the rules governing the scheme and shall abide by them.
    (ii) I am not at present getting any financial assistance from the ICSSR, University, U.G.C, or from any other agency for the purpose of the intended visit.
    (iii) The material required by me is not available in the libraries of the city/town where I am residing/working.
    (iv) I have/have not been previously awarded a Study Grant by the ICSSR.
    (v) The information given in the form is true and correct.

In the event of any information being found to be false, the application may not be considered.

Date: Signature of the Applicant

Certificate of the Registrar of the University /Head of the Institution/ Department.

*(i) Shri/Shrimati/Kumari is registered for Ph.D. for the topic mentioned in this application. The date of registration and the name of his/her Supervisor/Guide is;

(ii) The application of Shri/Shrimati/Kumari is forwarded for consideration. It is certified that the information given in the application has been found to be correct.

Signature of the Registrar/
Head of the Institute/Department
(with rubber stamp)

NOTE

The application for Study Grant will be considered only if it is accompanied by the following documents for consideration :

(i) Detailed elaboration of the research proposal: principal concerns, the methodology, etc.
(ii) Progress of the work already done on the research proposal (with recommendation of Supervisor/Guide in case of Ph.D. scholars).
(iii) True copy of the Registration Certificate for Ph.D.
(iv) List of Publications to be consulted.
(v) In case Study Grant has been accepted previously by any of the ICSSR Centres, please also enclose a detailed report of the work (duly approved by the Supervisor) accomplished during the Study Grant.
(vi) Any other information which the scholar may like to give in support of the application.

I. STUDY GRANT : GENERAL INSTRUCTION

The scholar should immediately acknowledge the receipt of the sanction letter and intimate probable date of arrival.

The scholar, with prior approval, can utilize sanctioned Study

*Starred item relates to only Ph. D. scholars.

Grant in more than one trip. However, the fare will be reimbursed for only one trip.

The scholar should report arrival to the office personally or by telephone between 9.30 a.m to 5.30 p.m on his first working day. NASSDOC Reading Room remains open on all working days except National Holidays.

Payment for second class/rail/bus-fare from place of residence, and per diem of Rs.30.00 will be made against bill submitted in the prescribed form. Bill processing would normally take seven days.

Payment will normally be made by an account payee crossed cheque drawn on United Commercial Bank, ICSSR Extension Counter, New Delhi after 15 days of arrival, on receipt of the library attendance certificate and progress report of the work done. If Study Grant is for more than 15 days and the payment is required in more than one instalment, only incoming fare and per diem for actual working days which should not be less than 15 days will be paid in the first instalment.

If cash payment is needed, it must be stated in the bill and collected personally from the Finance Division.

Following Centres entertain Study Grant application for their respective area of operation indicated against each:

A: Delhi

Director, National Social Science
Documentation Centre
35 Ferozeshah Road, New Delhi-100 001.
(for all places except those covered by the following Centres)

B: ICSSR Regionel Centres

1. Bombay :	The Director, ICSSR Regional Centre, Vidyanagri, Kalina, Bombay, Maharashtra-400 098.
2 Calcutta:	The Hony. Director. ICSSR Regional Centre, 10 Jadunath Sarkar Road, Culcutta, West Bengal-700 029
3. Chandigarh:	The Hony. Director, ICSSR Regional Centre, Panjab University Library Building,

Panjab University,
Chandigarh-160 014.

4. Hyderabad : The Hony. Director, ICSSR Regional Centre, Osmania University Library, Hyderabad, Andhra Pradesh-500 007

5. Shillong: The Hony. Director, ICSSR Regional Centre, NEHU Library Building, Mayurbhanj House, Shillong-793 003.

C: Institutional Centre

1. Ahmedabad : Director, Sardar Patel Institute of Economic and Social Research, Post Box No.4062, Navrangpura, Ahmedabad-380 009.

II. INDIAN COUNCIL OF HISTORICAL RESEARCH (ICHR)

Some of Broad Priorities

The Council has taken a broad view of history so as to include in its fold the history of art, literature, philosophy, science and technology, epigraphy, numismatics, archaeology, socio-economic formations and allied subjects.

With a view to encouraging research in certain significant but hitherto less explored aspects of history, the Council has identified from time to time, certain areas in which work may be undertaken by the scholars so as to contribute towards the better understanding of our history. These include:

Studies of Social and Economic formation;
History of the peasantry and agrarian relations;
Urban studies;
Industrialisation;

History of the different regions of India and editing/calendaring/ translation of sources.

The above list is purely illustrative and should not be held to exclude other themes of historical impotance. The Council also supports researches in the history of other countries.

The programmes assisted are:

Fellowship

The fellowship programme of the Council will cover the following categories:

(a) Fellowships for historians doing research in India,
(b) Fellowships for Indian historians doing research outside India,
(c) Fellowships for foriegn scholars to conduct research study in history in India, and
(d) National Fellowships.

Fellowships for Historians doing Research in India

Eligibility

These fellowships will be extended to historians in universities, colleges and other Institutions who have established their reputation for research, or who have the potential for professional growth. Fellowship will normally be granted to those who are already based in an academic institute on a regular basis. However, women who are housewives and who are otherwise qualified may apply. Initially, the fellowship scheme will apply to post-doctral work but in special cases fellowship may also be extended to those taking up doctoral work or likely to complete their doctoral work in the near future. M.Phil/Ph.D. students will be considered eligible for a junior fellowship of the Council. M.Phil students will be eligible for grant of fellowships for a period of one year only. They may apply to the Council after completing six months of their registration.

Amount of Fellowships

1. Junior/Doctoral Fellowship of Rs. 800 p.m and contingent grant tenable for two and half years initially, is granted to a scholar doing Ph.D. (contingency Rs.3000 p.a w.e.f 1-1-1987). Extension of fellowship for one year may be granted in exceptional cases after evaluation of the previous work.

2. Post-Doctoral Fellowship of Rs. 1200 p.m and contingency tenable for two years initially is granted to scholar of history of doing post-doctoral research work (contingencies from Rs.3000 to Rs.5000 p.a).
3. Pay-Protection Fellowship is granted to College/University Teachers and to scholars having the same academic status. The salary of the scholar is protected and contingent grant given. It is tenable for two years initially, (contingency Rs.5000 p.a).
4. Fellowship of Rs.1500, Rs.2000, Rs.2500 p.m tenable for 2 years is awarded to the historians under this. The historians are categorised as under:

   (a) University readers/Independent research scholars of equivalent experience and status are granted Rs,1500 p.m for two years initially.
   (b) Retired University Professors/Senior independent scholars with equivalent experience and status are granted Rs.2000 p.m depending on the merit of each case.

In addition to the above contingent grant is also awarded to the scholar keeping in view the nature of study/area of specialization ranging from Rs. 5000 p.a. to Rs. 8000 p.a. Besides, a senior fellow is provided with a research assistant, typist and travel expenses to visit archival repositories for the collection of material. Senior fellow will be required to submit annual progress report in triplicate for assessment by the Council.

5. The Counicl also awards national fellowships to eminent historians who wish to work on projects of special historical importance (Fellowship: Rs. 3000 p.m; contingencies; Rs. 10,000 p.a; and secretarial assistance of Rs. 1000 p.m for a period of three years (The total number of National fellows would not exceed ten at a time).
6. Very senior scholars (no longer in service) may be offered the designation as "Historian Emeritus" with an honorarium of Rs.12,000 p.a.

Duration

The duration of the research fellowship shall ordinarily be two years, extendable in exceptional cases to the third year. A detailed review of the work done will be made at the end of the each year and further continuance of the fellowship will be decided thereupon.

Selection

A historian eligible under the above rule may apply for a research fellowship, through the institution where he/she is working, in the prescribed form, submitting five copies of detailed note/synopsis on his/her research proposal and his/her bio-data. The application shall be considered by the ICHR in accordance with such procedures as may be laid down from time to time and research fellowship will be awarded if the Council considers the applicant to be eligible and approves of his research proposal.

Remuneration

During the term of full-time fellowship, the historian shall receive the same salary as he was drawing before the award, if he is an employee of a university or a teaching or research institution having UGC scales. If he is in the service of Government or any organisation other than a unversity, his status shall be equated with that of a lecturer, reader or professor under a university and the salary payable to him shall be fixed accordingly.While doing so the ICHR shall take into account any amount drawn by the fellow from his parent organisation either in the shape of leave salary or otherwise so that his total salary during the period of fellowship does not exceed that drawn by him prior to taking up the fellowship. The fellow will be entitled to the allowances admissible in the institution of affiliation. (Housewives selected for the fellowship will get a consolidated honorarium of Rs. 500 per month.)

Contingent Grant

In addition to the salaries and allowances, etc, under Rule 5 above, each research fellow shall be given a contingent grant equal to the actual expenditure incurred or Rs. 5000 a year, whichever is less. This grant will cover expenditure on such items as TA/DA for Journeys connected with pursuit of the fellowship, purchase of books, secretarial assistance, stationery, etc.(Those who will be doing part-time research work in addition to their existing duties shall also be given such contingent grant.)

Institutional Affiliation

(a) Every research fellow shall be attached to an institution of his choice and approved by the ICHR through which the fellowship amount shall be disbursed. During the period of such attachment, (the fellow shall be treated as an employee of the institution for all administrative purposes and) the rules of the institution shall apply in the matter of drawal of TA/DA, holiday and contingent expenditure. It should be clearly understood that the fellowship is not in the nature of deputation and no liability will be attached to the ICHR or to the institution concerned for payment of any contribution towards leave salary, pension, medical attendance, etc. The Council will, however, pay the employer's share of contribution in accordance with the rules of the contributory Provident Fund to which the fellow may be subscribing.

(b) The amount of the fellowship shall be paid to the institution in advance in yearly instalments.

(c) The institution shall provide to the fellow facilities of accommodation, including furniture, library and research facilities and messenger services. For this the ICHR shall pay to the institution overhead charges of five per cent of the Grants-in-aid sanctioned under these Rules.

The amount of these overhead charges shall be paid after the conclusion of the fellowship and the receipt of audited statement of accounts and utilisation certificate.

Progress Reports

The research fellow shall submit a yearly progress report in triplicate to the institution which shall forward it to the ICHR alongwith a statement of expenditure during the preceding one year and an estimate of the expenditure likely to be incurred during twelve months. The subsequent instalment will be released only on receipt of these documents.

Other Conditions

(a) A research fellow shall engage himself on his research work on a whole-time basis and shall not accept, during the period of fellowship, any other assignment without prior permisson of the ICHR.

(b) Unless the ICHR decides otherwise, all equipments purchased out of the contingent grant shall be transferred to it after the completion of the work. The books purchased upto a limit of Rs. 1000 (Rupees one thousand only) out of the funds of the Council may be retained by the scholar concerned.

(c) Termination: the ICHR may terminate fellowship, after giving one month's notice. if it is of the view that the progress is not satisfactory or that the research fellow has seriously violated the rules and conditions of this fellowship. Whenever an awared of fellowship, contingency grant or honorarium is made by the ICHR,the scholar must join ICHR fellowship or intimate utilisation of contingent grant or begin drawing honorarium within six months of the decision. Otherwise the decision could be deem to have lapsed.

Travel Grant or Contingent Grant

The above rules apply also to travel grant (within India or contingent grant without fellowship) in connection with doctoral and post-doctoral work.

Final Report

On conclusion of the fellowship and in any case not later than six months thereafter, the research fellow shall submit a complete copy of his work alongwith an abstract incorporating the main conclusions reached by him for books/articles published with an aid of the research material collected during the tenure of ICHR fellowship. Due acknowledgement of ICHR grant must be made and reprint sent to the Council for its record.

Fellowship for Historians doing Research Outside India

Research Fellowship may be awarded to Indian historians who, in connection with their ongoing research projects, need to collect material and data from other countries. In such cases, the ICHR will extend such financial help as is determined in each case after taking all the factors into consideration. All the Rules from 2 to 10 above shall apply for such cases. The amount of research fellowship inclusive of salary, travel costs, contingent expenditure etc. shall be determined separately in each after taking all the relevent circumstances in to consideration.

Fellowships for Foreign Scholars to Conduct Research Studies in History in India

Research Fellowship may be awarded by the Council to overseas scholars specially those belonging to Asian, African and Latin American countries, who desire to carry out research studies in India.

All the rules applicable for fellowship to Indian Scholars from rules 2 to 10 will apply here in these cases also. However, remuneration of such fellows and contingent grant shall be determined by Council separately in each case after taking all relevant circumstances into consideration.

III. INDIAN COUNCIL OF PHILOSOPHICAL RESEARCH (ICPR)

The main objective of the ICPR fellowship scheme is to promote research in philosophy at various levels by providing opportunities to scholars, including young scholars, to engage themselves on a whole-time basis, in important research projects suggested by them, preferably in the major areas of investigation or in the Council's own project.

Fellowship

The categories of fellowships, eligibility, terms and conditions there-of, etc, are as follows:

Senior Fellowships

Senior fellowships are awarded to well known senior, professional scholars in philosophy who have made a significant contribution to the study of philosophy and related subjects as evidenced from publication of their research papers and books.

General Fellowships

The general fellowships are of two kinds:One meant for scholars who are carrying on research in recognized institutions of higher learning leading to a doctoral degree and the other is meant for scholars who are either teaching or carrying on post-doctoral research. They are provided to scholars who have shown significant promise and competence for independent research work as shown by their publications in the form of books and research articles.

Short-term Fellowships

Short-term fellowships are awarded for a duration of three months, extendable by a period of another three months in deserving cases, to enable scholars to engage themselves on whole-time research to finalize the results of the research work.

Residential Fellowships

Residential fellowships are meant to facilitate the scholars who wish to consult the library at ICPR's Academic Centre, Butler Palace, Lucknow in connection with their on-going research projects. The selected scholars can avail of these fellowships during their leave of absence from their places of work/holidays. The fellowship is available for a maximum period of sixty days in a financial year. The selected Fellows can avail of the sixty days period at one stretch or can avail of it in parts. However, they will be provided with a first class rail fare from their place of work to Academic Centre, Butler Palace, Lucknow and back, only once.

Besides providing accommodation to the selected scholars, the Council will pay a daily allowance @ Rs. 75 per day. In case the Council is not able to provide them accommodation, they will be paid a daily allowance @ Rs.100 per day.

Fellowships for Preparing Learning Material

Fellowships for Preparing Learning Material are awarded to scholars who are renowned in their areas of research and related disciplines to enable them to prepare learning material (text-books, supplementary reading materials, pictorial presentations, slides, exhibition materials, etc,) in their areas of specializations for university and college students. The fellowship does not carry any contingency grant. However, typing and stationery charges upto a maximum of Rs.1000 for the entire duration of the fellowship will be reimbursed to the scholar by the Council.

General Conditions

Aplications for the award of fellowships may be submitted in the prescribed proforma at any time of the year. However, the applications will be scrutinized by the Council only once a year during January to March. In case of employed scholars the application should be sent through their employers.

The salary and the allowances of the employed scholars will be protected. In case of unemployed scholars, a consolidated fellowship amount ranging from Rs. 1000 to Rs.2500 per month, depending upon the merit of each case, will be paid.

Senior Fellowships, General Fellowships and Short-term Fellowships carry a contingency grant of Rs.10,000, Rs. 5,000 and Rs. 2,000 respectively per year.

Senior Fellowships, General Fellowships and Fellowships for Preparing Learning Material are awarded for a period of two years. However, in deserving cases fellowships may be extended for a period of one more year.

The Council reserves the first right to publish finished research project of the awardee. In case the Council decides not to publish it, the awardee may get it published anywhere else but he/she will have to acknowledge that the work was carried out under a fellowship provided by the Council.

The Council's decision regarding the award of fellowships and related matters is final.

IV UNIVERSITY GRANTS COMMISSION (UGC)

1.01 With a view to promoting research in humanities and social sciences, the University Grants Commission provides financial assistance to university and college teachers for research or learned work in their respective fields of specialisation. The Commission's support for research in the humanities and social sciences is available at present in the following disciplines.

1.02 Research on inter-disciplinary basis purticularly in areas which have remained relatively neglected but which are of crucial importance to the social and economic life of the country will receive priority. An illustrative list of such areas is given in Annexure 1. Teachers may also send proposals in other areas depending upon their interest and aptitude. These proposals would also be considered for financial support by the Commission.

1.03 Assistance from the Commission to permanent teachers working in university, college or a institution approved under Section 2 (f) and Section 12(A) of the UGC Act is available for minor research projects which could be completed in a year or two as well as for major research projects which may take up to three years.

1.04 Assistance is generally provided to a teacher or a department for one project at a time in cluding the projects approved by the UGC and other funding agencies.

1.05 Application for assistance for a project should be made in the prescribed form obtainable from the office of the University Grants Commission. The form, complete in all respects, should be sent to the Secretary, University Grants Commission, Bahdur Shah Zafar Marg, New Delhi, through the head of institution where the teacher is employed (Annexure-2). Before forwarding the application, the head of the institution should ensure that the teacher is holding a permanent post in the college/university where he is working and the institution is eligible to receive UGC grant (please see Para 1.03).

1.06 The head of the institution may also ensure that the application is not a recipient of any other award/grant for the same project from the UGC or from any other agency. If so, details thereof may please he indicated.

1.07 A synopsis of the project indicating (1) the problem to be investigated; (2) objectives of the project; (3) hypotheses; (4) research design and methodology; (5) tools to be used in the collection of data; (6) significance of the study; (7) its relevance to the present-day problems and needs of the society and the country and (8) its likely contribution to knowledge, may please be attached with the application form.

1.08 Grant is sanctioned for a project by the Commission on the advice of experts. The Commission's decision is communicated in respect of only those projects which are approved for financial assistance.

1.09 Entire grant approved for the project is released to the institution (university/college) in suitable instalments depending on the progress of the work.

1.10 On receipt of the amount of the grant from the Commission, the institution will immediately advance the entire amount to the researcher.

1.11 The amount for TA/DA for field work shall be determined on the merit of each case by the Commission on the advice of the experts. For the payment of TA/DA, the rules in vogue in the college/university where the teacher is employed, will be followed.

1.12 (i) Grants sanctioned under the scheme are meant to cover only direct expenditure on the project and not any expenditure which would normally be met by the university/college out of its own resources.

(ii) Any expenditure incurred prior to the issue of the sanction letter will not be an admissible charge on the grants sanctioned for the project.

1.13 Reallocation of funds from one item to another of the approved budget is not permissible without the prior approval of the Commission.

1.14 Six monthly report on the progress of the work done along with the statement of expenditure shall be furnished to the Commission by the researcher through the head of the department/institution concerned.

1.15 Grant is to be utilised within the period specified for the purpose by the Commission. This period may be extended in exceptional cases where specific requests are received from the researcher/department through the head of the institution atleast three months before the expiry of the period specified in the first instance.

1.16 Any amount left unspent at the end of the approved period shall be refunded to the Commission, through a demand draft drawn in favour of the Secretary, UGC.

1.17 Within two months of the expiry of the period approved for the utilisation of the grant, a consolidated report of the work done by the researcher with a summary of the findings in about 1000 words, the audited statement of expenditure and the utilisation certificate should be sent to Commission by the researcher through the institution concerned. A copy of the final report of the project shall be sent to the Commission when cyclostyled or printed.

1.18 On completion of the project, any apparatus or equipment purchased with the Commission's asssistance will become the property of the institution where the teacher is employed.

1.19 Prior approval of the UGC will not be necessary for publishing the results of the study on the projects supported by the Commission. However , in all such cases, the investigator should acknowledge the contribution made by the staff appointed for the project and the support received from the UGC. The universities may, if they so desire, consider the publication of the final reports on the approved project under the scheme of "publication of research works including doctoral theses" for which a fixed amount is placed at their disposal for the plan period by the UGC. Such reports could also be published in learned journals.

1.20 The recipients of the grant may not be allowed to leave the institution either on transfer, resignation or retirement etc. unless the accounts are settled by them and the unspent balance, if any, is properly handed over to the head of the institution for onward transmission to the Commission.

Schemes

Supports for Minor Research Projects

2.01 Under this scheme, financial assistance ranging from Rs.500 to Rs.10,000 may be provided to a teacher who wishes to undertake, alongwith teaching work, a minor research project or an investigation for a doctoral degree under approved supervision.

2.02 Assistance is available for items like field work, preparation/ cyclostyling/printing of questionnaire, computation work, equipment, books and journals which are specially required for the proposed project, but which are not normally available to the teacher in the institution where he is employed.

2.03 Assistance is also provided for typing, stationery, and contingencies which will be limited to ten per cent of the total approved grant.

2.04 Grant under this scheme is available to individual teachers and is neither transferable nor available to the college for appoinment of any staff or for meeting expenditure on items of a recurring nature.

2.05 Books and journals purchased with the Commission's Assistance may be retained by the teacher after the completion of the project.

2.06 The entire grant approved for the project will be released to the university/college in two instalments-50 per cent of the grant as first instalment and the balance on receipt of the statement of expenditure duly signed and verified by the Registrar/Principal for the first instalment.

Support for Major Research Projects

3.01 The University Grants Commission provides financial support to teachers—working as well as superannuated—in the universities and colleges with fecilities for post-graduate studies and research to enable them to take up intensive and indepth studies in specific areas in the humanities and social sciences. The superannuated teacher is entitled to an honorarium of Rs.750 per month as the principal investigator of the project, in addition to such other fecilities as may be recommended as a part of the project. Normally, no research project from a superannuated teacher is considered in this scheme if the teacher concerned cannot complete the project before attaining the age of 65 years.

3.02 Research project may be undertaken by an individual teacher or by a group of teachers or by a department as a whole. The Commission also considers research investigations which cut across various diciplines in the same university or college and if necessary, concerned or interested departments in other institutions. In case a project is undertaken jointly by a group of teachers, one of the teachers will function as the principal investigator and he will be responsible for all matters pertaining to the project.

3.03 Assistance under the programmes is made available from the Commission for appointment of junior research fellows, research associates, visits to libraries, field work, purchase of apparatus and equipment, books and journals, postage, stationery, computation work, preparation/cyclostyling/printing of questionnaire, contingencies and similar other items needed for the project.

3.04 The duration of the project will be up to a priod of three years In special cases, however, the period of Assistance can be extended up to five years.

3.05 On completion of the project, books and journals, procured with UGC Assistance will become the property of the institution where the project has been undertaken.

3.06 Grant approved by the Commission for the project will be released to the institution concerned in suitable instalments depending on the progress of the work. Progress report of the work done shall be furnished to the Commission every six months by the teacher. It should be accompanied by the statement of expenditure actually incurred on the project and an estimate of expenditure during the next six months. No further instalment of grant shall be released in the absence of satisfactory progress report. The Commission shall be informed well in time about any unexpected difficulties that may arise in the implementation of the project.

Priority Areas of Research : An Illustrative List

A list of priority areas of research in the Humanities and Social Sciences is given at the end. These areas have been identified by the UGC Panels in different disciplines. This list is not exhaustive; it is merely illustrative and will be under constant revision.

Research Associateships

Research Associateships are awarded by the Commission centrally and by the universities etc. every year with a view to provide an opportunity to research students and teachers who have shown extraordinary talent and competence to take up research work independently or on project assignments in Science, Humanities including Social Sciences and Engineering and Technology.

Eligibility

Research Associateships are intended for persons preferably below the age of 45 years who have doctorate degree and have published research work to their credit and have already shown evidence of independent research work. In case of women candidates, the age limit is 55 years.

Emoluments

Research Associateships are awarded in four slabs and carry emoluments at the following rates:

(i) Rs. 2200-100-2700
(ii) Rs. 2700-100-3200
(iii) Rs. 3200-100-3700
(iv) Rs. 2700-125-4325

(These rates will be effective from 1-4-1987)

A research Associate shall complete his tenure in the same slab which he is placed at the time of selection.

Contingency

The Research Associateship carries a contingency grant of Rs.5,000 p.a for contingent expenditure in case of Humanities and Social Sciences and Rs. 7.500 p.a in case of Sciences, Engineering and Technology.

Duration

Associateship will be tenable initially for a period of three years extendable for another term in the same slab for a period not exceeding two years.

Allowances and Other Facilities

(a) *House Rent Allowance*

(1) Single seated flat-type accommodation should be provided to the associates as far as possible. Research Associates not accommodated as above, would be entitled to house rent allowence on the same basis as is admissible to another staff of the University/Institution receiving equalent emoluments as per rules of the University/Institution concerned.
(2) Research Associates who have not been provided with

accommodation as above but have been accommodated in a hostel recognised/maintained by the University/Institution may be reimbursed the hostel fee.

(b) *Medical Fecilities*

Research Associates are entitled for health-care facilities as admissible to other staff of similar level of the University/Institution

(c) *Readers Allowance*

Readers Allowence @ Rs.400 p.m is admissible to blind Research Associates.

(d) *Leave*

(1) He/She shall be entitled to all leave as per rules of the institution.
(2) He/She in special cases, be allowed by the Commission leave without associateship for a period not exceeding three months during the tenure of award on the recommendations of the Head of the Institution concerned. The period of leave without associateship will count towards the tenure of associateship.

Benefits to Host Institution

The Commission has decided that the host institution where Research Associates are placed would be given a grant equal to 10 per cent of the total associateship component for providing infrastractural facilities (Stores, purchase, technical and clerical Assistance, repair and supply of electricity, water, gas, etc.)

Conditions of Award

(a) The Associateships are generally tenable at any University Institution approved under the University Grants Commission Act.
(b) He/She shall do whole-time research work in a subject chosen by him and approved by the Univercity/Institution concerned.

Scholarships and Fellowships

For the developement of research in Universities and Colleges, UGC awards scholarships in various subjects. In any given time more than 3500 fellowships are operational under this scheme. These fellowships will be awarded only to those research scholars who have qualified in national level tests conducted by the U.G.C, CSIR, GATE, etc. Tests conducted at all India level in some selected subjects by JNU and Indian Institute of Science, Bangalore have been accredicted as equivalent to national tests for this purpose.

6.2.22 Teachers of outstanding eminence are awarded national fellowships for a specified period to devote themselves exclusively to research and writing. Under the scheme of Research Scientists, 200 positions have been created in the grades of lectures, Readers and Professors in order to provide opportunities to those who wish to pursue research as a career. Selections under this scheme are made directly by the Commission.

Miscellaneous Programmes

Coaching classes for Competitive Examinations for Weaker Sections amongst Minority Communities.

6.2.23 The Commission provides Assistance to 14 Universities and 39 Colleges for organising coaching classes for competitive examinations for weaker sections among the minority communities.

Facilities for Sheduled Castes/Scheduled Tribes

6.2.24 In addition to the Jr. Research Fellowships reserved for Scheduled Castes/Scheduled Tribes out of the total number of such fellowship instituted in various universities, the Commission is directly awarding every year 50 fellowships exclusively for Scheduled Castes and Scheduled Tribes. Smilarly, the Commission has reserved 40 research Associateships for Scheduled Castes and Scheduled Tribes. In order to provide opportunities to teachers in affiliated colleges belonging to Scheduled Castes/Scheduled Tribes for improving their qualifications by doing M.Phil./Ph.D.. the Commission has instituted 50 teacher fellowships every year.

Women's Studies

6.2.25 The Commission has been providing financial Assistance to universities for undertaking well-defined projects for research in women's studies and also for the development of curriculam at the undergraduate and postgraduate levels and relevant extension activities. The Commission has also created 40 positions of part-time research associateship for women candidates in Science and Humanities including Social Sciences and Engineering and Technology. Twenty-eight research projects relating to the themes of women's studies were approved for assistance upto November 1988. Also the Standing Committee on women's studies, after examining various proposals, recommended, assistance to some selected universities and colleges to set up centres/cells for women's studies.

Bilateral Exchange Programmes

6.2.27 The Commission continues to implement various items under the Cultural Exchange Programmes assigned to it from time to time. These programmes involve exchange of teachers, development of bilateral academic links between institutions of higher education, joint seminars, scholarships and fellowships and assignment of foreign language teachers to unversities in India. During the year 1987-88, 75 Indian teachers were able to undertake visits abroad under these programmes and 70 foriegn scholars visited India.

ANNEXURE-1

PRIORITY AREAS OF RESEARCH : AN ILLUSTRATIVE LIST

Economics

1. Development of Indian economy since Independence
2. Inter-regional planning problems
3. Export promotion and import substitution of India
4. Economics of energy
5. Poverty in India
6. Unemployement and employment of India
7. Area planning
8. Working of the mixed economy
9. Mobilisation of fiscal and physical resources
10. Economics of distributive justice
11. Public distribution system
12. Economics of Scale
13. Manpower Planning
14. Cost benefit analysis of Public expenditure
15. Prices and production in agriculture
16. Technological change and agricultural development: income distribution
17. Transport economics : modes of transport, cost pricing and allocation of resources between different modes of transport, traffic flow, cost benefit appraisal, fare and freight policy, and exsisting deficiencies in transport planning.

Commerce and Mangement

1. Commercial viability of public enterprices
2. Public distribution system and consumerism
3. Industrial policy including licensing and control
4. Technology transfer and collaboration
5. Project Planning and appraisal
6. Managerial and supervisory effectiveness
7. Depreciation theory and practices
8. Inflation Accounting

9. Working capital management
10. Trade policy including import substitution and export promotion
11. Agro-Industry
12. Human Resource accounting
13. Problems of Corporate sector
14. Problems of small business
15. Transport economics
16. Industrial relations and personnel management.

ANNEXURE-2

UNIVERSITY GRANTS COMMISSION
Bahadur Shah Zafar Marg, New Delhi

APPLICATION FORM FOR SUPPORT FOR MINOR RESEARCH PROJECT

(*Note* : Application is to be sent in duplicate)

1. Name of the teacher
   (in block letters)
   (i) Date of birth
   (ii) Qualification and designation
2. Name of the institution where the teacher is employed:
   (i) (a) department of
       (b) University of
       (c) College affiliated to
           the University of
   (ii) Whether the University/College/Institution is approved under Section 2(f) and Section 12(A) of the UGC Act? YES/NO (please check)
   (iii) Whether the teacher is working on a permanent basis? YES/NO (please check)
3. Academic Experience:
   (a) Research experience Years
   (b) Teaching experience Years
   (c) In case the teacher holds a doctoral degree, please indicate:
       (i) Title of the thesis
       (ii) Year of the award of degree
       (iii) Name of the University which awarded the degree
       (iv) Whether the thesis has been published? If so, the year of publication and the name of the publisher
   (d) Details of publications:
       (i) Number of papers published
       (ii) Number of papers accepted for publication
       (iii) Number of books published
       (iv) Number of books under publication (please give the detailed information on a separate sheet of paper)

4. Particulars of the proposed research project:
   (a) Subject
   (b) Title of the project (in block letters)

(A synopsis of the project indicating (1) the problem to be investigated; (2) objectives of the projects; (3) hypotheses; (4) research design and methodology; (5) tools to be used in the collection of the data; (6) significance of the study; (7) its relevance to the present day problems and needs of the society and the country; and (8) its likely contribution to knowledge, may please be attached with the application.)

   (c) Details of inter-departmental cooperation, if any
   (d) Whether the project has been approved by the University for the doctoral degree; if so, please indicate :
      (i) Date of registration;
      (ii) Name and designation of the supervisor approved by the University;
      (iii) Name of the University where registerd;
   (e) Name and designation of the associates, if any.

5. Financial Assistance sought:

Items	Amount required Rs.
Total	

(A statement giving details of various items required for the project may please be attached with the application. In case assistance is required for field work, details thereof indicating the places to be visited, purpose of the visit and approximate expenditure on travel and collection of data and manuscripts etc. may also be given in the statement.)

6. Whether the teacher has received support for the present project or a similar project from UGC, under major or minor scheme of Support for Research or from any other agency. If so, please indicate:
   (a) Name of the agency from which assistance was received;
   (b) Sanction letter number and date under which the assistance was approved;
   (c) Amount approved and utilised;
   (d) Title of the project for which Assistance was approved;
   (e) In case the project was completed, whether the report on

the project has been published/cyclostyled or if the candidate was working for the doctoral degree, whether the thesis was submitted and accepted by the University for the award of degree;

(A summary of the report/thesis in about 1000 words may please be attached with the application).

(f) If the project has not been completed, please state the reason;

7. Whether the teacher has already submitted the present project or similar project to the UGC under major or minor scheme of Support for Research or to any other agency? If so, please indicate the name of the agencies and their decision on the proposal; and

8. Any other information relevant to the above research project which the teacher may like to give in support of his/her application

Certified that I have read the rules governing the scheme and shall abide by them in case the award is made to me. It is further certified that the information given above is correct to the best of my knowledge.

(Signature of the Applicant)

FOR USE IN THE UNIVERSITY/COLLEGE OFFICE

It is certified that facilities for working on the above project will be provided to .... in the Department of .... in the University/College.

It is further certified that equipment and books etc. for which assistance has been asked for, by the teacher, are not available for his/her use in the institution and that the teacher is not at present in receipt of a similar grant from the University, Unversity Grants Commission or any other agency. The institution agrees to abide by the rules governing the scheme, if the UGC provides assistance to the teacher for the project.

(Signature: Head of the Department)

(Signature: Head of the Institution)

UNIVERSITY GRANTS COMMISSION
Bahadur Shah Zafar Marg, New Delhi

APPLICATION FORM FOR SUPPORT FOR MAJOR RESEARCH PROJECT

(*Note:* The Proposal is to be sent in quadruplicate)

PART A

1. Name, date of birth, qualification, designation and address of
   (i) Principal investigator:
   (ii)
   (iii)
2. Name of the institution where the project will be undertaken:
   (a) Department of .... University of
   (b) College .... affiliated to the University of

3. (a) Whether the University/College/Institution is approved under Section 2(f) and Section 12(A) of the UGC Act? YES/NO (please check)
   (b) Whether the Principal investigator is working as a teacher on a permanent basis in the University/College? YES/NO (please check)
4. C.V. of the principal investigator:
   (a) Research experience Years
   (b) Teaching experience Years

Research degree	Year of award	University	Title of the Study
Ph.D			
D.Litt			
Any other (please specify)			

(d) Details of publications:
   (i) Number of pages published
   (ii) Number of papers accepted for publication
   (iii) Number of books published

(iv) Number of books under publication (please give detailed information on a separate sheet of paper).

PART B

1. Details of the proposed work:
   (a) Subject
   (b) Title of the project (in block letters)
   (c) Duration
   (d) Details of inter-departmental cooperation, if any

(A synopsis of the project indicating (1) the problem to be investigated; (2) objectives of the project; (3) hypotheses; (4) research design and methodology; (5) tools to be used in the collection of data; (6) significance of the study; (7) its relevance to the present day problems and needs of the society and the country and (8) its likely contribution to knowledge, may please be attached with the application.)

2. Are you aware of the work done or being done on the above project or on a similar or allied project in any other institution in the country? If so, please attach a note indicating the present status of research in the area in which you now propose to work and also the gaps which you now propose to cover. Please indicate the serial number of enclosure which gives this information.

3. Financial assistance required:

(1) Recurring:

(a) For Research
(b) More staff

Estimated Expenditure

Designation	No.of Positions	Remuneration Rs.	Years I	II	III	Total Rs.
Research Associate						
Junior Research Fellow						
Investigator						
Total:						

(2) **Non-Recurring**

Items	Total Estimated Expenditure
(i) Books and journals	Rs.
(ii) Computation	
(iii) Stationery and postage	
(iv) Printing of questionnaire, if needed	
(v) Equipment, if needed	
(vi) Field Work/Travel	
(vii) Other expenses (please specify)	
Total	
Total estimated expenditure (R and NR) Rs.	

4. Whether the teacher has received support for the present project or a similar project from UGC, under major or minor scheme of Support for Research or from any other agency? If so, please indicate:

(a) Name of the agency from which assistance was received;

(b) Sanction letter number and date under which assistance was approved;

(c) Amount approved and utilised;

(d) Title of the project for which assistance was approved;

(e) In case the project was completed, whether the report on the project has been published/cyclostyled or if the candidate was working for the doctoral degree, whether the thesis was submitted and accepted by the University for the award of degree;

(A summary of the report/thesis in about 1,000 words may please be attached with the application).

(f) If the project has not been completed, please state the reasons;

5. Whether the teacher has already submitted the present project or a similar project to the UGC under major or minor scheme of Support for Research or to any other agency? If so, please indicate the name of the agencies and their decision on the proposal; and

6. Any other information which the investigator may like to give in support of his proposal which may be helpful in evaluating it.

I/We certify that :

(a) General physical facilities, such as furniture, space etc. are available in the Department/College.

(b) I/We shall abide by the rules governing the scheme in case assistance is provided to me/us by the University Grants Commission for the above project.

(c) In case the above research project or an allied project receives assistance from any other source, I/We shall inform the University Grants Commission accordingly.

(d) Information given above is correct to the best of my/our knowledge.

(e) I/We shall complete the project within the stipulated period. If I/We fail to do so and if the UGC is not satisfied with the progress of the research project, the Commission may terminate the project immediatly and ask for the refund of the amount received by me/us.

Name and Signature of (a) Principal Investigator
(b) Other investigators

FOR USE IN THE UNIVERSITY/COLLEGE OFFICE

Facilities for the above project to..in the Departement and the University/College. The proposal has our full support. This institution agrees to abide by the rules governing the scheme, if the project is approved by the UGC for assistance.

Name and Signature of (a) Head of the Deptt.
(b) Head of the Institution

APPENDIX-IX

EDUCATION OF WOMEN AND GIRLS IN INDIA: A CASE STUDY

Educational enrolments in India are depressed because of the slow progress in the education of girls ; but there is a growing sensitivity to educate this half of the population. Progress will depend upon a number of social, cultural and institutional factors.

One of the main labours of girls is providing sibling care.Creches or nurseries, either attached or near to elementary schools, release working-class girls from a major preoccupation with child-care so that they can attend school.

A girl in rural India works on an average nine hours a day and 315 days in the year, surviving on less nutritional food and struggling against prejudice and discrimination. Nonetheless, despite such evidence, there is continued reluctance to view girls as productive workers. This can be attributed directly to certain assumptions regarding a women's role and that of the school, which is regarded as an institution primarily for boys.

Irrespective of socio-economic background, the ideal of feminine roles usually conflicts with the ideal of modern education; for their survival families build on docile aspects of womanliness. While middle class families allow girls access to certain kinds of courses, in a poverty situation, schooling is a seen as a poor investment providing no sure access to better employment. Despite their role in survival, girls are deprived of any free time during adolescence, and there are severe restrictions on the kind of food a girl can eat.

In October 1978, the minimum legal age of marriage for girls was raised to 18 and 21 for boys. Despite this, a recent study found that 10 million girls below age 11 were married. Child marriages are associated with low educational enrolments and high female and maternal morality.

Adapted from a case study written by Malavika Karlekar for a book to be published by the IBE.

Access to Education

In a situation where families restrict a girl's mobility, particularly after adolescence, easy access to a primary school is essential to ensure at least a few years of schooling.

In the Indain context among certain social categories, co-education at any level is unacceptable and depresses girls' enrolment. Their education depends substantially on whether they are taught by women or not, and single-sex schools are pre-condition for the mass schooling of girls. Yet, recent figures show that only about 10 to 15 per cent of all institutions are segregated.

Dependence on one individual teacher means that in the event of his or her illness, absence or even transfer, children are left on their own. Many schools exist as thatched huts, tents or just open spaces. In such situations, parents would be reluctant to expose their daughters to a potentially 'unsure' environment.

The existence of daily and yearly school time-tables which ignore the work patterns of households deter the participation of children. The problem can be lessened by the introduction of multiple point entries at different ages in specially organized primary schools, where teaching is organised using innovative techniques. Scholarships, mid-day meals and free books are also possible incentives.

Bias

Inflexible teaching methods and single date entry into school inhibit enrolments. The school institutionalizes specific norms such as uniform age at enrolment, sequential promotion on the basis of examinations, teaching from prescribed textbooks within a certain time period, and a philosophy of punishment and reward. In most cases, educational planners and administrators and authors of textbooks are men from middle-classes urban backgrounds, whose assumptions are based on children (boys) reared in the same environments.

Biases in textbooks and syllabi are now increasingly recognized. Whether a textbook teaches mathematics or English, it is a powerful medium for the perpetuation of stereotypes and role models. A 1986 study of the Hindi textbooks found that the ratio of boy-centred stories to girl-centred stories was 21:0. In thirteen English-language textbooks, the proportion was eighty-one to nine. Further, books in both languages portray boys as courageous, achieving and interested in science and technology, whereas girls are invariably portrayed in menial and subordinate roles.

Textbook revision and in-service programmes for teachers have been initiated in several parts of the country, but teachers must still cope with completing courses within an inflexible time schedule, resuming in a some what singleminded focus on the content of books and rote learning.

There are 41 girls to each 100 boys in science courses, and only 6 girls to a 100 boys in engineering and technology courses. Thus, far fewer girls enter science and technology than would be reasonable to expect, both in school and higher education. Important non-academic factors and situations influence girls' choices at the age of 16 or 17 related to social and family expectations.

Signs of Change

Social and family perceptions are slowly changing: considerable behind-the scenes activities and intrafamilial dramas are leading to a growing cohort of self-confident, aware young women.

A changing social environment has also encouraged a more positive approach recognizing that 'women as victims should be replaced by the notion of women's empowerment'.

An important innovation is the government-initiated Mahila Samakhya (Women Speak of Equality) Programme. This programme goes beyond literacy to recognize and promote overall development. Most importantly, women must articulate their own demands, work towards a resolution of their problems, and co-operate with peers and colleagues in problem-solving. Flexibility encourages women to participate in literacy programmes, to work for more child-care centres, to establish new village-based learning units and to organize networks across villages. Thus the programme's. basic philosophy is self-reliance arising out of a fundamental belief in the capacity to mobilize, discuss and then move towards action.

The Mahila Samakhya Programme is targeted towards rural women and the less privileged: in short, mainly those who have been by-passed or marginalised by the formal system of education, so that an increasing number of Indian women are taking charge of their own lives. At the other end of the spectrum, the slow yet definite movement of more privileged girls into competitive male-dominated areas of study and work confirms an erosion of traditional values. Expectations have indeed begun to rise.

APPENDIX-X

WOMEN'S LITERARY WORKS

Women's studies is often said to be the only growth area in academics and the bastion of radical thought after the collapse of the Communist world. Whatever the reasons for the avalanche of books on feminism or gender studies, they do dominated the 11th World Book Fair in New Delhi.

But like all fields with specialisations and sub-specialisation, the range was enormous from women on women, the male backlash, critical studies in women's literature and different aspects of gender and its meaning in a fast changing world.

Perhaps the biggest section within women's studies was a revival of women writers and critical reassessment of their works from George Eliot down to Virginia Woolf, Angela Carter and Rebacca West. Most of their work has been pioneered by the Virago Press which was not represented by a single Indian publisher or distributor in the fair.

The quickest way was to stick closely to the foreign publishers who had a special corner for women's studies and literature, including originals. But the literature available in women's fiction is vast and one needs to be clear about whether one requires academically oriented titles like Jane Austen's *Pride and Prejudice* or Virginia Woolf's *To The Lighthouse* or contemporary fiction like Toni Morrison's *Jazz* that is read for pleasure.

Given the nature of our book buying habits that tend to be more academically oriented, most of the literature books displayed were those directly prescribed in courses with very little of the more vibrant women writers like Terry McMillan, Alice Walter, Gloria Kaylor, Label Allende available or at least prominently displayed. If women writers' works outside the academic fold were present, they were basically those of the dead and famous or those who have 'arrived' like the Nobel Prize winner Nadine Gordimer and Tony Morrison, whose works were available at special Indian prices.

But Penguin Books and Kali for Women had Indian Women's fiction and some reprinted here which were available in a number of books stalls because the distinction between publishers and distributors was very thin at the Fair—a difference one must always bear in mind in India.

By far the best buy in women's fiction was *Breaking Ice,* An Anthology of Contemporary African-American fiction published by Vintage and edited by Terry McMillan who rivals Toni Morrison for the sheer force of her language and metaphor on the condition of the black American women. McMillan has brought together not merely the leading American women writers—There are also some men writing on women's issues—but those still emerging and who will be heard in the years to come.

Fiction, however, is a small component of women's literature; most of it is concentrated on gender studies or the impact of women in different fields—or the lack of of it and the reasons for its absence. In gender studies that fit into a wide cross-section of academic requirements in history, economics and sociology, the best bet was Polity Press represented by Dass Media and distributed by some of the leading booksellers.

Some new titles like the *Polity Reader In Gender Studies, Imagining Women, Defining Women, Inventing Women, Science, Gender and Technology, Beyond The Family, Familiar Exploitation, A New Analysis of Marriage In Contemporary Western Countries* and *The Transformation of Intimacy* had arrived—sadly the quantities received are rather small and the prices were high—which would fit into courses in cross-cultural studies. There were many other titles that could not be slotted into one subject or another like *Feminine Sentences: Essays on Women and Culture* which could fit into sociology and politics and perhaps other social sciences in a loose kind of way.

What is striking about serious feminist literature—as distinct from the rather hackneyed antimale chauvinist pig titles—is the emphasis on theory rather than empirical studies on women's exploitation and their second-class status in a male-dominated world. The "sex war" themes are now over and done with, and there is a distinct shift towards feminist theory, cultural and literary analysis, sociology and art, history and women's relationship to modern and post-podern culture.

Apparently, publishers have realised that titles like *Women Resistance and Revolution; Rights and Wrongs of Women; The Past Is Before Us; Vindication of the Rights of Women* have little lasting value in a fast changing world—hence the shifts towards more substantive studies like the classic, *The Second Sex* that, in some ways, started the women's revolution and still continues to lead the way. Feminist literature is a vast field now and the Book Fair gave some idea of how much there is to cover.

What of our own? Except for Kali for Women, no Indian publisher has developed an independent women's studies programme although women's writings have been anthologised in literary, political and sociological studies.

Kali's emphasis is on women in the Third World and within this frame it has published in social sciences and humanities, including some fiction, pamphlets and monographs. The slant is distinctly academic with titles like *Issues and Ideology in the Indian Women's Movement; Muslim Women in India; Political and Private Realities; Staying Alive; Women, Ecology and Survival in India* and *Recasting Women:Essays in Colonial History.* Perhaps the lead title would be Radha Kumar's *The History of Doing: An Illustrated Account of the Women's Movement In India* which studies the contribution of women activities in the natural struggle, and later in raising mass consciousness against women's inequality.

APPENDIX-XI

COUNCIL OF EUROPE: EDUCATION OF WOMEN IN AUSTRIA

Women under-represented in higher education

According to data published by the Ministry for Science and Research, women are under-represented in higher education—except for first-year students. The per centage of women is :first-year students: 49.7 per cent; graduates: 42.9 per cent; Junior lectures: 20.2 per cent: assistant staff under contract: 30.9 per cent; persons qualified to apply for a professorship *(Habilitation):* 11.9 per cent; Senior lecturers: 7.9 per cent; extraordinary professors: 4.8 per cent; ordinary (full) professors: 2.7 per cent.

In the humanities and social sciences female students far outnumber male students (for example 87 per cent in the case of future interpreters), whereas in science and technology few female students are to be found (2.9 per cent in electrical engineering). There is no research evidence, however, that girls from girls schools do better than girls from co-educational schools when it comes to science and technology. Some 46 per cent of the male students succeed in their studies as compared to 40 per cent of the women.

A study commissioned by the "Austrian University Journal" revealed the following proportion of men compared to women in academic staff:

— 5.2:1 for Austria as a whole;
— 3.2:1 for the University of Salzburg and the Vienna College of Veterinary Surgery;
— 25.7: 1 for the College of Mining.

In a doctoral thesis Renate Augusta , of the Vienna Institute for Industrial Management, compared men and women in history teacher training (considered a typically female domain) and in computer studies aiming at a career in industry (considered a male domain). She found that men wanting to qualify as history teachers were not at all concerned about career prospects, whereas women in computer studies were much more career-minded than their male colleagues, taking their father as a model and trying to adopt male values.

Among the reasons for the underrepresentation of women in higher education, the *Austrian University Journal* listed the following:

— As organised at present, higher education and research in Austria are not attractive for women. Research approaches often correspond to male ways of thinking.
— Many professors still have prejudices against women in matters of research. They claim that women are too emotional and not rational enough in their approach.
— Women often lack "tacit knowledge" about career development. How to fight for adequate working conditions? How and where to apply for research grants? Which research topics enjoy priority so that publications may rouse interest? How to be invited to lecture at a prestigious congress? How to bargain from a position of sientific strength? Who are the opinion leaders in one's own subjects and how best to attract their attention?Women often do not have this information, because they have limited access to career networks. They also lack a certain ruthlessness in the persuit of a career.
— It can be difficult to reconcile the demands of family and of career.

The Ministry envisages the following measures to alleviate these problems:

— tighter control of recruitment and promotion criteria so as to ensure that women get a fare chance;
— special grants for women preparing a doctoral thesis or qualifying for a professorship;
— special quotas for teaching activities concerning topics of interest for women;
— the appoinment by each university of a person responsible for securing equal opportunities for women, This person would take part in all meetings where staff matters are discussed and decided and be entitled to intervene, make requests and have disagreements recorded in the minutes. No decision would be valid if the person is not present. If the person uses her veto, the body in question has to discuss and decide a second time. If the committee decides not to change its decision, the matter may be brought before the Minister; and

— once adopted, the Federal Equal Opportunities Act will forbid any form of discrimination and will set up an Equal Opportunities Committe responsible for making recommendations on how to improve the career prospects of women. The Minister will be obliged to report at regular intervals about progress made.

Osterreichische Hochschulzeitung, 9-10/1993;
Memorandum Zur Aufklarung die Univeritatsreform
by Prof. Dr Erhard Busek
(Michael Vorbeck)

Descriptors: career development; discrimination; equal opportunity; higher education; positive discrimination; research; women; Austria

APPENDIX-XII-1

1995 WORLD CONFERENCE ON WOMEN

The Member States of the United Nations, by General Assembly resolution 45/129, Economic and Social Council resolution 1990/12 and Commission on the Status of Women resolution 36/8A, agreed to hold the Fourth World Conference on Women: Action for Equality, Development and Peace, from 4 to 15 September 1995 at Beijing, China. Moreover, the Commission on the Status of Women, recalling successful forums for non-Governmental organizations held at Mexico, Copenhagen, and Nairobi, agreed in its resolution 36/8C that the Conference should be proceeded by a forum for non-Governmental organizations (NGOs). This forum will take place from 31 August to 12 September 1995, also at Beijing and will be coordinated by an NGO Forum Fecilitating Committee under the auspices of the Conference of Non-Governmental Organizations in consultative Status with the Economic and Social Council (CONGO)

The primary task of the World Conference will be to analyse and adopt two documents: the World Survey on the Role of Women in Development, and the Platform for Action. The debates will focus on the process of change in the situation of women, by reviewing and appraising the progress achieved in the implementation of the Nairobi Forward-looking Strategies for the Advancement of Women, adopted at the 1985 Third World Conference on Women. That progress will be considered in the light of sweeping changes taking place world-wide and their effects on the criteria that steer the course of development. Another goal of the Conference will be to mobilize men and women at all levels of the social structure to work towards the achievement of the objectives identified as key areas in the Platform for Action adopted at Beijing, which will aim at accelerating the implementation of the Nairobi Strategies.

APPENDIX XII-2

WOMEN'S STUDIES PROJECT

Family Health International has begun a five-year programme of research to determine the impact of family planning on women's lives in developing countries. The U.S. Agency for International Development awarded FHI an $8.6 million agreement to manage the project, which began in October.

Research has examined the impact of family planning services on infant health, demographic trends, health-care costs and many other related subjects, says Dr. Theodore M. King, FHI's president and chief operating officer.

"With this project, we hope to examine the benefit of family planning on numerous aspects of women's lives, including self-esteem, education and autonomy", Dr. King says. An ultimate goal of the project is to provide leaders in developing countries with research to help shape their national health policies and programme.

Source: Network 14/(3) February 1994, Family Health International P.O. Box 13950, North Carolina, U.S.A.

APPENDIX-XIII

WORKING WOMEN IN INDIA

The 1991 Census shows that 23 per cent of the women in India are working as against 19.6 per cent in 1981. Kerala has one of the lowest employment rates for women in the country. Seventeen per cent of women (It has reached the highest percentage of literacy in the country) of the country are economically employed.

The number of working women in the country, including those doing unpaid work, has gone up by 42 per cent in the decade.

North-eastern States of India have the highest employment rates for women. Sikkim heads the list with 53 per cent of the women economically employed. The percentage of the working women in the other States of the region is Mizoram 44 per cent, Arunachal Pradesh 40 per cent, Nagaland 39 per cent and Manipur 37.5 per cent.

Other States with respectable number of women earning a livelihood are Andhra Pradesh 35 per cent, Himachal and Madhya Pradesh 33 per cent each, Tamil Nadu 31 per cent , Karnataka 29 per cent , Gujarat and Rajasthan 27 per cent each. Way down the employment ladder for Women is Punjab where just 6.8 per cent of the women are perceived to be gainfully employed. Haryana is little better with 11.3 per cent.

The female work participation rate is higher in rural areas rather than in urban areas. It is estimated that over 27 per cent of the women in the rural areas work as against 10 per cent in urban areas. In rural areas, the largest number of women are working in agriculture, followed by household industries, weaving, handicrafts, tailoring, forestry (collecting and carrying wood and minor forest produce) and sale of fish. There are of not many women engaged in their own enterprises of manufacturing a commodity or running a shop.

In urban areas, the largest number of women are employed in the construction industry, followed by those in Government services as nurses and teachers. Women are largely more in low-paid jobs and in manual labour.

In the 1981 Census, just 10 per cent of the households were headed by women though some areas like the north-east 30 to 35

per cent were headed by women.
Source: Cooperative Development Group, NDDB, Anand.

The number of girls who opted for engineering on completing higher secondary school education was one per cent in 1975, and has gone upto ten per cent in 1990. The total number is estimated at 18,875.26.1 per cent of them are unemployed . None of the major private industrial firm preferred women mechanical engineers. The overall number of women engineers has gone up more enrolling at specialized institution like the IIT and the Regional Engineering Colleges remains low.

The largest population of women engineers is in Tamil Nadu and Karnataka , Maharashtra, Madhya Pradesh , Andhra Pradesh, Gujarat, West Bengal and Uttar Pradesh come next. Electronics is the most preferred branch among women. Electrical and civil engineering come next. Computer science, chemical and mechanical engineering come later.

Data on the job status shows that 66.3 per cent are employed, 2.4 per cent are self-employed, 5.2 per cent are post-graduate students. Among the employed, 40 per cent are those who graduated during 1989 and 1990, indicating a high rate among the recent entrants in the job market. The highest number of jobless are in Kerala. Civil engineers are the most among unemployed. The largest number of unemployed are in the educational institutions (26.9 per cent), Government and civil services account for 22 per cent, public sector 18.9 per cent, large private industry12.7 per cent, small scale industrial units among private sector 9.1 per cent and the Government R&D 8.9 per cent.

APPENDIX-XIV

FOCAL POINTS/BODIES DEALING WITH QUESTIONS RELATING TO WOMEN'S DEVELOPMENT ISSUES

I. UNITED NATIONS

The Division for the Advancement of Women

Centre for Social Development and Humanitarian Affairs, United Nations Office at Vienna, Vienna International Centre

P.O Box 500
A-1400 Vienna, Austria
Tel:(431)21131-4270
Fax : (431)232156
Telx:135612

United Nations Office at Vienna (UNOV)
Liasion Office
Room S-2925
United Nations Headquarters
New York, NY10017, USA
Tel : (212)963 5634
Fax : (212)963 4185

The *Division for the Advancement of Women,* part of the Centre for Social Development and Humanitarian Affairs located in Vienna, Austria, is the United Nations system's focal point for all activities relating to women. Its programmes relate particularly to monitoring appraising implementations of the *Nairobi Forword-looking Strategies* adopted by consensus at the 1985 Nairobi World Conference which concluded the United Nations Decade for Women:Equality, Development and Peace. The Division acts as secretariat both for the Commission on the Status of Women and for the Committee on the Elimination of Discrimination against Women.

The Division also undertakes research studies and coordinates research, expert group meetings and advisory seminars, particularly on priority themes selected for each year by the Commission on the Status of Women (see list below). It also publishes periodicals, such as *Women 2000* and the *Data Highlights* series women. A complete list of publications is available from the Division.

The Division maintains a major data bank on Women. The *Women's Information System* is a computerized bibliographic data bank comprising some 2,000 United Nations documents which represent much of what the United Nations system has produced on paper on women's issues since January 1985. This data is readily available to all users, from Governments to individuals, by contacting the Reference Room of the Division at the telephone/telex/fax numbers listed above, with specific requests. Users in Vienna enjoy immediate visual access to documents described in the data bank for users from afar, a mailing list of publishers provided along with the printout:

Commission on The Status of Women
c/o Division for the Advancement of Women
(see address above)

The 45 members Commission on the Status of Women was set up in 1946 to promote women's rights in political, economic, social, and educational fields and to make recommendations on problems requiring immediate attention. To this end, it collects and analyses data to monitor the status of women around the world and prepares recommendations and reports on issues which affect women including their role in development

Committee on the Eliminations of Discrimination against Women(CEDAW)
c/o Division for the Advancement of Women
(see address above)

The United Nations Committee on the Elimination of Discriminate against Women is composed of 23 experts (jurists, lawyers, teachers, diplomats and experts on women's affairs), acting in their individual capacities rather than as representatives of Governments. Elected by States that has ratified the Convention, it is their job to monitor implementation of the 1979 Convention on the Elimination of All Forms of Discrimination against Women.

Department of Public Information (DPI)
Project Manager for Women's Issues
United Nations Room S-1040

New York, NY, 1017 USA
Tel : (212) 963-0352
Fax : (212)963-4556

The Department of Public Information Produces printed information products, films and videos as well as radio and television programmes on women, organizes special events, conducts briefings, responds to request for informations and maintains active liaison with the media and organizations dealing with topics related to women.

United Nations International Research and Training Institute for the Advancement of Women (INSTRAW)

P.O. Box : 21747
Santo Domingo, Dominican Republic
Tel :(809) 685 2111
Fax : (809)685 2117
New York Liaision Office
Tel :(212)963,5684

The International Research and Training Institute for the Advancement of Women was created by the Economic and Social Council in response to the 1975 World Conference call for a United Nations body to develop and expand research, training and information activities related to women and development. It serves as a clearing -house for research and informations and fosters coordination of individual and institutional research and training efforts for women. Located in Santo Domingo in the Dominican Republic , INSTRAW is completely financed by voluntary contributions.

Department of International Economic and Social Affairs (DIESA)

Statistical Office
Room DC 2-1554
United Nations
New York, NY,10017, USA
Tel:(1)(212) 963-4939
Telex: (1) (212)963-4116

DIESA maintains the United Nations Women's Indicators and Statistics Database for microcomputers (Wistat) which is a focal point for compilation of statistics on women from throughout the United

Nations system. It is available on dikette as a machine readable sales product and may be requested from the above address.

United Nations Development Fund for Women (UNIFEM)

304 East 45th Street, 6th floor
New York, NY, 10017, USA
Tel :(1) (212) 906-6400
Fax :(1) (212) 906-6705
Cable :UNDEVPRO New York

Originally called the Voluntary Fund for the United Nations Decade for Women, UNIFEM was created in 1976 to provide direct support for women's projects, and to promote the inclusion of women in the decision-making processes of mainstream development programmes. Financed by voluntary contributions from over 100 donor contries, international and non-governmental organizations and private individuals, UNIFEM has improved the lives of ten of thousands of poor women throughout the world by providing them with access to credit training and technologies.

United Nations Development Programme (UNDP)

Director, Division for Women in Development
1 United Nations Plaza
New York, NY, 110017, USA
Tel: (1) (212)906-5082
Fax: (212) 906-5365
Cable : UNDEVPRO New York

The United Nations Development Programme is the world's largest grant development Assistance organization with a network of field offices in 112 developing countries. With UNDP there is a special Division for Women in Development which maintains a close working relationship with the field offices and promotes concrete action to ensure the participation of women in UNDP funded projects . It also assists governments in integrating women into their development activities.

United Nations Population Fund (UNFPA)

Special Unit For Women, Population and Development
220 East 42nd Street
New York, NY 10017, USA

Tel : (1) (212) 297-5141
Fax : (1) (212)297-4095
Telex: 422031

UNFPA was established in 1969 and has always sought to ensure that its programmes and projects increased women's opportunities to paticipate in development as decision-makers, programme planners and community workers. In 1975, UNFPA became one of the first UN bodies to issue guidelines for involving women in population and development activities and now has a special unit for women, as well as an advisory panel of women to provide expertise on the systematic integration of women's concerns into all development programme.

United Nations International Children's Emergency Fund (UNICEF)
Women in Development Section
3 United Nations Plaza
New York , NY 10017, USA
Tel :(212)326-7000
Fax :(212)8887465
Telex :239521

Established in 1946 as the United Nations International Children's Emergency Fund to aid children in post-World War II Europe, UNICEF today serves 128 countries because of the obvious links, both biological and socio-economic, between women and children, UNICEF is a strong advocate for movements in the status of women.

United Nations Environment Programme (UNEP)
Focal Point for Women and the Environment
1889 F Street, N.W.
Washington, D.C 20006, USA
Tel :(1) (202) 289-8456
Fax :000-120-237-107- 47
Telex : 89-506 UNIFOCEN WSH

Office of the United Nations High Commissioner for Refugees (UNHCR)
Senior Coordinator for Refugee Women
Case Postale 2500
CH-1211 Geneva 2 Depot

Tel :(41)(22)739-81 11
Telex :28741 HCR CH Geneva (Switzerland)

United Nations Relief and Works Agency for Palestine Refugees in the Near East (UNRWA)

Chief, Office of the Commissioner General,
Vienna International Centre
P.O Box 700
A-1400 Vienna, Austria
Tel :(43) (1) 211310
Fax :(43) (1)2307487
Telex : 135310 UNRWA A

World Food Programme (WFP)

Policy Development Officer
Office of the Executive Director
Via Cristobo Colombo, 426
00145 Rome, Italy
Tel.: (39) (6) 57971
Fax: (39) (6) 57975652
Telex: 626675 WFP

World Food Council (WFC)

Senior Economic Affairs Officer
Via delle Terme di Caracalla
00100 Rome, Italy
Tel.: (39) (6) 57971
Fax: (39) (6) 574-5091
Telex: 610181 FAO I

United Nations Centre for Science and Technology for Development

Associate Economic Officer
1 United Nations Plaza
DC1-1044
New York, NY 10017, USA
Tel.: (1) (212) 963-8603
Fax: (1) (212) 963-1267

United Nations Institute for Training and Research (UNITAR)
Under-Secretary-General
801 United Nations Plaza
New York, NY 10017, USA
Tel.: (1) (212) 963-86212
Fax: (1) (212) 697-8660

United Nations University (UNU)
Vice Rector, Programme Division
Toho Seimei Building
15-1 Shibuya 2-chome
Shibuya-ku, Tokyo 150, Japan
Tel.: (81) (3) 499-2811
Fax: (81) (3) 499-2828
Telex: J25442

Food and Agriculture Organization of the United Nations (FAO)
Chief, Women in Agricultural Production
and Rural Development Service
Via delle Terme di Caracalla
00100 Rome, Italy
Tel: (39) (6) 57971
Fax: (39) (6) 5146 172
(39) (6) 5797 3152
Telex:610181 FAO I

United Nations Educational, Scientific and Cultural Organization (UNESCO)
Co-ordinator for Activities relating to
the Status of Women
7, place de Fontenoy
75700, Paris, France
Tel.: (33) (1) 4568 10 00
Fax: (33) (1) 4567 16 90
Telex: 270 602 PARIS
204 461 PARIS

International Civil Aviation Organization (ICAO)
Chief, External Relations Office
Suite 327

1000 Sherbrooke Street West
Montreal, Quebec H3A 2R2, Canada
Tel.: (514) 285-8219
Fax: (514) 288-4772
Telex: 05-24513

World Health Organization (WHO)
Director
20, Avenue Appia
1211 Geneva 27, Switzerland
Tel.: (41) (22) 791 21 11
Telex: 41 54 16

World Bank
Chief, Women in Development Division
1818 H Street, N.W
Washington, D.C. 20433, USA
Tel.: (1) (202) 477-1234
Fax: (1) (202) 477-6391
Telex: RCA 248423

International Monetary Fund (IMF)
Director
700 19th Street, N.W.
Washington, D.C. 20431, USA
Tel.: (1) (202) 623-7000
Fax: (1) 202) 623-4661
Telex: RCA 248331 IMF UR

Universal Postal Union (UPU)
Director-General
Bureau International de l'Union
Postale universelle
Case postale
3000 Berne 15, Switzerland
Tel.: (31) 43 22 11
Fax: (41) (31) 43 22 10
Telex: 912761 UPU CH

International Telecommunications Union (ITU)
Secretary-General
Palais des Nations
1211 Geneva 20, Switzerland
Tel.: (41) (22) 730 51 11
Fax: +(41) (22) 733 72 56
Telex: 42100 UIT CH

World Meteorological Organization (WMO)
Executive Assistant to the Secretary-General
41 Avenue Giuseppe-Motta
Geneva, Switzerland
Tel.: (41) (22) 730 81 11
Fax: (41) (22) 734 23 26
Telex: 23260

International Maritime Organization (IMO)
Focal Point for Women-in-Development
4 Albert Embankment
London SE1 7SR, England
Tel.: (44) (1) 735 7611
Telex: 23588

World Intellectual Property Organization (WIPO)
Head, Section for Relations with Int'l Organizations and Promotion of Innovation in Developing Countries
34 Chemin des Colombettes
1211 Geneva 20, Switzerland
Tel.: (41) (22) 730 91 11
Fax: (41) (22) 733 54 28
Telex: 412 912 ompi ch

International Fund for Agriculture Development (IFAD)
Technical Adviser, Women in Development
Via del Serafico, 107
00142 Rome, Italy
Tel: (39) (6) 54591
Fax: (39) (6) 5043463
Telex: 620330

United Nations Industrial Development Organization (UNIDO)
Co-ordinator, Unit for Integration of Women in Industrial Development
P.O. Box 300
Vienna International Centre
A-1400, Vienna, Austria
Tel.: (43) (1) 211310
Fax: (43) (1) 232156
Telex: 135612

International Atomic Energy Agency (IAEA)
Division of Nuclear Power
P.O. Box 100
Vienna International Centre
A-1400 Vienna, Austria
Tel.: (43) (1) 23600
Fax: (43) (1) 234564
Telex: 1-12645 atom a

General Agreement on Tariffs and Trade (GATT)
Director, External Division
Centre Willam Rappard
154, Rue de Lausanne
1211 Geneva 21, Switzerland
Tel.: (41) (22) 739 51 11
Fax: (41) (22) 731 42 06
Telex: 412-324 gatt ch

International Trade Centre UNCTAD/GATT (ITC)
External Relations Officer
Palais des Nations
1211 Geneva 10, Switzerland
Tel.: (41) (22) 730 01 11
Fax: (41) (22) 733 44 39
Telex: 28 90 52 ITC-CH

International Labour Office (ILO), 4 route des Morillons, 1211 Geneva,
Switzerland.

OECD Development Centre, 94 rue Chardon-Lagache, 75016 Paris, France.

United Nations Centre for Social Development and Humanitarian Affairs (UNOV/CSDHA),
Division for the Advancement of Women, Vienna International Centre, PO Box 500, A-1400 Vienna, Austria.

United Nations Non-Governmental Liaison Service,
United Nations, Geneva and New York.

II INTERNATIONAL AND INTERGOVERNMENTAL ORANISATIONS

Council of Europe, BP 431 R6, 670006, Strasbourg Cedex, France.

European Economic Community, rue de la Loi, B-1049 Brussels, Belgium.

III INTERNATIONAL NGOs

ACORD, Francis House, Francis Street, London SW1P 1DQ., England

Asian and Pacific Development Centre (APDC), Kuala Lumpur, Malaysia.

Association of African Women for Research and Development (AAWORD),
C/o CODESRIA, BP 3304, Dakar, Senegal.

Commission on the Churches' Participation in Development (CCPD), World Council of Churches, 150 Route de, Ferney, 1211 Geneva 20, Switzerland

Development Alternatives with Women for a New Era (DAWN),
APDEC, Pesiaran Duta, PO Box 12224, Kuala Lumpur, Malaysia.

Debt Crisis Network,
1901 Q St., NW,
Washington DC 20009. USA

Depthnews Women's Feature Service,
PO Box 1843
Manila, Philippines.

Environment Liaison Centre (ELC),
PO Box 72461
Nairobi, Kenya.

Interfaith Action for Economic Justice,
110 Maryland Avenue, NE, Washington DC
20002, USA.

International Alliance of Women,
Alemannengasse
42, CH-4058 Basel.

International Center for Research on Women,
1717 Massachusetts Avenue, N.W., Suite 501,
Washington DC 20036., USA.

International Coalition for Development Action (ICDA),
22 rue des Bollandistes, 1040 Brussels,
Belgium.

International Confederation of Free Trade Unions
(ICFTU), c/o Trade Union Congress, 23-28
Gt. Russell St. London WC1B 3LS, England.

International Cooperation for Development and Solidarity (CIDSE),
1 Ave. des Arts, Boite 6, B-1040 Brussels, Belgium.

International Council of Jewish Women
19 Rue de Teheran,
75008, Paris, France.

International Council of Voluntary Agencies (ICVA),
13 rue Gautier, 1201 Geneva, Switzerland.

International Council of Women,
13 rue Caumartin, 75009 Paris, France.

International Council on Social Welfare,
Koestlergsse, 1/29, A-1060 Vienna, Austria.

International Federation of University Women,
37 Quai Wilson, 1201 Geneva, Switzerland.

International Federation of Women in Legal Careers,
6, via R. Giovagnoli, 00152 Rome, Italy.

International Women's Tribune Centre,
777 UN Plaza, New York 10017, USA.

International Women's Development Agency,
139, Hoddle St., Richmond,Vic 3121, Australia

International Organisation of Consumer Unions,
POB 1045, 10830 Penang, Malaysia.

ISIS/WICCE Women's International Cross-Cultural
Exchange, 29 rue des Gares, 1201 Geneva, Switzerland.

Lutheran World Federation,
150 Route de Ferney,
1211 Geneva 20, Switzerland

Medical Women's International Association,
Herbert-Lewin-Strasse 5,D-5000 Cologne 41, Germany.

NGO Working Group on Refugee Women,
C/o Norwegian Refegee Council, Pilestredet 15
B. Oslo, N-0164, Norway.

Third World Network,
87 Cantonment Road,
10250 Penang, Malaysia.

Women's International League for Peace and Freedom,
Case postale 28 CH-1211
I rue de-Varembe, CH-1211 Geneva 20, Switzerland.

World Association of Girl Guides and Girl Scouts,
12c Lyndhurst Road, London NW 3 5PQ, England.

World Assoclation for the School as an Instrument of Peace,
5, rue du Simplon, 1207 Geneva, Switzerland.

World Federation of Methodist Women,
777 UN Plaza, New York NY 10017, USA.

World Union of Catholic Women's Organisations,
20 rue Notre-Dame des Champs, 75006 Paris, France.

Youth for Development and Cooperation (YDC),
21 Leiliegracht, 1016 GR Amsterdam, Netherlands.

Zonta International,
557 West Randolph Street,
Chicago Ill. 60606-2284, USA.

IV NATIONAL (GOVERNMENTAL AND NGO)

Australian Council for Overseas Aid (Australia)
(ACFOA), GPO Box 1562, Canberra, Australia.

International Women's Development Agency,
139 Hoddle St., Richmond, Vic. 3121, Australia.

Bangladesh Institute for Development Studies (Bangladesh)
17/E, Agargaon, Dhaka, Bangladesh.

National Centre for Development Corporation (NCOS)
76 rue de Laeken, 1000 Brussels, Belgium.

Ibase, Instituto Bresileiro de Analises, Brazil
Sociaise Economicas, 155 Av. Nilo Pecanha,
20020 Rio de Janeiro, Brazil.

Canadition International Development Agency (CIDA), Canade
200 Promenade du Portage, Hull, Quebec, Canada K1A 0G4.

Canadian Council for International Cooperation,
One Nicholas Street, Ottawa, Canada.

Danish International Development Agency (FINNIDA), Denmark
Asiatisk Plats 2, DK-1448,
Copenhagen, Denmark.

Finnish International Development Agency (FINNIDA), Finland
POB 276, 00171, Helsinki, Finland.

Finish United Nations Association,
Unioninkatu
45 B, SF-00170, Helsinki, Finland.

Centre de recherche of d'information pour le developpement (CRID), 49 rue de la Glaciere, 75013 Paris, France.

IRELAND
Trocaire, 169 Booterstown Avenue,
Blackrock, Co. Dublin, Ireland.

NETHERLANDS
Forum on Debt and Development (FONDAD),
Noordeinde 107 A. 2514 GE,
the Hague, Netherlands.

Netherlands Organisation for International Development (NOVIB),
Amaliastraat 7, 2514 Jc
The Hague, Netherlands.

Women's Health Action Foundation
P. O. Box 4263, 1009 A.G.
Amsterdam, Netherlands.

NORWAY
NIEO Network, St, Olavsgt. 29,
N-0166, Oslo, Norway.

Norwegian Agency for Development (NORAD),
POB 8142, Dep. 0033, Oslo 1, Norway.

PERU DESCO (Centre de estudios y promocion del desarollo), 110 Leon de la Fuente, Lima 17, Peru.

PHILIPPINES
(Depthnews, POB 1843, Manila.
Freedom from Debt Coalition, University of the Philippines, Room 301, Alumni Center,
Quezon City, 978226 Philippines.

IBON Data Bank,
P.O. Box S-447, Sta. Mesa,
Manila, Philippines.

SWEDEN
Development Forum of the Swedish Churches,
Gotgatan 3 NB, S-75222, Uppsala, Sweden.

Swedish International Development Agency (SIDA),
Birger Jarlsgatan 61,S-10525 Stockholm, Sweden.

SWITZERLAND
Third World Information Service (i3w),
Monbijoustrasse 31, Berne, Switzerland.

UGANDA
The Grail, P.O. Box 14267, Kampala, Uganda.

UNITED KINGDOM
Catholic Fund for Overseas

Development (CAFOD), 2, Garden Close,
Stockwell Road, London SW99TY, England

Catholic Institute for International Relations (CIIR),
22 Coleman Fields, London N1 7AF, England.
Institute for Development Studies, University of Sussex, UK.

Minority Rights Group,
29 Craven Street,
London WC2N 5NT, England.

Overseas Development Institute,
Regent's College, Inner Circle, Regent's Park,
London NW1 4NS, England.

Oxfam, 274 Banbury Road, Oxford
OX2 7DZ, England.

War on Want, 37-39 Great Guildford Street,
London SE1 9BT, England.

World Development Movement
(WDM), Bedford
Chambers, Covent Garden, London
WC2E 8HA, England.

UNITED STATES OF AMERICA
Association for Women in
Development, 2607 North 24th Street,
Arlington Va. 22207, USA.

Bread for the World, 802 Rhode Island Ave.
NE, Washington DC 20018, USA.

Coalition for Women in International Development,
1815 H. Street NW, Washington DC 20433, USA.

Inter Action, 200 Park Ave. South, Suite 1114,
New York, NY 10003, USA.

Interfaith Action for Economic Justice,
110 Maryland Ave. NE, Washington DC 20002, USA.

Overseas Development Council,
1717 Massachussetts Ave. NW, Suite 501,
Washington DC 20036, USA.

The Development Gap,
1400 Eye St. NW,
Suite 520, Washington DC 20005, USA.

US Agency for International Development (USAID),
320 21st St. N.W. Washington DC 20523, USA.

US Debt Crisis Network,
1400 Eye St. Nw,
Suite 520, Washington DC 20005, USA.

Women's Foreign Policy Council,
1133 Broadway,
New York, NY 10010, USA.

World Development Journal,
1717 Mass. Ave.
NW, Washington DC 20036, USA.

IV. REGIONAL FOCAL POINTS

AFRICA: African Training and Research Centre
for Women (ATRCW)
Economic Commission for Africa (ECA)
P.O.Box 3001,
Addis Ababa, Ethiopia
TEL: (251) 151-7200
FAX: (251) 151-4416

Women's Working Group for Africa
c/o FEMNET
P.O. Box 54562,
Nairobi, Kenya
TEL:(254-2) 44-02-99 FAX: (254-2) 44-38-68

WESTERN ASIA: Women and Development Programme,
Economic and Social Commission for Western Asia (ESCWA),
P.O. Box 950629,
Amman, Jordan
TEL: (962-6) 694-351
FAX: (962-6) 694-980

Women's Working Group for Westem Asia
2 rue du Lycee El Menzah IV
2080 Ariana, Tunisia
TEL: (216-1) 25-98-70 FAX: (216-1) 34-233

ASIA/PACIFIC: Women and Development Programme,
Economic and Social Commission for Asia and the Pacific (ESCAP)
United Nations Building
Rajadamnern Avenue
Bangkok 10200, Thailand
TEL : (66-2) 282-9161-200
FAX: (66-2) 282-9602

Women's Caucus for Asia and the Pacific
C/o AWHRC (Asia Women's Human Rights Council)
P.O. Box 190
1099 Manila, Philippines
TEL/FAX: (63-2) 921-5571
and'or
C/o APWLD (Asia and Pacific Forum on Women, Law and Development)
P.O. Box 12224
Kuala Lumpur, Malaysia
TEL: (60-3) 255-0648/9
FAX: (60-3) 254-1371

L. AMERICA/ CARIBBEAN: Women and Development Programme
Economic Commission for Latin America and the Caribbean (ECLAC)
Edificio Naciones Unidas,
Casilla 179-D
Santiago, Chile
TEL: (56-2) 210-2000
FAX: (56-2) 208-0252
Women's Working Group for
Latin America/Caribbean
C/o Flora Tristan
Parque Herman Velarde #42

	Lima 1, Peru TEL: (51-14) 33-06-94 FAX: (51-14) 33-90-60
EUROPE/ N. AMERICA	Focal Point for Women **Economic Commission for Europe (ECE)** Palais des Nations, 1211 Geneva, Switzerland TEL: (41-22) 917-1234 FAX: (41-22) 917-0036 Women's Working Group for Europe and North America 2 Chemin des Usses CH 1246 Corsier, Switzerland TEL: (41-22) 751-20-58 FAX: (41-22) 751-26-85
CHINA:	All-China Women's Federation 50 Deng Shi Kou Beijing, China 100730 TEL: (86-1) 512-7711-x280 FAX: (86-1) 513-6044

V. INDIA

A. WOMEN'S STUDIES CELLS

Andhra Pradesh
P.G. College of
Social Work,
Hyderabad- 500004

Montessory Mahila
P.G. College,
Vijaywada-520008.

Anvesh Research Centre for Women's Studies
Osmania University Campus
Hyderabad - 868489

University of Hyderabad
Women's Study cell
Department of History
School of Social Science
Gachi - Borali
Hyderabad - 500134

Assam

Gauhati University
Women's Studies Research Centre
Guwahati - 781014

Bihar

SS.L.N.T.H. College
Centre for Women's Development Studies
Dhanbad - 82600

Delhi

National Council of Educational
Research and Training,
Department of Women's Studies
Sri Aurobindo Marg
New Delhi - 110016

Jount Women's Programme
146, Jangpura
New Delhi-110014

Gujarat

Ahmedabad Women's Action
48 Somnathnagar
Vijaynagar Road, Navarangpura
Ahmedabad - 380013

Self-Employed Women's Association (Sewa)
Opposite Lokmanya Tilak Bang
Bhadra
Ahmedabad - 380001

Gujarat University
Department of Sociology

School of Social Sciences
Women's Study Cell
Ahmedabad - 38001

Haryana
M and N College,
Yamunanagar-135001.

Jammu and Kashmir
Model Institute of Education and Research
Child and Social Welfare Wings
Centre for Women Development and Studies
B.C. Road
Jammu - 18000

Karnataka
NMKRV First Grade College for Women
Jayanagar
Bangalore -560011

Mysore University Institute of Development Studies
Centre for Women's Studies, Mysore -570005

Kerala
All Saints College,
Trivandrum-695514

College for Women
Trivandrum-695514

Iqbal College,
Trivandrum - 695363

Government College for Women
Women's Studies Cell
Trivandrum - 695014

Madhya Pradesh
Sociology Deptt.
Barkatullah Vishwavidyalaya
Bhopal-462026

Maharashtra

Women's Centre
104-B, Sunrise Apartment, Nehru Road, Vakola
Santa Cruz (E)
Bombay - 400052

Tara Institute of Social Sciences
Women's Studies Unit
P.B. No 8313
Sion - Trambay Road
Deonar
Bombay - 400088

Orissa

Ganjam College
Ganjam - 761026

Rajasthan

Sociology Deptt.
Jodhpur University
Jodhpur-342001.

Savitri College
Ajmer-305001

Tamil Nadu

Avinashalingam
Institute for Home Science and
Higher Education
for Women,
Coimbatore-641043.

Holy Cross College
Tiruchirapalli-620002

Lady Doak College,
Madurai-625002.

Seethalakshmi
Ramaswamy College,
Tiruchirapalli-620002

Stella Mary's College
Madras-600086.

Tamilnadu
Mother Teresa Women's University
Kodaikanal-624102

Uttar Pradesh
ANDMM Mahavidyalaya
Kanpur-208012
B.N.K.B.P.G. College
Akbarpur,
Faizabad-224122

Hindu College,
Moradabad-244001

INM(PG) College,
Meerut - 250002

S.D. College
Muzaffarnagar-251001

West Bengal
Jadavpur University
School of Women's Studies
Calcutta - 700032

SPONSORED BY UNIVERSITY GRANTS COMMISSION WOMEN'S STUDIES CENTRES

Andhra Pradesh

1. Andhra University
   Visakhapatnam-530003

2. Nagarjuna University
   Nagarjuna Nagar-522500

3. Shri. Padmavati
   Vishwavidyalayam
   Tirupati-517502

4. University of Hyderabad
   Hyderabad - 500004

Assam

5. Gauhati University
   Guwahati - 781014

Bihar

6. Sundervati Mahila
   Mahavidyalaya,
   Bhagalpur - 812007

Chandigarh

7. Panjab University
   Chandigarh - 160014

Delhi

8. University of Delhi
   Delhi-110007

Goa

9. Goa University
   Jaleigao Plateau,
   Goa - 403005

Gujarat

10. Bhavnagar University
    Bhavnagar-364002

11. Gujarat University
    Ahmedabad-380009

12. M.S. University of
    Baroda,
    Baroda-390002

Haryana

13. Kurukshetra University
    Kurukshetra - 132119

Jammu and Kashmir

14. University of Jammu
    Jammu Tawi-180001

15. University of Kashmir
    Srinagar
    (J and K)- 190006

Karnataka

16. Gulburga University
    Gulbarga - 585106

17. Karnataka University
    Dharwad - 580003

18. Mysore University
    Mysore-570006

Kerala

19. Kerala University
    Trivandrum - 695581

Madhya Pradesh

20. Devi Ahilya Vishwavidyalaya,
    Indore-452001

21. Rani Durgavati Vishwavidyalaya Jabalpur - 482001

Maharashtra

22. Amravati University Amravati-494602

23. S.N.D.T. Women's University Bombay-400049

24. Tata Institute of Social Sciences Bombay - 400088

25. University of Poona Pune - 411007.

Orissa

26. Berhampur University Berhampur - 760007

Rajasthan

27. University of Rajasthan Jaipur-302004

Tamil Nadu

28. Alagappa University Karaikudi - 623003

Uttar Pradesh

29. Banaras Hindu University Varanasi - 221005

West Bengal

30. Calcutta University Calcutta - 700073

31. Jadavpur University Calcutta - 700032

V. INDIA
DOCUMENTATION CENTRES

Assam

Dibrugarh University
Dibrugarh
Assam - 786004

Delhi

Centre for Women's Development Studies Library
25, Bhai Vir Singh Marg,
New Delhi - 110011

Indian Social Institute Library
10, Institutional Area
Lodi Road
New Delhi - 110003

Jagori
B-5 Housing Corporation Society, South Ext. I
New Delhi - 110049

Jigyasa (Library) Institute of Social Studies Trust
5, Deen Dayal Upadhyay Marg, New Delhi - 110002

Women's Studies and Development Centre,
Chhatra Marg
Delhi - 110007

Voluntary Health Association of India Library
40, Institutional Area
South of IIT
New Delhi - 110016

Margaret Cousins Memorial Library, All India Women's Conference
6, Bhagwan Das Road
New Delhi - 110001

Gujarat

Women Households Development Studies Information Centre
MS University of Baroda
Baroda, Gujarat - 390002

Karnataka

Centre for Education and Documentation
No. 8, Palmgrove Road,
Austin Town
Karnataka - 560047

Kerala

Kerala Shastra Sahiya Parishat
Rubin D. Cruz Documentation Centre, Parishat Bhavan,
Anayara Post, Trivandrum,
Kerala - 695001

Maharashtra

Centre for Documentation and Research on Women
'Kedar', 86/11 -B, Kanchar Gall, Evandawane
Pune, Maharashtra - 411004

Centre for Education and Documentation
3, Suleman Chambers,
4, Battery Street

SELECT BIBLIOGRAPHY ON WOMEN'S EDUCATION AND ALLIED TOPICS

I Recent Indian Doctoral Dissertations

Aruna, Krupadanam, A.O., 1993, *Women's Education: A Study of Impact of Certain Socio-economic Factors on the Education of Adult Rural Women,* Osmania University, Hyderabad.

Amrik Singh and Altbach, eds. 1974, *The Higher Learning in India*, Vikas Delhi, p. 180-201.

Anon, 1977, Women Education Commission on Higher Education, *University News* 15 (6) p. 144-145

Anon, 1983, *Women's Education in India: The Regional Dimension,* National Institute of Educational Planning and Administration, New Delhi.

Badgujar, A.D., 1992, *The Work Value of Undergraduate Students with Reference to Sex, Socio-Economic Status and Family.* Saurashtra University, Rajkot.

Banda, Sarojana, 1992, *A Study of the Status of Women as Depicted in the Text Books Offered at School Level in Andhra Pradesh*, Osmania University, Hyderabad.

Bhagwat, Sunita, 1992, *Preparation of a Package of Divergent Production Type in Mathematics and to Study the Effectiveness of the Package against the Sex Difference and Levels of Intelligence for Std. VII Students in Pune City*, S.N.D.T. Women's University, Bombay.

Desai, N., 1969, *Socio-Economic Background of Married Women Students of the University and Their Educational Problems,* Research Study financnced by National Council of Educational Research and Training, New Delhi and SNDT Women's University, Bombay.

Duggal, Janak, 1993, *Access of Scheduled Caste Girls to Elementary Education in Rural Haryana: A Study of Socio-Economic Problems in the Universalisation of Elementary Education*, Jamia Millia Islamia, New Delhi.

Updates Bilbiography included in *Women's Education in India*, CICIL-13

Garima Singh, 1992, *Barriers to Girls' Education: A Critical Study of Varanasi Region,* Banaras Hindu University, Varanasi.

Gursaranjit Kaur, 1993, *Effect of Training on Some Biochemical Parameters of Female Players,* Punjabi University, Patiala.

Gupta, Promila, 1969, Pioneer in Women's Education, *University News* 7(3), p. 18-19.

Israney, S.M., 1989, Institutional barriers to Women Students in Indian Higher Education, *University News* 27(32), p. 10-13.

Parabhsharan Kaur, 1993, *A Comparative Study of Some Psychological Characteristics of Women Hockey Players Playing at Different Field Position,* Punjabi University, Patiala.

Rajeswari, V., 1993, *Gender Inclusive Curriculum in the Textbooks of Tamil Nadu*, Mother Teresa Women's University, Kodaikanal.

Sodhi, Harlean Kaur, 1993, *Impact of Adult Education Programme on the Attitude of Rural Women in Relation to Their Age, Religion, Family Type and Socio-Economic Status*, Punjabi University, Patiala.

Srinath, Krishna, 1993, *Empowering Rural Women Through Extension Education: An Action Research in a Fishing Village*, Sri Avinashilingam Institute for Home Science and Higher Education for Women, Coimbatore.

Surya Kumari, A., 1987, Women's Studies and the Mother Teresa Women's University, *University News,* 25(32), p. 7-9.

Swarnalatha, A., 1992, *Status of Women and Fertility Behaviour*. Sri Venkateswara University, Tirupati.

Syamala, Moka, 1993, *A study of the Dynamism of the Female Students of Higher Education with Special Reference to Their Social, Political and Academic Activities: Their Attitudes and Aspirations*, Andhra University, Hyderabad.

Vijender Kumar, 1992, *Study of College Social Systems, Sex roles, Personality and Attitudes towards Physical Activity among Male/ Female Athletes and Non-athletes*, Kurukshetra University, Kurukshetra.

Tewari, Ratna, 1994, *Participation of Women in Fisheries and Impact of Modernisation on Them,* S.N.D.T. Women's University, Bombay.

Trivedi, Jyoti H., 1989, Future images of women's universities, *University News* 27 (32), p 5-9.

II. Recent Books and Other Documents

Aggarwal, J.C., 1992, *Yearbook of Indian Education 1990-91: World Overview,* Doaba, Delhi.

Aggarwal, J.C. and Agrawal, S.P., 1991, *Documentation Encyclopaedia of UNESCO and Education,* Concept Publishing Company, New Delhi, 799 p, CICIL-16, 2 vols.

Aggarwal, J.C. and Agrawal, S.P., 1992, *Educational Planning in India : With a slant to Educational Financing and Administration, vol I : Reports of Committees and Commissions, Five Year Plans, Statistics and Tables*, Concept Puslishing Company, New Delhi, 490 p, CICIL-39.

Agrawal, S.P., 1964, *Education for International Understanding: A Bibliography,* Indian National Commission for Cooperation with UNESCO, New Delhi, 1959, INC Bibliography Series, 1.

Agrawal, S.P., 1985, *India since Independence*, rev. edn, Publications Division, Ministry of Information and Broadcasting, New Delhi, 137p.

Agrawal, S.P., 1993, *Development/Digression Diary of India: 3D Companion Volume to Information India 1990-91*, Concept Publishing Company, New Delhi, 144 p, CICIL -45.

Agrawal, S.P., 1993, *Development/Digression Diary of India: 3D Companion Volume to Information India 1991-92*, Concept Publishing Company, New Delhi, 296p, CICIL - 46.

Agrawal, S.P., 1994, *Development/Digression Diary of India: 3D Companion Volume to Information India 1992-93,* Concept Publishing Company, New Delhi, CICIL (in Press).

Agrawal, S.P., 1994, *Indian Writings on Education 1947-1979: An Indicator to Indian Educational Journals Grouped by Subject Descriptors,* Concept Publishing Company, New Delhi, CICIL (in Press).

Agrawal, S.P., and Aggarwal, J.C., 1988, *UNESCO and Social Sciences: Retrospect and Prospect*, Concept Publishing Company, New Delhi, 366p, CICIL-3.

Agrawal, S.P., and Aggarwal, J.C., 1989, *Information India, 1988: Global Veiw*, Concept Publishing Company, New Delhi, 220 p, CICIL-12.

Agrawal, S.P. and Aggrawal, J.C., 1990, *Information India, 1989-90: Global View*, Concept Publishing Company, New Delhi, 530 p, CICIL-24.

Agrawal, S.P., and Aggarwal, J.C., 1990, *National Policy on Education:*

Agenda for India 2001, Concept Publishing Company, New Delhi, 153 p.

Agrawal, S.P. and Aggarwal, J.C., 1991, *Second Historical Survey of Educational Developments in India: Select Documents, 1985-1989,* Concept Publishing Company, New Delhi, 460 p, CICIL - 15.

Agrawal, S.P. and Aggarwal, J.C., 1992, *Indian Writings on Education: An Indicator to Indian Educational Journals Grouped by Subject Descriptors, 1979 to 1986,* Concept Publishing Company, New Delhi, 736p, CICIL - 28.

Agrawal, S.P. and Aggarwal, J.C., 1992, *Information India, 1990-91: Global View*, Concept Publishing Company, New Delhi, 510p, CICIL-30.

Agrawal, S.P. and Aggarwal, J.C., 1992, *Women's Education in India : Historical Review, Present Status and Perspective Plan with Statistical Indicators aud Index to Scholarly Writings in Indian Educational Journals,* Concept Publishing Company, New Delhi, 316p, CICIL -13.

Agrawal, S.P. and Aggarwal, J.C., 1993, *Information India, 1991-92: Global View,* Concept Publishing Company, New Delhi, 576 p, CICIL-47.

Agrawal, S.P. and Aggarwal, J.C., 1994, *Information India, 1992-93: Global View,* Concept Publishing Company, New Delhi, CICIL (in Press).

Agrawal, S.P. and Aggarwal, J.C., 1994, *Third Historical Survey of Educational Developments in India, 1990-1992*, Concept Publishing Company, New Delhi, CICIL (in press).

Agrawal, S.P. and Naresh Kanta, 1990, *Child Education in India: Index to Scholarly Writings in Indian Educational Journals and News-papers since Independence,* Concept Publishing Company, New Delhi, 115 p, CICIL - 20.

Alic, Margaret, 1990, *Hypatia's Heritage: A History of Women in Science from Antiquity to the Late Nineteenth Century,* Women's Press, London.

Amrik Singh and Altbach, eds., 1974, *The Higher Learning in India,* Vikas, Delhi, p 180-201.

Anand, Anita, 1982, Rethinking Women and Development: The Case for Feminisim, *Convergence* 15 (1).

Anon, 1977, Women Education Commission on Higher Education, *University News* 15 (6) p. 144-145.

Anon, 1982, *Women and Development: Guidelines for Programme and*

Anon = Authorship (Personal) not established

Project Planning, United Nations, Economic Commission for Latin America and the Caribbean, Santiago.

Anon, 1983, *Women's Education in India: The Regional Dimension,* National Institute of Educational Planning and Administration, New Delhi.

Anon, 1984, *Men and Women in School Texbooks: A National Survey on Sex Biases in Zambian Textbooks in Primary and Junior Secondary Schools and Their Implications for Education in Zambia,* UNESCO, Paris, 43p, ED-841 ws/25.

Anon, 1985, *The State of the World's Women,* United Nations, Department of Public Information, New York.

Anon, 1986, *The Nairobi Forword-Looking Strategies for the Advancement of Women,* United Nations DPI/DESI, New York.

Anon, 1986, *Refugee and Displaced Women in Independent African States*, Economic Commission for Africa, African Training and Research Centre for Women.

Anon, 1986, *Simultaneous Education for Women and Girls*, UNESCO/ PROAP, Bangkok, 63p.

Anon, 1986, Women Fighting Discrimination in Jobs and Schooling, *China Reconstructs,* March, p 35.

Anon, 1987, *Institutions Engaged in Research on Women: Asia- Pacific,* UNESCO/ PROAP, Bangkok, 134p, RUSHSAP Directories, No. 1.

Anon, 1987, *Linking Energy with Survival: A Guide to Energy, Environment and Rural Women's Work*, International Labour Organisation, Geneva.

Anon, 1987, *Women Social Scientists: Asia - Pacific*, UNESCO/PROAP, Bangkok, 319p, RUSHSAP Directories, No. 2.

Anon, 1988, *Participation of Women in Political Life and in the Decision-Making Process*, International Centre for Parliamentary Documentation, Inter-Parliamentary Union, Reports and Documents, No. 15.

Anon, 1989, *Convention on the Elimination of All Forms of Discrimination aganist Women,* United Nations, Department of Public Information, New York, DP1/ 1993.

Anon, 1989, *Engendering Adjustment for the 1990s: Report of a Commonwealth Expert Group on Women and Structural Adjustment,* Commonwealth Secretariat, London.

Anon, 1989, *Female Adult Illiteracy*, United Nations, Division for the Advancement of Women, Centre for the Social Development and Humanitarian Affairs, Washington D.C., Data Highlights, No. 6.

Anon, 1989, Gender Planning in the Third World, *World Development,* November, p 1802

Anon, 1989, *Gender and Development: Combating Gender Blindness,* NGO/EC Liaison Committee, Brussels.

Anon, 1989, Women and Movement Politics in India, *Asian Survey,* October, p 943.

Anon, 1989, *Women in Development: Guidelines by Sector,* United Nations, New York, DPI/1032.

Anon, 1989, *Women in Development: Project Achievement Reports,* United Nations Development Programme, New York.

Anon, 1989, *Women in High-Level Political Decision-Making: A Global Analysis,* United Nations Expert Group Meeting, August 1989, United Nations, New York, EGM/EPPDM/1989-WP.2.

Anon, 1989, *Women in Norwegian Politics,* Royal Ministry of Foreign Affairs/Royal Ministry of Consumer Affairs/Government Administration, 9 p.

Anon, 1989, *Women in Politics: Still the Exception*, United Nations , Department of Public Information, New York, U.N. Focus, DPI/1012.

Anon, 1989, *World Survey on the Role of Women in Development 1989,* United Nations, Centre for Social Development and Humanitarian Affairs, Vienna.

Anon, 1990, *Functional Literacy and Civil Education among Rural Women*, UNESCO/PROAP, Bangkok, 46 p.

Anon, 1990, The Hidden Power of Women, *Development and Cooperation,* January, German Foundation for International Development.

Anon, 1990, *Literacy: Tool for Empowering Women,* United Nations, Department of Public Information, New York, UN Focus, DPI/1075.

Anon, 1990, *Plus Project Literacy: Special Report on Family Literacy,* National Centre for Family Literacy, Pittsburg.

Anon, 1990, *The State of the World Population*, United Nations Population, Fund.

Anon, 1990, *Women's Education: Findings for Demographic and Health Survey:* Paper Presented to World Conference on Education for All, Jomitien, Thailand, March 5-9, 1990, Demographic and World Survey Programme.

Anon, 1990, *Women's Participation in Higher Education: China, Nepal and the Philippines*, UNESCO/PROAP, Bangkok, 162 p.

Anon, 1990, *Writing for Women: Civic Education,* UNESCO/PROAP, Bangkok, 78 p.

Anon, 1991, *Mahila Samakhya: Education for Women's Equality*, Ministry of Human Resource Development, Department of Education, New Delhi.

Anon, 1991, *The World's Women, 1970-1990: Trends and Statistics*, United Nations, Statistical Office of the Department of International Economic and Social Affairs and Division for the Advancement of Women, New York.

Anon, 1992, *Women in Authority: The Ideal and the Reality*, International Labour Office, Geneva.

Anon, 1993, *Breaking Boundaries: Women, Free Trade and Economic Integration*, Alt-WID, Centre of Concern, Washington.

Anon, 1993, *Ours by Rights: Women's Rights as Human Rights, International Conference: Linking Hands for Changing Laws: Women's Rights as Human Rights around the World*, 1992 September, Toranto (Canada), Zed Books Ltd., London; North-South Institute.

Apte, Bal, 1977, *Educational Change*, Akhil Bharatiya Vidyarthi Parishad, Delhi.

Ballara, Marcela, 1992, *Women and Literacy*, Zed Books Ltd, London; United Nations Non-Governmental Liaison Service, Women and World Development Series.

Basu, Aparna, 1982, *Essays in the History of Indian Education*, Concept Publishing Company, New Delhi, 115 p.

Bhasin, Kamla, 1971, *The Position of Women in India*, Orient House, New Delhi.

Bhasin, Kamla, 1985, Illiteracy, Women and Development, *Adult Education and Development* 24, p 95-105.

Birto, A., 1990, Literacy and Family Health in Cape Verde, *People* 17 (2), International Planned Parenthood Federation, London.

Biswas, A. and Agrawal, S.P., 1971, *Indian Educational Documents since Independence: Committees, Commissions and Conferences*, Academic Publishers, New Delhi, 639 p.

Biswas, A. and Agrawal, S.P., 1986, *Development of Education in India: A Historical Survey of Educational Documents before and after Independence*, Concept Publishing Company, New Delhi, 936 p.

Boylan, Esther R., 1991, *Women and Disability*, Zed Books Ltd., London; United Nations Non-Governmental Liaison Service, Women and World Development Series.

Calledois, F., 1989, *Women's Literacy for Development: A Brief Overview of the Situation*, Paper Presented at the Symposium on Women and Literacy: Yesterday, Today and Tomorrow, June 10, 1989, Hasselby Slot.

Desai, N., 1969, *Socio-Economic Background of Married Women Students of the University and Their Educational Problems*, Research Study Financed by National Council of Educational Research and Training, New Delhi and SNDT Women's University, Bombay.

Dhar, Suneeta, 1991, *Tenets of Women's Learning*, Report of the National Seminar, Bhubaneswar.

Gaber-Kantz, Elaine and Horsman, Jenng, 1988, Is It Her Voice if She Speaks Their Words, *Canadian Women Studies*.

Grant, Rebecca and Newland, Kathleen, eds., 1991, *Gender and International Relations*, Open University Press, Milton Keynes, 176 p

Gupta, O.P. 1993, *Higher Education in India since Independence: UGC and Its Approach*, Concept Publishing Company, New Delhi, 312 p. CICIL-42.

Gupta, Promila, 1969, Pioneer in Women's Education, *University News* 7(3), p-18-19.

Hall, Eve, 1988, *Vocational Training for Women Refugees in Africa: Guidelines from Selected Field Projects*, International Labour Organisation, Geneva, Training Policies Discussion Paper No. 26.

Hasan, S.N., 1976, *Education and Social Change*, Ministry of Education, New Delhi.

Hensman, Roluni, 1988, *The Gender Division of Labour in Manufacturing Industry: A Case Study in India*, Institute of Development Studies, Brighton, 31 p.

Hewlett, Sylvia, 1986, *A Lesser Life: The Myth of Women's Liberation in the USA*, Warner Books, New York.

Israney, S.M., 1989, Institutional Barriers to Women Students in Indian Higher Education, *University News* 27(32), p 10-13.

Indira, R., 1989, *Women in Technical Education*, Sharda Prakshan, New Delhi.

Jabre, B., 1988, *Women's Education in Africa*, UNESCO/UNICEF Cooperative Programme, Paris, Digest No. 26.

Jacquette, Jane S., ed., 1989, *The Women's Movement in Latin America: Feminism and the Transition to Democracy*, Unwin Hyman, Boston.

Jena, Kalendi, 1994, Progress of Educated Tribal Women, *Men in India* 74 (1) March, p 81-86.

Joekes, Susan, 1987, *Women in the World Economy: An INSTRAW Study*, Oxford University Press, Oxford, 161 p.

Junge, B.J. and Tegegne, D., 1985, The Effects of Liberation from Illiteracy on the Lives of 31 Women: A Case Study, *Journal of Reading* 28 (7), p 606-613, IRA, Delaware.

Kabeer, Laila, 1994, *Reversed Realites: Gender Hierarchies in Development Thought,* Verso, London, 240 p.

Kandiyoti, Deniz, 1988, *Women and Rural Development Policies: The Changing Agenda,* Institute of Development Studies, Brighton, 18 p.

King , E., 1990, *Educating Girls and Women: Investing in Development,* World Bank, Washington, D.C.

Kotite, Phyllis, ed., 1989, *Women's Education Looks Forward: Programmes, Experiences, Strategies,* UNESCO, Paris, 119 p, annexes.

Kurrien, John, 1988, *Education for Girls and Women in India with Special Emphasis on the Poor and Their Employment,* Background Paper Prepared for the World Bank, Washington, D.C.

Linda, Agneta, 1989, *Literacy as a Tool for Empowerment of Women: Women's Participation in the Literacy Programmes of the Third World,* Paper Presented at the Symposium on Women and Literacy : Yesterday, Today and Tomorrow, Stockholm.

Linda, Agneta 1990, A Tool for Empowerment of Women, *Voices Rising* 5(1), p 4-5, Toronto.

Lycklama a Nijeholt, Geertje, 1992, *Women and the Meaning of Development: Approaches and Consequences,* Institute of Development Studies, Brighton, 24 p.

Mc Call, C., 1987, Women and Literacy: The Cuban Exprience, *Journal of Reading,* 30 (4), p 318-324, IRA, Delaware.

Maquire, 1994, *Doing Participatory Research: A Feminist Approach,* Centre for International Education, Amherst, Massachusetts.

Martin, Forbes, 1992, *Refugee Women,* Zed Books Ltd., London, Women and World Development Series.

Michel, Andree, 1986, *Down with Stereotypes: Eliminating Sexism from Children's Literature and School Textbooks,* UNESCO, Paris, 105 p.

Michel, Andree, 1986, *Positive Acton for the Benefit of Women,* Council of Europe, Strasbourg.

Miles, Rosalind, 1990, *The Women's History of the World,* Palladin, London.

Molyneux, M., 1985, *Mobilization without Emancipation,* Feminist Studies, London.

Morgan, Fideles, 1989, *A Masogynist's Sourcebook,* Jonathan Cape, London.

Nickese, R.S., et al, 1988, An Intergenerational Adult Literacy Project: A Family Intervention/Prevention Model, *Journal of Reading* 31(7) p 634-642, IRA, Delaware.

Nuna, S.C. 1986, *Spread of Famale Literacy in India, 1901-1981,*

National Institute of Educational Planning and Administration, New Delhi.

Nuna, Sheel, 1990, *Women and Development,* National Institute of Educational Planning and Administration, New Delhi.

Oak, A.W., 1988, *Status of Women in Education,* Indian Publications, Ambala Cantt.

Overholt, C., 1988, *Gender Role in Development Projects,* Kumarian Press, West Hartford, Conn.

Radcliffe, Sarah A. and Townsend, Janet, 1988, *Gender in the Third World: A Geographical Bibliography of Recent Works,* Institute of Development Studies, Brighton, 90 p.

Radha Kumar, 1992, *Gender, Politics and Identity at Times of Crisis: The Agitations around Sati-Daha in India*, Institute of Development Studies, Brighton, 37 p.

Ramdas, Lalita, 1985, Illiteracy, Women and Developemnt, *Adult Education and Development* 24, p 85-105.

Ramdas, Lalita, 1989, Women and Literacy: A Quest for Justice, *Prospects* 19 (4), p 519-530, UNESCO, Paris.

Ramdas, Lalita, 1990, Women and Litracy: A Quest for Justice, *Convergence* 23 (1).

Raza, Moonis and Malhotra, Nirmal, 1991, *Higher Education in India: A Comprehensive Bibliography*, Concept Publishing Company, New Delhi 477 p.

Reddy, R.C., 1988, *Changing Status of Educated Working Women: A Case Study,* Daya Publishers, Delhi.

Rix, Sara, ed., 1988, *The American Woman, 1988-1989: A Status Report,* W.W. Norton, New York.

Rockhill, Kathleen, 1988, Emancipatory Literacy, *Canadian Woman Studies* 9 (3-4).

Rodda, Annabel, 1991, *Women and the Environment,* Zed Books Ltd., London; United Nations Non-Governmental Liaison Services, Women and World Development Series.

Sadik, Nafis, 1989, *Investing in Womens: The Focus of the 90's,* United Nations Population Fund.

Saha, B.V., 1979, Education and Social Change among Tribals in India, *Sociological Bulletin* 28 (1-2).

Sharma, Prem Lata, 1988, *Rural Women in Education: A Study in Under-achievement,* Sterling, New Delhi.

Shirali, Kishwar Ahmed, 1988, Ganga Devi: A Question of Literacy and Development, *Canadian Women Studies* 9 (3-4).

Shrestha, S.M., 1986, *Women's Literacy Programme in Afghanistan,* UNDP/UNESCO, Paris, Project AFC/79/002.

Shrivastava, Kavita and Sharma, Jaya, 1991, *Training Rural Women for Literacy,* Institute of Development Studies, Jaipur.

Stromquist, Nelly, 1986, Empowering Women through Education: Lessons from International Cooperation, *Convergence* 19 (4).

Stromquist, Nelly, 1987, Empowering Women through Education: Lessons for International Cooperation, *Adult Education and Developement* 28.

Stromquist, Nelly, 1987, *The State and the Education of Women towards a Theoretical Understanding* 'mimeo.'

Stromquist, Nelly, 1990, Women and Literacy Promises and Constraints, *Media Development* 37(1), p10-13, World Association for Christian Communication, Geneva.

Suryakumari, A., 1987, Women's Studies and the Mother Teresa Women's University, *University News* 25 (32) , p 7-9.

Talesra, Hemlata, 1989, *Higher Education among Men, National,* New Delhi.

Thakur, B.S. and Agrawal, Binod C., 1989, *Media Utilisation for the Development of Women and Children,* Concept Publishing Company, New Delhi, 195 p CICIL-8.

Townsend, Janet, 1988, *Women in Developing Countries: A Select Annotated Bibliography for Development Organisations,* Institute of Development Studies, Brighton, 189 p.

Trivedi, Jyoti H., 1989, Future Images of Women's University, *University News* 27(32), p 5-9.

Varghese, Mariamma A., 1990, *Women Administrator in Education,* Vikas, New Delhi.

Vickers, Jeanne, 1991, *Women and the World Economic Crises,* Zed Books Ltd., London; United Nations Non-Governmental Liaison Services, Women and World Development Series.

Waring, Marilyn, 1988, *If Women Counted,* Harper and Row Publishers, San Francisco.

Young, K., ed., 1988, *Women and Economic Development: Local, Regional and National Planning Strategies,* UNESCO, Paris.

Young, Kate, 1989, *Serving Two Masters : Third World Women,* Allied Publishers, New Delhi, 219 p.

Young, Kate, 1993, *Planning Development with Women: Making a World of Difference,* Macmillan, London, 187 p.

INDEX

Acord, 378

ANDMM Mahavidyalaya, Kanpur, 391

Adedeji, Adebayo, 204

Adult education, 46-47;
  Universalization, 68-69

Adult Education Centres for Women, 27

Adult Education, Directorate of, 21, 47, 67

Advancement of Women, Division for Centre for Social Development Affairs, United Nations Office at Vienna, 368

Afghanistan, enrolment of girls in secondary school, 207; literacy rate for women, 205;-adult, 208

Africa, economic crisis, effect on education, 204-05; educational sex gap, 297;

Literacy rate, 248; women's organizations, 385

African Training and Research Centre for Women (ATRCW), 385

Agatsya, 279

Ahmedabad Women's Action, 388

Alagappa University, Karaikudi, 393

All-China Women's Federation, 387

All India Council for Technical Education (AICTE), 65

All India Educational Survey (1986), 58

All Saints College, Kerala, 389

Allende, Label, 358

Amravati University, 393

Andhra Pradesh, employment rate for women 366-67; literacy rate, 39;-, female, 39

Andhra University, 392

Anganwadi (ICDS), 48-49

Anvesh Research Centre for Women's Studies, 387

Apala, 279

Arunachal Pradesh, employment rate for women, 366; literacy rate, 22

Asia, education and sex gap, 297

Asia and the Pacific, Women & Dev. Programme 86

Asian and Pacific Development Centre (APDC), 378

Association of African Women for Research and Development, 378

Association of Asian Social Science Research Councils (AASSREC), 310

Atharvaveda, 279

Augusta, Renate, 361

Australian Council for Overseas Aid (Australia), 381

Avinashalingam Institute for Home Science and Higher Education for Women, Coimbtore, 390

Awareness generation projects for rural and poor women, 303

B.N.K.B.P.G. College, Akbarpur, 391

Badaun, Uttar Pradesh, female literacy, 23

Banaras Hindu University, 393

Bandhu, 279

Bangladesh Institute for Development Studies, 381

Barkatullah Vishwavidyalaya, Bhopal, 389

Behrampur University, 392

Benin, Women Literacy rate, 205

Bhavnagar University, 392

Bhutan, education of girl child, 212; recommendation of the SAARC Workshop 212-13

Bihar, 60; literacy rate, 22;-female, 23-24

Bihar Education Project, 20

Bolivia, expenditure on education, 204

Brahadaranyaka, 280

Bread for the World, Washington DC, 384

Bulgaria, women/men enrolment in higher education, 203

Burkina Faso, adult women literacy rate, 208

C.R. Polytechnic, Rohtak, 282

Calcutta University, 393

Canadian Council for International Co-operation, 382
Canadian International Development Agency (CIDA), 381
Caribbean, education and sex-gap; literacy rate for men and women, 206-297
Carter Angela, 358
Catholic Fund for Overseas, 383
Catholic Institute for International Relations, 383
Central Advisory Board of Education (CABE), 63, 72
Central Advisory Board of Education Committee, 6
Central Board of Secondary Education, 65
Centre for Documentation and Research on Women, Pune, 394
Centre for Education and Documentation, Bombay, 394
Centre for Education and Documentation, Karnataka, 394
Centre de Researche d' Information pour le Development (CRID), 382
Centre for Social Development and Humanitarian Affairs, UN Office at Vienna, 368
Centre for Women's Development Studies Litrary, New Delhi, 40, 394
Centre for Women's Studies, Madras, 394
Chandigarh, non formal education of girls, 285-86
Chile, economic crisis, effect on education, 205
Co-alition for women in International Development, USA, 384
College for women, Thiruvananthapuram, 38
Commission on the Churches Participation in Development, 378
Commission on the Status of Women, 230, 264-66, 368-69; resolution adopted by, 244-45, 364
Condensed courses of Education for Adult Women, 301
Constitution of India, Article 45, 56
Continuing Education Centre, 43
Convention on the Elimination of All Forms of Discrimination Against Women, 232, 243, 264, 368-69
Costa Rica, economic crisis, effect on education, 205; expenditure on education, 204
Council of Europe, 378

DIETS, 21, 67
Danish International Development Agency, 382
Dass Media, 359
Debt Crisis Network, 379
Declaration on the Elimination of Discrimination Against Women, 256
Delhi, female literacy rate, 24
Delhi University, 392
Demographic Health Survey, 227
Depthnews Women's Feature Service, 379
Development Alternatives with Women for a New Era (DAWN), 378
Development (CAFOD), 383
Development Forum of Swedish Churches, 383
Development Gap, the , 384
Development Research Community Service Centre, Calcutta, 395
Development, Women's role, 226-27
Devi Ahilya Vishwavidyalaya, Indore, 75, 392
Dibrugarh University, 394
Documentation Centres, India, 394-95
Dominica, Women/Men higher education, 203

Early Childhood Care and Education (ECCE), 27, 31-32, 49, 54, 61-62, 73
Economic Commission for Africa, 204, 385
Economic Commission for Europe, 387
Economic Commission for Latin America and the Caribbean (ECLAC), 386
Economic crisis, effect on education 203-05, 208
Economic and Social Commission for Asia and Pacific (ESCAP) 386
Economic and Social Commission for Western Asia (ESCWA), 385
Economic and Social Council resolution, 364
Education, Department, Human Resource Development Ministry, 17, 20, 48, 61, 65, 70
Education Directorate, 63, 73
Education for Women's Equality, 63-70, 74 *see also* Mahila Samakhya
education work for prevention of atrocities against womne, 303
educational heirarchy, representation of women, 45

elementary education, universalization, 68-69
Eliot, George, 358
Employment cum Income Generating Units, 301
Environment Liasion Centre (ELC), 379
Equal Opportunities Committee, 363
equal opportunities in education for women and girls, 257
European Economic Community, 378

Family Health Intrnational, 365
Federal Equal Opportunities Act, 363
Finnish International Development Agency (FINNIDA), 382
Finnish United Nations Association, 382
Food and Agriculture Organisation of the United Nations, 374
Forum on Debt and Development, Netherlands, 382
Fourth U.N. Development Decade, 244, 247
Framework for Action to meet Basic Learning Needs, 260
Freedom from Debt Coalition, Philippines. 383

Ganjam College, Orissa, 390
Gargi, 280
General Agreement on Tariffs and Trade (GATT), 377
General Awareness Programmes for the Society, 221
Girl Child, availability of schooling, 32
Goa University, 392
Gordimer, Nadine, 358
Government College for Women, Thiruvananthapuram. 389
Grail, the Uganda, 383
Guahati University, 392
Gujarat, employment rate for women 366-67; Mahila Samakhya Programme, 46
Gujarat University, 392; Sociology Department, School of Social Sciences, Women's Study Cell, 389
Gulbarga University, 392
Guatemala, women's role in development. 227

Harvard University, 208
Haryana, employment rate for women, 366; Primary education, 20
Himachal Pradesh, employment rate for women, 366
Hindu College, Moradabad, 391
Holy Cross College, Tiruchirapalli, 390
Howrah Teachers Forum, 20
Human Resource Development, Ministry, 17
Hyderabad University, 392

IBON Data Bank, 383
INM (PG) College, Meerut, 391
Ibase, Instituto Bresileiro de Analises, Brazil, 381
India, Documentation Centres, 394-95; female literacy rate, 64; Saarc Workshop recommendations, 213-16;-education, 213, health, 214, legislation, 216; resocialisation, 214-15; women development issues, bodies dealing with, 387-95
Indian Council for Agricultural Research, 65
Indian Council for Historical Research, 65, 328; fellowships for historians doing research in India, 329-33; fellowships for historians doing research outside India, 333-34
Indian Council for Medical Research, 65
Indian Council for Philosophical Research (ICPR), 334, fellowships, 334-36
Indian Council for Social Science Research, 65, 307; application forms, 312-27; contingency grants, 309; fellowships, 308-09; international colloboration, 310; publications grants scheme, 310; research grants, 307; study grants, 309
Indian Social Institute Library, New Delhi, 394
Indo-Dutch Programme of Alternatives in Development, 310
Indo-Soviet Commission for co-operation in Social Sciences, 310
Indrani, 279
Information and Broadcasting, Ministry, 21, 51
Institute of Education, 75
Integrated Child Development Scheme and creches, 202-03
Integrated Education for the Disabled, scheme, 26
Inter Action, 384
Interfaith action for Economic Justice, 379, 384
Inter-Ministerial Committee for Women's

Education, 20
International Alliance for Women, 379
International Atomic Energy Agency (IAEA), 377
International Centre for Research on Women, 379
International Civil Aviation Organization (ICAO), 374
International Co-alition for Development Action, 379
International confederation of Free Trade Unions, 379
International Co-operation for Development and Solidiarity (ICDS), 379
International Council for Adult Education, 258
International Council of Jewish Women, 379
International Council on Social Welfare, 380
International Council of Voluntary Agencies, 379
International Council of Women, 380
International Development Agency, 65, 247
International Development Strategies, 237, 244
International Economic and Social Affairs, Department of (DIESA), 370
International Federation of Social Science Organisations (IFSSO), 310
International Federation of University Women, 380
International Federation of Women in Legal Careers, 380
International Fund for Agricultural Development (IFAD), 376
International and Intergovernmental Organisations, 378
International Labour Office, 377
International Literacy, Year, 1990, 257-59
International Maritime Organisation, 376
International Monetary Fund, 375
International Non-Governmental Organisations, 378-81
International Organisation of Consumer Unions, 380
International Research and Training Institute for Advanement of women, 264
International Social Science Council, 310
International Task Force on Literacy, 258
International Telecommunication Union, 376
International Trade Centre UNCTAD/GATT (ITC), 377
International Women's Development Agency, 380-81
International Women's Tribune Centre, 380
International Women's year, 1975, 263, 266
Iqbal College, Thiruvananthapuram, 389
Izquierdo, Munoz, 227

Jadavpur University, 393; School of Women Studies, 391
Jagori, New Delhi, 394
Jamaica, expenditure on education, 204
Jammu University, 392
Janaka, 280
Janardhan Committee see Central Advisory Board of Education Committee
Jigyasa Institute of Social Studies Trust, New Delhi, 394
Jodhpur University, Sociology Department, 390

Kaksivan, 279
Kali for women, 358, 360
Karnataka, employment rate for women, 366-67; Mahila Samakhya Programme, 46
Karnataka University, 392
Kashmir University, 392
Kaylor, Gloria, 358
Kerala, employment rate for women, 366; literacy rate, 22; female, 24, 27
Kerala Shastra Sahitya Parishat, Thiruvananthapuram, 394
Kerala University, 392
Katyayani, 280
King, Theodore M., 365
Kottayam, female literacy, 23
Kurukshetra University, 392

Labour force, women's participation, 228-29
Lady Doak College, 390
Latin America, education and sex gap, 297; literacy rate for men and women, 206
Lesotho, women/men enrolment in higher education, 203
literacy rate for men and women, gap between 206-08; India, 22-23; male, 23
Lopamudra, 279
Luthern World Federation, 380
Lyngdoh, H.S., 60

M and N College, Yamunagar, 389
M.S. University of Baroda, 392

Madhya Pradesh, employment rate for women, 366-67; literacy rate, 39; female, 23, 39; teacher education curriculam, 75-77

Mahabharata, 280

Maharashtra, employment rate for women, 367

Mahila Samakhya Project (Education for women's Equality), 19-20, 25-32, 42, 61, 63-70, 74, 357

Mahila, Samriddhi Yojana, 302

Maitreyi, 280

Maldives, Saarc Workshop recommendations, 216-17

Mali, economic crisis, effect on education, 204

Manipur, employment rate for women, 366

Manusmriti, 280

Margaret Cousins Memorial Library, New Delhi, 394

Media, role in Women's education, 41, 43

Medical Women's International Association, 380

Meghalaya, female literacy rate, 24

Mexico, 227-28

Mcmillan, Terry, 358-59

Minority Right Group, 383

Mishra, Ashok Kumar, 60

Mizoram, employment rate for women, 366; literacy rate, 24

Model Institute of Education and Research, Centre for Women Development Studies, 389

Mongolia, Women/men higher education, 203

Montessory Mahila P.G. College, Vijayawada, 387

Morrison, Tony, 358-59

Mother Teresa Women's University, Kodaikanal, 391

Mysore University, 392; Institute of Development Studies, Centre for Women Studies, 389

NGO Forum Facilitating Committee, 364

NGO Working Group on Refugee Women, 380

NIEO Network, Norway, 382

NMKRV First Grade College for Women, 389

Nagaland, employment rate for women, 366

Nairobi Forward Looking strategies for Advancement of Women, 231, 241, 244, 247, 256-57, 264-66, 364, 368

National Centre for Development Corporation, Belgium, 381

National Commission on Women, 51

National Convention on the Rights of the Child, 222

National Council for Educational Research and Training, 20-21, 39-41, 44, 58, 67, 75, 304-05; Women's Cell, 39-41, 44, 47, 388

National Development Plan, Eight , 217

National Health Policy, 210

National Institute of Educational Planning and Administration (NIEPA), 6, 44, 47

National Literacy Mission, 47

National Open School, 21

National Perspective Plan for Women, 213

National Policy on Child Labour, 210

National Policy on Education, 6, 17, 19, 56, 62; Review Committee, 6, 62

National Workshop, 1987, 210

Navodaya Vidyalayas, 18

Nepal, adult women litracy rate, 208

Nepal, SAARC Workshop recommendations, 217-19

Netherlands Organisation for International Development, 382

Non-formal education for girls, centres, 27; difficulties and suggestions for improvement, 288-92; methods for collection of data, 283-84; salient features of the programme in states, 284-88

Non Governmental Organisations in Consultative Status with the Economic and Social Council (CONGO), 364

Non-Governmental Organisations, role, 261-62

Norwegian Agency for Development (NORAD), 382

OECD Development Centre, 377

Office of the United Nations High Commission for Rufugees (UNHCR), 372-73

Operation Blackboard, 18, 50

Overseas Development Council, 384

Overseas Development Institute, 384

Oxfam, England, 384

P.G. College of Social Work, Hyderabad, 387

Pakistan, enrolment of girls in secondary schools, 207

Panama, Woman/men enrolment in higher

education, 203
Panchayati Raj Institutions, 49
Panini, 280
Penguin Books, 358
Peru Desco, 383
Planning Commission, 73
Polity Press, 359
Poverty Population Growth Environmental Stress, Problem and education of girls, UNICEF report on, 253-55
Poona University, 393
Portugal, Women/men enrolment in higher education, 203
Programme of Action to Mitigate the Social Costs of Adjustment (PAMSCAD), Ghana, 208
Public Information, Department of, 369
Punjab, employment rate for women, 366; literacy rate, 24, 27
Punjab University, 392

Qatar, women/men enrolment in higher education, 203

Radha Kumar, 360
Rajasthan, literacy rate, 22, 39;—female, 23, 27, 39; employment rate for women, 366-67
Rajasthan University, 393
Ramamurti, Acharya, 25
Ramamurti Review Committee on Education *see* National Policy on Education Policy on Education, Review Committee
Ramayana, 280
Ranade, R.D., 280
Rani Durgavati Vishwavidyalaya, 393
Rashtriya Mahilakosh (National Credit Fund for Women), 302
Reddy, N. Janardhana, 72
Rigveda, 279-80
Romasa, 279
rural women, education, 205-06

S.D. College, Muzaffar Nagar, 391
S.N.D.T. University, 393
S.S.L. N.T.H. College, Centre for Women Development Studies, 388
Samaveda, 279
Satapatha Brahmana, 280
Savitri College, Ajmer, 390
Scheduled Castes and Scheduled Tribes, literacy rate, 61
School of Women's Studies, Jadavpur University, 391
Second SAARC Ministerial Meeting of Women in Development, 210
Seetholakshmi Ramaswamy College, 390
Self Employed Women's Association (SEWA), Ahmedabad, 388
Shram Shakti Report, 41
Shramik Vidyapeeths, 19
Shri Padmavati Vishwavidyalaya, 392
Sikkim, employment rate for women, 366; literacy, 24
Siprabandhu, 279
Socio cultural and economic factors, influence on women education, 28-29
Somalia, adult women literacy rate, 208; economic crisis, effect on education, 204
South Asia Association of Regional Countries, 68; Audio Visual Exchange Programmes, 222; Workshop, 1988, 210
Special Component Plan, 74
Special Education and Extension Services, NCERT, 281
Srutabandhu, 279
Standing Committee on Women's Studies, 19
State Institute of Education, Chandigarh, 282-84
States Reorganisation Commission, 64
Stella Mary's College, 391
Subandhu, 279
Sudan, literacy rate for men and women, 206
Sundarvati Mahila Mahavidyalaya, 392
Support to Training and Employment Programme for Women (STEP), 301
Swedish International Development Agency (SIDA), 383

Tago, economic crisis, effect on education, 204
Tamil Nadu, employment rate for women, 366-67; female literacy rate, 27
Tara Institute of Social Science, Women's study unit, Bombay, 390
Tata Institute of Social Sciences, Bombay, 393
Teacher Education, Department of, 281
Third World Information Services, Switzerland, 383
Third World Network, 380
Total Literacy Campaign, 69

Traingle Research Institute, 227-28
Tribal Sub-Plan, 74
Trindad and Tobago, Women education, 227
Tripura, female literacy rate, 24
Trocaire, Ireland, 382

UN Decade for Women, 256
UN Declaration of the Rights of the Child, 222
US Agency for International Development, 385
US Debt Crisis Network, 385
United Nations, 222, 236, 248, 256-57, 293; bodies dealing with questions relating women development issues, 368-78
United Nations Centre for Social Development and Humanitarian Affairs (UNOV/CSDHA), 378
United Nations Centre for Science and Technology for Development, 373
United Nations Children's Fund (UNICEF), 19, 204, 258-59, 372
United Nations Decade for women's Equality, Development and Peace, 1976-85, 263-64, 368
United Nations Development Fund for Women (UNIFEM), 263, 371
United Nations Development Project, 259, 371
United Nations Division for the Advancement of Women, 266
United Nations Educational Scientific and Cultural Organisations (UNESCO), 201, 203, 248, 257-58, 293; Plan of Action for Eradication of illiteracy by the year 2000, 258-59
United Nations Environmental Programme, 372
United Nations General Assembly, 263-64
United Nationsl Industrial Development Organisation (UNIDO), 377
United Nations Institute for Training and Research (UNITAR), 374
United Nations International Children's Emergency fund *see* (United Nations Children's Fund (UNICEF)
United Nations International Research and Training Institute for Advancement of Women (INSTRAW), 370
United Nations Non-Governmental Liasion Service, 378
United Nations Population Fund, 266, 371-72
United Nations Office, Vienna, 368
United Nations Relief and Works Agency for Palestine Refugees in Near East (UNRWA), 373
United Nations University (UNU), 374
United Nations Voluntary Fund for Women *see* United Nations Development Fund for Women
Universal Covenant Rights; Economic, Social and Cultural Rights, 257
Universal Declaration of Human Rights, 248, 256-57
Universal Postal Union, 375
University Grants Commission, 19, 44-45, 53, 336-47; bilateral exchange programmes, 345; facilities for SC ST, 344; priority areas of research scholarships, schemes, 339;—, support for minor research projects 339-40;—, support for major research projects, 340; womens studies, 345;—sponsored women's studies centres, 392-95; Women's cell, 47
Uttar Pradesh, 60, female literacy rate, 23, 39; Mahila Samabhya Programme, 46

Vasukara, 279
Village Education Committees, 49
Vintage, 359
Virago Press, 358
Vocational Education, 43
Vocation Education bureaus, 65
Vocational Training Programme, 301
Voluntary Health Association of India Library, New Delhi, 394

Walter, Alice, 358
War on Want, London, 384
West Bengal, non-formal education of girls, 24
West, Rebacca, 358
Women, biases in textbooks, 356-57; changes in social environment, 357
Women's caucus for Asia and the Pacific, 386
Women's Centre, Maharashtra, 390
Women and Child Development, Department, 21, 73
Women and Develop Programme, Asia and Pacific, 386; Latin America and the Caribbean, 386; Western Asia, 385
Women, discrimination against, in literacy

and education, 223-24
Women, empowerment, 45-46; economic, 301
Women's Health Action Foundation, 382
Women's Households Development Studies Information Centre, Baroda, 394
Women's Information System, 369
Women's International Cross Cultural, 390
Women and international economy, 241
Women's International League for Peace and freedom, 380
Women's Library, Calcutta, 395
Women literacy, Access to, 356; for future, 208-09; and health and sanitation, 233; motivation, 225-26; obstacles 224-25; and poverty population Growth and Environmental stress, probem of 253-55; and productivity, 228; and self employment, 228; and social change, 226; social development, impact on, 250; and sustainable development, 228-29
Women's measures in favour, 251
Women's organisations and international agencies, relationship, 236
Women, participation in labour force, 228-29
Women, role in development, 226-27
women, status, in Indian society, implications for education, 28-29
Women's Studies and Development Centre, Delhi, 394
Women's Studies Research Centre, Guahati University, 388
Women's Studies, research and development, 44, 67-68; centres, 44, 50,52-53;- India, 387-95; UGC sponsored, 392-95; courses, 45
Women, vocational education, 41, 43
Womens' working group for Africa, 385
Women's Working Group for Europe and North America, 387
Women's Working Group for Latin America Caribbean, 386
Women's Working Group for Western Asia, 386
Woolf, Virginia, 358
World Association of Girls Guides and Girls Scouts, 381
World Association for the School as an Instrument of Peace, 381
World Bank, 259, 375
World Conference to Review and Appraise the Achievements of the United Nations Decade for Women: Equality, Development and Peace, 1985, Nairobi, 256
World Declaration on Education for All, 259-60
World Development Journal, USA. 385
World Development Movement, 384
World Federation of Methodist Women, 381
World Food Council, 373
World Food Programme, 373
World Health Organisation, 315
World Intellectual Property Organisation, 376
World Meteorological Organisation, 376
World Union of Catholic Women's Organisation, 381

Yajnavalkya, 280
Yajurveda, 279
Yami, 280
Yemen, economic crisis, effect on education, 204
Youth for Development and Co-operation, 381

Zaire, expenditure on education, 204
Zambia, expenditure on education, 205
Zonta International, 381

CICIL LIST

CONCEPTS IN COMMUNICATION, INFORMATICS & LIBRARIANSHIP

(CICIL)

General Editor: **S.P. AGRAWAL**

CICIL-1 Development of Library Services in India: Social Science Information
S.P. Agrawal Rs. 150

CICIL-2 Development of Documentation in India: Social Science Information
S.P. Agrawal Rs. 250

CICIL-3 UNESCO and Social Sciences: Retrospect and Prospect
S.P. Agrawal and **J.C. Aggarwal** Rs. 250

CICIL-4 INDIANA : A Bibliography of Bibliographical Sources
M.K. Jain Rs. 200

CICIL-5 Dimensions of Library and Information Science: Kaula Festschrift
V. Venkatappaiah (Eds.) Rs. 600

CICIL-6 Book Numbers: Some Indian Methods
M.P. Satija and **S.P. Agrawal** Rs. 100

CICIL-7 National Policy for University Libraries in India: Problems and Perspectives
N.B. Inamdar and **L.S. Ramaiah** (Ed.) Rs. 250

CICIL-8 Media Utilisation for the Development of Women and Children
B.S. Thakur and **Binod C. Agrawal** Rs. 150

CICIL-9 Terrorism: An Annotated Bibliography
Susheela Bhan (Ed.) Rs. 275

CICIL-10 Transnational Library Relations: The Indo-American Experience
M.B. Konnur Rs. 175

CICIL-11 Geography of Marketing and Commercial Activities in India (Documentation on Research Information)
R.S. Dixit Rs. 130

CICIL-12 Information India 1988: Global View
S.P. Agrawal and **J.C. Aggarwal** Rs. 200

CICIL-13 Women's Education in India: Historical Review, Present Status and Perspective Plan
S.P. Agrawal and **J.C. Aggarwal** Rs. 360

CICIL-14 Cultural Communication in India: Role and Impact of Phonograms
J.M. Ojha Rs. 220

CICIL-15 Second Historical Survey of Educational Development in India: Select Documents 1985-1989
S.P. Agrawal and **J.C. Aggarwal** Rs. 490

CICIL-16 Documentation Encyclopaedia of UNESCO and Education
J.C. Aggarwal and **S.P. Agrawal** Rs. 800 (set of 2 parts)

CICIL-17 Attitude Towards Information: A Study of Post-Graduate Teachers and Researchers in Social Sciences
N.G. Satish (in press)

CICIL-18 Librarianship and Bureaucratic Organisation: A Study in the Sociology of Library Profession in India
P.K. Jayaswal Rs. 175

CICIL-19 Literature Search
K.A. Isaac Rs. 150

CICIL-20 Child Education in India: Index to Scholarly Writings in Indian Educational Journals and Newspapers since independence
S.P. Agrawal and **Naresh Kanta** Rs. 100

CICIL-21 Lok Sabha and Vidhan Sabha Elections in India 1989 & 1990: Process and Results with Comparative Study of Manifestos
S.P. Agrawal and **J.C. Aggarwal** Rs. 250

CICIL-22 Islamic Studies in India: A Survey of Human, Institutional and Documentary Sources
Mohamed Taher Rs. 180

CICIL-23 Panchayati Raj: An Annotated Bibliography
N.B. Inamdar, N.G. Satish and **Anil Takalkar** 290

CICIL-24 Information India 1989-90: Global View
S.P. Agrawal and **J.C. Aggarwal** Rs. 500

CICIL-25 First Handbook of Psychological and Social Instruments
Udai Pareek and **T. Venkateswara Rao** Rs. 500

CICIL-26 Educational and Social Uplift of Backward Classes: At What Cost and How? Mandal Commission and After
S.P. Agrawal and **J.C. Aggarwal** Rs. 275

CICIL-27 Mass Media and New Horizons: Impact of TV & Video an Urban Milieu
H.R. Trivedi Rs. 180

CICIL-28 Indian Writings on Education : An Indicator to Indian Educational Journals Grouped by Subject Deseriptors 1979 to 1986 (in two parts)
S.P. Agarwal Rs. 900 (per set)

CICIL-29 Nation in Crisis
S.P. Agrawal and **J.C. Aggarwal** Rs. 200

CICIL-30 Information India 1990-91: Global View
S.P. Agrawal and **J.C. Aggarwal** Rs. 500

CICIL-31 Development of University Libraries in India after Independence
O.P. Gupta Rs. 270

CICIL-32 Handbook on Child : With Historical Background
Pramila Pandit Barooah Rs. 320

CICIL-33 Weaker Section in Indian Society : Undiscovered Past, Uncertain Present and Unpredictable Future : Index to Writings in Indian Scholarly Journals and 10 National Newspapers Classi-

fied under 1500 Descriptors 1886-1990
S.P. Agrawal and **Rajeev Kumar Sharma** Rs. 600

CICIL-34 Communication Informatics and Librarianship in India : An Introductory Guide to Publications Based on a Survey of Libraries in Capital City of India
S.P. Agrawal and **Pushpa Rani Sharma** Rs. 720

CICIL-35 Problems of Collection Development in Special Libraries
M.S. Sridhar Rs. 225

CICIL-36 National Information Resources for Social Sciences in India : Mobilisation, Dispersal and International Enhancement
S.P. Agrawal Rs. 225

CICIL-37 Modern History of Punjab : A Look Back into Ancient Peaceful Punjab Focusing Confrontation and Failures Leadingto Present Punjab Problem, and a Peep Ahead : Relevant Select Documents
J.C. Aggarwal and **S.P. Agrawal** Rs. 400

CICIL-38 India Information Sources : Economics and Business
Kyllikki Ruokonen and Manohar Lal Rs.

CICIL-39 Educational Planning in India : With a Slant to Educational Financing and Administration, Vol. 1, Reports of Committees and Commissions, Five Year Plans, Statistical Tables
J.C. Aggarwal and **S.P. Agrawal** Rs. 650

CICIL-40 Integrated Library System : Two Case Studies : Latin America and India
Maria Luiza Rigo Pasquarelli, Rosaly Favero Krzyanowski, Ines Maria M. Imperatriz and **S.P. Agrawal** Rs. 160

CICIL-41 Social Science Information in India: Effort towards Bibliographical Control
S.D. Vyas Rs. 300

CICIL-42 Higher Education in India Since Independence: U.G.C. and Its Approach
O.P. Gupta Rs. 360

CICIL-43 Government and Politics in India: A Bibliographical Study of Contemporary Scenario Chronicling Rajiv Gandhi Era
S.P. Agrawal and **Rajeev Kumar Sharma** Rs. 500

CICIL-44 Second Handbook of Psychological and Social Instruments
D.M. Pestonjee Rs. 300

CICIL-45 Development/Digression Diary of India; 3D Companion Volume to Information India: 1990-91
S.P. Agrawal Rs. 200

CICIL-46 Development/Digression Diary of India; 3D Companion Volume to Information India: 1991-92
S.P. Agrawal Rs. 300

CICIL-47 Information India 1991-92: Global View
S.P. Agrawal and **J.C. Aggarwal** Rs. 500

CICIL-48 Committees and Commissions in India 1974, A Concept's Project, Compiled by a team of professionals guided by Virender

Kumar (Vol. 12) Rs. 450

CICIL-49 Committees and Commissions in India 1975, A Concept's Project, Compiled by a team of professionals guided by Virender Kumar (Vol. 13) Rs. 450

CICIL-50 Committees and Commissions in India 1976, A Concept's Project, Compiled by a team of professionals guided Virender Kumar (Vol. 14) Rs. 450

CICIL-51 Committees and Commissions in India 1977, A Concept's Project, Compiled by a team of professionals guided by Virender Kumar (Vol. 15) (in four parts) Rs. 450 each

CICIL-52 Committees and Commissions in India 1978, A Concept's Project, Compiled by a team of professionals guided by Virender Kumar (Vol. 16) (in two parts) Rs. 450 each

CICIL-53 Subject Guide to Communication, Informatics and Librarianship in India (Based on a Survey of Library Holdings in Capital City of India)
S.P. Agrawal and **Pushpa Rani Sharma** Rs. 400

CICIL-54 Restructurring of Library and Information Science Curriculum
A. Tejomurty Rs. 250

CICIL-55 Committees and Commissions in India 1979, A Concept's Project, Compiled by a team of professionals guided by Virender Kumar (Vol. 17) (in two parts) Rs. 450 each

CICIL-56 Committees and Commissions in India 1980, A Concept's Project, Compiled by a team of professionals guided by Virender Kumar (Vol. 18) (in two parts) Rs. 450 each

CICIL-57 Third Historical Survey of Educational Development in India
S.P. Agrawal and **J.C. Aggarwal** Rs. 700

CICIL-58 Model Library Legislation
Velaga Venkatappaiah Rs. 400

CICIL-59 Indian Library and Information Science Literature (1990-91)
Sewa Singh Rs. 525

CICIL-60 Librarianship and Library Science in India
Mohamed Taher and **Donald Gordon Davis, Jr.** Rs. 350

CICIL-61 Comprehensive Glossary for Library & Information Science by
O.P. Gupta Rs.300

CICIL-62 Information India 1992-93:
S.P. Agrawal and **J. C. Aggarwal** Rs. 500

CICIL-63 Automation of Libraries and Information Science
R.K. Shukla Rs. 250

CICIL-64 Modern History of Jammu and Kashmir
J.C. Aggarwal and **S.P. Agrawal** Rs. 1500 (per set of 2 vols.)

CICIL-65 Library and Information Science: Emerging Trends:
Sister M. Esperanza, A. C. Rs. 250

CICIL-66 Mental Retardation in India (A Bibliography)
S. Venkatesan and **V.G.D. Vepuri** Rs. 275

CICIL-67 Information India 1993-94: Global View
S.P. Agrawal and **J.C. Aggarwal** Rs. 500

CICIL-68 Information Behaviour of Scientists and Engineers:

M.S. Sridhar Rs. 500

CICIL-69 Uttarakhand: Past, Present and Future
J.C. Aggarwal and **S.P. Agrawal** Rs. 750

CICIL-70 National Information System in Education: A Comparative Study
S. L. Verma Rs. 650